Henry Frye

HENRY FRYE

*North Carolina's First
African American
Chief Justice*

Howard E. Covington, Jr.

McFarland & Company, Inc., Publishers
Jefferson, North Carolina, and London

Library of Congress Cataloguing-in-Publication Data

Covington, Howard E.
    Henry Frye : North Carolina's first African American chief
justice / Howard E. Covington, Jr.
        p.   cm.
    Includes bibliographical references and index.

    ISBN 978-0-7864-7575-9
    softcover : acid free paper ∞

    1. Frye, Henry Ell.   2. African American judges—
North Carolina—Biography.   I. Title.
KF373.F79C68 2013
347.756'035092—dc23
    [B]   2013006961

British Library cataloguing data are available

Cover photograph: Portrait of Justice Frye (courtesy Frye family)

Manufactured in the United States of America

*McFarland & Company, Inc., Publishers
 Box 611, Jefferson, North Carolina 28640
 www.mcfarlandpub.com*

For Gloria

Table of Contents

Preface

My life first intersected with Henry Frye's in the early years of my career as a reporter covering state government and politics for the *Charlotte Observer*. I was new to Raleigh in 1969 when Frye became the first African American in modern times to be elected to the North Carolina General Assembly. He was a big part of the stories that we reporters wrote that day in mid–January as the legislature launched its biennial session. In the coming years, the increasingly important presence of African Americans in the legislature, in state politics, in business, and civic life became one of the most significant continuing news stories of the second half of the twentieth century.

I departed newspaper work in the mid-eighties for private ventures, including the writing of history and biography of twentieth-century individuals and enterprises. I often found myself in archives and manuscript collections in libraries in North Carolina and elsewhere as I pursued an understanding of the lives of public figures like former governor and senator Terry Sanford and bankers and businessmen whose institutions had shaped North Carolina in the twentieth century. Along the way it became exceedingly clear that the shelves were virtually empty of books about the role African Americans played in the life of North Carolina as the state moved from the era of segregation into greater participation in modern society.

In time, I became committed to the notion that once I had the opportunity I would focus my attention on a black person whose life had not only made a difference in the way we live today but whose story would also give readers a broader perspective of a revolutionary time in the life of the state. After some sleeve tugging on my part, Henry and Shirley Frye agreed to let me into their lives in such a way that I could make a start in presenting what has been a largely untold narrative.

There were a number of men and women who because of their activism emerged in the 1960s to be identified on air and in print as "civil rights leaders." It was really an artificial and indefinite description because there were far more people like the Fryes who never led a march but who were "leaders" nonetheless. This group, small at first and then larger as the years passed, diligently applied their time and talents to spanning the racial divide during a difficult and delicate time. As the following pages show, the Fryes were among the early ones who devoted themselves to the challenges of overcoming generations of discrimination long after the streets were quiet and American society had moved on to other social justice issues.

The number of times that they broke the color line, or their presence changed the way we live, are too numerous to list here. That, in fact, is a part of what this book is about. Most important, the Fryes understood that the marches and protests were just the beginning of the end of the Jim Crow era. In the years ahead, the movement would require people to become involved in the full range of political, social, and civic undertakings and to remind whites and blacks alike that society would be improved for all only as long as people stayed the course.

I am grateful to the Fryes for their generosity of time and their abundance of patience with the writing process. They allowed me to return to their kitchen table time and again as I searched for the details that make history come alive. By the end of my research, I had recorded more than 150 interviews with them and their contemporaries, from childhood friends to Henry's colleagues on the state supreme court. I also drew upon interviews of African Americans collected more than twenty years ago by the Southern Oral History Program. The Greensboro Voices collection of interviews from this era at the University of North Carolina at Greensboro also was especially helpful. Other assistance came from archivists at the North Carolina Collection and the Southern Historical Collection located in Wilson Library on the UNC campus in Chapel Hill. Gloria Pitts, the university archivist at N.C. A&T State University, dug deeply in her collection to fill my requests while Jason Tomberlin at the North Carolina Collection, Elise Allison at the Greensboro Historical Museum, and Kim Cumber at the state archives were helpful in securing photographs.

I am grateful for the sponsorship of this project by the N.C. Supreme Court Historical Society, which allowed me to receive financial support from the Z. Smith Reynolds Foundation and the Tannenbaum-Sternberger Foundation. This book would not have been possible without the encouragement of Greensboro's best friend, Jim Melvin at the Joseph M. Bryan Foundation, who provided financial assistance and continued motivation to see its completion so it could become a resource for students in the Guilford County schools.

My constant companion in this and other projects has been my wife, Gloria. Her reading interests run to subjects other than history and biography, but she has been a devoted cheerleader and her careful reading of my pages has saved me from editorial embarrassment more than once. My thanks to her and others in my family for their encouragement and love.

Introduction

On a Sunday morning at midsummer in 1957, First Lieutenant Henry E. Frye was in the congregation at the Dexter Avenue Baptist Church in Montgomery, Alabama, and the Reverend Dr. Martin Luther King, Jr., was in the pulpit. King had recently emerged as one of the best-known African Americans in the country, and Frye's reserve duties at nearby Maxwell Air Force Base presented him with an opportunity to hear the young minister everyone was talking about. As he left the church at the close of services, Frye stopped to speak to King as he stood greeting parishoners on the high staircase at the front of the church. The golden dome of the Alabama state capitol, where the Confederacy was born, loomed overhead atop a hillside two blocks away.

Frye's brief encounter with King established a resolve to see that his home state of North Carolina lived up to the ambition of its motto, *Esse Quam Videri* ("To be rather than to seem [to be]"). It was a high-minded statement that had been adopted in 1893 at a time when African Americans held public office and shared in political power. That didn't last long. In 1898, following a brutally racist political campaign that included the armed overthrow of elected officials in Wilmington, North Carolina, voters elected legislators who wrote new constitutional amendments that effectively stripped African Americans of their right to vote. The amendments were approved by the voters two years later.

African Americans were still laboring under the weight of those amendments in the mid–1950s. The summer before Frye traveled to Montgomery, he heard a clerk in the registrar's office in Ellerbe, his hometown in Richmond County, tell him he wasn't eligible to vote. Although he was a summa cum laude college graduate and an air force officer, he was informed he had not passed the state's literacy test, and was therefore unqualified.

Just over a decade later, North Carolina would learn of Henry Frye when he was elected to the state house of representatives and became the first man of color in a position to affect the affairs of citizens throughout North Carolina. One of the first things he did was to introduce legislation to remove the discriminatory amendments from the state constitution. Before his career in public office ended in 2000, he would preside over the state supreme court and, as chief justice, manage the state's judiciary, the third branch of government.

Looking back over a half-century since that day in Montgomery, the journey of America out of the Jim Crow era appears to follow a fairly straight line. It begins with the rulings in *Brown vs. Board of Education* to desegregate public schools, passes through the advances brought by the 1964 Civil Rights Act, the subsequent Voting Rights Act, equal housing and fair employment legislation and on to the integration of African Americans into all phases of life and society. One barrier after another fell, loosing an unbroken stream of opportunity up to the election of a president of the United States in 2008.

Henry Frye, and his wife, Shirley, were part of this seismic shift in social and political change in the twentieth century. They grew up under legal segregation, helped bring it to an end, and built on new opportunities as they presented themselves in the state's political and civic affairs. As a result, the second half of the twentieth century produced countless "firsts" for African Americans like the Fryes, for whom virtually every door was one to be opened for the first time.

Henry Frye pushed on many doors. It began early in the law school at the University of North Carolina, where he was the first African American to enroll and graduate after three years of study. In the fall of 1962, he was the first African American appointed to serve in the office of a U.S. attorney in North Carolina. He and civil rights attorney Julius Chambers became the first African Americans admitted as members of the N.C. Bar Association. Then came his years in the General Assembly, where he chaired committees and succeeded to membership on the state's budget-making authority. None of his achievements was more important than his eighteen years on the state supreme court that ended with service as chief justice.

Henry Frye did not set out to become one of the most applauded African Americans in North Carolina. When he and Shirley began their lives together in 1956, his plan was to become a lawyer. She was a public school teacher. At the time, the most extraordinary thing that set them apart from other young African Americans with talent and ambition was a determination to make their homes in North Carolina rather than join the stream of friends and family who were still leaving the South for something "better" beyond the Mason-Dixon line. The heavy overcoat that Henry wore as a freshman in college was a hand-me-down from an uncle living in New York.

Frye did propose to make a difference. And he had big dreams. Even as he and Shirley were living from one paycheck to the next, he was talking about organizing a bank in Greensboro to serve African Americans. He believed in an institution that could produce jobs and help folks build a home and make a community better. He saw economic justice as a full partner with social justice. His ambition was all the more remarkable considering his background. Like Shirley, he had grown up on a farm in rural North Carolina in a home without electric power or running water. It was not the kind of place that produced future bankers, or future lawyers for that matter. But Greensboro National Bank opened for business in 1971.

Yet, as Frye's career in business, politics, and public life demonstrates, the transition from Jim Crow to the supreme court was not as neat as it appears through the window of time. There were hidden shoals in this river of change that required deft navigational skills and a steady hand. Major victories were followed by years of dulling resistance and complacency, and legal maneuvering to prevent the inevitable. While the black community tried mightily to maintain an appearance of unanimity, there were those who viewed as a threat the destruction of the familiar boundaries of segregation. African Americans of a certain age still resist talking critically of the internal debate from those days.

Frye was not a marcher, and only a fair politician on the stump when one got down to basics. He was quiet, reserved, some said aloof and all too calm. He often needed Shirley at his elbow to put names to faces in a crowd. The law was his real love, and as an associate justice he was the one who most enjoyed digging into the intricacies of complicated cases. One of the first decisions he wrote after joining the N.C. Supreme Court, *Meiselman v. Meiselman*, remains a standard in the defense of minority shareholders in closely held corporations.

The future for African Americans in the late 1960s was no more certain or straightforward than it had been for newly freed salves a century before. If African Americans were to realize the gains of the civil rights movement, then the future would require skill, intelligence, and determination played out in the chambers and halls of state government, including the N.C. House of Representatives which, in January 1969, had not heard the voice of a black man spoken from the floor for nearly seventy years.

1

Hen'rell

His family called him Hen'rell and so did the neighbors who came to know the fourth son and the eighth of the twelve children that Walter and Pearl Frye raised on their small farm at the edge of Ellerbe, North Carolina. His proper name was Henry Ell Frye, but family members and others created a blended name that rolled nicely off the tongue. So, until Henry Ell Frye left his friends and family there on the edge of the Carolina Sandhills, he was simply Hen'rell.

When Henry was born at home on August 1, 1932, with the help of a local midwife Sain Davis—Miss Sain as she was called—Walter and Pearl Frye were already well known around the rural crossroads in Mineral Springs township on the north end of Richmond County not far from where the Yadkin River becomes the Pee Dee and rolls on into South Carolina. The family lived in a four-room house that sat on a ridge southeast of town about a half mile beyond Ellerbe (Colored) High School. (There was an Ellerbe school for whites within the town limits.) The house wasn't much; there was no electricity or running water, children slept three to the bed, and the family set out buckets to catch the rainwater that dripped through holes in the roof. But it was their own, along with forty-six acres and a barn out back.

Walter Asbury Frye was a strong man of medium height and impressive build with a quiet disposition and serious intent. He made his living in the stands of long leaf pine that once covered the Carolina coastal plain for as far as the eye could see. The old growth had produced trees with tops that reached more than a hundred feet into the sky, but much of that was gone by the time Walter and Pearl arrived in Richmond County from South Carolina in the early 1920s. Nonetheless, timber production remained a steady and profitable enterprise. The two had met at her home, near Elgin, South Carolina, when Frye followed his boss man home and fell in love with his sister. Frye was an independent sort whose boldness breached the boundaries of racial familiarity set by whites in the Jim Crow South, but whites who knew him didn't seem to mind Frye's audacity. They considered him to be a master sawyer who could salvage every usable splinter out of logs as big around as a well-fed sow when he squared them with a huge, high-speed blade before peeling off boards into stacks of rough lumber. His formal education had ended in about the fifth grade — the same as his wife — but he could read and write well enough. Most important, practical uses of math came easily. It was said that he could stand behind a truckload of saw logs and accurately calculate how many board feet would be in the pile when he was through.[1]

While Walter Frye was busy on the farm or at the sawmill much of the week, Pearl was occupied at home. Any extra time she had after feeding, clothing, and keeping up with her large family was devoted to praising the Lord on Sundays. Religion was as much a part of life as cornbread at suppertime. No meal began without thanking God for the bounty on the table. On Sundays, Bible verses augmented prayers and her youngsters vied to be first with the shortest one, "Jesus wept." Everyone, that is everyone except her husband, was in church on Sunday morning. She also was known for her talents in the kitchen. If folks were going to visit, they usually arrived around mealtime. Despite the crowded and simple accommodations in the house, she seemed to always have room for one more. She also made sure that cookies, molasses bread, or some other treat awaited the children after they had walked the half-mile home from school. She treated the teachers to egg custard pies.[2]

From time to time, the extended family included three generations. Walter Frye's father, Atlas, occasionally drove over in a buggy. He was from near Salisbury in Rowan County originally, and that may have been where his son was born. Later, after Atlas Frye died, grandmother Frye lived with the family. She called her son "Bud." Pearl's youngest brother, Vernon, and one of her cousins named Bill were part of the extended family living at the Frye home.

The Frye family's world didn't extend much beyond a tight radius around Ellerbe. There were occasional trips to Rockingham, a thriving county-seat city a dozen miles away whose commerce was driven by the area's farmers and thriving textile mills. Walter Frye's idea of relaxation was hunting. On Saturday nights he liked to sip on a couple of bottles of Orange Crush and eat saltines coated with peanut butter. From time to time, when Henry was older, Walter Frye would load the children into the back of his stake-body truck and head out for a day on the coast at Atlantic Beach, a black enclave just north of Myrtle Beach, South Carolina. Henry and his siblings didn't venture far into the surf. They lost their chance to learn to swim after a neighbor's son drowned in the local swimming hole.

Two nearby churches and the schoolhouse were the most important places outside of the Frye home. Pearl Frye believed that education smoothed the road to the future even if it meant following the paved highway from Ellerbe south to Rockingham and on to the train station at Hamlet. Over the years, she saw her sons and daughters graduate from school and then head out to New York City as part of the Great Migration of African Americans away from the South. It had begun in the teens and would continue until the 1970s. The first to leave was her oldest daughter, Luvertus, whom everyone called "Sweet." She got married and settled in Brooklyn. Sons Walter and T.C. went north after World War II. One by one, from the late 1930s through the war years of the 1940s and into the 1950s, nearly all of the Frye children packed their belongings and boarded the train with a meal of fried chicken that would tide them over until they could reached a part of America where skin color didn't bar entrance to the dining car.

Walter and Pearl Frye raised a family of 12 children on a small farm outside of Ellerbe in Richmond County, North Carolina (courtesy Frye family).

The Frye children were better prepared for their journey than many poor black teenagers in the South. Scipio Booker Timothy Easterling, the principal at Ellerbe (Colored), saw to that. He had arrived in Richmond County at about the time Henry was born. Easterling was a tall and imposing man with a body conditioned by his training on the football squad at Shaw University in Raleigh, where he earned his degree.[3] When Easterling reached Ellerbe he found a Rosenwald school with each of the four rooms occupied by little more than a teacher and a pot-bellied stove. From year to year, he secured more teachers and improvements to the building, including new classroom additions that extended out from each side. By the time Henry graduated in 1949, Easterling had eleven teachers for the grammar grades through high school, one for each of his classrooms, and indoor running water. His high school students were trained in French, chemistry, biology, algebra, economics and sociology, American history, citizenship, and a handful of other courses, including agriculture and home economics.[4] If they wanted to go to college, and those who stayed in class long enough to graduate often did, then his wife, Hilda, would find them a slot in a college somewhere.

But it was New York, or anything north of Baltimore, Maryland, that became a destination for the Frye children; the North offered jobs that did not require work in the fields from before daylight to dark, or "can't see to can't see," as Henry remembered his father's description of a workday. Little else was available in Richmond County. The one cotton mill in Ellerbe only hired a few blacks and they were assigned the dirtiest of jobs or janitorial work. The same was true of the large mills in Rockingham. Teaching and preaching offered something better, but that required college degrees and the older Frye boys didn't take to college, although some had tried. Instead, they left first for the army and then, after a brief hiatus back in Ellerbe, went to find jobs elsewhere. In time, their homes in New York City became the beach-head for family and friends who followed them north. This out-migration drained Richmond County of many of those who could have contributed to the future of the region. During the 1930s, the African American population in Richmond County dropped by about a fourth.[5]

Leaving home meant young black men and women could escape the combined burden of life on the farm and the discrimination of Jim Crow laws and customs, which mandated "separate but equal" status for African Americans that was rarely equal. Blacks and whites lived within hailing distance of one another along the dirt road that passed in front of the Frye home. During the week, whether at the sawmill or in the fields, these neighbors lived easily with one another. They shared the same dipper in the water pail and sat up nights sitting side by side and stoking the fires under the tobacco barns. That changed on Saturdays and Sundays when folks went to town. Whites and blacks trod separate paths on the streets of Ellerbe and Rockingham and deference to whites trumped everything else. Ola, Henry's sister, could buy an ice cream cone at the drug store, but she and the other black children had to go outside to eat it. On special occasions, when the family went to Rockingham for a Saturday at the movie theater, Henry could get a ticket to see a Tom Mix western, but he and others of his color sat in the balcony. Race even trumped service at the post office. Whites confidently stepped to the front of the line while blacks stood aside and waited without public complaint before asking for their mail. That really galled Henry.[6]

Forty African Americans had once held public office in Richmond County. That was before the election of 1898 when Cameron Morrison, a young lawyer from Rockingham who was still in his twenties, mounted a campaign for white supremacy that culminated in a parade and mass meeting the Saturday before election day that featured a Confederate veteran holding aloft a banner that read, "The Whites Will Rule the Land or Die." The Raleigh *News and Observer* declared that Morrison's work in Richmond "permeated the whole east, carried thirty counties, and saved the state for democracy."[7]

On occasion, Walter Frye violated social conventions. One day, he and young Henry were at the courthouse in Rockingham where the elder Frye had gone to conduct business with an influential white man, J. Elsie Webb, an Ellerbe lawyer and well-connected politician. Frye had known Webb since his early days in the county when he was running a sawmill for Webb's father, a large landowner and farmer who had less education than his black contractor. Henry saw Webb first and pointed him out to his father, who called to him from across the room, using his first name. This was something blacks just didn't do. Henry cautioned his father, who dismissed his son's concern saying, "Oh that's just Elsie. I've known him since he was a boy." Walter Frye was not intimidated by white supremacists. He once climbed into his truck and drove into Ellerbe to see the Ku Klux Klan march through town. His family warned against it, but he said no one was going to scare him off the streets.[8]

Walter Frye's relative ease and confidence in dealing with whites meant he was called on by other blacks when they needed help. With a nod from Frye, a neighbor could get credit at a local store or fill his gas tank at the service station. White merchants knew Walter Frye was good for the amount due. Others depended on Frye for work. Each year, he recruited a picking crew for one of the white growers whose peach orchards spread across the rolling hills north of Ellerbe. The Elbertas, Hiley, and Georgia Belles grew to perfection in the Richmond County soil, making the county the top peach producer in the state.

Most of the growers hired blacks as pickers where work in the trees was hot and uncomfortable. The loose peach fuzz could fill every crevice of a man's body with discomforting efficiency. Whites got the jobs out of the sun in the packing sheds. Frye took no regard of skin color. On his crew, whites and blacks worked together in the fields and in the sheds. It caused some conversation, but no one challenged Frye's arrangement. Young Henry worked on the crew one summer, but after a day's work in the trees he asked for a transfer to the packing shed.

Frye's entrepreneurial style afforded him a rare and valued independence in a world owned and managed by whites. It meant he was not beholden to any man, white or black, and unlike most of his neighbors, he maintained control of his life. His freedom came at a price. When a timber man offered him a salary of $60 a week to run his mill, Frye turned him down, despite the attraction of good wages. He told his son he didn't want to be tied to one job and would rather take his chances with freelance work, even when times were tight and he didn't even have the cash to renew the license for his truck. If work was slow, he could always haul timber to the mills or sell firewood to folks in town. By the late 1950s, Frye was operating his own sawmill and was working more than forty acres of melons, tobacco, and beans that he farmed on halves with the owner.

Walter Frye taught his children sound morals, the virtues of responsibility, and the value of hard work. He also tried to teach Henry how to plow
a straight furrow with the mule and later told him it was a good thing he was
a good student because he'd never make a living as a farmer. Pearl Frye was
a loving and caring person and she instilled her faith in God in her son. He
was in Sunday school every week at Sydney Grove Baptist. Except for the one
Sunday a month when the Baptist circuit rider was in the pulpit, the family
got its weekly preaching at Sneed Grove AME Zion church that was just across
the road. Henry also drew lessons from neighbors like Elias Dove, who occasionally worked at the mill with Walter Frye, regularly ate Pearl Frye's cooking,
and dispensed wisdom to passersby. When Henry complained about not being
able to accomplish some task or another, Mister Elias would tell him, "You
can make it. The mail man did." Years later, Henry said, "If you wanted to
know the truth about something, or if people were bragging one way or the
other, you asked Mister Elias and if he knew he would tell you. You could
depend on him like that."[9]

Henry took to the church in a way that pleased his mother, who began
to think he would make a fine minister some day. He and a friend, Frederick
Terry, who would become a clergyman, were always together in Sunday
school. On one winter's day, all of Ellerbe was stilled by a heavy snowfall.
Nonetheless, the two boys showed up at the Baptist church, let themselves
in, lit a fire in the stove, and waited for the others to arrive. When it became
clear they were going to be the only two on hand, they completed the lesson
they had prepared by themselves. Each year, families in the community gathered at the church on New Year's Eve for Watch Night, a prelude for obser-
vance of Emancipation Day on January 2, the date that Abraham Lincoln had
signed his Emancipation Proclamation in 1863. The politics of the occasion
was lost on Henry, who remembered only the singing and praying that went
on past midnight, but he was not clear on the significance of it all.[10]

African Americans didn't participate in public life in Richmond County,
or elsewhere in North Carolina for that matter. The whites had taken care of
that in 1900 with the passage of amendments to the state constitution that
effectively disenfranchised black voters. The haunting past of Morrison's white
supremacy was still very real. Morrison himself had gone on to be elected
governor in 1920, not long before the Fryes moved to Ellerbe. Nobody in the
Frye family voted, or had tried to register. Even as late as the 1950s, when
blacks made up a third of the county's population, only 6 percent of Richmond
County's registered voters were African Americans.[11]

Walter Frye stuck to his business, not the public's, and it was through
enterprise and hard work that he was able to expand his farm and build a new
house that the family moved into just before Henry began high school. The
house had six rooms instead of four, was protected by a sound roof, and most

important, thanks to rural electrification, was wired for electricity. Henry ran from room to room flipping the light switches and marveling at the convenience, grateful that he no longer had to depend on the kerosene lanterns to accompany him and his books at night. Additional rooms also meant more comfortable sleeping arrangements. With the extra space, the children only slept two in a bed instead of three. And electric power warranted the purchase of a refrigerator, an appliance that everyone called the Frigidaire. A radio soon followed and the family listened to the daily news reports about the war — the two eldest sons were in the military — with the announcer closing each show with "and so goes the story of today and remember that FD on your fertilizer bag means Fair Deal."

The family also enjoyed the regular radio broadcasts of gospel musicians such as the Dixie Hummingbirds, a South Carolina group that had relocated to Philadelphia, and the Selah Jubilee Singers. The Singers had been organized in Brooklyn but in the 1940s moved south to North Carolina. Their weekly program was broadcast over Raleigh's WPTF, a high-power station that covered much of central and eastern North Carolina. Both of the gospel groups toured the East Coast performing at churches and larger venues, such as Raleigh's Memorial Auditorium, where the Fryes saw them both on the same night.

Gospel singers could draw a crowd and S.B.T. Easterling handled bookings for some of the best-known groups in the South that performed at country churches around Ellerbe. The Dixie Hummingbirds came, so did the Five Blind Boys of Alabama and Sister Rosetta Thorpe. There were no public accommodations for blacks so the performers stayed in private homes and usually found themselves at Pearl Frye's table for one of her delicious meals. Easterling himself sang with a group called the Five Travelers that, for a time, included Henry's brother T. C.

Adults other than Mister Elias offered encouragement to promising youngsters like Henry and his friend Frederick, but none of those in the community shaped lives like the Easterlings and his teachers. It was the largest black school in the county school system with about 225 children in the elementary grades and another 125 or more in the high school. (There also were high schools for African Americans in the Rockingham and Hamlet city school systems.) It was one of 4,977 schools built in the 1920s for African Americans by the Julius Rosenwald Fund. Under the arrangements with the fund, which helped build 800 schools in North Carolina, parents of prospective students contributed cash or sweat equity. Ellerbe's blacks provided $1,275 in labor, money, and materials that was combined with $1,100 from the Rosenwald Fund and $4,476 from Richmond County to pay for the school. During the Depression, a four-room addition was built and paid for by the Works Progress Administration.[12]

Walter and Pearl Frye's children attended Ellerbe (Colored) High School that was built with money from the Rosenwald Fund in the 1920s. It was enlarged and expanded over the years through the energy and ingenuity of principal S.B.T. Easterling. In a small building at the rear of the school Henry Frye and other boys took classes in agriculture. The school's privies were behind at the edge of the school property.

Easterling wasn't the school's first principal, but he came along shortly after the school opened to replace a preacher named Julius McRae whom parents deemed ill suited to control a bunch of rowdy country boys. When Easterling arrived he announced he was afraid of only two things—a rattlesnake and a woman with a knife. If students misbehaved in his school, they could expect a whipping, no matter how big they were. Easterling would remain in the job for forty years. He was a tall, sturdy man with a deep baritone voice. His mere presence commanded attention and respect. Although Henry had known Easterling since he was a child, he was in his final year of high school before Henry began to feel comfortable in his presence. Easterling taught chemistry while his wife, Hilda, made sure students did all they could to finish four years of English. She also was the school's de facto guidance counselor and found ways for more than one of the Frye children to go to college.

The Easterlings lived a double life. For nine months out of the year the Easterlings largely controlled their own circumstances, albeit within the social boundaries of Ellerbe, where their situation was better than most blacks. They received regular paychecks and lived in a small frame house at the edge of town and enjoyed modern conveniences, including a telephone. The Easterlings had three children — two sons and a daughter — and all were given names that began with the letters S, B, and T. They were raised amid books, music, and occasional trips to museums in Raleigh. When school ended, and the paychecks stopped coming, the family moved to Philadelphia or New York where Hilda took a job as a maid. Her husband worked as a laborer, including one summer as a member of a road crew laying asphalt. His co-workers called him "School Boy."[13]

Like Walter Frye, Easterling successfully negotiated the complications and discrimination of Jim Crow. At the school, and among blacks throughout much of the county — his high school students came from miles away — Easterling's position as a leader was without dispute. The respect he enjoyed in the school carried out into the community where parents responded to his call to improve their school with money raised from bake sales, raffles, and May Day celebrations. Teachers and parents chipped in and collected donations to pay for an activity bus and the swings and seesaws in the playground. Chest-high stone columns guarded the front drive; the schoolyard was landscaped and kept in good order. The neat appearance of the grounds was in stark contrast to what was found at the other one- and two-teacher schools for blacks where erosion contoured the schoolyards and broken windowpanes went unrepaired.

To the whites who paid his salary and controlled his budget, he was Professor Easterling. Neither he nor his teachers ever published their first names: This partial anonymity encouraged students to address them with a courtesy title and frustrated whites who refused to do the same. His daily challenges were almost overwhelming. The per-pupil allotment for his school was two-thirds of the average spent on students in the county's white schools. The students' textbooks were hand-me-downs from the white schools, just like the school buses. The engines on those old buses were hard to start on cold mornings and often broke down on the long routes that student drivers—including Henry—followed around the county. Children from at least one of the school's four routes were late each day.[14]

In September and part of October, classes were held for only half a day. Many of the students came from sharecropper families and harvest time trumped education. The classrooms were crowded and students sat at a mixture of single and double desks. Light from a single bulb in each classroom, hanging from a cord overhead, was all that cut through the gloom of overcast skies. Henry was beginning his first year of high school in 1946 when a water line was installed following a survey by the county health officer and sanitation inspector who noted the school's "deplorable physical and unsanitary conditions." Even with running water, students and faculty used privies that stood at the edge of the schoolyard behind the building.

Despite these disadvantages, education was happening inside, once Easterling had satisfied the prevailing notion among whites that academic achievement for black children was secondary to vocational training. The boys were required to take agriculture and shop; the girls had two years of home economics. Easterling made practical use of it all. Boys crafted the tables and chairs in the home economics classroom and the girls occasionally provided a hot meal at midday. At the same time, S.B.T. and Hilda Easterling cultivated the ambitions of those who showed promise of making something of themselves off the farm. This uplifting attitude was shared by the Ellerbe teachers, all of whom had college degrees by the mid–1940s and were devoted to the school. Two-thirds of them had been in his classrooms for more than ten years. It was a remarkable team of educators.

Among Henry Frye's favorites were Richmond E. McIntyre, who taught the eighth grade and coached the boys' basketball team. Another was John E. Forte. He taught agriculture and organized the county's only On Farm Training Program for blacks. Forte also sponsored a chapter of the New Farmers of America, the alternative to the white-only Future Farmers of America. McIntyre was a precise, disciplined bachelor who was always immaculately dressed. Henry was twelve when he joined a Boy Scout troop that McIntyre had organized. It met weekly at the school and boys were expected to be ready at 8 P.M. sharp. Nothing happened until the second hand reached twelve, and the meeting was called to order immediately. Each boy was expected to not only know the Scout oath, but should be able to explain each part of it. Forte had an inviting manner, however, and talked to Henry and his friends about their ambitions and their dreams. Henry went from wanting to become an army general to the hero he discovered in the last book he read. He struggled a bit with the mechanics of the shop class requirements, but Forte was patient and saw him excel in the New Farmers chapter.

New Farmers of America was about more than agriculture. Students learned parliamentary procedure and competed in public speaking with boys from other chapters around the state. The winners of the regional contests then went on to statewide finals that were held each year in Greensboro on the campus of the Negro Agricultural and Technical College of North Carolina (later North Carolina Agricultural and Technical State University). During his final year in high school, Frye won first place with a recitation of Edwin Markham's "The Man with the Hoe," a narrative poem about a worker's hardships. He recruited a classmate to illustrate his declamation by standing on stage with him dressed in bib overalls and leaning on a hoe.

Within the walls of Easterling's school, the opportunities were limitless for creative and energetic youngsters who were eager to learn. He and his teachers talked about the future for their students with optimism and hope. Their textbooks may have been ragged and used, but Hilda Easterling told her students that the information inside would be useful to them around the world. Her husband often recited simple aphorisms—"when the going gets tough, the tough get going"—and reinforced the message with a weekly chapel program. If a black person of note was anywhere near Ellerbe, Easterling detoured him to the school to speak to his students. It was the first time any of his students would see a college president, such as Benjamin Mays from Morehouse College in Atlanta, or a corporate executive like C. C. Spaulding, the head of North Carolina Mutual Life Insurance Company, the largest black-owned business in the world, which was based in Durham. "In addition to that," Frye recalled, "were graduates of the school who came back. He would introduce them, say what type of student they were, and then the person would tell what he was doing. It was inspirational."

Students who faced second-class status in their own community gained an appreciation of black leaders and philosophers who had challenged that world. They learned about Booker T. Washington's lessons of self-help and industry and W.E.B. Du Bois's description of the "Talented Tenth." They were introduced to the ambitions of Marcus Garvey and the works of black writers and artists. Easterling had a low tolerance for idleness. His suggestions for school activities were never dismissed out of hand. One day Henry was sitting idle with his friends when the principal observed there wasn't a single senior boy in the chorus. The chorus had an ample supply of tenors at the next scheduled practice.

Henry enjoyed his education. He was a voracious reader and consumed everything, from comic books to the classic tales of King Arthur and his court. There weren't many books at home but Easterling allowed Henry and his older sister Ola to select books from the school library and carry them home to read during the summer. Their choices also included textbooks that they would use in the coming year. Henry also read — and sold — *Grit*, a weekly journal written for rural readers, and the Norfolk (Va.) *Journal and Guide*, the largest black newspaper circulating in the Carolinas. He also subscribed to *The Crisis*, the publication of the National Association for the Advancement of Colored People (NAACP).

Chapters of the NAACP were first organized in North Carolina in 1912. By the end of World War II, the organization was active in all the major cities in the state and even in more remote locations such as nearby Hamlet and Southern Pines. The NAACP launched a statewide voter registration drive in 1948 and was prepared to march on Raleigh to press newly elected Governor Kerr Scott with its demands when the governor persuaded state President Kelly Alexander of Charlotte to call it off. Scott met privately with an NAACP delegation that wanted equal education and employment and an end to discrimination in public transportation.[15]

Henry was only a teenager but he believed in the inevitability of change in the South's social order. He was impressed with the writings of the NAACP's national director, Walter White, who wrote accounts of a trip through the South where he passed for white because of his light-colored skin. Emboldened by what he had learned from Easterling, and what he had seen in his father's interaction in a segregated world, Henry began selling NAACP memberships, collecting $5 from the few who dared to join. It was risky for him and for those who handed over cash payments that he sent on to the NAACP national headquarters in New York. While the group did not have a particularly high profile in North Carolina, whites regarded it as subversive and a dangerous threat to the status quo. Henry was in high school when rumors reached the county school offices in Rockingham that Hilda Easterling had been elected to a statewide post with the NAACP. She was called before the superintendent, who threatened her job if such was the case. She told him the story was false: She had been elected to a position with the North Carolina Teachers Association, the NCTA, a statewide organization of black educators.

As Henry neared the end of his high school years, he began thinking of going on to college. Purely on a lark, he wrote for a catalog for Harvard University, even though he knew that was beyond his reach. One sister had gone to Hampton Institute in Virginia, another had attended Fayetteville State Teachers College. His oldest brother, Walter, had enrolled as a student at N.C. Agricultural and Technical College in Greensboro (later N.C. A&T State University) before leaving for the army. John Forte was pushing Henry toward Greensboro and A&T, his alma mater, rather than North Carolina College (later North Carolina Central University), the Durham school that was the only state-supported liberal arts college for blacks in the nation. On graduation day, with Henry leading his class as valedictorian, S.B.T. Easterling announced that Frye had been awarded a Sears Roebuck college scholarship of $100. The money would be enough to cover his first quarter.

Henry Frye was going to college, which, for Walter Frye, was all to the good. He warned his son from time to time that as slow as he was in the field, he had best find something to do besides farming.

2

Aggie Pride

When Henry Frye arrived in 1949 to enroll as a freshman at A&T College in Greensboro, he found a city that fancied itself as part of the New South that progressive newspaper editors had been promising for fifty years. That was about the same amount of time that had passed since the A&T faculty began welcoming young men onto the campus. For most of those years, A&T had been the larger of three academic islands for African Americans on the city's east side. Nearby were the private girls' school, Bennett College, founded and nurtured by Methodists, and the small, struggling Immanuel Lutheran. They existed as springboards of opportunity in Greensboro's tattered and ignored southeastern corner where only the main thoroughfares were paved and more than half of the residents lived in dilapidated houses. Breadwinners did the best they could with menial jobs that paid the lowest wages in town.

Henry had just turned seventeen when he reached the campus, and the surroundings were not totally unfamiliar. He had performed on the stage at the school's Richard B. Harrison Auditorium when the annual gatherings of the New Farmers of America had brought high school students to the campus. In the summer of 1947, the national NFA meeting had attracted a crowd of more than 500 teenagers. Frye was confident he could make his way as a college student, thanks to the instruction and support that he had received from his teachers in Ellerbe. He was less certain whether he could stay long enough to earn a degree. The Sears scholarship he planned to use to cover tuition had evaporated in a disappointing misunderstanding. As a result, Walter Frye told his son to wait for word from home before cashing the hundred-dollar check he had written for the down payment on college fees. For much of a week, Henry's status remained in limbo as he checked daily with the office of the college's bursar, Nathaniel C. Webster. Finally, just as the deadline for payments was upon him, he got word his father's check would clear the bank.[1]

A&T dominated the north side of East Market Street about ten blocks from downtown Greensboro. The campus's western boundary began a few blocks east of the Southern railroad tracks and continued on for about a quarter mile to Benbow Road. The main campus had changed little since the 1920s, when founding president James B. Dudley was still in charge and the school received a $600,000 appropriation for new buildings, thanks to state bonds promoted by Governor Cameron Morrison to add new buildings and make permanent improvements at all of the state institutions. Part of this money had paid for a dormitory that Dudley and the trustees dedicated in the governor's name. Now, twenty-five years later, Morrison Hall was in need of repair. Four years before Frye arrived, students had created an embarrassing disturbance for Dudley's successor, Ferdinand D. Bluford, when they complained loudly and publicly that the Morrison basement collected water when it rained. The continuing seepage was not only uncomfortable, they also said it was unhealthy after one resident developed pneumonia.[2]

More recently, the campus had grown by fifty-plus acres after the federal government decommissioned the army's Overseas Replacement Depot and A&T took over the hospital section of the base, where it joined the campus on the north side. Included in the transfer were some two hundred buildings, most of which had been erected hastily in 1942 to house, feed, and train soldiers for World War II. (A local judge had drafted A&T students for the construction crews.[3]) In 1949, student housing was at such a premium that Frye and other freshmen were assigned bunks in one of these old structures. Some of the former hospital wards had been refitted as shops and classrooms for the school's mechanical arts courses. Enrollment in non-degree vocational courses had swelled with veterans eager to take advantage of the benefits of the GI Bill.

Though the campus was ragged around the edges, A&T remained the pride of alumni, many of them school teachers and agricultural extension agents working in the rural reaches of North Carolina who guided students like Frye to Greensboro. In the years to come, A&T graduates— men and women — would strengthen the black middle class all around the nation. From its classrooms would come lawyers, businessmen, college professors, and even an astronaut. They would become the solid center and build a foundation for the uplifting of African Americans in the second half of the twentieth century after the protests, marches and demonstrations had dismantled Jim Crow discrimination.

In 1949, President Bluford held out some hope that the state's new governor, W. Kerr Scott, would send some catch-up money to A&T during his four years in office. The leaders of the NAACP, in a surprising surge of boldness, had confronted Scott earlier in the year to remind him of their help in his upset of the Democratic Party establishment that allowed him to win the governorship in 1948. Bluford was adept at courting the white politicians, and he was particularly fond of Scott, a former state commissioner of agriculture.[4] Scott did not disappoint. Henry Frye would be among the first of the A&T men to sleep in the rooms of Scott Hall, a 500-room dormitory that opened in 1951. It was one of ten new buildings, including a new home for the president, that would be added to the campus during Scott's term.

Bluford presided over a campus where youths were encouraged by faculty members with degrees from some of the most prestigious universities in the nation to learn and grow and believe in the future. Academic achievement was regarded with respect and young men and women could talk about building a future upon the power of their intellect rather than the strength of their backs. A&T's teachers cared about their students' success and took whatever measures they could to see that they left the school prepared for life, even if it was learning a manual trade in the school's mechanical arts department. For most students, their time on the campus would provide their first exposure to art, live theater, classical music, literature, and even indoor plumbing.

Bluford was just one year shy of a quarter century of service as A&T's president. He had come to the campus in 1912 to teach English and had served as a dean and later as vice president under Dudley at a time when A&T was little more than a trade school that turned out shoemakers, tailors, brick masons, and workers in something called "domestic science." He had been the unanimous choice of the trustees to replace Dudley following the president's death in 1925. Gradually, building upon the meager gains of one year after another, Bluford expanded the curriculum and hired faculty to support instruction in the arts and sciences.[5] By the late 1940s, A&T was training engineers, chemists, biologists, agronomists, and teachers, although the instruction of tailors, masons, auto mechanics, steamfitters, and welders remained a mainstay of the curriculum. On the same stage where he presented diplomas to graduates in the arts and sciences at commencement each June, he handed out technical degrees to those who had completed requirements as tradesmen. These programs were on the wane. By the time Henry Frye graduated in 1953, the school of mechanic arts had been reorganized as the college's school of engineering.

Bluford was a large man with a full round face, broad facial features, and light tufts of white hair on his otherwise bald head. A constant and dignified presence on the campus, he addressed faculty members and students alike with courtesy, and he expected the same in return. He didn't tolerate indifference, sloth, or tardiness. If students weren't seated and ready to learn when a class was due to begin, instructors reported their absences to his office. Likewise, if an instructor failed to arrive on time, Bluford was known to appear at the classroom door, inquire as to the subject matter, and begin teaching that day's lessons himself. He responded quickly and decisively to those whose actions and performance made his life uncomfortable; students and teachers who created disturbances on his campus didn't last long. Those who raised the ruckus in 1945 over the conditions in Morrison Hall weren't asked to return the following year. Two years later, a department head who publicly challenged Bluford's allocation of funds among the departments wasn't on campus at the start of the next term. Dismissals came with a blessing delivered in his deep baritone voice: "I am happy, therefore, to dismiss you from this institution of higher learning."[6]

Henry Frye was one of nine hundred new students in the fall of 1949. A third of them were women; a fourth of them, mostly men, were seeking training in a trade. The number of veterans on hand was down from the previous year, however. Two-thirds of the freshman class was from North Carolina. Many came from rural communities and farm towns like Ellerbe and homes without modern conveniences. In 1950, when Governor Scott toured the campus, he asked about 400 students in a group if their homes were without electrical service; a dozen raised their hands.[7] For these young men and women, a chance at a college education meant their lives might be different from what their mothers and fathers had known. The future wasn't going to be determined by the weather, as Henry's new friend Velma Speight described it. Back on her father's farm near Snow Hill in eastern North Carolina, life was dictated by whether it was rain or shine, not talent and ability.

Speight was trapped between fright and anger when the bus that carried her to Greensboro reached the station downtown in mid–September just before classes began. She was only fifteen, her hair was in pigtails, and her bobby socks and red shoes completed a picture of pure innocence. She had been tormented throughout her long bus ride west by boys who sang out, "What's greener than grass in the spring? A freshman." They had watched through the open windows of the bus as her father pulled $1.50 from a pocket in his overalls and presented it to her with parting words to not come home until Christmas. During freshman orientation she recognized one of those who had been taunting her and realized that he was just as green as she was and whose bluster disguised his own nervousness.[8]

Henry's accommodations in the former army barracks offered little in the way of privacy, but he wasn't in a position to be picky. In addition to his studies, he had to worry about how he was going to accumulate the nearly four hundred dollars he would need to cover the cost of his first year in college. He signed up with the *Greensboro Daily News* to deliver a paper route and learned early on to collect at the first of the month when the veterans on campus got their government checks. He also "inherited" a job as a porter at the Sternberger Hospital for Women and Children on Summit Avenue. His mentor from high school, J. E. Forte, had held the same job when he was a student and it was handed down from one man to another. Forte arranged for Frye to join in the legacy. His duties at the hospital occupied his afternoons during the week and was part time on the weekends, with chores that included washing dishes, buffing floors, carrying meals to patients, and whatever else was asked of him.

Aside from his work at the hospital and excursions to retail stores on Elm Street, Greensboro's main thoroughfare, Frye had little contact with the rest of white Greensboro. He remained close to a world whose center was Market Street as it passed by the A&T campus where African American businesses created an unbroken row of one and two story buildings. A popular spot with students was David "Boss" Webster's grill and newsstand; it was a block or two east of the railroad tracks. David's brother was the bursar at A&T. While Webster ostensibly ran a newsstand, his fried bologna sandwiches fed thousands of A&T men over the years. There was an inordinate number of beauty parlors, evidence of the proximity of a girls' school and the coeds at A&T; a small grocery; a laundry; a pool hall; a diner or two—the Royal Garden Café was an all-night eatery—the Palace theater; and McNair's drug store. Doctors, dentists and other professional men, such as the agents for North Carolina Mutual insurance, had offices in the rooms within the hustle and bustle of the retail commerce.

Members of the A&T faculty had substantial homes fronting the campus near the president's house that stood across from Dudley Memorial Building, a stately columned structure that housed the administrative offices and the college library. This fringe of respectability faded quickly within a block or two. An A&T sociologist reported a few years before Frye arrived that a nearby section called the "Bull Pen" was a collection of dilapidated shotgun houses amid "poverty, disease, crime, and dependency in the area flanked by the railroad tracks."[9]

Greensboro was considered to be more progressive in its race relations than many southern cities. Some attributed that to the Quakers who had been early settlers, and to the number of colleges in the community. In addition to A&T, Bennett, and Immanuel Lutheran, Greensboro was home to the Woman's College of the University of North Carolina; Greensboro College, a four-year liberal arts school for women that was supported by the Methodists; and the Quakers' own Guilford College. Nonetheless, the city remained as rigidly segregated as any city in the Deep South and periodic protests over discrimination in public accommodations had been ineffective. An effort to force open seating at the theaters in 1937 had broken down after a short time. Blacks returned to the balcony. "In Greensboro, the two races seldom associate except under conditions of clear social distinction, such as the master-servant relationship. For violation of the code, both parties are subject to punishment from the white group—the white offender in terms of ostracism and the Negro of intimidation," Donald W. Wyatt wrote in *This Be Their Destiny*, a study of black youth in three cities. The maids and laborers left southeast Greensboro daily for their jobs elsewhere, and returned home to an area of town where whites, even elected officials, seldom appeared.

Greensboro blacks had attempted to win representation at City Hall in the 1930s, but without success. As a result, east Greensboro suffered from serious public neglect. There were a few paved streets and a neighborhood of nice homes, mostly along Benbow Road where the professors, preachers, doctors, and others with steady incomes lived. Yet, while these houses approached middle-class respectability, the area was surrounded by rental houses in poor repair. Half of the children who used the Windsor Community Center lived in broken-down homes, nearly a fourth of which didn't have running water. "Slums! Slums! Slums! Slums!!" a columnist in *The Future Outlook*, a weekly newspaper that was published for African Americans, wrote the week A&T prepared to begin the 1949-1950 academic year. "That's all you see for blocks around the East Market Street section. What's this city and city council have to happen to them to awaken them to the fact that these slums were condemned time and time again."

The writer of the newspaper column was a white businessman named Ralph Johns who ran a clothing store on East Market Street. He was expressing his frustration at the black elites on Benbow Road who had complained loudly about a housing development that had been proposed by a private contractor, W. H. Weaver, who wanted to build 256 units of affordable housing. "In all of the history of the Negro American, they have been fighting side by side, trying to conquer the many evils that were trying to tear them apart and weaken them; they've stood all that was pushed upon them. Now a small matter like housing has cropped up; it threatens to envelop the Negro people like a monstrous octopus stretching its tentacles to choke them, one by one. Both sides are wrong, and both sides are right ... but the real issue isn't housing, it's slums, slums, slums!!!"[10]

None of this mattered to Henry Frye. He had not come to A&T to change Greensboro or the world. Public protest was not part of the student DNA, for whites or blacks, in the late 1940s and early 1950s. He didn't believe that segregation could be sustained and thought that change was on the way. When would that happen? He was not sure, although he was aware that cracks had begun to appear in the system. He believed that when change did come it would be because of the ballot, or the courts, but certainly not in the streets. For the present, Frye abided by the social restrictions of the day and threw his energy into recording the best grades possible to earn a degree in the school of agriculture. His selection of a major was made with little conviction and mostly in deference to his sponsor, Mister Forte.[11]

He was just completing orientation when he fell in with a group of classmates who, in the years ahead, would shape his life as well as the future of A&T. They were a tight clique that shared similar family stories: They had all grown up on the farm, with the limited offerings of rural life, the children of hard-working parents who were sacrificing for their education. The group included Velma Speight, David McElveen, James Bridgett, Gloria Swann, and

Frye. Frye and the other boys had already become friends when Speight had confronted Bridgett, the boy who had taunted her on the bus. Bridgett was from Williamston, a county-seat town deep in eastern North Carolina. He and Henry would serve in the N.C. Student Legislature together and work together on the *Ayantee*, the A&T yearbook. McElveen was from South Carolina, and, like Henry, would graduate with a commission in the United States Air Force. They attended church together and joined the same social fraternity. McElveen would become president of both the junior and senior classes. Swann was from just outside of Danville, Virginia, and, like Speight, would become a math major and a teacher. She was one of the brightest in the group.

The five became fast friends as they studied together and helped one another through the freshmen and sophomore courses that they had in common. Henry's notes and recollections of lectures were considered as good as a tape recording of the real thing; he could recite the professor's words verbatim. They shared their dreams and concerns and counseled one another as they chose their majors. Speight had come to A&T to prepare herself for running the family farm in Greene County. Warmoth Gibbs, the dean of the school of education and sciences, took an interest and steered her to a counselor who encouraged her to change her major to math based on the high grades she had posted in high school. The men joined the debate team and by the time they were upperclassmen they were members of Alpha Kappa Mu, the national academic honors society. Bridgett was one of the most gregarious in the bunch and established beachheads in a number of campus organizations, including the *Register*, the student newspaper, and the *Ayantee*, where Speight served as an editor. While McElveen emerged as the campus politician, Frye was comfortable with positions of lower rank in his fraternity and other organizations. If Bridgett was the organizer, and McElveen the candidate, then Frye was the thoughtful counselor. Gloria Swann called him "the adviser."[12]

Henry strayed from his friends in one pursuit in particular. Beginning with his freshman year, and continuing until he was a senior, he was a performing member of the Richard B. Harrison Players. As a freshman, he was chosen for the part of Leo, one of the supporting roles in Lillian Helman's play *The Little Foxes*. The campus newspaper gave him a favorable review: "Mr. Frye, too, is new with the Richard B. Harrison players though you might never

Opposite, top: As a freshman at N.C. A&T in 1949, Henry Frye joined the Richard B. Harrison Players and won a speaking part in its fall production of *The Little Foxes*. He is standing third from the left (courtesy Frye family). *Opposite, bottom:* Henry Frye was elected speaker pro tempore at the state student legislature that met in the fall of 1952. The event included college students from black and white campuses across North Carolina. It was a unique, racially integrated program that students pushed forward against opposition from some state officials.

have guessed by his splendid performance."[13] Later he had a part in *The Corn is Green*. He enjoyed the stage enough to compete for speaking parts in productions at Bennett College, where A&T men were imported for roles. In one play he was required to smoke a cigar. A non-smoker, Frye practiced for weeks, but never got the hang of using tobacco. His distaste for smoking was so evident that a promoter for a cigarette manufacturer refused to hire him to give away free samples to students, a common promotional practice of the day.

The Bennett campus was an enclave just a few blocks south of East Market Street. The school had been founded by the African Methodist Episcopal church in the years after the Civil War to teach emancipated slaves. The student body had included men and women until 1928, when David D. Jones became president. He narrowed the curriculum and developed Bennett as a liberal arts school for women and as a sister institution to Morehouse College, a prestigious men's school in Atlanta. Bennett girls came from the families of the black elite and middle class and the school cultivated a reputation as an institution that turned out young women of social grace as well as academic achievement.

Bennett's rules were strict. Students were allowed only one movie date a week and regular visitation was limited to eighty minutes, beginning at 4:15 P.M., Monday through Saturday. Men were asked not to telephone until after 9 P.M. The regular switchboard closed at 10 P.M. for all except seniors, who could take calls until 11.[14] No student was allowed to leave campus unless she was properly dressed, which meant a hat, pocketbook, pearls, and gloves. The pearls were the symbol of womanhood. Henry had arranged a date with a Bennett girl when Velma Speight told him he ought to call her friend E. Shirley Taylor, who had been asking about him recently. Henry was interested, but he passed on Velma's suggestion. His sense of chivalry precluded withdrawing his earlier invitation and breaching Bennett's rules of decorum.

Edith Shirley Taylor had not planned on attending A&T. Her choice was North Carolina College in Durham, but there was not enough money in her family for her and a sister to attend college at the same time. She postponed her plans and agreed to help a family friend open a barbecue restaurant in Greensboro. Her parents were anxious about the arrangement. They finally gave their consent after they found her a place to stay on Benbow Road in the home of Bessie Lee, a strong responsible woman who was caring for her ailing husband. Shirley's mother told Mrs. Lee that when her daughter was in Greensboro, she was hers. Mrs. Lee took the instruction literally and became a second mother. She also convinced Shirley that A&T was where she needed to study, not that school in Durham. She joined the freshman class in 1950.[15]

Like Henry, Velma, and the others, Shirley had grown up on a farm; she had three sisters and a brother. The Taylor farm was near Fremont in Wayne

County near Goldsboro, and her father, Ed Lenzie, knew his way around a field. He trained purebred horses and produced hams that won blue ribbons at the state fair. State extension agents talked about his success with crops of tobacco and cotton. He only finished four years of school but he could help his daughter with her algebra homework. Shirley's mother was a high school graduate. She took care of the home and began each day wearing a clean, starched, white apron over her dress. Shirley's parents were devoted Christians who disapproved of dancing or any sort of common behavior for girls such as riding on wagons, picking cotton, or being seen at the annual tobacco markets. It wasn't ladylike. On her first date, Shirley's father drove her to her high school prom and waited outside to drive her safely home. While Shirley's sisters helped their mother with the cooking and chores around the house, Shirley kept the books for her father's produce business. On weekends, he went door-to-door in Goldsboro selling vegetables and flowers in the white neighborhoods. The closest she came to farm work was milking the family cow when her father became seriously ill. The experience did not go well and forever spoiled her taste for whole milk.

She graduated at the top of her class at Friendship High School with a lofty ambition to be like Pauline Frederick, the lone female broadcaster of the day. She had discovered Frederick during the early mornings in the barn where the radio kept her company on the milking stool. Friendship school, with grades from elementary to high school, had been called Fremont Training School until Shirley's father and other parents took exception to the name. His children needed an education, not training, he said. Shirley's teachers were impressed with her talent and intelligence, and they directed her attention to North Carolina College on the belief that she was best suited for a liberal arts education. When she got to Greensboro, she believed A&T was for students of agriculture, and she had never met a farmer who left a favorable impression. She wanted to be a teacher and had even started her training in high school. In her senior year, a teacher in the elementary grades fell ill and the principal of the consolidated school asked Shirley to take her place. She was a substitute teacher long enough to qualify for pay of six dollars a day.

Because of Velma and Gloria's close friendship with Henry, Shirley — her friends called her E. Shirley — thought he was already spoken for. The two young women assured her that Henry was only a friend. Velma laughed aloud at the thought of spending the rest of her life with a scholar — a nerd in later vernacular — like him. Shirley saw something more in the studious young man, they later confessed. One impressionable evening was at a party sponsored by Beta Kappa Chi, the scientific honor society, when Shirley lost her date to an over indulgence in liquor. Looking about the room, she saw Henry sitting at a table playing bid whist, a card game that stole hours of his time. He was enjoying himself with his friends, and she envied the girl who had come with someone as composed and well-mannered as that. When he finally asked her for a date, she demurred and was a bit coy, saying she'd let him know later in the week. She had planned to accept when she saw him at a Wednesday class, but Henry was absent. Friday came without seeing him and she feared she had lost her opportunity. She asked a mutual friend to pin a note to his door in Scott Hall saying she would like to be his date. He picked her up at Mrs. Lee's on October 11, 1952, the day before her birthday.

Henry was regarded as a serious student by his friends, and rightly so. His grades were among the best in his class. During his sophomore year he flirted with the idea of accepting a scholarship and transferring to Tuskegee Institute in Alabama to study veterinary medicine. He passed on the offer but did transfer out of agriculture to the school of education and science, where he chose biology as his major and became a student of the talented and demanding Dr. Isaac Miller, a young chemistry professor with a Ph.D. in biochemistry. Frye excelled in Miller's classes. In addition to the scientific honorary society, he was a member of the American Chemical Society and his high grades made him eligible to attend a national meeting of Alpha Kappa Mu in Pine Bluff, Arkansas. Dean Gibbs had helped organize AKM in 1937 along with others from institutions like A&T across the South when Phi Beta Kappa had chapters only on white campuses. Henry's sister Ola, who had transferred to A&T in 1950, heard from her classmates that they would pass on taking a course if they saw Henry sitting in the classroom because they knew he would set the curve too high for them to compete. Henry's first opportunity to take notice of Shirley was when he wrote on behalf of AKM to invite her to become a member.[16]

Frye's teachers in Ellerbe kept track of their prize graduate's college record. In April 1952, he was invited to speak at the dedication of a new high school building on a program that included the district's congressman, C. B. Deane, and the entirety of the county's education and political establishment. Frye was asked to give the "sentiments of appreciation" from the alumni.

Henry's academic achievements didn't preclude a social life. He was an attractive man, tall, and well proportioned. He wore a thin mustache, short cropped hair, and had lean features. He was considered to be a fine dancer and one of the best-dressed men on campus. He had arrived in Greensboro without much of a sense for fashion, but one of the student tailors who lived in his barracks that first year raised his consciousness about his appearance. One day, when Henry headed out the door wearing mismatched clothes, his friend asked if he couldn't do better. He also followed the advice of D. D. McDade, a white merchant who owned a men's clothing store on Elm Street. When Henry's "personal tailor" commented that a heavy woolen overcoat he had inherited from an uncle in New York was not appropriate for everyday use, Henry went to see McDade and picked out a lighter gabardine model that McDade allowed him to pay for in weekly installments. When he was inducted into his social fraternity, Kappa Alpha Psi, McDade loaned him several suits to wear while he was "on line" and expected to dress with uncommon good taste during the week leading up to his formal initiation.

Selecting a social fraternity was no idle exercise. A man's choice established an association and entrée into African American society that lasted a lifetime. At A&T, only students with a grade point average of at least 2.5 (on a 3-point scale) were eligible to join fraternities, and members worked hard to establish a fraternity's credentials as a service organization. There was still plenty of time left for partying on special occasions during the year. There were no off-campus houses, but members claimed space for their own in the dormitory. McElveen and Frye applied to be Kappas (founded at Indiana University in 1911) because of the chapter's high academic standing. Bridgett joined Omega Psi Phi (founded at Howard University in 1911), which was known for its gregarious membership. Taylor and Speight's sorority was Alpha Kappa Alpha, another favorite of black elites around the country.[17]

By the time of their senior year, the group of five was now a group of six. Shirley Taylor was allowed to join after she had become Henry's regular companion. She had started a year behind the others, but by taking courses in the summer she caught up and planned to graduate with the Class of 1953. She fit in easily. Her grades were high, as was her interest in campus affairs. Dean Gibbs sought her out to edit the *Register* during one summer session and in the following academic year she wrote a column titled "A Thought For Each Day." Her offerings included uplifting commentary such as, "You are one of the fortunate ones who live in the dawn of a new age." She also wrote a feature story about a chemistry professor who was working to keep North Carolina cows from giving bitter milk.[18] This crowd controlled the *Ayantee*. Henry was "literary editor" and his staff included Taylor and Swann. Frye, Speight, Swann, and McElveen were among the eleven chosen as outstanding seniors.

In late November in 1951 and 1952, Frye was one of a dozen or so in the A&T delegation to the N.C. Student Legislature. McElveen joined him one year, as did Speight and Taylor. The mock legislature had been organized for college students in the late 1930s and held its sessions in the House and Senate chambers in the State Capitol. It was perhaps the only place in North Carolina where white and black students met in public on equal footing. The racial integration of the program had not come without controversy. The 1945 session dissolved into a dogfight over a bill offered by a University of North Carolina student that, if approved, would include representatives from the black schools at the next annual gathering. The debate was such that the session carried over an extra day before the bill finally passed 110–48, despite warnings of repercussions from Secretary of State Thad Eure. Wake Forest

College didn't send a delegation the following year when the first African Americans attended, and a reception for the students at the governor's mansion was cancelled, but that appeared to be the only deviation from the past.[19] By the time Frye began his participation, Wake Forest had rejoined and students from the campuses at A&T, North Carolina College, Shaw University in Raleigh and Johnson C. Smith in Charlotte were competing for the various legislative offices.

The 1952 session opened November 20 in Raleigh with Frye as his delegation's candidate for a legislative office. When the horse-trading for votes ended on the first day, he emerged with enough support to be chosen speaker pro tempore of the House, the second highest office in that body. The *Ayantee* published a photo of Frye presiding from the speaker's chair, his hand on the gavel, as he ended a forensic free-for-all on the floor with the declaration, "Everybody's out of order, except me." He introduced one bill, on a subject long forgotten, but he was so well prepared in his debate that opponents

The Palace Theater was one of the popular destinations on East Market Street in the commercial district across from the North Carolina A&T campus in Greensboro. This picture was made in 1946, three years before Henry arrived at the campus (© Carol Martin Collection/Greensboro Historical Museum).

finally gave up, saying that if any member asked further questions, Frye would be on his feet all day. The bill passed.[20]

Henry and his friends concocted strategies to put one another into campus positions during evening bull sessions on the steps of the dining hall, or at the women's dormitory where Velma was a student advisor. If they stayed past curfew, Velma, who worked for the dean of women, arranged for herself, Gloria, and Shirley to be excused from the deadline. Most of their conniving related to the usual campus politics, but on at least one occasion they went after something more profound. In the fall of 1952, they engineered the selection of a dark-skinned girl to be Miss A&T. All students knew the old saw: "If you are light, you're all right; if you are brown, stick around; if you are black, get back." They set out to challenge the negative stereotype of a truly black woman. Working with friends in the organizations that presented nominees for the honor, they arranged for all of the candidates in 1952 to be of a darker hue than in prior years. Their efforts ended a succession of light-skinned women as the campus beauty. They also took up other campus concerns—Bridgett complained about the restrictions put on men in the new

Elm Street in December 1950. The retail center of Greensboro was about ten blocks west of the A&T campus. Henry Frye found a friendly haberdasher who sold him an overcoat on the promise of weekly payments (© Carol Martin Collection/Greensboro Historical Museum).

Scott Hall, an issue he raised in the *Register*—and, from time to time, they carried their complaints to President Bluford. Usually, they left without satisfaction. His standard answer was, "We're working on that," and nothing would happen.

Bluford did not push the boundaries of the limits to his authority, and he had a long history of dealing with those who embarrassed him with difficult questions. He was especially sensitive to the opinions of important white businessmen in Greensboro and political appointees out of Raleigh who, with a phone call or two, determined his fate, and that of the school. Even some blacks called Bluford the last of "the handkerchief heads," because of his unrelenting efforts to curry favor with those in authority.[21] Rather than push for more support for his under-funded school, he made sure that he sent money back to Raleigh at the end of the fiscal year. He believed it demonstrated sound management and his keen sense of responsibility. He told those who worked closely with him that he knew about the derisive comments from fellow blacks and that white politicians called him "cotton top" but, he said in private, "Every time they called me that, I slap up a new building."[22]

The president's maneuvering was no different from the challenges facing any administrator dependent on white support. As an elder among the college leaders of the day, Bluford was aware that even Dr. Mordecai W. Johnson, the president of prestigious Howard University, had moved to end a sit-in campaign at Washington, D.C., restaurants in 1944 after the direct-action campaigns led to criticism of Howard from congressional leaders who controlled 60 percent of Howard's funding. Johnson gave speeches in defense of African American rights, but political reality would not permit him to support the students when they attempted to eat wherever they chose in the nation's capital.[23]

There had been minor dustups under Bluford, who quietly eliminated potential embarrassment. Shortly before Frye arrived in Greensboro, a young A&T English instructor, Eugene Stanley, had become an officer in James Farmer's new Congress On Racial Equality while in his first year as an associate professor. He didn't return to the campus in the fall of 1947 after he participated in the CORE-sponsored Journey of Reconciliation that involved whites and blacks riding buses together through the South to test a recent U.S. Supreme Court decision desegregating interstate transportation. When they reached North Carolina, some of the riders were threatened in Chapel Hill and then later arrested in Asheville.[24]

There were stories that Bluford's concern over white reaction led him to discourage faculty members from joining the NAACP, which was considered to be the "radical" political group. If that was the case, he did nothing to stop Frye and a handful of others from organizing a NAACP student chapter. The group only met a few times, but it was no less engaged than the NAACP chapter in Greensboro, which, at that time, was moribund. Political action was the domain of the Greensboro Citizens Association, a group of professionals and businessmen who in 1951 mounted the first successful campaign to elect an African American to the city council.

For the most part, A&T students and faculty steered clear of public debate over civil rights or challenges to the segregated world around them. That made all the more memorable a chapel meeting that Frye attended as an upperclassman that was called to hear about a case in nearby Caswell County. Matt Ingram was a young African American who had been charged with assault on a white woman after she accused him of "leering" at her from fifty feet away. Ingram was given a six-month jail term. His case drew international attention and became an example of the inequities of Southern justice. Ernest Frederick Upchurch, a bold white lawyer in Roxboro, eventually took his case and won a reversal of the conviction in the N.C. Supreme Court. The court ruled "we cannot convict him solely for what may have been on his mind. Human law does not reach that far."[25]

Frye understood that Bluford's situation was not that different from what was required of his high school principal. S. B. T. Easterling fumed in private about the injustices visited on his faculty and his school, but he never took offense in public. Both men submitted to white authority and got something, knowing that if they stepped outside accepted behavior that they would be out of a job, replaced by someone who was perhaps even more subservient.

Bluford was not alone in accepting the status quo and avoiding issues that could make his life difficult. Faculty families enjoyed a comfortable upper middle-class lifestyle with steady jobs, good pay, and a rank atop the social ladder in east Greensboro. At campus events, a faculty member's pedigree was open to inspection and approval. In 1949, when Lucille Piggott came to Greensboro with her husband, Bert, who was A&T's new assistant football coach, she was asked by the wives at a faculty affair, "What is your school?" Young, and newly married, but not intimidated by the condescension implied in the question, Piggott replied, "Alton [Illinois] High School." The next morning, she was standing in the line at registration with the rest of the freshmen, taking her first steps to earning a Ph.D.[26]

Frye, Bridgett, and McElveen approached graduation in June 1953 with the eager anticipation of service in the Air Force as second lieutenants. A&T was a federal land-grant institution and participation in ROTC was required of men in their freshman and sophomore years. The campus had a proud military history. During World War I it trained more African Americans for service than any other land-grant college of its kind. One hundred students and faculty were with the 15th New York infantry, the famous black regiment that fought with French and Senegalese troops in the most advanced section of western front at Thonn.[27]

Once Frye had finished the required service for lower classmen he had planned to leave his uniform behind until McElveen convinced him that he should enroll in the advanced Air Force ROTC program that was beginning its first year as he became a junior. The Air Force component of the ROTC program had begun in the 1920s, but had faded out of existence during the Depression. It was revived in 1946, but only at white schools. In 1950, A&T was one of the first black schools with an engineering program and it was chosen to participate. Frye's decision came too late for him to enroll in classes in the fall of 1950 but he added air science to his studies in the next quarter. In his senior year, he was a squadron commander in the Arnold Air Society and, like McElveen, received his commission as a second lieutenant at graduation.

The world that was waiting for the Class of 1953 was pregnant with change, especially in the South. Graduation day on June 1 came less than a month after Dr. William Hampton had been reelected to the Greensboro City Council after leading the balloting in the first primary. African Americans also had been elected in municipal elections in Durham and Chapel Hill.

Henry Frye joined the Air Force Reserve Officers Training Corps as an A&T upperclassman. Upon graduation he was commissioned as a second lieutenant and later served on active duty in Korea and Japan (courtesy Frye family).

There was some expectation that the U.S. Supreme Court would render its decision in the school desegregation cases before it left for its summer break on June 15. (The decision did not come until May 1954.) The bishop of the Catholic church in North Carolina had banned racial segregation, and on the Sunday before graduation ceremonies in Greensboro he was in the tiny town of Newton Grove where white and black congregations were merging, although not peacefully. The bishop was only able to complete mass with the help of sheriff's deputies who kept angry white parishioners from storming the church.[28]

Frye was among 11 who completed degrees with highest honors in A&T's 1953 class of 411 graduates. He received the intercollegiate dramatic association award for his participation in the Richard B. Harrison Players. He and Velma Speight were presented with the Fellowship Council award for four years of meritorious service in religious activities. (Frye led a Sunday school in

Harrison Auditorium.) The immediate past president of Tuskegee Institute, Dr. F. D. Patterson, was the principal speaker for students, faculty, and family who gathered in the shade of the tall oaks on the quadrangle of the A&T campus for the ceremonies. The day before, commencement speakers at Shaw University in Raleigh and in Durham at North Carolina College had spoken of the duality of America and the curse of racial segregation. "America cannot lead as long as any segment of its population has a second class status," Congressman Adam Clayton Powell of New York had said in his speech at Shaw. "This country must fight to save itself and this must be done by the Negro people." Patterson's call upon the A&T faithful was more muted. He told students to "speak for man" and went on to praise the Marshall Plan that had helped rehabilitate Europe.[79]

The Frye family was on hand from Ellerbe. There was some consternation back home, however, when word spread that one of Ellerbe (Colored) High School's most outstanding graduates was not going into the ministry. Nor did it appear that he was going to be a teacher. Those were the two professions considered best for a college-educated black man. Henry wasn't sure what lay ahead, but he was leaning toward a career — perhaps medicine — in which he would use his studies in biology and chemistry. As pleased as he was of the academic honors and the service awards that he had achieved, he was proudest of the silver bar that Shirley Taylor pinned on his uniform as one of the eighteen graduates of the Air Force ROTC program. Before anything else, he was first going to be an officer and a gentleman in the American military forces.

He didn't have orders in hand, so first he had to find a job. After a brief stay in Ellerbe, he did what his brothers and sisters and thousands of other young African Americans had done before him. He boarded the train for New York City with a box of food prepared by his mother.

3

"It was going to be slow"

It was one of those mornings typical of late spring. The temperatures were cool, in the low fifties, when the students arrived in Washington Elementary School on May 17, 1954. Youngsters in grades one through six settled into their chairs and chattered among themselves. Shirley Taylor's second graders were as excited as any group of youngsters anticipating their summer vacation. It was just a few weeks away.

Taylor's students knew her well. Most of them had been in her student-teaching class the year before as she finished practice-teaching requirements to qualify for graduation from A&T. At the end of the school year, in May 1953, Washington's principal, Dr. John Leary, had pulled her aside and sat with her as she completed a job application to teach in the Greensboro schools in the coming year. Leary wanted to keep Taylor at Washington Elementary. She was that good. When school opened that fall, he assigned her to a second grade classroom with the students who had been with her in the spring.[1]

Leary knew Taylor as more than just another one of Dr. Warmoth Gibbs's promising A&T graduates. She was the surrogate daughter of Mrs. Bessie Lee, the woman who ran the cafeteria at his school and was one of his adversaries at the bridge table. Mrs. Lee had integrated Taylor into life along Benbow Road, where her neighbors included Leary, owners of East Market Street businesses, A&T faculty, and professional men like physician George Evans and dentist W.L.T. Miller. Not long after she arrived in Greensboro, Taylor joined Mrs. Lee's church, and by the time she was a sophomore, she was running the Bethel AME Girl Scout troop. In her junior year, she was in charge of cookie sales for all of Greensboro's African American Girl Scout troops. Each morning, on her way to classes at A&T, she stopped by Washington school to post the daily lunch menu on the bulletin board. By the time she was a senior, Mrs. Lee and her friends all had an opinion about the right man for her. It was Henry Frye, that tall boy from Ellerbe who had finished at the top of his class.

Miss Taylor's second graders were well into their Monday lessons that May morning in 1954 when, shortly after 10 A.M., Chief Justice Earl Warren

38

began reading the U.S. Supreme Court's long-awaited decision in *Brown v. Board of Education*. Without dissent, the Court outlawed segregation in public schools and demolished the separate-but-equal standard set in 1896 in *Plessy v. Ferguson*. That case carried a curious Greensboro historical footnote. Homer Plessy's lawyer was Albion Tourgée, an Ohio man and Union officer who had come to Greensboro after the Civil War to recover from war wounds. He had once lived not far from Washington School and during Reconstruction had served as a superior court judge. The Court's decision in *Brown* was on the wire services within minutes after Warren finished his recital; John Leary learned about it in a newscast heard over his office radio before the second graders were on their way to eat their lunch. Leary and the teachers talked of little else for the balance of the day.[2]

The decision was a stunning interruption in the lives of all in the South, especially whites who believed a dual society was the legal, and natural, order of things. By the time the temperature had warmed to the high seventies on the afternoon of the 17th, most white politicians had reacted with everything from fuming disappointment to belligerent promises of judicial disobedience. In contrast, the comments of Greensboro's men of position and influence were calm and civil. Most remarkable of all was the statement from Leary's boss, city school Superintendent Benjamin L. Smith. "It is unthinkable that we will try to abrogate the laws of the United States of America," Smith said, "and it is also unthinkable that the public schools should be abolished."[3] By the end of the day, the threat of ending public education to bypass the Court and keep whites and blacks apart was being bandied about by the most rabid segregationists.

Local newspaper reporters cast their lines for public comment from African Americans but didn't reel in the proclamations of victory or loud amens they may have anticipated. The Reverend James T. Douglas was pastor of St. James Presbyterian Church and about the only black preacher in Greensboro who used his pulpit to talk about something other than heaven and how to get there. "It is a blessing to the country, but I think we've got to face up to the fact that it will take clear thinking and down-to-earth human relationships," Douglas said, his satisfaction tailored by a reasoned deference to reality. Bennett College President David D. Jones, the newest member of the city school board, said he believed the community would stand up to the challenges presented by the Court. The only titled person of color who declined the newspaper's offer to comment was A&T's President Ferdinand Bluford. The remarks of Bluford's second in command, Warmoth Gibbs, were understated, to say the least. He said he appreciated the Court's "gradual approach."

One day later, on the evening of May 18, the Greensboro school board became the first in the South to instruct its superintendent to begin working on compliance with the Court's decision. Smith had a formal board response ready to go; he had anticipated the decision and for weeks had been working on the proper wording with his chairman, D. Edward Hudgins, an Oxford-educated lawyer. What they crafted expressed no judgment; it matter-of-factly recognized the new law of the land. Hudgins went further in his public remarks. "We must not fight or attempt to circumvent this decision. If I as a member of this board failed to take notice of the Court's decision, I would feel that I'm failing in my duty; that I would be derelict in my duty as a board member if I should not take a stand."[4] One board member, Howard Holderness, the head of one of the city's largest institutions, Jefferson Standard Life Insurance Company, voted no, saying the statement was premature. Lost in the discussion was the fact that for nearly six years the city schools had been educating racially mixed student bodies at the hospitals for victims of polio and cerebral palsy.

Once folks caught their breath, the implications of the Court's decision became personal. In a woman-on-the-street story published on Wednesday by the *Greensboro Record*, the afternoon newspaper, a mother and former schoolteacher said she believed in integration in theory but wouldn't want her children going to a school with African Americans. Another female raised the specter of whites and blacks dancing together, a condition she saw as on the slippery slope to mixed marriages.[5]

Some of the state's leading politicians were no more tolerant. Once again, as had happened fours years earlier, the Court had tossed a bomb into the closing days of a political campaign. In 1950, it had been the decision desegregating law schools at public universities. That one had come in the midst of the Democratic primary contest for the U.S. Senate. The Willis Smith–Frank Graham race would devolve into racial politics of the worst sort.[6] Now, another Senate primary was underway. Alton Lennon, the Wilmington man who had been named to fill the late Senator Smith's unexpired term, and former Governor Kerr Scott were in a close race. Lennon immediately accused Scott of opposing segregation and warned that "agitators" were already in the state to stir up trouble. Scott was more reserved but he stated his preference for a dual school system.[7] In a curious turn of events, President Dwight D. Eisenhower, the Republican who had put Earl Warren on the Court, was in Charlotte on May 18 and the president was silent on the most important question facing the South. He was there to celebrate the 179th anniversary of the signing of the Mecklenburg Declaration of Independence and, in his brief address, he stayed within the boundaries of the political turmoil of the eighteenth, not the twentieth, century. He had a picnic lunch with the mayor and the state's first Republican congressman in modern times, and was not asked a single question about the Court's decision.[8]

As the rhetoric became more furious in the South, Greensboro looked like an eddy in a rushing stream of racial one-upmanship. The city's Junior

Chamber of Commerce, a Jaycee chapter with one hundred fifty members, heartily endorsed the school board's action.[9] Toward the end of the week that included Decision Day, the members of the city's Exchange Club, as hearty a band of burghers and small businessmen as any, refused to go along with their president, who wanted the club to ask the governor for a special legislative session to suspend the sale of $50 million in school bonds that had been approved prior to the Court's decision. The response from those responsible for the schools outside of Greensboro in Guilford County was unenthusiastic, but not obstructionist. The county superintendent initially expressed compliance with the law. About ten days later, his board officially reserved comment on the decision until after the Court had spoken to implementation following further hearings set for the fall. At its monthly meeting on May 28, the county board acted as if nothing had happened to change education as they saw it. Members followed their regular agenda and approved the renaming of a school in the Summerfield community, where African Americans were regularly assigned, in honor of Duella Laughlin, a long-time teacher there. It postponed action of renaming Gibsonville Negro School in honor of another African American, Ralph Bunche, the United Nations diplomat and Nobel Peace laureate in 1950.[10]

The racial integration of public schools would become the South's longest-running news story. *Brown* remained on the front page for a few more days and then became a familiar item on the daily news agenda, popping to the fore with successive steps for decades to come. In May 1954, it was understood that nothing was going to happen immediately. Even the Court had said as much. When change did come, John Leary's teachers, many of them young and eager like Shirley Taylor, believed they would have their students ready.

Leary was a dedicated educator who ran one of the finest schools in the state. He had a staff of talented and caring teachers and his program was soundly supported by Superintendent Smith. There were no second-hand books or cast-off furniture at Washington Elementary.[11] The notion that black teachers and principals feared integration because they could not compete for jobs with white teachers—a line promoted by an unnamed Guilford County school source—was dismissed as preposterous. "There was no turmoil," Shirley Taylor Frye recalled many years later. "They were all excited about what was going on. Thurgood Marshall (the lead lawyer in the *Brown* case) was everybody's idol at that time. Most of it was the white folk are not going to let (integration) happen. It was going to be slow."[12]

Taylor's bravado disguised a tinge of uncertainty, a condition that was rare for her. Earlier in the school year she had talked with Leary about her future as a teacher. Routine classroom work was not providing the professional stimulation that she wanted out of a career in education, she told him. Leary asked if she had ever considered teaching children with mental disabilities.

She became enthusiastic about the prospect as they talked about a challenge that would provide an outlet for her creativity. Together, they had surveyed the literature and Taylor found that the best men in the field were at Syracuse University in New York. She made plans to take courses there as a special summer student rather than formally enroll as a candidate for a graduate degree. Taylor was cautious. She was not sure her A&T training had adequately prepared her to pass the Miller Analogies Test, the standard for admission to a regular graduate program.[13]

Money for her further study was available from the state. North Carolina was a year away from a court order desegregating the Consolidated University of North Carolina, so rather than open classrooms to African Americans seeking post-graduate training at the white institutions, the state paid tuition for blacks to attend out-of-state schools. Taylor was stubborn. She was not going to be part of a plan that facilitated segregation. Her summer studies hung in the balance until Leary secured a grant of $500 for her from the Greensboro Kiwanis Club to cover her travel expenses and tuition.[14]

The trip itself was an adventure. She had traveled out of state with the A&T debate team, but this time she was on her own, alone. She booked a sleeper berth for Syracuse, New York. When the train reached New York City she thought she was at her destination only to learn she had another two hundred fifty miles to go. The summer proved to be everything she had hoped for. Moreover, she discovered that her concern about the adequacy of A&T education was unfounded. Once she was toe-to-toe with white peers, she did fine. It was the same lesson Henry Frye had learned when he found himself competing with white ROTC candidates at summer camp.

African Americans were commonplace on the Syracuse campus. In her first year, she shared a room in a dormitory with another black teacher, a woman from Durham who was continuing her studies in library science. Taylor finished the summer session with A's in all three of her courses. The next summer, in 1955, she returned as a regular graduate student after posting good grades on the qualifying exams to become a candidate for a master's degree, which she was awarded at the end of her last summer of classes in 1958.

The experience was not without its troubling moments. In her final semester, a visiting professor stopped her after class and questioned her work on a recent assignment. Who had written her paper for her, he asked? Why, no one, Taylor replied; she had written it herself. He could not believe a young black woman from a school he had never heard of could produce such quality work. Taylor got an A in the course. Meanwhile, she found encouraging support from her classmates. In one class, fellow students challenged their instructor after his joke included the punch line, "nigger in the woodpile." Taylor heard the tasteless remark, but she did not respond. Others in the class called the man to account for his offensive language and he apologized. She ignored her mother's caution about always having the last word. "I said, 'I look at that terminology as an adjective. I thought you were describing yourself.'" She then put the incident behind her. "It was one of those things that I was not going to allow to interfere with what I went there to do. I wasn't going there to fight any battles, so I just let it roll off."[15]

When Taylor began her studies in 1954, Henry Frye was in South Korea wearing a sidearm and serving as the duty officer in charge of an air force ammunition dump about seventy miles south of Seoul. Daily combat for the United Nations forces in Korea had ended a few weeks after Shirley had pinned a lieutenant's bar on his collar at A&T graduation ceremonies in June 1953. The suspension in hostilities was welcomed by the world, but it left Frye and his fellow ROTC graduates in limbo. The air force wasn't ready to ship more men to the Far East, so Frye was left with an uncertain future that made him imminently unemployable.

He said goodbye to Shirley and headed to New York City in search of a job. He took up temporary residence with a sister on Hancock Street in the Bedford-Stuyvesant section of Brooklyn and began knocking on doors. Employers interested in his academic background were put off by his military commitment. He was simply overqualified for other jobs. Finally, he bumped into another A&T grad who told him a slaughterhouse was hiring, and for the next five months or so, the future chief justice of the N.C. Supreme Court earned union wages as he shuttled the skinned hides of sheep and calves around a slaughterhouse that supplied Armour and Company. His orders from the air force came through in December at about the same time he found a job as an assistant in a hospital laboratory. He saw Shirley in December, when she was in New York to visit her sister, before he left in January 1954 for Lackland Air Force Base in San Antonio, Texas, for his officer orientation. From there he went to Lowry Air Force Base near Denver to learn how to run an ammunition depot. He and Shirley did see not one another until late spring when he had a month's leave before he reported to his post in Korea.[16]

Frye spent most of his furlough in Ellerbe, lending a hand to his family. During his senior year at A&T, a fire had destroyed the Frye home. The cause was never determined, but it might have been arson. Henry's sister Ola was at home one night when she heard a noise outside. She checked, saw nothing amiss, and went back to bed. A short time later, the barn was consumed in flames and the roof collapsed, killing Walter Frye's mules. Not long after the barn fire, the house burned to the ground. Ola believed it was arson and the culprit was a man Walter Frye had embarrassed by giving refuge to the man's daughter, who claimed she was being abused. Another cause may have been faulty wiring.[17] Instead of rebuilding the house, the Fryes—Henry's youngest brother Elbert was still at home — moved a half mile closer to town into a smaller rental house that was short on conveniences, including a reliable supply of clean water. Walter Frye hauled in water after the well had become contaminated.

Henry worked with a neighbor, Evans Terry, and his former agriculture teacher, J. E. Forte, to put in a quarter mile of water line to connect the Frye and Terry homes to the Ellerbe town service that had been extended only as far as the new school that had opened in 1952. Before he left, the Fryes would no longer worry about drinking from water barrels. Henry considered his labor and investment in materials to be a gift for his mother. When the stream of water began to flow into the kitchen sink he had never in his life been more proud.[18]

Frye was a good officer and was promoted to first lieutenant before he completed his tour of duty. His active service was uneventful. In Korea, where he was stationed for three months before being reassigned to Japan, he relied on a senior non-commissioned officer who was more proficient at managing munitions than any newly minted junior officer. His duties in Japan followed a humdrum routine that was broken by opportunities to see the countryside and have some contact with the Japanese, but that first assignment taught a valuable life lesson.

When Frye arrived at his duty station, the installation was under the command of a white warrant officer. He was a man with twenty years in the service and Frye was faced with a choice. He could exercise his privilege of rank and take over, or defer to the man's experience. "I had a whole lot of book learning, but I didn't know anything," Frye recalled. "I said I want you to keep on running it, just like you have been doing, but I said I want to meet with you in the morning before you start and again in the afternoon and I want you to teach me everything you know about this. And that made him feel good. By the time he left, I knew what I was doing. Boy, if he had said, 'OK, it is your show, you go ahead and run it,' I would have made all kind of mistakes. And you are dealing with ammunition, bombs, 250-, 500-, 1,000-pound bombs. I would have been lost."[19]

The Jim Crow South was literally and figuratively a world away, and while he was in uniform nobody made any fuss about Frye's skin color. As undergraduates back in Greensboro, he and his ROTC buddies had wondered if they would be given the same respect as white officers. They had talked about what they would do if an enlisted man refused to salute. Frye never had a chance to find out. Any slights were minor and infrequent. Once, after he reported for duty at Lackland Air Force Base, he joined fellow officers for a dinner off the base in San Antonio. They entered one restaurant and were told it was for whites only. They left and went elsewhere. During his time in Denver, he bought a used 1951 Chevrolet and signed up for membership in the American Automobile Association, thus skirting the association's aversion to enrolling black members in the South. He was interested for the roadside service, not the route tips; the routine listing of public accommodations was useless information for African Americans traveling in the South.[20]

The post-war years had produced cars and highways to accommodate Americans in a hurry. White travelers had little difficulty enjoying the new freedom of the road, but the situation was different for African Americans driving in the South. "When we were driving anywhere, you had to think about where you could use a rest room," Frye said. "[The] Esso station was somewhere you could use a rest room, but not all of them. So if I was driving to somewhere I went regularly, I found out where the Esso stations were. To play safe, I would always buy some gas and almost in the same breath ask, where is your bathroom. Nine times out of ten it worked. But in a few cases, they said, we don't have one or we don't have one for colored. I [then] said forget about the gas."

On trips to visit family in the North, Frye was guided by directions from his brothers who knew the route. "People used to drive to New York from Greensboro and Ellerbe. In Richmond, Virginia, there was a black restaurant that became well known as a place to stop and eat. You planned your trip on that. Once you got to the New Jersey Turnpike you could use the restrooms and everything else. Once you got to the turnpike you were up North. You were free. Until you got there you didn't know what you were going to run into.

"In Baltimore, they said when black folk got to Baltimore they figured they were up north. But when white folks got to Baltimore they felt they were down south. That is not a good place to be. Above there, OK. Below there, you knew your place so you didn't try. Washington, D.C., was just like the South. In the train, you sat in the front of the train and the back of the bus just like in the South."[21]

In the Far East, he was generally the only black officer around, and race was not an issue. The Japanese seemed to be suspicious of all Americans, no matter whether they were black or white.[22]

Fifty years later, Frye compressed his time in Japan into two memories. The first was a recollection of a fellow officer who was a lawyer and who spent his weekends in the stockade teaching uneducated servicemen how to read and write. Up to that time, he subscribed to his mother's conviction that lawyers were liars whose job was to get guilty people out of trouble. He also met a young Japanese interpreter and guide, Hideki Imamura, who was working with Baptist missionaries. Imamura led him and some fellow officers on a hike to the top of one of the peaks of Mt. Aso, the world's largest active volcano that dominates the southern island of Kyushu. On Frye's return to the United States in December 1955, he spent a few days in California before traveling on to North Carolina and a segregated world that had changed little during his two years in the Far East.

Shirley posted a letter to Henry on virtually every day that he was in uniform. Writing him became a part of her daily routine. He was not so regular with his replies, but when a letter did arrive, she shared portions related to his experience overseas with her Girl Scout troop. There was little risk of embarrassment if the teenagers stumbled onto something personal. Frye was not a romantic. In fact, he had told Shirley when he headed overseas that she should not wait for him. He said he wanted to make a fresh start when he was released from active duty. She dated other men, much to the concern of Mrs. Lee and her friends on Benbow Road, who reminded her regularly that Henry Frye was the man for her to marry. Privately, she agreed with them.[23]

In January 1956, Frye was in more of a quandary about his future than he had been two years earlier. Upon graduation, he at least had the knowledge that military service would occupy the next two years. As his service in Japan was coming to an end, he considered staying in the military, but the air force wanted another four years, or nothing. That was too long, so he opted to honor the balance of his military obligation with service in the reserves. Back in civilian clothes, he returned to Ellerbe, but he was anxious about every minute that he remained dependent on his family. He looked for a job in Greensboro and helped his father at his sawmill to earn a bit of money. Short on cash, he cut his trips to Greensboro to see Shirley to every other weekend. One Sunday, he was pacing the floor at home when his mother told him to stop stewing about Shirley Taylor and go see her. He called to be sure she was home, and when he arrived he told her he had come to talk about planning their life together. "I assumed he was asking to marry me," Shirley said some years later.[24]

They compromised on a wedding date in August. Shirley wanted to wait a year, but once Henry made up his mind about anything he was ready to act. They made plans to go to Fremont to speak with her family. When they got to the Taylor home, Henry paid his respects to Shirley's mother and then pulled off his suit coat and headed out to the field to meet her father. Ed Lenzie Taylor was cropping tobacco and he took to Henry's initiative and readiness for hard work. When they returned for the evening meal, he told his wife, "That boy's all right."

Henry had no luck in finding a job in Greensboro. Sales seemed a likely extension of his prior work experience. He had been selling something — newspaper subscriptions, seeds, and NAACP memberships — since he was a youngster. He answered a help-wanted listing in the Greensboro newspaper and was told to come for an interview. Once he got there, however, he was left to sit and wait. He finally asked a receptionist about the interview he had been invited to attend. She left and a man returned to complain that Frye had not told him he was black. Frye said he didn't know it mattered. "He said we are going to hire some colored salesmen, but we are going to do that on Saturday." He was invited to return that weekend. He didn't.[25]

Once again, any job had to be a temporary arrangement since he planned to use his GI Bill benefits to pay for further study. The Benbow Road crowd pegged him for a doctor. He wasn't that interested in medicine but dentistry looked promising for a man with a background in the sciences. Teaching was also an option. Some of his A&T professors, especially his chemistry teacher, Dr. Isaac Miller, had left a profound impression. He didn't know which way to turn.

Henry could not afford too many visits to Greensboro without a job to pay his bills. When he stayed overnight he usually got a room at the Magnolia House, a small hotel run by the Gist family. It was near the Bennett College campus and the only decent place in Greensboro for African American travelers. The food prepared by Mrs. Gist was always good and the clientele was diverse. The Magnolia's guests included businessmen, educators visiting the nearby campuses, and well known musicians, such as trumpeter Louis Armstrong when he played dates in Greensboro.

His choices for professional schooling were better in 1956 than when he had graduated in 1953. While he was in the air force, the trustees of the University of North Carolina had ended a half-dozen years of bootless legal appeals to avoid desegregation. Three African Americans were admitted as undergraduates at Chapel Hill in 1955 and seven others were in graduate programs.[26] With dentistry as the most attractive option, Henry and Shirley drove to Chapel Hill to speak with the dean of the dental school. The trip was a disappointment. He discovered that while his college record was excellent, he would need two more courses in physical chemistry to qualify for admission. He was encouraged to fill the gap and apply in a year.

Henry also had considered law school but had been discouraged by one attorney with whom he had talked. "I remember the kind of questions he had asked me," Frye said many years later. "He said, 'Is anybody in your family a lawyer?' I said, 'No.' He said, 'Is anybody in your family in business?' I said, 'No.' He said, 'Well, how are you going to get business?' I said, 'I don't know.' He asked me about my background. I said I was a biology major, with a chemistry minor with air science. He didn't encourage me at all. So I had thought that maybe that was the wrong area to go into."

Greensboro had four black lawyers in 1956. Herbert Parks was self-taught and had been licensed well before he had to face the discipline of modern bar examinations. He handled bastardy cases and a few criminal matters. His summations were worth a visit to court; some times he mistook the jury for the congregations he preached to on Sundays. At the other end of the professional spectrum was Mrs. Elreta Alexander. She was a graduate of A&T

and, in 1945, was the first African American female to graduate from the Columbia University School of Law. She was licensed in New York and within a year had moved to Greensboro with her husband, a doctor. The city's other black lawyers were Major S. High and J. Kenneth Lee, who were closer in age to Frye.[27]

Frye knew Lee from his visits with Shirley at Lee's aunt's house on Benbow Road. A man of modest size, lively and personable, Lee was a bundle of energy. He was as much an entrepreneur as he was a lawyer. After graduating from A&T in 1946 he taught engineering to undergraduates during the day and ran a night school in radio repair for vets on the GI Bill. In 1949, students at the makeshift law school at North Carolina College in Durham had sued for a place in the whites-only law school at Chapel Hill. The NAACP took up the case and successfully argued that the law school at Durham was not equal to the one at Chapel Hill. When it appeared the original plaintiffs might graduate at North Carolina College before the suit would run its course, the NAACP's Thurgood Marshall recruited two more plaintiffs from the law school. His picks were Harvey Beech from Kinston, and his roommate, Kenneth Lee, who had yet to finish his first year of courses. In 1951, the federal court ruled in favor of the plaintiffs; Lee, Beech and three others entered the UNC law school in September. Lee finished his course work and took the bar examination in the summer of 1952. Lee and Beech became the first of their race to earn an academic degree from the University of North Carolina.[28]

E. Shirley Taylor met Henry Frye when she was a freshman, and the two dated throughout their college years. At graduation, she pinned the bars of a second lieutenant on his uniform (courtesy Frye family).

Like Frye, Lee had grown up poor and undereducated in Richmond County schools. He knew something about Ellerbe and the people who came from up that way, and he liked what he had seen of Frye. Years later, he said Frye was "an old honest country boy, and smart." When Lee heard that others had discouraged Frye from attending law school because of his academic training as a scientist, he scoffed and pointed a finger at his own degree in engineering. "Don't worry about that stuff," Lee told him. "Get out there and do a good job."

That was all Frye needed. He and Shirley headed back to Chapel Hill and an appointment with Dean Henry Brandis at the law school. The reception was different from five years earlier when Lee's admission ticket was a court order. Brandis was welcoming, and encouraging. The two

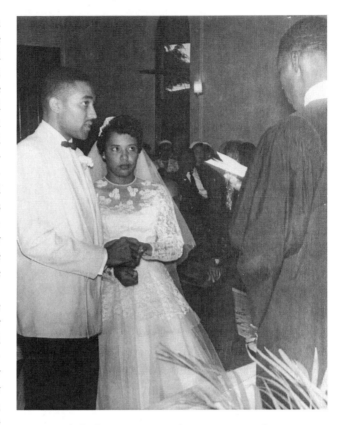

Henry and Shirley were married in August 1956 in a ceremony officiated by the Reverend Frederick Terry (right). Earlier in the day, Terry and Henry Frye had tried unsuccessfully to register to vote in their hometown of Ellerbe (courtesy Frye family).

saw Brandis on Friday; Henry got an application for admission in the mail on Monday. He sailed past the admission exams and had his acceptance letter by the end of May 1956. In the meantime, he returned to New York where an employment agency helped him land a job as a lab assistant at Felton Chemical Company, a firm that supplied the food and drug industry with flavorings and perfumes.

Henry and Shirley's wedding day was August 25. That would leave them about a week for a honeymoon before Henry was due to begin classes in Chapel Hill. On the morning of the wedding, Henry was in Ellerbe while Shirley busied herself in Greensboro before the ceremonies set for 5 P.M. at Bethel AME Church. Bethel's minister, the Reverend Melvin Swann, and Henry's childhood friend from Ellerbe, who was now the Reverend Frederick Terry, were officiating. While Frye was at A&T and in the Air Force, Terry had finished at Shaw University in Raleigh and begun his studies at seminary. This would be his first wedding.[29]

Before they left for Greensboro, Frye and Terry drove to the Ellerbe town hall where they planned to register to vote. A clerk was on duty on Saturdays and this would be Henry's last opportunity to take care of matters before heading on to Chapel Hill. The two gave their mission no more thought than if they were going in to collect the mail. The clerk brought them up short when he took their names and began asking questions about former presidents of the United States, and if they could name a certain number of signers of the Declaration of Independence. Frye was stunned. He didn't try to answer and said he didn't believe he was required to do so. The clerk told him he was only following instructions. They had to pass a literacy test and he pointed to a book on the counter before him as his authority.[30]

The state constitution did include such a provision. It was part of a package of amendments adopted in 1900 after Democrats regained control of the state after literally and figuratively running Republicans and African Americans out of public office. The provision stipulated that any prospective voter "shall be able to read and write any section of the Constitution in the English language." Registrars had used that provision to reduce African American political participation to next to nothing, especially in "black belt" counties where the majority black population could make an appreciable difference in elections. Over the years, Richmond County had effectively discouraged African Americans from voting. In 1940, of the 8,746 voters in the county, only 68 of them were black. None of the Fryes were registered to vote, as far as Henry knew. By the mid–1950s, there were still only a handful of blacks on the rolls in Richmond County. In the Mineral Springs precincts that included Ellerbe, about a third of the residents but only about 6 percent of the registered voters were black.[31]

Of course, discrimination was nothing new for Frye or Terry. They had seen it — and experienced it — all of their lives. At the same time, they found the clerk's justification for dismissing the applications of two college graduates as illiterates to be unbelievable. They left the office, and then Frye turned around and went back inside. There must be a mistake, he said. The clerk must have questioned his application, he said, because he had been out of the state working in New York of late. No, the clerk replied. There was no mistake. Recalling the incident years later, Frye said the man told him: "Oh no, I know your father, Walter Frye, and you are the one admitted to the law school at Chapel Hill."

"So you are turning me down," Frye said.

"Yes," the man said, "You didn't pass the literacy test."

Henry was still deeply disturbed about the insult more than five hours later as he stood with Terry at the front of Bethel AME Church and watched Shirley walk down the aisle on the arm of her father in a glorious dress of Chantilly lace and tulle over satin. In her hand was a white Bible topped with a white orchid. Henry was in white formal wear. There was an orchid in his lapel. Just as his bride reached the chancel, he leaned in to whisper to her, "Do you know they wouldn't let me register to vote today?" She smiled back and said, "Can we talk about that a little later?"[32]

4

Law School

Henry E. Frye walked up the steps of Manning Hall on the campus of the University of North Carolina in September 1956 and became the first African American to enter the university's law school as a first-year student. This footnote in history was far less important to Frye than his desire to convince his mother he had made the right decision. The son that Pearl Frye had hoped to see in a clerical robe was set on becoming a lawyer. Frye was determined to overcome her belief that a man of the law could never be as honorable as a man of the cloth.

Frye was one of thirteen African Americans among the nearly 7,000 white students on the campus, and he was the only one of his race among the 105 first-year students in the law school. His arrival on campus was unremarkable, especially for the law school, where classes had been racially integrated since the fall of 1951. He wasn't alone. George Green of Raleigh, a transfer to the law school, was beginning his third year. Nonetheless, Frye was isolated, but probably no more so than when he was on active duty in Japan or Korea. He reminded himself that he was in law school to make good grades, not fast friends.

Manning Hall sits in the heart of the campus at the east end of a quadrangle just off Polk Place, the long sloping lawn between South Building, which was the university's administrative center, and the impressive hulk of the campus library. It had been the home of the law school since the building opened in 1923. When Frye arrived, the school's faculty was composed of men, most of whom had been teaching in Chapel Hill since the 1920s and 1930s. Some of them had helped North Carolina's attorney general prepare his arguments in favor of separate-but-equal schools before the U.S. Supreme Court. It would be another year before a "young man," Daniel H. Pollitt, a former marine and left-leaning lawyer in his mid-thirties, would join the faculty and fill the vacancy created when Professor William Aycock was named chancellor of the university. Pollitt would add some spice to Frye's studies during his last two years.

The Chapel Hill campus was clothed in the traditions of the Old South, and most of them were antagonistic to African Americans. The university administration, mindful of a board of trustees that opposed desegregation at every step, had come along grudgingly in accommodating the blacks admitted to the campus by orders of the federal courts. Students, meanwhile, appeared more open to change. Beginning in 1951, students speaking through campus organizations had accepted desegregation and challenged the foot-dragging by those in South Building. When undergraduates learned in the fall of 1951 that J. Kenneth Lee and the other African Americans in the law school had been excluded from regular student seating at Kenan Stadium, they had confronted Chancellor Robert B. House with their petitions of protest. An editorial in the *Daily Tar Heel* had argued that segregated seating "is thoroughly repugnant to the cardinal principle for which this venerable citadel of democracy and freedom has so long stood."[1] House brushed aside the student protest and said the social customs of the South would be obeyed. He told the students, "The university can go no faster than the forces that control it will allow."[2]

The administration had further embarrassed itself when it assigned dormitory space to Lee and two others. The three had the entire top floor of Steele Hall, where they enjoyed ample space for themselves, as well as a number of guests, at a time when white students were sleeping in dormitory basements or going without a bed. The African Americans took their meals at the campus cafeteria in Lenoir Hall, but usually sat at tables apart from the others. This public separation masked quiet, private collaboration with some of their white peers. Lee later recalled that he wouldn't have made it through the year without the help of students who slipped into Steele Hall to share lecture notes and participate in a study group. Of course, there were incidents that left scars. Harvey Beech never forgot the student, whose last name also began with B, who refused to walk beside him when they lined up in pairs at graduation to receive diplomas. Nor would he forget another from far back among the Rs who readily took his place.[3]

A federal court had forced admission of black undergraduates in 1955, the year before Frye arrived. There had been a bit of a stir on campus. Student body president Don Fowler declared that the majority of the students were opposed to integration and supported the trustees' legal challenges to desegregation, despite the statements to the contrary from student organizations. That was the extent of the objections made public, however. In September 1956, Chapel Hill was such a model of acceptance that a documentary film crew for a Ford Foundation subsidiary was on hand to record the peaceful integration of a Southern college campus.[4] Eight months earlier, a mob in Tuscaloosa had confronted Autherine Lucy when she attempted to enroll at the University of Alabama.

Frye arrived unencumbered of any call upon the university beyond a seat in the classroom and the attention of his professors. He planned to commute from Greensboro, where he and Shirley had rented a house on Gorrell Street that was owned by Kenneth Lee's sister Lillian. The seven-room bungalow was in a neat, well-trimmed neighborhood just west of South Benbow Road, across from St. Mary's Catholic Church. It came fully furnished; Shirley didn't even have to unpack wedding gifts. They were fresh from a three-day honeymoon at the home of Henry's aunt and uncle in the rural reaches of Virginia near the Tye River community, a hamlet about twenty-five miles north of Lynchburg. The cost was little more than gas up and back. The two were quite short on cash; Shirley's first paycheck for the 1956-1957 school year wouldn't arrive until well after Labor Day. In the meantime, they were living on Henry's GI benefits of $135 a month.[5]

Before his law classes started, Henry had unfinished business back in Ellerbe. The clerk's refusal to register him to vote remained an insulting injustice that demanded attention, and quickly. The statewide referendum on the so-called Pearsall Plan, a legislative device designed to stall full integration of public schools in North Carolina, was set for September 8. He wanted to cast his vote against it. As soon as he could, he set out for Richmond County, where he paid a call on the chairman of the county's board of elections. The man apologized when he heard what had happened; he told Frye to try again. On his second visit to the Ellerbe office, he was met by a different clerk, a woman this time, who asked if he was the man who had been turned away before. Frye said yes. She asked him to write a passage from the state constitution and promptly added his name to the rolls as a Democrat.[6]

Henry had put in a call to his father's old friend, attorney Elsie Webb, to tell him about what had happened. That may have had something to do with the different attitude he found on his return visit. Frye would not have fared as well in some North Carolina counties. Just a few months earlier, in May 1956, a registrar, who apparently was working from a script similar to the one that confronted Henry on his first visit, had refused to register Ernest Ivey in Halifax County. Among the questions posed to Ivey, who was as undeniably literate as Frye, was, "On what date each year does Congress convene?"[7]

There was no question which political party Frye would adopt for his own. The Democratic Party's response to the Great Depression under President Franklin Roosevelt, promoted by his wife, Eleanor, had shaken poor African Americans free from their moorings in the Republican Party that had held fast for nearly seventy-five years. When Henry was in New York, earlier in the summer, he had developed a friendship with the young minister at the church he attended. The man could not understand how any African American could vote for a Democrat. "He went all the way back to Lincoln and the Republicans during Reconstruction and how the Democrats took over and almost enslaved blacks all over again in 1900. He said he'd die before he voted for anyone other than a Republican," Frye later recalled. "I knew about Franklin Roosevelt and I couldn't see how you could vote Republican." After all, it was FDR and the New Deal that had brought electricity to the Frye farm in Richmond County.[8]

When Frye arrived in Chapel Hill, three years had passed since he had seen the inside of a college classroom. Still, he believed he was ready. He was confident he could make the grade in law, despite his background in science, and his experience in the air force had only reinforced his confidence that he could compete with whites. Nonetheless, what lay ahead of him in law school would be different; cultural biases did not inhabit the pure sciences that had been the foundation of his undergraduate degree. That was not always the case with history, economics, and the law.

Much like his white peers, Frye discovered he was more comfortable in some courses than he was in others. He easily grasped the concepts of criminal law, for example. Professor Albert Coates carried his students through the particulars, probing each point of an offense for its foundation. Consider the crime of breaking and entering, Coates would say. If the defendant had one foot inside a house, and went no farther, was that entering? If the door was cracked open, and someone entered uninvited, did that amount to a breaking? Frye could visualize the criminal law and its application. At the same time, the scholar in him rose to the challenges in his legal methods course where students learned how to mine the law found in court decisions from across the land. The courses he found most difficult were those that simply had no connection with his personal experience. He knew nothing about business, and was totally unfamiliar with corporations and how they were organized. "The things that my contracts teacher thought were simple, I thought were complicated," Frye said. "The ones he thought were complicated, I thought were simple. I was glad to get out of contracts." The study of future interests in property was founded in English common law and precepts that had developed over centuries of settling contests of feudal estates sent him to the history books. "Sometimes," he said, "the articles [assigned to be read] or the professor would talk about king this of England. That was difficult. I had to spend a lot of time trying to understand the English feudal system."[9]

His decision to commute to classes in Chapel Hill from Greensboro eased his social concerns, but it meant he spent roughly three hours a day in a car, when he otherwise could be reading cases in the law library. His study time was curtailed even further by the need to supplement Shirley's paycheck. On the weekends, he grabbed a bag of samples of Watkins products—soaps, oils, and seasonings—and made his way through the neighborhood selling items door-to-door. Frye's easy temperament, gracious manner, and clean looks facilitated his introduction. Once inside a home, however, he had to compete with the interruptions of children and the constant distraction of a television set that always seemed to be on. He was seasoned by years of direct sales, from seeds and *Grit* readers back in Ellerbe to the vets in the A&T housing who were on his paper route. "If you do it long enough," he said years later, "you learn who won't pay."[10]

On weekdays during that first year, Frye arose early and prepared for the day's classes while Shirley cooked breakfast. At around 6:30 A.M., he usually joined one or two other law students who lived in Greensboro to share a ride to Chapel Hill. A regular companion was Robert Blum. From time to time, another Greensboro commuter, Max Ballinger, joined them. Both of his traveling companions were white and, like him, students in their first year.

Blum had grown up in Memphis and was about four years younger than Frye. His parents had moved to Greensboro by the time he graduated from Vanderbilt University and Frye was completing his two years of military service. The two met in Chapel Hill and decided to make the daily drive together, but the arrangement lasted only their first year. Frye was a stickler for punctuality; Blum less so. He told Frye not to worry about being late, which happened often enough to become a real bother for Frye. No one noticed who was tardy, Blum assured him. Frye believed everyone noticed when the only black man arrived late to class. During his subsequent years, Frye rented a room in a dormitory and stayed over in Chapel Hill when his schedule was tight.[11]

Blum and Frye grew comfortable with one another during the year they shuttled to and from classes together. The experience awakened Blum to the challenges his friend faced in a society that clearly did not include him in its mainstream. Even if Frye had wanted to socialize outside of class with him or any other students, there was no place besides the campus cafeteria for them to go. None of eateries on Franklin Street admitted blacks. From time to time, the two talked about desegregation and the South's racial conundrum, but Frye didn't dwell on the subject. Nonetheless, Blum saw a fire that smoldered beneath Frye's calm demeanor and uncomplaining manner. When students began the lunch-counter sit-ins in Greensboro in 1960, he called Frye to see if he had provoked them. It was not that Frye was unconcerned about current issues, but, for the moment, at least, his attention was focused on the cases up for discussion in the next class. "He was a good student," recalled Blum. "Henry was working very hard to navigate through law school, in a white community, in times that were difficult. He wanted to make the least of it as possible."[12]

Frye responded to Jim Crow the way he would later approach his role in affecting change. He wanted to make his efforts count. In Richmond County he had challenged a dull and bigoted clerk, and he did something about it. Registering to vote was a personal victory; he had simply stood up for his rights. He had done all he could. Frye believed the world was changing, but a first-year law student wasn't going to move things forward by picking fights. As he put it, he was focused on "getting my degree and getting out of there. I wasn't too interested in socializing, going out at night, drinking beer."[13]

The civil rights movement barely had a name in 1956. Rather than witnessing a movement, the nation was experiencing only flashpoints. Some were startling in their ferocity, such as the mob Autherine Lucy faced in Tuscaloosa. Others were all but ignored. One of North Carolina's early cases of civil disobedience was the arrest of a group of African Americans in Greensboro who played on a city-owned golf course that was only open to whites. And the movement did not have a leader until December 1956, just as Henry and Shirley were preparing for their first Christmas together. In that month, the seating restrictions on city-owned buses came down in Montgomery, Alabama, and a young Baptist minister named Martin Luther King, Jr., brought to a close a year-long boycott. The victory came after the U.S. Supreme Court ruled unconstitutional the segregated seating required by Alabama law, but it was the drama of African Americans defiantly walking to work rather than riding in humiliation that gave the nation a visual image of the courage of people opposed to the injustices of segregation. Within a matter of weeks of the end of the boycott, King became the voice and face of the movement.

At the same time, Southern segregationists were consolidating their positions. The campaign by whites in favor of massive resistance to desegregation of public schools was heading toward the closing of public schools in Virginia. That would have suited some in North Carolina, too, where changes in state law and the constitution under the Pearsall Plan made that possible, if whites fully exercised their options. The mood in North Carolina was subdued, compared to other Southern states, but voters had demonstrated what could happen to racial moderates who stepped out of line. Two North Carolina congressmen who refused to sign the so-called Southern Manifesto, a resolution that denounced the Supreme Court and pledged resistance to integration, failed to win re-nomination in 1956. One of the casualties was Richmond County's Charles B. Deane. He had represented the Eighth District for ten years.[14]

Three years after Greensboro school officials had made their bold statements, the makeup of the Greensboro city schools remained unchanged as Henry finished his first year in law school. Shirley and her fellow teachers had worked after hours on school days to prepare students for integration of classrooms. The Washington Street Parent-Teacher Association had counseled parents on their responsibility to remain current with their children's schoolwork, if there was to be hope of a smooth transition. In the late summer of 1957, when Greensboro school officials finally made new school assignments, it was clear the school board was interested in integrating only a few classrooms in all-white schools. The token steps were a deep disappointment to African Americans, who had expected more.[15]

Shirley had taken a break from her studies at Syracuse University to get married in 1956. In the summer of 1957, she continued her work toward a graduate degree. Grants from two Greensboro civic groups—the Kiwanis Club and the Junior League—had paid her expenses for the first two years; this time she was on her own. The Greensboro schools program for children with special needs was not exactly experimental, but close to it. Classroom teachers used rudimentary methods, at best, to determine if one of their students was mentally disabled and needed reassignment to Shirley's care or that of the one white teacher who taught children with special needs. The assignments made by uninformed teachers were so clumsy that Shirley discovered one of her students wasn't disabled, he was just a slow learner. The boy returned to regular classes, graduated and ended up building one of the largest auto dealerships in the state of Maryland.

Her classroom was one of just a few in the state for mentally disabled African American children, as she discovered when she and her principal, John Leary, attended a meeting to form a state association for retarded children. The meeting was held at the state's Caswell Training Center in Kinston, a tobacco town deep in eastern North Carolina not far from where Shirley was raised. Attending the conference with them were Dr. George Evans and his wife, Marguerite, who was a nurse. After the morning session adjourned, they were moving along with the group of educators to lunch in the cafeteria when they were stopped and told African Americans were not allowed to be seated with the rest of those attending the meeting. When Evans protested, he was asked if they were Native Americans. "[Dr. Evans] said, 'No we are not Indians.'" Shirley recalled. "They could have passed for Indians, but I don't think I could have. I don't have any Indian features. But we ate. On the way back, Dr. Evans said, 'Can you believe what we just ran into?'"[16]

Leary's light complexion admitted him to stores in downtown Greensboro whose owners would have never served most of the darker-skinned teachers in his school. Passing for white proved helpful when he was traveling with Frye and other teachers to attend state meetings. If they happened to be on the road at mealtime, and they could not find a restaurant or diner that would admit them, Leary would park the car, take a seat at a restaurant, and order sandwiches to go.[17]

When Shirley left for Syracuse in the summer of 1957, Henry stayed behind in Greensboro. He owed two weeks of his summer break from law school to the U.S. Air Force. He was excited about his orders that called for him to report for duty at the Air University at Maxwell Air Force Base in Montgomery, Alabama.

By the time Henry got to Alabama, Dr. Martin Luther King, Jr., had become one of the best-known public figures of the day. Since the end of the boycott in December 1956, King's picture had appeared on the cover of *Time* magazine, and the *New York Times* magazine had produced a long article on the boycott that was mostly a profile of its leader. Lawrence Spivak invited him to appear on the *Meet the Press* television show. He had gone on an international tour where he was greeted warmly by Kwame Nkrumah, the president of Ghana, the first independent nation in sub–Saharan Africa, before traveling on to Rome, Geneva, and London. Just two months earlier, on May 17, 1957, King spoke at a mass meeting in Washington to celebrate the *Brown* decision, where he turned the phrase "Give us the ballot" into a rousing refrain. While King was in Washington, he spent two hours with Vice President Richard Nixon talking about the civil rights bill that was pending in the Senate. One of the principal features of the bill was an extension of federal protection to voting rights. Republicans hoped the bill, which was being fought by southern Democrats, would help enroll African American voters.[18]

Henry Frye hoped that when he got to Alabama he would be able to hear the preacher everyone was talking about. On the Sunday of his first weekend in Montgomery, he made his way to King's church, Dexter Avenue Baptist, and joined the congregation for the morning's service. The crush of the year's events had often taken King away from his home pulpit, but he was there for most of July and August. On July 14, he began a series of sermons that spoke to the psychological challenges to healthy relationships of all persons, but which played especially upon the well-being of African Americans trying to cope with the deadening effects of life in a segregated society. King's first sermon dealt with feelings of inferiority. He moved on to dealing with fear, and closed with a sermon on controlling one's ego, or self-centeredness, as he called it. He drew heavily for the series upon the writings of Henry Emerson Fosdick's essay, "The Principle of Self-Acceptance."[19]

King had a preaching style that Frye might have adopted if he had gone into the ministry. Frye liked sermons with intellectual heft. He could do without the rousing, emotional exuberance found in most black churches. He longed for a message that made him think about himself, his life, and his world. King was his kind of preacher. His delivery was like controlled heat; he never shouted, but he preached like someone who could. He didn't talk down to his congregation. Rather, he assumed his listeners appreciated proper diction, had an understanding of good grammar, and had read a book or two. King's sermons were founded on scripture, and he kept the Lord at the center of his message, but he also talked about the quotidian difficulties of real life, especially if you lived in a nation that measured your worth by the color of your skin.[20]

As he finished his sermon on July 14, King said that it was not the environment, nor circumstances, that determined an individual's true character, but it was how a person responded to the challenges of the world. King used language that morning that twenty-five years later would become a familiar call of his protégé, an A&T graduate named Jesse Jackson. "I say to you this morning," King said from the Dexter Avenue pulpit, as the heat of the Alabama summer poured in the open windows, "you should go out with the assurance that you belong and you count and that you are somebody because God loves you. And that becomes a hope. That is the vital part."[21] Years later, Frye wasn't sure if he had heard King on the 14th, or had been on hand for one of the other sermons in his series, but the message became part of his mental inventory.

The Dexter Avenue church sits at the foot of a hill at a side street and fronts on the broad avenue leading to the steps of the Alabama State Capitol. The front door of the church opens onto a high porch, and the raised entrance offers a clear view of the domed pile, just a few blocks away, where, in 1861, Jefferson Davis had taken the oath of office as president of the Confederate States of America. King was standing at the church door at the conclusion of the service, greeting worshippers, as Frye joined the procession moving toward him. He grasped the minister's hand, and the two talked for a minute or two, before Frye continued on down the steps to the street below.

One King sermon wasn't enough to satisfy. Frye wanted to hear more, so, late in the afternoon, he drove to a country church where, he had learned during the morning service, King was scheduled to speak at a mass meeting related to the ongoing desegregation efforts of his Montgomery Improvement Association. Frye had plans he could not change for the evening, but he hoped that he could remain at the rally long enough to hear this exciting young minister at least once again.

The church was full and every seat was taken when Frye arrived. The only space he could find was on a staircase leading to the balcony. "They were singing, praying, and talking," he recalled. "Reverend [Ralph] Abernathy was warming people up for when Dr. King got there. I remember him saying, 'They tell us we have got to do it gradually, gradually. If I am in the ditch and a man has his foot on my neck, I don't want him to turn me loose gradually, I want him to turn me loose now.' I had to leave right after that. I didn't get to hear Dr. King speak."[22] Less than a year later, on February 11, 1958, King spoke at Bennett College in Greensboro, which arranged a hall for him after he was denied venues at A&T and black churches. Henry and Shirley did not hear him on that occasion.

Whatever lingering doubts Frye had about his capacity to succeed in law school dissipated with the posting of an initial round of grades. Professors identified students by a number, rather than by name, but despite the procedure the word spread that Frye was among those with As on his early exams. His success had not come easily. He studied hard to remain current on the cases featured in the classroom discussion. Whenever he and Shirley were in the car together, she read cases aloud while he drove. When he couldn't get to the law school library on weekends, he and Blum arranged admission to the one at the Guilford County courthouse in Greensboro. A's and B's came to Frye in his first year and, in his second year, he was in the top 10 percent of his class, which qualified him to write for the *North Carolina Law Review*.

Student writers contributed to the "Notes and Comments" section of the *Law Review*, a quarterly publication that analyzed legal concepts, court rulings, and other particulars about the law. Only the best students were eligible to participate and the top student in the third-year class served as editor-in-chief. For his first article, Frye chose a case that quite literally was close to home.

In the spring of 1957, the N.C. Supreme Court had rendered a decision in *State v. Cooke*. The case turned on a relatively narrow point — the limits on a trial court to amend an arrest warrant — but *Cooke* carried more freight than was evident in the prosaic title. Indeed, this was the trespassing case that had been brought against Greensboro dentist George Simkins, Jr., and his friends for playing golf on a city-owned course that had been leased to a private operator who denied privileges to African Americans. When the case was heard in superior court, the original warrant had been changed to say that the trespass had occurred on premises of "Gillespie Park Golf Club Inc." rather than "Gillespie Park Golf Club." The court held these were separate entities and ruled that the change amounted to the charging of a different crime. The convictions were thrown out.

Frye's commentary on *Cooke* was published in Volume 37 of the *Review*, released in the spring of 1958. It ran for thirteen paragraphs and included thirty-eight footnotes. His analysis focused on the legal point at issue before the court; there was no hint that *Cooke* concerned one of the state's first acts of protest at the segregated facilities of the Greensboro parks and recreation department.[23] The case he chose for his second effort for the *Law Review* was even more commonplace. He wrote about the legal intricacies of forgery and false identity. If Frye's intent was to avoid political statements while in law school, he was an overachiever.[24]

Talking some years later about the social dimensions of his law school experience, Frye downplayed the difficulties that he faced because of his race. Were his classmates supportive, he was asked. Generally, yes, he said, but he and other African Americans called the law school the "ice box," because of the cold shoulders they received from many classmates. Yet, in a quiet, steady, unobtrusive way that raised no tempers, Frye was raising the bar for black achievement and respect. After seven years of integration in the law school, he was the first African American to be published in the *Law Review*. His peers recognized his ability, and he was nominated as an officer in the Law

School Association, although Frye immediately withdrew his name from consideration.[25]

Integration of the law school remained a delicate matter, especially for social events. Law School Dean Henry Brandis had held that events were open to all students, which presented a quandary for planners of the annual Barristers Ball, a social affair with formal wear and a sit-down dinner. Not every venue allowed black guests, so each year the social chair had to determine if race was going to be a consideration. In advance of the event in Frye's second or third year, a white student asked Frye and law professor Dan Pollitt to join him for lunch. They met in the neutral territory of Lenoir Hall and ever so gently the man got around to asking about Henry and Shirley's plans for the ball. Henry toyed with his inquisitor for a time, knowing full well what he was about, but finally allowed that he and Shirley would not be attending.

A few days after their lunch meeting, Pollitt asked the white student why it had been necessary for him to be there. The man's reply set him back. "He said, well he was interested in politics and didn't want to be seen eating at Lenoir hall with a black student but it would be OK if it was with a professor. I was there to protect his political future."[26]

State politicians of all stripes played to the white majority. State Attorney General Malcolm Seawell was the speaker at the Law Review banquet in the spring of 1959 and defended the adoption of the Pearsall Plan, which blacks saw as only a delaying tactic of integration. He had spoken about militant activity, and declared that the NAACP represented "a great danger to continued public education."[27] The speech was an affront to Frye, who was present at the dinner, and he considered walking out during Seawell's speech. "I decided to stay and see what the end was going to be," he said.

Pollitt liked Frye and welcomed the chance to advise him on his work for the *Law Review*. Henry reciprocated and warmed to Pollitt, who was far more approachable than the senior members of the faculty. Pollitt had an easy manner and usually wore a wry smile. He was talkative, smart, very *liberal*, and endowed with a generous inventory of arresting tales. (As a marine serving in the South Pacific, he once found himself in hand-to-hand combat armed only with a canteen.) He had come to teaching from the law offices of Joseph Rauh, one of the founders of Americans for Democratic Action. In the early 1950s, he and Rauh had represented defendants such as writer Lillian Hellman, who had been charged in loyalty cases during the Red Scare.

Pollitt arrived in Chapel Hill after a stint on the law faculty at the University of Arkansas. He left there when he was asked to swear he wasn't a member of any subversive organizations. At the time, one of the organizations on the Arkansas attorney general's list was the NAACP. Pollitt had been a member for years. UNC Chancellor House was supposed to collect Pollitt's signature on a similar loyalty oath before putting him on the state payroll in

North Carolina. When the question arose during the employment interview, House fumbled among his papers and then declared he couldn't find the necessary form. A short time later, House retired and William Aycock, House's successor, never raised the subject again.[28]

In the summer of 1958, Henry and Shirley both went to Syracuse University. While Shirley finished up her work on her master's degree, Henry took courses in damages, casualty insurance, and legal writing in the university's law school. He came home with two A's and a B. When he got to Chapel Hill to begin his third year, the number of black students on the campus had doubled. Of the twenty-six, five were in law school, three were in the medical school, and two were in the school of social work, while nine were in other post-graduate programs. The balance was undergraduates. Among the five in the law school was Mrs. Sylvia X. Allen. She was a native of Cuba in her mid-thirties, the mother of six children, and the wife of a practicing physician in Fayetteville. Her presence bothered one of the two white women in the law school. They complained to Brandis that Allen rested from her commute to class from her home seventy-five miles away by taking naps on the couch in the women's lounge. Pollitt said one of the women told Brandis, "The nigra comes in and lies down on the pillow. We don't like it. Can't you stop it?" Brandis responded that if Allen's use of the couch was such a bother, then the complainer could use the women's lounge in nearby Lenoir Hall. (Allen graduated in 1962. She was the first black woman to earn a degree from the law school and later served as an assistant district attorney in Fayetteville before joining the N.C. Justice Department as an assistant attorney general in 1977.[29])

Not long after the start of his third year, Frye approached Pollitt for advice on an appropriate case or cases to use as a subject for his next *Review* commentary. Pollitt responded bluntly: "Henry, you are the only black man in this law class. You have written two articles. Get you a good racial discrimination case." When he returned for approval on his choice, Pollitt was delighted. Frye had looked into a federal appeals court decision that had denied relief for black railway workers who were losing their jobs as a result of discriminatory action by the Brotherhood of Locomotive Firemen and Enginemen. The legal issues involved were tied up in a tangle of cases that begged for description and analysis. Pollitt knew the issue well. He and Rauh had represented A. Philip Randolph, the founder of the Brotherhood of Sleeping Car Porters and an outspoken advocate for equal rights.

"[The unions] were trying to protect the jobs of the black firemen in the southeastern United States when they were changing from coal to diesel," Pollitt recalled. "It had been a black job when they shoveled coal and it became a white man's job when they turned a knob. They were trying to get rid of the blacks; we were trying to save them. There was lots of litigation and eight or nine cases in a short period of time and it was pretty confusing. I suggested he do blacks and Railway Labor Act. He did that and did a very good job. It was pretty important, especially to the readers of the *Law Review*."[30]

Frye's research took him to cases in a variety of state courts, as well as the record in the appeals court that had denied the workers membership in a union that, by law, was responsible for representing their interests. Frye buried himself in the law library as he approached his deadline. When he planned to work late he called Shirley to let her know his plans. At the time, the two were living in Chapel Hill and sharing a house with a medical student and his wife. Shirley had joined him in the spring of 1959 after she was forced into a leave of absence by school rules that prohibited expectant mothers from working in classrooms. The two were excited about their prospects for a family. Henry had once told Shirley he wanted twelve children. She wanted a number less than that. They were expecting the birth of their first child just a few weeks after Henry's graduation in May.

Henry became so absorbed in his work at the library that he was still there well past the time that Shirley expected him to be home. There was no way for her to contact him as the hours wore on, so she was left to wonder about his whereabouts. He finally arrived about dawn, with his work completed. After sorting out the cases, Frye concluded that the appeals court was lagging behind cases resolved in other states. His final sentence was not the language to launch a public protest. Again, he was a lawyer-to-be, his words uncluttered by emotion. "In denying relief in the principal case," he wrote, "the court has failed to forge the missing link in the chain of judicial remedies necessitated by the problems of racial discrimination in union membership."[31]

Henry Frye received the law school's juris doctor degree at graduation ceremonies in May 1959. At the time, it was only awarded to those students who graduated with honors. None of his family was on hand to witness his success as the first African American to complete his entire law education at the university. Henry had advised his parents against coming, telling them it was too much of a struggle to get onto the campus and get seated among the crowd. It was only after he discovered Shirley had invited her relatives that he realized his mistake. His parents would not miss any other event confirming their son's achievements as long as they were alive.[32]

Frye had the academic qualifications to be a lawyer, but he needed a license from the N.C. State Bar before he could hang out a shingle and begin his law practice. The bar examination was held each year in late July, and he had two months to get ready. Some graduates paid for tutorials to refresh themselves on subjects from one or two years back. Frye didn't have the money for outside help, but he did have Kenneth Lee, who loaned him space in an office at 427 S. Benbow Road that he shared with Dr. Alvin Blount. Frye settled in a small room between the two professionals and began reading the general statutes from the first volume to the last. He read steadily, and occasionally took a break to sit in on trials underway at the courthouse downtown. From time to time, Lee paid him to complete some legal research.

The bar examination was held in Raleigh over a period of three days. Frye was anxious after the first day, especially after he heard others talking about a case referenced on the test. Their answer was not the one he had supplied. There was at least one pleasant surprise. One of the questions dealt with negligence and Frye's answer was informed by what he had learned from one of the cases on trial that he had observed earlier in the summer. After a week of waiting, the letter from the State Bar arrived in late August. It began, "Congratulations" and Frye doesn't remember what came after that. He knew he had made it.

Weeks passed after he received his notification, and he had heard nothing further, even though he knew others who had received their licenses. Finally, Frye received a letter from the director of the State Bar informing him that he had missed an interview at the State Bar's office in Raleigh. The licensing process required personal certification of a prospective lawyer's moral character. That was usually done with a personal interview that was often routine and conducted by a State Bar designee in a candidate's hometown. Frye called Ed Cannon, the State Bar's executive director and the man with whom he supposedly was scheduled for an interview. Frye told Cannon he had not received a notice of a meeting; Cannon gave him a date for a new appointment.

Cannon's reputation preceded him. He was known for his racial bias and intimidating manner, all of which was reinforced for African Americans by the large, war-torn, Confederate battle flag hanging on his office wall. African Americans believed that their examinations were marked with an N and that only one or two were allowed to pass the bar exam each year. The only time more than two had passed was the year when Cannon was out of the country attending an American Bar Association meeting in London.

Cannon merely reflected the attitudes of the elders of the state's legal fraternity who had supported the university trustees' opposition to integration of the law school in 1951. A member of the state Board of Law Examiners testified for UNC and stated that black lawyers didn't need the experience offered at the law school in Chapel Hill because they would only have black clients.[33] Harvey Beech, the 1952 graduate, ran into that same antagonism during his interview in the licensing process. He and Kenneth Lee, who graduated that same year, were cross-examined on the politics of Michael H. Ross, the white student who had walked with Beech at graduation. Beech said he was asked if he knew whether Ross was a "communist."

Cannon's reception of Frye was no more cordial. After a few preliminary questions, Cannon asked if Frye had ever visited at a certain street address in Charlotte. Frye said he had been to Charlotte, but he didn't remember that address. He responded as best he could to a few more of Cannon's questions before he realized that Cannon was inquiring about the location of the state offices of the NAACP. By this time, Frye's temper was rising. It was rare, but he was building to a real boil that day.

"Old dumb me," Frye said many years later, "I made a mistake. He said, 'Are you a member of the NAACP?' I said, 'No, sir. I haven't paid my dues yet.' I didn't need to add that last part. All I needed to say was, 'No sir,' and that would have been the end of my interview, but, by this time, I was pretty warm."

Cannon pursued the NAACP angle further and then he asked Frye about a lawsuit brought by Greensboro attorney Elreta Alexander, the state's only black female lawyer. During the course of the questioning, Frye told Cannon that he had been advised by experienced lawyers that one shouldn't believe everything that was stated in a pleading. At that stage of a legal action, the facts are not established and the document includes unproven allegations. He thought nothing more about his reply, but when he returned to Greensboro a phone message from Alexander was waiting for him. By the time he got to her office just off East Market Street, she was furious. She accused Frye of telling Cannon that she had advised him to put false statements in a formal legal pleading.

"I don't know what he told her," Frye said, "but I stood there and that lady chewed me up one side and down the other. Every time I would start to explain, she would cut me off. The one word [from her] that I remember is she said, 'You talk too much.'"

Cannon's call provoked Alexander to withdraw her endorsement of Frye's application for a license. He replaced her recommendation with one from Major High, who was Kenneth Lee's associate. Of course, Lee would have obliged him, although a recommendation from Lee would have been as provocative as one from Thurgood Marshall. At the time, Lee was engaged in desegregation cases.

More time passed, and Frye still heard nothing. The delay from the State Bar was not only an insult, but Cannon's foot-dragging was turning into a serious financial problem. Henry and Shirley had counted on his income from a law practice, modest though it might be. He finally telephoned Elsie Webb in Rockingham and explained his predicament. Webb told him to call the chair of the board of law examiners, who happened to be a lawyer in Rockingham. "I went to him and told him what had happened," Frye said. "He said if I didn't get my license by such and such a date, that I was to get back in touch with him."

This license arrived soon thereafter. It was dated November 13, 1959. Henry Frye was finally a lawyer.[34]

5

Henry Frye, Esquire

In the weeks after Henry Frye opened his law office, only a few clients visited the small space he occupied midway between Dr. Alvin Blount's examining room and Kenneth Lee's law office in the one-story Benbow Professional Building on Greensboro's east side. One day, Blount pulled Frye aside and offered an observation. He told the young lawyer that he had heard people talking about legal advice they had received in their telephone conversations with Frye. That was no way to do business, Blount said. If people were serious about legal representation then they ought to see him in person. After all, as Abraham Lincoln said, "A lawyer's stock in trade is his time and advice." By offering counsel over the phone, Frye wasn't getting paid when his help was beneficial, and if a caller's problem wasn't resolved to satisfaction, then his ersatz clients would be mad and discourage others from calling on him in the future.

Frye had a lot to learn about being a lawyer. He might have a law degree, even one received with honors, and he might know the law well enough to research and write a brief for the U.S. Supreme Court, but three years of serious study hadn't done a thing toward teaching him how to earn a living.

Blount liked Frye.[1] The doctor had opened his practice in Greensboro in the early 1950s just about the time Frye was graduating from A&T. He, too, was an A&T graduate, with a major in chemistry, and he was a Kappa. "Kenneth and I felt we were the senior fellows among our fraternity brothers, and we tried to pass along the best advice we could," Blount said some years later. Even after Blount abused Frye of his naiveté, the law practice didn't exactly flourish. Frye struggled through the early months with only an occasional client. He often relied on work passed along by Lee, who paid well. At one point, Frye's bank account was empty after he paid office rent and his secretary's wages. In order to make ends meet at home, he asked his secretary to lend him a portion of her pay. When the school year ended, and Shirley's paycheck stopped coming, the Fryes took advantage of special bank loans designed to help teachers on a nine-month pay schedule make it through the summer months.[2]

Frye was one of only a handful of black lawyers in Greensboro at the start of 1960. Closest in age was Major S. High, a 1953 UNC law graduate. He had developed a specialty in title work and stayed busy with referrals from the savings and loan company that Lee had recently organized. A few blocks west of Lee's Benbow Road office were the East Market Street offices of Elreta Alexander (later Alexander-Ralston). She was frequently the only African American, and the only woman, who appeared with any regularity in court. Her associate was Herbert Parks, the self-taught lawyer and part-time minister who sometimes turned out in a swallow-tailed coat and wing collar. Henry Frye was only five years old when Parks got his law license in 1937. He was just beginning high school when Mrs. Alexander made history as the first black female to earn a law degree from Columbia University.

Frye struggled in those early days not only because of his lack of experience, but because of the nature and prejudices of his neighbors. When African Americans got in trouble with the law they usually turned to white lawyers for help. The assumption was that a white lawyer was better received in court. Elreta Alexander once asked a judge if her white client was at a disadvantage because she was representing him.[3] As for civil work, there wasn't much in the way of private enterprise in east Greensboro upon which a lawyer could build a practice. Most black-owned businesses were mom-and-pop operations that required few legal services. Those who owned an enterprise large enough to need representation also tended to go to the white firms. One of Lee's clients hired a white firm to represent his company, but then hired Lee to keep an eye on the white lawyers. Lee once observed that if black lawyers got just a fourth of the business in east Greensboro, he and his colleagues would all be wealthy.[4]

Lee was the best known of Greensboro's black lawyers, largely because of his court appearances in civil rights cases. He had challenged the city's leasing of the golf course to an operator who restricted play to whites only, and he had represented black parents in their applications to have children admitted to all-white schools. Lee carried some of the work load of Conrad Pearson of Durham, who was the NAACP's lead counsel in North Carolina, but, after five years of handling civil rights cases, Lee was ready to move on to other work. He could not afford the NAACP's standard rate of $35 a day for court work and no compensation for research, travel, or expenses. At the same time, he felt compelled to accept civil rights cases, when he was called upon. Pearson and the NAACP's Thurgood Marshall reminded him that they were the reason he had a law degree. By 1960, however, Lee was deeply involved in more lucrative affairs. His American Federal Savings and Loan Association, the first black-owned institution of its kind in the city, had opened in late June 1959. Lee also was working with a group of investors to open a country club for African American golfers on land purchased from Burlington Industries. The large spread on Greensboro's east side had once been a recreation area for the company's black employees.[5]

Lee was the NAACP's man in Greensboro when, on the afternoon of February 1, 1960, four A&T students walked into the F. W. Woolworth store on Elm Street, purchased a few personal items, and then sat down at the lunch counter and ordered a cup of coffee. They were told they would not be served and were asked to leave, after a black employee behind the counter scolded them for their presumptuous behavior. They remained seated on the counter stools until the store closed and then left, only to return the next day and politely renew their request for service. They were met with the same cold shoulder from store employees, but they, and their supporters, stayed at the counter for the rest of the day, and the next day, and the next day. Students from area colleges and universities fell in behind them and took places at the counter. Their actions gave life to a non-violent demonstration that historians later credited with invigorating the civil rights movement across the South.

Like most people in Greensboro, Henry and Shirley Frye learned about the Woolworth sit-in (at first it was called "sit-down") when they picked up the afternoon paper on February 2. Shirley arrived home from school at about the time the *Greensboro Record* fell onto the doorstep of the rental house on Cambridge Street that the Fryes had moved into after their son, Henry Jr., was born in July 1959 while Henry was preparing to take the bar exam. News of the students' action came as a surprise and was met with concern by many in east Greensboro. Dr. John Leary, Shirley's principal at Washington Street Elementary School, told her and the other teachers that the young men didn't know what they were doing, but they deserved the support of the community, nonetheless. One of her fellow teachers was dating an A&T professor. She kept the others current on the students' activities.[6]

The four college students had initiated the sit-in on their own, drawing much of their early courage from Ralph Johns, the white merchant on East Market Street. Henry Frye had been in and out of Johns's store on East Market Street when he was an undergraduate nearly a decade earlier. His place was just west of the railroad tracks from the campus. It was a convenient stopping point for students on their way to larger establishments on Elm Street, Greensboro's main shopping district. Johns catered to the men at A&T, was a lively conversationalist and, for a white man, he held a decidedly different point of view on race. Even conservatives in the NAACP, of which he was a member, considered his ideas too "radical." A frequent topic around the store was the onerous burden of Jim Crow and what could be done about it. After nearly a decade of encouraging young black men to act on their beliefs, Johns had finally found four young men willing to be bold and audacious.[7]

Over the next few months, as the sit-ins and sidewalk picketing continued in early months of 1960, Frye was sitting in on the strategy sessions held in Lee's office. In attendance were the leading figures of east Greensboro—doctors, educators, and preachers mostly—who made up the leadership of the Greensboro Citizens Association. This was the group advising those negotiating on behalf of the student demonstrators with white businessmen and others who were eager to see the demonstrations end as soon as possible. Frye was quiet and reserved. For the time being, at least, the issues were not legal, so his professional advice was not solicited. Aside from a few arrests in late April, police generally kept the opposing parties apart and prevented confrontations. Clearly he was a junior member, but those who were just getting to know him were impressed by his calm demeanor and serious attention to all sides of the items up for discussion. Some saw him as too cautious. That didn't include Blount, who believed Frye was just drawing on an innate analytical nature that had served him well when he was a college debater. "I think you would say he wanted to know the truth about things and let's see if we can work this thing out so everybody benefits," Blount recalled.[8]

The steady pressure applied by the college students, who were supplanted in the summer months by high school volunteers, eventually led to a resolution in July 1960 when Woolworth, S. H. Kress, and the Meyer's Department Store began offering service to all customers. The end came none too soon for downtown merchants who were already beginning to worry about the viability of their businesses. The demonstrations had done nothing to enhance the image of Elm Street, which many considered outdated and uninviting to shoppers who had begun favoring the convenience of stores in the city's new shopping center on West Friendly Avenue. The Greensboro city leaders were already talking about a bold plan of renovation and renewal that they hoped would save the heart of the city from atrophy.

One of those that Frye came to know well during the months of negotiations was Hobart Jarrett. He was a Bennett College humanities professor and one of the principals in the talks that led to the integration of the dime stores. Jarrett was an engaging man and a skillful advocate. Twenty-five years earlier he had been a member of the debate team from Wiley College, a small African American school in Texas, when it surprised the nation by capturing the national debate championships. He chaired the Greensboro Citizens Association and he drew Frye into the association's work by asking him to lead a committee to register voters for the upcoming 1960 elections.

The association had been formed a little more than a decade earlier to clean up politics as it was practiced in east Greensboro, and to organize voters behind black candidates. It had been responsible for the election of the first African American to the city council in 1951, and when Dr. William Hampton ran as an incumbent two years later he led the ticket in the first primary. African Americans won modest concessions from city hall during Hampton's years on the council as he drew attention to unpaved streets and other inequities in city services. Meanwhile, the association demonstrated an independence from white politicians who were used to bartering for black votes on Election Day, hiring "drivers" whose job was to get their friends to the polls.[9]

As a homegrown organization, the citizens association avoided the anger, resentment, and suspicion that whites heaped on the NAACP, which was said to represent the "radical element," especially in the wake of the *Brown* decision. If whites believed the worst about the NAACP, the association's new president in Greensboro, Dr. George Simkins, Jr., did nothing to disabuse them of that opinion. Simkins's experience with the golf course trespass case had left him distrustful of the courts and governmental institutions dominated by whites. His outrage over Jim Crow was a renewable fuel. It drove his challenges to the status quo and would sustain him over thirty years of agitation to gain a greater voice for African Americans in local affairs.

The NAACP was caught in something of a no-man's land in Greensboro in the late 1950s. Simkins had picked up the leadership of the local chapter from the Reverend Edwin R. Edmonds, who had left the city in 1959, after he lost a part-time campus ministry position at A&T. Edmonds believed that A&T President Warmoth Gibbs, who had succeeded Ferdinand Bluford upon his death in 1957, had knuckled under to whites to eliminate his job and cost him part of his livelihood.[10] At the same time that the organization was anathema to whites, Edmonds didn't enjoy universal admiration from African Americans. He complained about the weak spines of Hampton and others, including school men like Leary, who, he said, didn't adequately represent the interests of Greensboro blacks. Simkins was just as feisty as Edmonds, but he enjoyed the independence of his dental practice and was protected from economic retaliation by whites. A strong-willed man, he brought the Greensboro branch under his control. In a short time, Simkins and the NAACP would become virtually synonymous.

Those who exercised influence in east Greensboro, including Simkins, were no more prepared for the challenge to segregation thrust upon them by the A&T students than were the whites in charge of the businesses downtown or in offices at city hall. Many were like Henry Frye, who believed that segregation was doomed, but the change would most likely come though the courts and Congress, and even the softening of people's hearts, rather than from direct action. Least prepared for the students was the NAACP, whose national office did not condone or promote direct action. When Simkins heard about what was happening, he called upon James Farmer's Congress on Racial Equality for help. CORE had a long history of forcing the issue of civil rights, beginning with the Journey for Reconciliation in 1947. Farmer dispatched a field worker to Greensboro. The students thanked him for his support, but said they wanted to keep their efforts free of outside influence.

"We respected them very much," one of the four, Ezell Blair, Jr., told writer Robert Penn Warren a few years later. "We wanted to destroy the old idea that Negroes had to be told everything to do by CORE or the NAACP."

The Greensboro Citizens Association respected the students' wishes and encouraged their independence. That was especially true of Jarrett, who inspired the same creativity and imagination in his classroom. Jarrett saw the need for the association to coordinate the various voices and energy in east Greensboro in order to present a unified front. Under his careful management, he brought together representatives of all manner of fraternal, civic, and social organizations.[11] Among those represented were the Greensboro Men's Club, which included the elite of the black business and professional community; the MCs, another men's group that was a notch or two down the social ladder from the men's club; the alumni chapters of the college fraternities and sororities that maintained a tight bond among their members; along with other organizations in the community. Jarrett wanted to hear from every group, large and small, that reflected a facet of African American life, from flower clubs and sewing circles to the NAACP. "You had people in there who were in position to help do a lot of things that needed to be done," Frye said some years later.[12]

The voter registration effort that Frye undertook on behalf of the association was initiated in the spring of 1960, just as the election season was beginning to ripen. The association's effort tracked with a renewed registration campaign promoted by Dr. Martin Luther King, Jr.'s Southern Christian Leadership Conference, and by the NAACP, which had a history of getting blacks on the voter rolls, especially in urban areas like Greensboro. Clearly there were gains to be made. In April 1960, a group of Jarrett's students at Bennett College contacted seventy residents who lived in the heart of east Greensboro and found only six were registered to vote. When John M. Brooks, the NAACP's director of voter registration, opened a voter registration drive at Bennett that month, he said only 5,000 of the 15,000 African Americans in Greensboro who were eligible to vote were registered.[13]

The voting power of African Americans in Greensboro had long been concentrated in three of the city's twenty-five precincts. One of these polling stations was at the Hayes-Taylor YMCA, a second was at Windsor Community Center in the heart of the Benbow Road neighborhood, and a third was at McIver School, which was central to the city's earliest black enclave called Warnersville that traced its founding to the days of Reconstruction. Frye set out to expand the influence of black voters on the east side when he and other African Americans showed up at the organizational meeting of a fourth precinct. They arrived in numbers sufficient to outvote whites and, for the first time, elected African Americans to the top precinct offices. The new chairman was Dr. W.L.T. Miller, a dentist who was Jarrett's closest ally in the negotiations over the lunch counters.[14]

The move came as a surprise to the whites of Precinct 8, which voted at Gillespie Park Elementary School, but change was inevitable. Whites had been leaving the old homes along Asheboro Street for newer subdivisions in other parts of town. African Americans, who already lived in adjacent neighborhoods, had simply moved in to replace them. The transition was underway by the mid-fifties when, in 1957, the city school board admitted black children from the neighborhood to what had been all-white Gillespie Park, a school that was closer to their homes than the one to which they had been previously assigned.

Voter interest was high in the spring of 1960. Massachusetts Senator John F. Kennedy's entrance into the Democratic presidential campaign in January had added excitement to a field that included Minnesota's Senator Hubert Humphrey and the Senate's majority leader, Lyndon B. Johnson of Texas. North Carolina voters were more focused on the Democratic Party's gubernatorial primary, a contest that was shaping up as a referendum on segregation. I. Beverly Lake, the former Wake Forest law professor and state assistant attorney general who had argued for continuing separate schools during the Court's consideration of the implementation of the *Brown* decision, cast himself as "the man who believes in the basic American freedoms—freedom of association, freedom of education, freedom of religion, freedom of private business." He said he was "the champion of a balanced budget, segregation, states' rights, and property rights."[15]

None of the gubernatorial candidates dared favor integration, but none openly declared themselves as opposed to racial change as did Lake. Candidates were learning how to use code words and phrases to connect with voters on this delicate issue. The NAACP was a favorite target for white politicians. One of Lake's opponents, John Larkins, accused the NAACP of "plans to provoke the white people of North Carolina to extreme anger."[16] The NAACP also crept into the primary contest to fill an open congressional seat in the district that included Greensboro. One of the Democratic candidates was state solicitor William Murdock from Durham. In 1957, he had prosecuted African Americans who had defied a local ordinance requiring separate service for blacks and whites at the Royal Ice Cream store in Durham. The NAACP remained his opponent, as it had been in this early sit-in case. "I feel we need men in Congress who have sufficient experience to do what they know and ought to do and will stand up against organized minorities." He said, "Letting them [organized minorites] throttle the economy was a crime."[17]

Frye didn't enroll in a particular candidate's campaign in the spring or the fall, although he and Shirley did go to hear Kennedy when he made a campaign stop in Raleigh that September. Frye saved his time for the voter registration effort, which he approached as a form of social justice without any political ambitions of his own. He and Shirley had agreed on a number of things when they had talked of marriage more than three years earlier. Two of those conditions were: He would not ask her to go back to Ellerbe to live, and he wouldn't get involved in politics. Work with the citizens association was simply civic duty. Of course, the exposure to people in the community was not bad for a budding law practice either. When Kenneth Lee was just getting started, he had run for the city council in a pack of candidates that included east Greensboro's favorite, the incumbent William Hampton, just as a way to get his name out in the community.

Henry's focus remained on the law and earning a living. In aid of expanding his legal experience, Henry, Shirley, and their one-year-old son packed themselves into a Renault and headed out for New York City in the summer of 1960 to visit family while Henry attended the annual meeting of the American Bar Association. While the N.C. Bar Association and the Guilford County Bar Association limited membership to whites only, there were no such restrictions at the ABA. He looked forward to meeting lawyers from around the country. They planned to treat themselves to lunch at the New York City's Waldorf-Astoria. When they finally got to a table in the hotel's famous restaurant, Peacock Alley, a venue of cosmopolitan elegance and style, they opened the menu and discovered that the only selection they could afford was a small salad. They had water to drink.[18]

A few days before the general election in the fall of 1960, a report in the *Greensboro Daily News* said that black voters in North Carolina were leaning toward the Republican presidential candidate, Richard Nixon. A month before the election, Jackie Robinson, the Brooklyn Dodger who had broken major league baseball's color barrier, was in Greensboro to speak to the NAACP state convention that drew about 1,750 attendees. He had told a Sunday afternoon crowd that Nixon was the best candidate; Kennedy wasn't "fit to be president of the United States." With Nixon as president, voters could count on a black person being part of a Nixon cabinet. The word from the NAACP's Clarence Mitchell was that blacks were cool to Kennedy because he was a Roman Catholic.[19] That all changed. Between Robinson's speech in Greensboro and the end of the month, the Kennedy campaign gave public support to the Reverend Martin Luther King, Jr., who was then housed in a Georgia jail. On the strength of that contact, the mood was different on Election Day.

There was little question that the Greensboro Citizens Association favored Kennedy and the Democratic nominee for governor, Terry Sanford, who had appealed to the group for its support. Jarrett was amused when he met with Sanford's representative, who was surprised to learn that Jarrett was a member of the NAACP. "He thought that the NAACP was something radical I suppose, and communistic," Jarrett later said. "At any rate, we assured him that everybody sitting in there and talking with him was a member of the NAACP and had been most of his life."[20] Based on its interviews with candidates or their representatives, the association prepared a list of favored candidates that was kept under wraps until the night before the election, when flyers carrying the endorsements were printed. The group published its selections on donated paper that passed through mimeograph machines found in the various business and professional offices around the community. The sample ballots were then distributed to poll workers who handed them out to voters the next day. The secrecy prevented candidates from capitalizing for their own purposes on the association's choices. At the time, a white candidate who didn't get the nod from the black organizations would often use the slight to arouse whites with the accusation of "bloc voting."[21]

Both Kennedy and Sanford were heavy favorites among black voters in Greensboro. Kennedy outpolled Nixon by as much as three and four to one in the precincts with the largest black registration. Even at Gillespie Park, a precinct with a balanced white-black registration, the vote was 1,146 for Kennedy and 828 for Nixon. It was white Democrats who couldn't stomach Kennedy; the Nixon ticket carried every other precinct in the city, except one that served the area around the Woman's College of the University of North Carolina (later University of North Carolina at Greensboro). Nixon carried the county with nearly 60 percent of the vote. Sanford also took a drubbing in white precincts. Altogether, 10,000 new voters were registered in Greensboro during the spring and fall campaigns and many of them were African Americans.

By the end of 1960, the Fryes had established themselves as likely candidates who might join the upper tier of the social and professional community in east Greensboro. They had little money and lived in a rented house, but they were well regarded within the community. Their introduction to the right people along Benbow Road had been facilitated by their connections with A&T and by Shirley's relationship with Mrs. Lee, whose home remained a hub of activity for those influential in school and community affairs. Henry's professional credentials, and his work with the citizens association, had brought him closer to those whose opinions mattered. Moreover, the Fryes were an attractive couple. Shirley was warm and inviting to all she met. No one was a stranger. Her easy and open manner, and a generous smile, complemented her husband's quiet reserve. Henry was generally upbeat, courteous and well spoken. His manners would make a mother proud. He had a youthful, well-scrubbed appearance that befit his twenty-eight years. For the time being, he had forsaken the thin mustache that he had worn from time to time during his years in law school.

Nothing recommended them more than their devotion to Providence Baptist Church. Religion was an important part of Henry's life, and Shirley was the product of a well-churched family, too. Henry had attended different churches during his college years and, when he was a senior, he had conducted a Sunday school program on campus at Harrison Auditorium. Shirley had joined Mrs. Lee's Methodist congregation after she moved to Greensboro. After they were married, Shirley attempted to sleep in on one Sunday but learned that her husband expected her to be with him at Sunday school after they joined Providence. Their attendance began not long before the arrival of a new, young minister, the Reverend Lorenzo Lynch. He replaced the Reverend J. W. Tynes, who had been the pastor at Providence for twenty-six years.

Providence was a historic community of believers that traced its roots to 1866 and a small wooden building that was built for Sunday services and for use as a school for freed slaves. This church was later replaced by a brick-and-mortar structure that was the first of its kind for African Americans in North Carolina. Three-quarters of a century later, the old brick church was still standing beside the Southern Railway tracks, about two blocks off the A&T campus on a dusty side street called Dean's Alley. The church attracted many of the community's academics and professionals. Such was the number of faculty members in the congregation that it was called "A&T Baptist Church." Tynes would often delay the start of his sermon in order to give President Bluford ample time to get to his pew. Tynes's daughter, Margaret, was a 1939 A&T graduate and a celebrated former member of the church choir. At the time of her father's retirement in the late 1950s, her singing career was winning international acclaim.[22]

Henry began his participation at the church by teaching a Sunday school class for teenagers; Shirley, drawing on her teaching experience, ran the vacation bible school in the summers. The Reverend Lynch was closer in age to the Fryes than Tynes, and he drew upon their support for taking the congregation in some new directions, away from what he later called "a stay-out-of-trouble theology." Lynch was more likely to talk about political issues that were often unsettling to the older, established members of Providence. "Middle class blacks didn't look back as we should," Lynch later recalled. "We were highly consumptuous in our life style. We had luxury cars and we didn't reach back to the black minority who suffered. Some of that middle class mentality had gripped that congregation." With Shirley's help, Lynch organized a nursery program for poor children. The Fryes clearly understood the needs of young parents, especially after their second son, Harlan, was born in July 1961. Henry chose the name to honor the first Justice John Marshall Harlan (Harlan II was his grandson), who cast the lone dissenting vote in the *Plessy v. Ferguson* decision that upheld Southern segregation laws in 1896.

Slowly, Henry Frye was building a law practice. His work with the citizens association, his visibility at church, and referrals from other attorneys had improved his situation. One day, he got a call from Dr. Samuel D. Proctor. He was the new president at A&T who had succeeded Warmoth Gibbs after his retirement in the summer of 1960. Gibbs was a mild-mannered academic, but he had distinguished himself during the sit-in demonstrations by standing firm in his support of the students, even against the wishes of Governor Luther Hodges, who wanted him to keep his students on campus and away from the lunch counters. "We teach our students how to think, not what to think," Gibbs had said. It was a statement that would become part of the legend of the sit-ins.[23]

Proctor was a new kind of leader for the school. He was young, just thirty-eight years old, and came from a background in the pulpit and college leadership. He left the presidency of Virginia Union to take the job in Greensboro. He had not been there long when he asked Frye to come to his office to talk about helping him with some estate planning, including new wills for himself and his wife. When Frye had documents ready for the final signatures, the president asked to handle the closing details in his office. Frye hesitated, only because he believed it would be easier to have the papers notarized and witnessed in his law office, but he agreed to the president's request. His reward for concierge service came when Proctor called in members of his administrative staff and praised Frye's service. "This young lawyer has done a good job," he told anyone within earshot. "If you don't have a will, you ought to get him to take care of you." The endorsement was as good as money in the bank.[24]

Frye was eager to increase his clientele for estates and commercial and real estate work. In those lean, early months, he had taken any kind of case that came his way. He had learned, through painful experience, however, that he had no taste for criminal defense work or divorces. He was mystified by clients who would not tell him the truth, or would withhold information, and then expect him to mount an effective defense. On at least one occasion, Frye arrived in court to discover the police already had his client's full confession. It was a valuable lesson in human nature. He learned early to look behind what a person said, or what he found on a piece of paper. Divorce cases were messy and seemed to always produce late-night calls to his home. As other work began to occupy more of his time, he cut back on criminal cases and eliminated domestic suits altogether.[25]

He wasn't immune to personal appeals. One day he received a call from a former schoolmate in Ellerbe. The man was in the federal prison in Atlanta and was asking for help. Henry was reluctant to go hear about his friend's troubles. Racial tensions were running high in the Deep South and traveling to Atlanta had its hazards. In addition, the likelihood of payment to compensate for his time was low. Frye also would be entering unfamiliar territory that would test his legal skills. Nonetheless, he took a night train to Atlanta, arriving the next morning.

He had not eaten breakfast when he got to Atlanta so he went to the station's diner for a meal. He seated himself and waited to be served. After being ignored for some time, an African American waitress finally motioned for him to come to another counter, the one that was reserved for blacks. Frye stayed where he was, telling the woman, "I am a lawyer and I know what I am doing." She finally took his order and brought him his food.

Frye ate his meal and then took a taxi to the prison, where he learned that the matter his friend wanted him to handle was nothing at all as he expected. He learned that during his stay in prison the man had converted to Islam and that he and other inmates were being denied access to the Koran and other Muslim literature. Frye was told that prison officials frowned on the requests of followers of Elijah Muhammad, the leader of the Black Muslims whose street image was of young black men, outfitted in angry scowls, dark suits, white shirts and black ties, as they passed out issues of *The Final Call*, the organization's newspaper. "I had never heard of a Black Muslim," Frye said many years later. He agreed to see what he could do.

Atlanta University was not far from the prison and Frye found a faculty member on the campus who gave him a quick overview of the Muslim religion, Elijah Muhammad, and the importance of the Koran to believers. He returned to the prison, made his case to the warden, who, he discovered, did not regard Black Muslims as a legitimate faith, but believed them to be troublemakers who advocated violence. Frye exhausted all the arguments he could bring to bear on his client's position, and then left for home feeling he had done all he could, and that wasn't very much. He learned a short time after he returned home that the warden had changed his mind. The Muslims got their Korans.

One of his largest fees in those early days came from a client from Asheboro who called upon him to perfect a title that one of the downtown white firms had given up on. The client, a white man, told Frye that he would pay him $500 if he were successful. Frye eagerly took the case and then he discovered the problem: There were gaps in lineage; heirs and others needed for a clear chain of title were either dead or missing. Frye began his search for the names he had and finally found a woman who directed him to a church cemetery where he was able to locate graves with dates of death that filled in some of the missing information. The woman also agreed to sign an affidavit outlining the sequence of the title transfers over the years. With this, Frye found a title insurance company that would guarantee the ownership. Almost giddy with his success, Frye called his client and presented him with his finished work. Clearly pleased with the lawyer's ingenuity and effort, the man began sending even more work Frye's way.[26]

All the while that Hobart Jarrett and the citizens association were negotiating to open the lunch counters, Dr. George Simkins, Jr., and a group of black doctors and dentists were seeking privileges to treat patients at Greensboro's two major hospitals, Moses Cone Memorial and Wesley Long Community. Wesley Long had a new $3 million facility that was to replace a modest cottage-style hospital. It was due to open in the latter part of 1961. In the spring of that year, the trustees of both institutions had refused to change rules and allow black doctors to treat their patients in the hospitals. Long did not admit any black patients; Cone accepted blacks only on referral in special cases from L. Richardson Memorial Hospital, a thirty-year-old facility built to serve African Americans in east Greensboro. Most medical professionals, white and black, considered it to be woefully inadequate.

Simkins had received encouragement for a legal challenge to this discriminatory policy from Jack Greenberg of the NAACP's Legal Defense Fund, which was looking for a case to follow on an earlier unsuccessful lawsuit involving a Wilmington, North Carolina, hospital. Even before the lunch counter sit-ins began, Simkins had appealed to Greenberg for advice on how to proceed. Simkins believed the restrictions were not only morally and legally wrong, but they also cost him and other medical men money when they had to turn the care of patients over to white physicians and dentists. The first step was to be denied the services of the two hospitals, both of which had been built with hefty amounts of federal aid under the 1947 Hill-Burton Act. Requests were submitted by Simkins and two other dentists and six physicians joined him. Among those lending support were Frye's mentors, Drs. Blount and Miller.[27]

Simkins's challenge to the white medical establishment created sufficient unease among his fellow black doctors and physicians that his plans for a lawsuit forcing integration failed to win an endorsement from the Greensboro Medical Society, the black counterpart of the all-white Guilford Medical Society. Some doctors feared their relationships with white physicians would be jeopardized. This lack of unity troubled Dr. Alvin Blount. He understood that blacks might fight among themselves over the best way to deal with issues, but in the end a unified front was considered essential. One of the best-known names missing from the list of potential plaintiffs was Dr. George Evans. He was one of the senior black physicians in the city and the first African American to be appointed to a public board, the Greensboro Housing Authority.[28]

Simkins pressed on, but cautiously. His criminal conviction for trespass on the golf course had been upheld by the federal courts because of sloppy legal work. This time he made the rounds of local lawyers to take a measure of both their interest and their ability. By the time he got to Benbow Professional Building, Henry Frye had done his homework. He told the doctors that the chances of succeeding with the lawsuit were good. When passed in 1947, the Hill-Burton Act had allowed for the use of federal money in segregated hospitals, but that was before the *Brown* decision invalidated the separate-but-equal provisions in the postwar law. Frye's assessment was that their suit would fail in the district court, where judges were reluctant to buck the prevailing local sentiment, but that decision would most likely be reversed on appeal. The U.S. Supreme Court had come close to desegregating hospitals in the Wilmington case, and there was a case to be built upon the dissents in that case that were written by Chief Justice Earl Warren and Associate Justices William O. Douglas and William Brennan. Frye said he would rest the challenge to the Greensboro hospitals on a stronger legal argument related to the use of federal funds in construction of the hospitals rather than the narrower point of law that had been presented earlier.[29]

The case raised difficult questions for Frye. Should the suit prevail, then winning would add to his reputation. It might even lead to further work on important civil rights cases from the Legal Defense Fund, which was then considering an increase in funding for civil rights work in the South. At the same time, Frye had barely a year of practical legal experience, and he was aware of the complications that might arise from his involvement in such a controversial case. There also was a question of control. Frye tried, unsuccessfully, to get a clear answer from the doctors on whether he would be in charge of the case, or whether he would to taking orders from the Legal Defense Fund. Frye believed he knew how to proceed and knew he would be uncomfortable with direction from someone who didn't have as much invested in its outcome as he did. By the end of his meeting with the doctors, Frye believed he had the group's endorsement to proceed.

Frye prepared the complaint and had it ready to file, but he heard nothing further from Simkins. Then, on February 13, 1962, Frye read a newspaper account of a lawsuit like the one he had drafted for the doctors that had been filed the day before, Lincoln's birthday, in federal district court by the NAACP's Conrad Pearson and Jack Greenberg of the Legal Defense Fund. Simkins never favored Frye with a call to explain why he was not included. In the end, Frye's analysis of the suit proved accurate. U.S. District Judge Edwin M. Stanley of Greensboro ruled in favor of the hospitals in December 1962, despite a brief on behalf of the plaintiffs submitted by the U.S. Justice Department. The Fourth Circuit Court of Appeals heard the case in April 1963 and on November 1, 1963, issued a decision, written by Chief Judge Simon E. Sobeloff, reversing Stanley. On March 2, 1964, the Supreme Court denied the hospitals' appeal for review, thus upholding the appeals court. *Simkins* did for medical care what *Brown* had done for education.

Simkins's snub of Frye created a tension between the two men that remained for years. Eventually, Frye learned that Simkins believed that Frye would have settled the lawsuit and negotiated an agreement to cover the Greensboro hospitals and doctors, rather than carry the case through the appellate process for a decision that would affect hospitals and doctors all across the land. Indeed, Frye had asked in his meeting with Simkins and the other doctors what their position would be if the hospitals offered to settle.

Years later, Frye said that his question to the doctors, though logical and appropriate under the circumstances, probably chilled any interest Simkins may have had in hiring him. "They were interested in setting a national precedent and I was interested in getting the job done," he said. "I was interested in getting black doctors to be able to work in the hospitals and treat patients." Of course, Frye was prepared to argue the case to conclusion.[30]

Frye's deliberative manner, his cautious demeanor, and his even disposition may have been off-putting to Simkins, who seemed to thrive on confrontation. Yet, the same personal characteristics that disturbed Simkins were considered assets by Hobart Jarrett and the Greensboro Citizens Association. It chose Frye to succeed Jarrett as president in the summer of 1961 when the Bennett professor left Greensboro to take a position at Brooklyn College in New York. Frye also had made a favorable impression on Durham banker John H. Wheeler, who was one of the most important African Americans in Democratic Party politics and a leading figure in the National Bankers Association, a trade group for black-owned financial institutions.

Wheeler's influence arose from his presidency of the Mechanics and Farmers Bank and his leadership of the Durham Committee on Negro Affairs. The DCNA had been making a difference in Durham's political life since the mid–1930s and Wheeler was its leader by the late 1950s. His bank was one of the oldest and most stable financial institutions in the country and its president was known far beyond Durham. In 1960, Wheeler had won a commitment from the Kennedys that the new administration would include African Americans in appointments made in the South. As the 1962 mid-term elections approached, Wheeler was still waiting on the White House to make good on that promise.

Wheeler liked what he saw in Henry Frye and, near the end of 1961, he asked the young lawyer to submit an application to the U.S. Justice Department for an appointment as assistant U.S. attorney in the Middle District of North Carolina. Frye did as requested, but he heard nothing further. With his law practice gaining ground, he had left the cramped quarters on Benbow Road for a new office on nearby Gorrell Street. That was when he got a call from Wheeler to anticipate an offer from the Justice Department soon. He left no doubt in Frye's mind that he was expected to accept.

Frye was a perfect candidate for such a position. He had an outstanding academic record, from both A&T and UNC, and his military record included a promotion to captain in the Air Force Reserves. He was the father of two and his wife was a schoolteacher. He was active in his church, and the presidency of the citizens association demonstrated support within his community. Simkins's failure to ask Frye to take the hospital lawsuit had relieved him of any political complications that might have arisen if he had been aligned with the Legal Defense Fund.

Frye had his concerns, however. It had taken him two years to build up a law practice. He knew that if the took the appointment that his hard-won clients would find other representation. The federal job paid well — the starting salary was $7,500 — but the professional momentum that he had gained in private practice would dissipate quickly. Frye didn't plan on staying for more than a couple of years, but even that might be too long. There was one important consolation. When he returned to private practice he would be the only black lawyer in the state who had experience in the federal judicial system. That could be valuable.

Wheeler's call came just before Thanksgiving in 1962. He might have heard something earlier but President Kennedy and his top advisors, which included his brother, Attorney General Robert Kennedy, had been preoccupied for most of the previous month with an international crisis involving Soviet missiles on their way to Cuba. The morning papers on Thanksgiving Day carried an unconfirmed report that the attorney general was appointing Frye as an assistant U.S. attorney. The newspaper account included a response from Frye's new boss, U.S. Attorney William Murdock of Durham, that matched the chill in the north winds that brought the season's first snow to the North Carolina Piedmont. This was the same Murdock who had made himself plain about his feelings about the NAACP in the 1960 congressional race. Asked by a reporter about the appointment, he only said he was aware that Frye had applied for the job. He didn't confirm the appointment until two days later, and issued no words of welcome to his new associate.[31]

The appointment created a political dustup that, while it lasted, gave Frye time to close his law office and find representation for clients whose work he could not complete. Kenneth Lee got his Asheboro man with the deep pockets. Just before Christmas, Judge Stanley rejected the Simkins case. An appeal was expected, but the Moses Cone trustees offered a concession. They agreed to allow black doctors to use the hospital. Simkins was appalled that the board continued to oppose opening its rooms and wards to African Americans.

Murdock clearly was not happy about the attorney general picking his district as one of five in which to put the first black assistant U.S. attorneys in the South. (The others were in Texas, Tennessee and, just the week before, in the eastern district of Virginia.) Short of resigning, there was nothing that he could do to avoid working with Frye. Nor could he say anything about the next shoe that dropped. His district was also getting the first African American to serve as a deputy U.S. marshal. Joseph C. Biggers of Durham had been cleared for that job. Kennedy had given Wheeler everything that he had asked for.

Murdock left the angry rhetoric to North Carolina's senior senator, Sam J. Ervin, Jr. Ervin was just finishing a busy year in which he led the opposition to a civil rights measure aimed at eliminating the poll tax and other devices designed to impede voter registration in the South. During a filibuster earlier in the spring, he mocked the requirements that had obstructed Frye and thousands of others who had been denied registration. During one four-hour performance on the Senate floor, Ervin had a sympathetic colleague measure the time it took for him to read a passage of the N.C. Constitution and then write it. He didn't say anything about answering arcane questions, as some registrars required or, on a whim, put to those they simply didn't like. A decade later, Ervin would emerge as a defender of individual liberties, but in 1962 he was the southern Democrats' chief strategist for defending segregation.[32]

U.S. Attorney General Robert Kennedy fulfilled a campaign promise to integrate Justice Department offices in the South. Henry Frye was appointed assistant U.S. attorney in the late fall of 1962 and was sworn into office by U.S. District Judge L. Richardson Preyer in January 1963 (courtesy North Carolina A&T State Foundation).

Ervin had finished a victorious political campaign in which he was re-elected by an easy margin in the face of Republican gains in other North Carolina races. He was not going to let the Kennedys off easy. The senator acknowledged that the attorney general had the authority to appoint Frye, but he bellowed that Kennedy's actions were "unprecedented, as far as I know."[33] Apparently, Ervin was more concerned about white backlash than a loss of the support of blacks at the polls. He repeatedly told reporters that neither he nor the state's other senator, B. Everett Jordan, had anything to do with the appointments.

It was all political theater. Ervin knew the appointments were coming, as did every other ranking Democrat from the governor's office to Capitol

Hill. The plan had been in the works for months. In fact, Wheeler had called the offices of both senators prior to the November elections and urged them to announce the appointments before the November election to shore up what was expected to be a weak turnout on Election Day. Writing her boss after taking Wheeler's call in mid–October, Ervin's assistant, Pat Shore, sent an urgent memo to Ervin telling him Frye's name was already cleared and Wheeler wanted "one of these appointments to show to the colored voters that constructive things are being done for the race in N.C."[34] It appears that the only concession Ervin wanted was deniability. Clearly, there were levers he could have pulled to thwart Kennedy, if he had wanted to make a fight of it. After a few days of huffing and puffing over the alleged slight by the attorney general, Ervin said nothing more.

While the senator had won by a comfortable margin in the November elections, the same could not be said for other Democrats. N.C. Republicans now had their second congressman, James T. Broyhill of Lenoir. He joined Charles Jonas of Lincolnton, who was re-elected for a seventh term. Both had defeated incumbent Democrats after Jonas was thrown into a match-up as a result of redistricting. In Guilford County, African Americans gave hefty majorities to Democrats, but the turnout in the key precincts did not show the same enthusiasm as in 1960. Republicans elected a sheriff, took control of the county board of commissioners, and swept away the Democratic majority in the state legislative races. Former state house speaker Joe Hunt had planned to launch a race for governor from the state senate until he was rejected. A newcomer, a Republican preacher who would serve but one term, won the seat. Hunt blamed the collapse of his political career on Governor Sanford. Local Republicans had capitalized on voter discontent over the tax program Sanford pushed through the legislature in 1961 to pay for his education program. The Reverend Charles Strong, Hunt's nemesis, said he got votes because of a tax revolt, but he also believed black voters had helped him win. In Precinct 8, the one Frye and the citizens association had focused on for a voter registration campaign early in 1962, Strong won by sixty votes.[35]

The same editions of the November 24, 1962, Greensboro papers that confirmed reports of Frye's appointment also carried front-page headlines about the arrest of sixty demonstrators who had attempted to eat a Thanksgiving meal at two popular downtown cafeterias. The students had resumed their protests against segregated service earlier in the fall. This time, the strategy was more confrontational, as students invited arrest and raised the stakes for the remainder of the white businesses that had not budged since the lunch counter sit-ins ended in the summer of 1960. Greensboro remained almost as segregated as it had been two years earlier. As the U.S. Civil Rights Commission reported, North Carolina's delay in abiding by the law of the land was not as great as that of states in the Deep South, but not by much. Among the questions that were raised in print about Frye's appointment was whether a court officer of the U.S. government could find a hotel room or be served a meal if he were traveling the district on behalf of the American people. Frye's hometown newspaper, the *Rockingham Post-Dispatch*, suggested that when Frye came to Richmond County for court appearances, "he can drive the 10 miles to Ellerbe and stay with his own folks." The biting and opinionated news article concluded, "Great is Bobby Kennedy."[36]

Ellerbe was proud of its native son. While Frye had not encouraged his family to come to his law school graduation, his mother and father and other family members were with him in Greensboro on January 10, 1963, when he took his oath of office from U.S. District Judge L. Richardson Preyer. A crowd of about fifty persons gathered in the courtroom at the federal building on West Market Street for the event. Frye was presented to the court by Roy G. Hall, Jr., the other assistant U.S. attorney in the office. Reporters were told Murdock was absent due to the illness of his father. Ola Stringer, Henry's sister, came with her parents. She watched her father sit quietly throughout the ceremony, his silence and a smile conveying his approval for a son he knew would never make much of a life as a farmer. "Dad was just very proud of him," she said. "He wouldn't say very much. He would sit back, and look at him, and smile. Any time he was pleased he would just sit and smile, which means you had his approval."[37]

The offices of the U.S. attorney, and the courtrooms, were on the second floor of a three-story building fashioned out of blocks of limestone that represented the best of 1930s government art deco architecture. The post office occupied most of the first floor. The building was just two blocks off the "Square," the intersection of Market and Elm streets, and a three-minute walk from the S&W cafeteria where the demonstrators had been arrested. Whatever public support Frye could offer to the students as president of the Greensboro Citizens Association had ended when he resigned and the organization chose the Reverend Otis Hairston as his replacement. That didn't mean the racial tension that was building in Greensboro was left behind when he reported for his first day of work.

6

"If not now, when?"

Before it was razed in the name of urban renewal in the mid–1960s, Trinity AME Zion Church on East Washington Street was an impressive gothic structure that for fifty years had offered the largest seating capacity of any church in east Greensboro. The pews could accommodate more than seven hundred worshippers inside an imposing building with a tall, square bell tower and arches at the front entrance. On the night of May 19, 1963, every pew was full, and people filled the aisles. Adults had turned out to show their support for the hundreds of young people, blacks and whites, who had been arrested during the preceding week in front of two movie theaters and two cafeterias whose owners steadfastly refused to serve customers of color. Henry and Shirley Frye were in the congregation.

The talk about the meeting at "Big Zion," as Trinity was known in the community, had begun two or three days earlier. Tension in Greensboro rose each time a parade of marching protestors arrived downtown. Most of these demonstrations began in the late afternoon or early evening, after students at A&T and Bennett College had finished their classes for the day. The young people formed up in a churchyard near the campuses and then moved out to the center of town to take up picketing stations outside the Mayfair and S&W cafeterias and the two Elm Street movie houses. Three years earlier, the sit-ins had produced only a handful of arrests. Now, things were different. By the time of the meeting at Big Zion, nearly a thousand young people were either in the county's jails or under guard at the former polio convalescent hospital on the edge of town.

After launching the sit-ins at lunch counters in 1960, the students in Greensboro now were part of a panorama of mass demonstrations that reached across the South. Earlier that May, what would be called the "Children's Crusade" had begun in Birmingham, Alabama. There had been a bombing in that city, and federal troops were poised and ready to prevent further violence. Street demonstrations had been renewed in Nashville. Closer to home, blacks maintained picket lines outside of eating establishments in Durham and Raleigh. The U.S. State Department was dealing with an embarrassing incident that had arisen two weeks earlier at the S&W in Raleigh when an African diplomat had been refused service. Greensboro had seen a thousand or more marchers on the streets of downtown at one time, but so far the city had not experienced anything like the police response in Birmingham that produced iconic pictures of high-pressure fire hoses and police dogs on attack.

The Greensboro demonstrations had been renewed on Thanksgiving Day 1962, the same day that word of Frye's appointment as an assistant in the U.S. attorney's office had been leaked to newspaper reporters. The marches had continued off and on — mostly off — for the next six months. It wasn't until May, after the publication of the shocking images from Birmingham, that large numbers of students returned to the streets in Greensboro. The marches continued daily in a choreographed performance between student leaders and a patient city police detective named William Jackson. Communication between the two camps was open and civil, even as the police filled the jails with those who entered establishments and refused to leave.

The marches had included a few adults, but this was a student movement. The elders worked on the fringes where they found some support from the city's chamber of commerce and merchants association, both of which had urged businesses to offer service to all. The response had been meager. Greensboro's McDonald's restaurant, a popular new drive-in on Summit Avenue, changed its whites-only policy after a brief protest. For the most part, Greensboro remained as segregated as always. Nearly a decade after *Brown*, only one-half of 1 percent of the 7,000 black students in the city schools sat in classrooms with whites. And all of them were enrolled at one school, Gillespie Park, where the first black students had been admitted in 1957, according to numbers compiled by a newly organized interracial group called the Greensboro Community Fellowship.[1]

On Sunday night, at Big Zion, the Fryes and the hundreds of others packed into the sanctuary were responding to the word from the white community that even the adults in east Greensboro were weary of the disruptions to daily life and the tarnishing of the city's erstwhile liberal reputation for tolerance and goodwill. "Responsible Negroes," it was said, did not condone these demonstrations. Those who turned out at Big Zion — from wage earners and domestics to professional people and academics — were there to say that just wasn't true. East Greensboro *did* care about the messages their children were carrying to the white-owned businesses on Elm Street. And they cared about the way their children were being treated in the jails, where most of them had chosen to remain rather than post bail.

The leading speaker that night was supposed to have been Dr. Charles Lyons, the head of the N.C. Teachers Association who had been on the front lines in Raleigh. Lyons was upstaged, as it were, by an unscheduled visit from James Farmer, the head of the CORE whose A&T chapter was organizing the daily marches. When dogs bite in Birmingham, Farmer told the crowd, the blood is spilled across the country. "Greensboro is not the worst city in the country," he said, "and not the worst in North Carolina. But as [CORE chapter president] Bill Thomas has said, Greensboro has got to be made to live up to its reputation as a liberal city. I think the city of Greensboro is deeply involved in this. Our kids need us right there marching beside them. Don't stop now. You're bound to win. If you want it bad enough, you'll get out in the streets for it."[2]

Farmer's call to the crowd was framed by other speakers, some of whom reported on the conditions of the students crammed into the old hospital buildings. Shirley Frye remembered the words of Pauline Foster, the principal of Bluford Elementary School, who told her friends and neighbors that the "youngsters," as she called them, deserved their support. And Farmer's refrain moved the crowd as well. "All over the country," he said, "the youth have been leading the demonstrations. But the segregationists have found out that when they start putting children in jail, then they'll have to get us too."[3]

The Fryes were among those conflicted about joining the "youngsters" on the streets, much less in jail. They and the other adults at Big Zion had considered the risk associated with public participation in the demonstrations. Those who were beholden to white employers or white institutions for their paychecks believed their jobs and their livelihood might be in jeopardy. Now, the moment of truth had arrived. There was a growing realization that no longer could they simply applaud and encourage, or contribute a dollar or a dime in aid of the cause, and still remain behind the veil.

Young Mel Swann was in the crowd that night. He was just beginning his teaching career at Principal A. H. Peeler's J. C. Price Elementary School. Swann had been a willing and eager participant in the marches, but he was warned not to go too far. One night, as he was seated in the middle of the street with students who had occupied the center of the Square, he felt a tap on his shoulder. He looked up to see one of his fellow teachers, a woman with far more years on the job. "She said, 'Mel Swann, Mr. Peeler is going to expect you to be in school in the morning. You had better get out of there. You don't need to be arrested.'"[4]

Henry Frye weighed his social and civic concern against his position in the U.S. attorney's office, where he had been employed for barely five months. His boss had not wanted him there in the first place, and he considered the consequences of the march that Farmer was urging him to take. What if it turned into an act of civil disobedience that could compromise an officer of the U.S. Justice Department? Moreover, he had never been one to participate in public demonstrations. That wasn't his style. He also wasn't quite settled in his commitment to non-violence, especially if some angry bystander spat in his face, or insulted his wife. Now might not be the time to be moved by the spirit. But then, he and Shirley reasoned together, if not now, when?[5]

So, the Fryes joined the people at Big Zion who left the church around 9:30 P.M. and formed into a column of four or five across that headed toward downtown. The group was silent as people marched under the leadership of nearly two dozen ministers, including the white rabbi of Greensboro's Temple Emanuel. Only the fall of their steps on the pavement could be heard. It was unnerving, Shirley later recalled, to hear nothing but the tramp of footsteps and the police who trailed along. The marchers continued to Elm Street where they turned north for a few blocks before heading back to Trinity. As he walked, Henry felt better and better about his decision to be part of the march. No one was arrested, but the point was made. The newspaper on Monday morning reported that, for the first time, adults in east Greensboro had shown in dramatic fashion their support for the students.

No one in his office commented on the march when Frye reported to work at the federal building. He didn't know if his co-workers, or his boss, were aware of his participation and just didn't express themselves, or if his effort to blend into the mass of marchers had succeeded. Indeed, he had been noticed. The director of the State Bureau of Investigation, Walter Anderson, filed a report to Governor Terry Sanford with details of the meeting at Trinity. He took note of the size of the crowd, Farmer's appearance, and he mentioned the name of only one marcher, whom he identified as "Herman Frye," an assistant to William Murdock in the U.S. attorney's office.[6]

William H. Murdock of Durham was fifty-seven years old and, before he was appointed to the federal job, he had spent nearly twenty years prosecuting criminals as solicitor in the state's Tenth District that included Durham and a few surrounding counties. He stood six-two and had served as a gunner's mate on an ammunition ship during World War II. In 1960, his plans for becoming a congressman had been spoiled by Horace Kornegay of Greensboro after Kornegay won the nomination in the Democratic Party primary. Kornegay's winning margin in the Sixth Congressional District, which included Durham, Guilford, and other counties, came out of Guilford County where Kornegay beat Murdock ten to one. In Frye's precinct, Kornegay received 859 votes to Murdock's 47. Murdock's appointment as U.S. attorney was his consolation prize.[7]

Reorganization of the U.S. attorney's office, after eight years under the Republicans, had taken the Democrats nearly a year to accomplish. Murdock kept one of the Republican appointees on for continuity but it was June in 1962 before he received approval for his first new assistant, Roy G. Hall, Jr. Frye's appointment by U.S. Attorney General Robert Kennedy was the next thing he heard from Washington. "I don't think [Murdock] was seeking any African American assistance," Hall said many years later.[8]

Murdock was what some called "a southern gentleman," and he was considered one of the best trial lawyers around. Having a black man in a position of authority in the federal courts challenged all manner of social mores, conventions, and traditions that were held dear by men of his generation. At the time of Frye's appointment, a newspaper reporter heard the first questions that were being raised about this peculiar situation: Where was Frye going to find a room and a meal when he was representing the government on the road and away from his home in Greensboro? No one spoke openly about the prospect of a black prosecutor cross-examining witnesses in the trial of white defendants.

Then, too, there were the questions that would arise in the confines of a working office where white female stenographers and office personnel would be required to come to Frye's office, seat themselves beside his desk, and take dictation.[9] Greensboro attorney McNeill Smith had hired a black secretary to help with his work as chair of the state advisory commission to the U.S. Civil Rights Commission and had been asked to move her to another office after the white secretaries in his law firm complained. Hall heard some catty comments from white lawyers about his new colleague, and even an apocryphal story that Frye's interest in the law had been spawned by his father, who, as a janitor in the federal building in Rockingham, brought old copies of the federal statutes home for his son to read. That story never reached Henry Frye and the image of a proud Walter Frye condescending to clean up after white folks brought a hearty laugh from his son when he heard it many years later.

If there was a stir among the women in the office over who would work with the stranger in their midst, Frye never heard about it. Nor did he remember any slights that interrupted his workday. Generally he bent to his tasks and left the socializing to others. It was the UNC Law School all over again. He knew the tensions were there but he was not going to give others any reason to make an issue of it, and he remembered the words of his one trusted friend in the building, U.S. District Judge Richardson Preyer. "Many eyes will be upon you and much will be expected of you," Preyer had told Frye when he was sworn in. Murdock may have been chilly, but he played his part without spite. In fact, he found a way to resolve his concerns, yet give Frye work of sufficient gravity to avoid complaints. Murdock buried Frye in bureaucratic paperwork.[10]

At the time, the federal government was finishing construction of a dam and reservoir near the headwaters of the Yadkin River outside of Wilkesboro. The town was in the foothills of the Blue Ridge, about seventy-five miles west of Greensboro, at the western edge of the district where African Americans were about as scarce as Democrats. The project was just before being dedicated in honor of former North Carolina governor and senator, W. Kerr Scott, when Frye came to work in the U.S. attorney's office. Frye's job was to handle the condemnation cases left behind by the government's taking of about four thousand acres of land for the project. It wasn't front-line duty in a Greensboro courtroom, but it was necessary and important work, and had to be done by someone. It was the kind of assignment that would logically have gone to a junior staff member with little trial experience.

Wilkes County was known for moonshine liquor and the fast cars that men like racing legend Junior Johnson, a Wilkes County native, used to haul it. The Kingston Trio had popularized another of Wilkes County's native sons. Tom Dula (Dooley to the singers) had murdered his fiancée Laura there before being tried and hanged in nearby Statesville in 1868. The local history was deep, and colorful. Standing outside the Wilkes County courthouse was an oak tree where British loyalists had met the same fate as Dula during the Revolutionary War. It was the land of Republicans — no Democratic candidate for governor had carried the county for more than twenty years — and only one in twenty residents were black.

Frye was starting from scratch. Except for what he had learned in law school, he knew nothing about the government's powers of eminent domain or the ins and outs of condemnation proceedings. He went back to school on the law, learning what he could from volumes of documents provided by the Justice Department's land division. From time to time, he was called to Washington for training with attorneys handling similar assignments in other districts. While he was there on one visit, he was lobbied by the division's chief, Assistant Attorney General Ramsey Clark, to consider a government career. On at least one occasion, Robert Kennedy spoke to the group, but he took no special notice of Frye. (Clark would later serve as attorney general under President Lyndon B. Johnson.[11])

Most of Frye's work included filing of the documents related to the government's taking of the land, and negotiating with landowners over settlement offers. Some who asked for formal meetings came to see him in Greensboro and he remembered the surprised expressions of those who entered his office and discovered he wasn't white. On the first occasion that required him to travel to Wilkesboro and stay overnight, he asked Murdock about accommodations. His boss told him he had a room at a hotel. Though Frye never asked, apparently someone in the office, perhaps Murdock, had made sure that the government's representative would not be embarrassed when he got to Wilkesboro. As far as he knew, Frye believed he was treated like any other guest during his stay. From time to time, he visited over lunch with a black agricultural extension agent in Wilkes County whom he had known from his days in the New Farmers of America.[12]

Frye settled into the routine of the job. The nominee from among the secretaries who was assigned to work with Frye learned that he was a picky writer who insisted that anything that went out over his signature was grammatically and typographically correct. His careful editing of the drafts of his letters often required retyping, which meant a complete overhaul in the day of typewriters and carbon paper. Over the months he was assigned some criminal cases, mostly plea arrangements with defendants. Occasionally, he conferred with federal law enforcement agents on the formalities of search warrants. He found the reputation of segregationist leanings was warranted among agents of the Federal Bureau of Investigation.

In time, Murdock grew more at ease with Frye's presence on his staff. He assigned him a few cases in federal courtrooms elsewhere in the district. He sent him to Winston-Salem to represent a postal employee involved in a traffic mishap. Frye surprised his boss in successfully defending the man, whom Murdock believed was probably guilty of something. On Frye's first trip to Rockingham in Richmond County, some of the folks from Ellerbe showed up in the courtroom to see the best-known graduate of Ellerbe (Colored) High School. Frye didn't have to worry about accommodations in Richmond County. He stayed with family. When he was in Durham, he would trade stories with Joseph Biggers, the deputy U.S. marshal who had broken the color line in that office in North Carolina. Frye believed Biggers probably had the tougher job; he had to escort white prisoners across South Carolina and Georgia to the federal prison in Atlanta.

Except for the march from Big Zion, Frye removed himself from public participation in the changes that were taking place around him. On one rare occasion, he parked his car on a side street and "patrolled" the sidewalks like other law enforcement officers as students marched from the campus into downtown. With only a few blacks in the city police department, and most of them in uniform, his guise probably didn't fool anyone. The demonstrations ended in mid-summer 1963 and Greensboro settled into an uneasy truce, with blacks focused more on the nation's capital and a march on Washington that the Reverend Martin Luther King, Jr., had scheduled for August.

Frye remained in touch with the Greensboro Citizens Association's Reverend Otis Hairston, one of the stalwarts of the movement in the city. Hairston had followed his father into the pulpit at Shiloh Baptist Church at about the same time Frye opened his law practice. Hairston succeeded Frye as chair of the association and was among the African Americans who negotiated with the whites at city hall for the end of segregation in downtown businesses. Frye also sat in on a discussion of measures undertaken by the Greensboro Citizens Emergency Committee, a group that Hairston organized to pressure white retail businesses to hire black sales clerks and treat all customers equally.

All in all, Frye's integration into Murdock's office went better than perhaps he or Murdock could have had anticipated. "It went smoothly because I knew the situation and he knew the situation, so both of us tried to handle things so that we didn't have confrontation," Frye said some time later. "That is the disadvantage, or advantage, of two Southerners who had grown up the same state and knew what things are like, and knew how to avoid confrontation and get some things done. That had a lot to do with it." The two even shared a few lunches together, although Frye said neither was entirely comfortable.[13]

Frye's appointment raised vexing questions for some within the Greensboro Bar Association, which had never accepted an African American into its membership. The bar groups in Winston-Salem and Charlotte had earlier dropped racial restrictions, although Wake County still limited membership to whites. In September 1963, the association received Frye's application for membership after he was encouraged to apply by Harper J. Elam III, a future Greensboro mayor whom everyone called Jack. Elam had spent five years as city attorney before becoming the first in-house counsel at Cone Mills Corporation in 1961. His efforts on Frye's behalf drew strong reaction from some members of the bar. Elam was steadfast in his support of Frye's membership and told those who protested that he would tender his own resignation if the bar did not accept Frye. A dissenter wrote Elam to tell him good riddance. The flurry was short-lived. Frye's application was accepted in October and the dropping of the racial barrier drew a modest reference in the local newspaper.[14] Henry's acceptance by his peers in the legal community didn't extend to Shirley, however. The Bar's auxiliary, composed of the wives of the members, didn't offer membership to Shirley until many years later, long after the time when an invitation would have been meaningful. She never joined.

Frye's job did not curtail all involvement in the community, where he was becoming known beyond the boundaries of east Greensboro. He was asked to become a member of the board of directors of the United Fund, he worked on behalf of the Boy Scouts, and he enjoyed the rousing annual membership drives led by David Morehead, the director of the Hayes-Taylor branch of the Young Men's Christian Association. The Y building at the edge of the A&T campus was one of the few locations in east Greensboro that members of the city's white establishment seemed to know how to find. Weekly meetings of a men's club started by Morehead, called the MCs, drew city officials and white businessmen from the other side of the tracks as luncheon speakers.

The Fryes also were a part of the Greensboro Community Fellowship, an interracial group led by businessman John R. Taylor and his wife, Betsy. Taylor was a missionary's son and a real estate developer; his wife was a Greensboro native and a volunteer leader in the Young Women's Christian Association, where interracial meetings had been held since the 1950s. The Taylors were well ahead of their time. Among John Taylor's businesses were two Holiday Inn motels. One was just north of Greensboro on U.S. 29 and another was on the south side of the city. They were among the first locations in the city that served all customers and the one place that the Fryes and other

African Americans frequented after Sunday services to enjoy a luncheon buf-
fet. One other spot where whites and blacks could socialize was the Taylors'
home in a country setting beside a small lake on the east side of the county.[15]

GCF had no official standing or political clout and depended on volunteers like the Fryes to make things happen. It had been formed in the 1950s
and was re-energized as the tensions grew in the spring of 1963. At one point,
the group bought a full-page ad in the morning newspaper in support of the
chamber of commerce and merchants' association resolutions on desegregation. It was paid for by one-dollar donations from the hundreds of people
whose names appeared in it.[16] For the most part, the group worked quietly to
unite whites and blacks and offer a place for the races to work through generations of separation. Shirley served as the secretary for a time, and she
helped organize a pre-school program of white and black children that was
held at Bennett College one year. Pairs of women, one white and the other
black, went door-to-door in east Greensboro to sign up students. The object
was to recruit a mixed-race classroom of children as a way to prepare them,
and their parents, to enter an interracial society.[17]

While Henry and Shirley had felt the sting of the Jim Crow South, they
also had witnessed positive interactions between whites and blacks in the
rural communities where they had grown up. It was a dimension of Southern
life that was virtually unknown by those who had been raised in the strict
confines of urban segregation. Walter Frye's association with white businessmen and political figures in Richmond County was not that far from the relationship that Shirley had experienced with her father in eastern North
Carolina. All of this left the Fryes impatient with the past, eager for the future,
and sometimes at odds with some of their own neighbors who remained wary
of whites and fearful for the changes that lay ahead. They pushed with a growing urgency to move the community along racially. Henry was surprised to
learn that even though the Taylors had spent years of working with blacks in
east Greensboro, no one there had ever invited the Taylors into their home.
Their first opportunity was a meeting that the Fryes hosted in their family
room.

The Fryes' optimism held fast, even when their lives were bruised by the
frustration and humiliation of discrimination. Among their friends outside
of east Greensboro were Hideki Imamura and his wife, Kikuko, a Japanese
couple living in Winston-Salem where Hideki was studying medicine at Wake
Forest University. Henry had met Hideki in Japan during his air force posting,
when Hideki led a weekend hiking excursion up Mt. Aso, a volcano near the
southern end of Japan's southern island of Kyushu. At the time, Hideki
was an interpreter for Baptist missionaries, one of whom was the sister of a
fellow air force officer. Hideki arrived in the United States after a tortuous
journey and entered Wake Forest, where he earned an undergraduate degree

and, finally, a medical degree in 1965. The Fryes invited the Imamuras to Greensboro for a meal and, to reciprocate, the Imamuras asked the Fryes and their two sons to attend church at Knollwood Baptist in Winston-Salem, where they were welcomed warmly. The day was to include a picnic at Tanglewood Park, the former country estate that tobacco man Will Reynolds had given to the city. Hideki Imamura was distressed to learn that while he and his family, who were foreigners, could come onto the grounds, the Fryes, who were American citizens, could not. Reynolds had stipulated in his will that the park was to be operated for whites only. The profound embarrassment felt by the Imamuras inspired Hideki to become active in race relations in his adopted homeland, where he subsequently created an impressive professional and civic resume. Henry Frye and writer Maya Angelou both offered eulogies at Hideki's funeral in 1997.[18]

After more than two years in the U.S. attorney's office, Frye was restless with what appeared to be a professional dead end. His position paid well, about $8,000 a year, and during his time on the government payroll he and Shirley had been able to buy their first home, a comfortable suburban split-level at 1920 Drexmore Avenue in a new subdivision called Benbow Park. The monthly mortgage payments came to just under a hundred dollars, which left them some money to furnish their home for the first time. (Each of the houses they had been renting had been furnished.) Henry's dim prospects for advancement were clear early on but he had stayed for two years out of respect for the effort that John Wheeler had put into gaining his appointment. He was bothered that when he left, there was little chance that another black man would be named to replace him. By the summer of 1965, the Kennedys were gone and there were no champions for blacks among southern Democrats.

At one point, Frye talked about his situation with Herbert Parks, the senior member of the black bar in Greensboro. Parks advised him to take advantage of his steady paycheck and use any spare money to invest in cheap houses that could be refurbished as rental units. This strategy offered no appeal to Frye, whatsoever. All in all, he was eager to return to a private law practice where he could perhaps take advantage of what he had gained from his experience. In August 1965, just as he turned thirty-three, Frye submitted his resignation. Murdock offered him a slight pay raise if he would stay, but it was not enticement enough. In private, Murdock had praised Frye's work to Roy Hall, Jr., but he never offered his good opinion to Frye.[19]

Two-plus years in the U.S. attorney's office made Frye a rarity among the hundred or so black lawyers in the state. He was the only one who could offer clients an insider's perspective of practice in the federal courts. That experience had come at a price, however. The clients that Frye had given up in 1962 to take the federal job had found other representation. He especially regretted the loss of the white businessman from Asheboro for whom he had cleared that tricky real estate title. The man was still developing property but he was comfortable with the service he was getting from Kenneth Lee. Frye also had missed a chance to be part of an initiative by the NAACP's Legal Defense Fund, which had chosen Frye's good friend, Julius Chambers, to underwrite a start-up practice in Charlotte to handle civil rights cases.[20]

He was looking for a broader practice than civil rights cases, both by choice and by necessity. "I wanted to make money and I wanted to make a difference and try to help people," he later recalled. "It was a split motive. There were things I knew I was going to lose money on." Most immediately, he needed a steady income to supplement Shirley's pay as a schoolteacher, which was about to end. She was pregnant and would have to leave at the end of her sixth month. When Daniel G. Sampson, the dean of the law school at North Carolina College in Durham (later North Carolina Central University), called him in the summer of 1965 and offered him a teaching job, he took it. Before he began the fall term, however, Frye opened a one-room office in a building occupied by two dentists at 107 S. Dudley Street. His teaching responsibilities would occupy him at least four days a week, but he still had Fridays and Saturdays to see clients.[21]

In addition to the career change, Henry and Shirley were facing another important decision. Their eldest son, Henry Jr., turned six in the summer of 1965 and would be entering public school in the fall. The Greensboro schools were operating under a freedom-of-choice school integration plan, which allowed parents to ask for their children to be assigned to a particular school. Henry asked Shirley to use her familiarity with the school system and find the best school available. The Fryes chose Brooks Elementary, a school with only two black children in a student body of several hundred. A decade after *Brown*, the Fryes found themselves in the same situation as other black parents who had to decide whether their child would be one to advance the cause of equal education.[22]

Henry, Shirley, and their friends had been talking about how to implement school desegregation since the decision had been issued ten years earlier. It was Henry's belief that the best way to achieve full integration was to work at it one grade at a time, and begin with the first grade. Within a dozen years, the old dual system would be gone, he believed. That had not happened, and Greensboro schools had assigned black students to formerly all-white schools only as parents stepped forward and asked to leave the comfort zone of all-black schools. The requests were not accepted without resistance. The school board balked in 1960 when the parents of Deborah Barnes asked that she attend Gillespie, which was about two blocks from their house, rather than an all-black school some distance away. Frye was prepared to make a legal challenge, but the case was never filed. Barnes was admitted as one of three blacks in the school.[23]

Now, what had begun for the Fryes as a forensic exercise on the steps of a classroom building at A&T was now a very personal decision. The Fryes based their choice on the facts. If Brooks was the best school available, then that was where their children would be educated. There was more to it, of course. "We decided that if our children were going to live in a world where they were going to know all people," Shirley later recalled, "we would place them in an integrated school." Some of their friends considered their decision a betrayal of loyalty to the black schools, but Shirley refused to listen to their complaints. The decision was the best for them, and for the son. "If they are going to have difficulty [with an integrated world], we wanted them to have it early so we could help develop them and mold them to see that all people were the same."

It was bold talk that masked private concerns that an otherwise happily adjusted black child, who suddenly found himself in a classroom filled with white children, would become confused about who he was. The parents didn't share their concerns with their sons. Rather, she said, "We had hoped that our behavior would be a good model for them." Nonetheless, Shirley was anxious as she and Henry prepared for the first parents meeting in Henry Jr.'s classroom. From her own experience in teaching first grade, she expected his teacher to subscribe to a traditional opening exercise and ask students to draw a picture of themselves. "We went to school that night and there were all these pictures on the bulletin board and that little brown face was in there." After the meeting, the teacher assured Shirley she had not prompted Henry Jr. in the creation of his self-portrait. "I didn't worry about him any more. We knew he knew who he was and we felt we had done the right thing by sending him to Brooks." Harlan followed his brother to Brooks and they finished their public schooling at predominantly white schools with both boys excelling at their respective high schools. When Harlan graduated from predominantly white Grimsley High School, his father was the commencement speaker.[24]

The state of North Carolina had never properly endowed the law school at North Carolina College in Durham, and by the time Frye arrived to meet his first class in mid–September 1965, the school was struggling for its very survival. It had been a bastard child since 1939 when it was created to give the appearance of separate-but-equal legal education for the state's African Americans. Its first dean was M. T. Van Hecke, the former dean at the law school in Chapel Hill. He added his work in Durham to his course load at the university. The school also had never been taken seriously by the state's educational establishment, and if Governor Dan Moore had his way, the school's days were numbered. The governor wanted it closed.

The school had never had a large number of students; its enrolled only three women in 1948. Its prospects faded even more in 1951 when the federal court desegregated the law school at Chapel Hill. The suit spelled out the inadequacies of the Durham school. Attorneys defending the state argued that the physical condition of the school was comparable, even though the 30,000 volumes in the law library were stacked one on top of the other and not readily available on shelves. The state also argued that the school's lower enrollment allowed for more specialized attention. The first students admitted to the Chapel Hill law school were transfers from Durham, and the school continued to supply second and third year students throughout the 1950s while maintaining a small number of students who finished their studies in Durham.

There were only thirty-one students enrolled in the law school in the fall of 1965 and the faculty still included white professors from Chapel Hill and Duke. Frye commuted to the campus four days a week and taught courses in civil and criminal procedure. Those subjects came easily to him and he especially liked teaching constitutional law. The course in future interests was no easier to teach than it had been to learn when he was in law school.

As Frye had hoped, the teaching job provided the transition he was looking for in a return to private practice. He enjoyed preparing for, and delivering, courses. His classes were relatively small, about twenty students each, and over the term he encountered aspiring attorneys who would make their own marks in the world. One was Clifton Johnson, who would go on to serve on the bench from the district court up to the appellate level. Eva Clayton, who later would be the first black woman elected to Congress from North Carolina, was another. He pushed his students to analyze the law, closely and critically, and he remained as much a stickler for proper grammar, punctuation, and clear writing as he was with his own work.

He ended his first year with an offer to return to Durham for another year. The experience had gone so well that he was beginning to think that he might find a permanent position at another law school. In the summer of 1966, he attended a meeting of the Association of American Law Schools. There, he ran into his mentor and former professor, Dan Pollitt, who did not know Frye was teaching in Durham. When Pollitt returned to Chapel Hill he recommended Frye for a vacancy at the UNC Law School, but his advice went unheeded. The school was looking for a teacher with a much higher academic profile.[25]

Henry Frye had begun his second year teaching in 1966 when the N.C. Bar Association turned down applications for membership from two black lawyers from Durham. One was from Henry M. "Mickey" Michaux, Jr., a 1964 graduate of the North Carolina College Law School. The other was his brother, Eric, who had just graduated from the Duke University Law School. Both had passed the bar exam the previous summer. Eric had succeeded on his first try, while it was his brother's third effort. The two were from a wealthy, well-connected Durham family with broad interests in business and real estate. During Dr. Martin Luther King, Jr.'s visits to Durham, he had stayed in the Michaux home. At King's urging, Eric had attended Boston University for his undergraduate degree before entering the Duke Law School. The Duke faculty encouraged him to apply for membership in the bar association, which only that summer had removed a "whites only" provision in its bylaws.[26]

African Americans had gained admission to a few of the local Bar organizations but they had given up on membership in the state association. Kenneth Lee had applied in the early 1950s, was turned down, and subsequently was involved in the organization of the N.C. Lawyers Association when the eight or ten black attorneys in the state could meet in the living room of a member's home.[27] In the early 1960s, the North Carolina lawyers had joined with black attorneys in South Carolina and Virginia to form the Southeastern Lawyers Association, which counted about 125 in its membership. About seventy-five of the members were from North Carolina.

Mickey Michaux believed the profession was rife with discrimination. He laid his lack of success at passing the bar examination to tactics of the same man who had delayed issuing Frye his law license, the State Bar's executive director, Ed Cannon. One year, Michaux was not notified that he was expected at the bar examination until the day before the testing was to begin. Michaux said such devices were one way that Cannon discouraged black candidates so he could limit their admission to the bar. "I remember being in [Cannon's] office," Mickey Michaux said some years later. "One of the first things that got your eye was one of the biggest, dirtiest Confederate flags you have ever seen in your life."[28]

The Michaux brothers offered their applications to the Bar association and in an appearance before the association's board of governors were asked if they were applying simply to break the color barrier, or to become participating members of the association. Eric told a *Charlotte Observer* reporter that he answered the question saying, "I told them that we came as both. I said that we came as lawyers but by birth and tradition we also were forced to come as Negroes." The board denied their applications.[29]

In response to the association's rejection of one of its graduates, the Duke law faculty voted in December 1966 to discontinue the continuing education classes conducted for lawyers on the Duke campus. The faculty at the UNC law school followed suit. In a curious turn, one of the dissenting votes at Chapel Hill came from Dan Pollitt. While Pollitt was sympathetic with the response of his colleagues, he said that, in good conscience, he couldn't ban the Bar association from campus at the same time that he was challenging the state's Speaker Ban Law that prohibited communists from speaking on school property.[30]

William F. Womble, from the prestigious Winston-Salem law firm Womble,

Carlyle, Sandridge and Rice, was the association's new president. Among those supporting his efforts to integrate the association were UNC Law School Dean J. Dickson Phillips, Jr., and his predecessor, Henry Brandis. There were others, including James B. McMillan of Charlotte, a future federal district judge and a recent past president of the association.[31] Womble tried to head off the dissent from the law schools, but to no avail. The disconnect with the law schools was more than symbolic. The association depended on faculty members at Duke, UNC, and Wake Forest to provide the core of its continuing legal education. In addition to refusing support for these courses, the Duke faculty also voted to no longer provide names of students for summer placement in North Carolina firms, an important opportunity to firms to try out future hires.

The response was to present more candidates for membership when the board of governors met again in the spring of 1967. Womble, McMillan, and others, including E. Osborne Ayscue from McMillan's firm in Charlotte, saw to it that the committee had applications from Henry Frye and Julius Chambers, both of whom were UNC graduates with outstanding professional

Henry Frye filed to run for the state house of representatives in 1966 using the $17.50 collected on his behalf by his students at the North Carolina College Law School. His wife accompanied him to pay his filing fee (courtesy Frye family).

records. Chambers was perhaps the better known of the two, since he had edited the *Law Review* in his final year at UNC and his name had been in the news in relation to the civil rights suits he was bringing in North Carolina. His application was accepted but for some reason, the committee stalled when it took up Frye's name. Those behind the effort arranged for additional endorsements and the two became the first black members of the N.C. Bar Association. In the summer of 1967, Frye and Chambers and their wives set out from Charlotte for the Grove Park Inn in Asheville, the usual mountain venue for the association's annual meeting. They arrived late and a bit shaken, however. Riding together from Charlotte they were involved in an automobile accident and had to return and get a second car.

When Frye had accepted the offer to teach, he told the dean that he was considering mounting a political campaign in the spring of 1966. So, it was no surprise to those in Durham when he announced as a candidate in the Democratic Party primary for one of Guilford County's six house seats in the N.C. General Assembly. He paid his filing fee of $17.50 with money that his law students had collected on his behalf. He finished seventh, a little more than 1,250 votes behind attorney James G. Exum, Jr., a white lawyer who was about Frye's age.

Shirley was crushed over the outcome; she had believed all those who had told her they would vote for her husband. The experience left her dispirited, even though her husband had tried to prepare her for defeat. Henry was typically philosophical; he called it a learning experience. "I knew that if I was going to win I was going to have to get much higher support in the white community," he said. "The question was how to do that."[32]

7

The Election

A newspaper reporter counting the number of African Americans elected to public office in North Carolina at the end of 1966 found only fourteen men who were members of local municipal authorities. A few others held appointments to school boards or a local housing commission.[1] Black candidates for the state legislature had been on the ballot since as early as 1948, but all had failed to win, even in Durham and Winston-Salem, which had the most effective black political organizations. As a result, no one paid much attention to Henry Frye's loss in 1966. He was just another casualty.

Greensboro had not elected an African American to any public office since 1961, when bail bondsman Waldo Falkener won re-election to the city council. He did not survive a primary election in 1963 when political rivalry within the black community left east Greensboro without a voice at city hall. Internal debate in the community on how best to marshal black votes had cost Falkener the election. It wouldn't happen again.

The politics in east Greensboro had run the gamut since Henry and Shirley Frye had arrived in Greensboro. They were upper classmen at A&T when a group of black doctors, businessmen, and ministers formed the Greensboro Citizens Association in an effort to unify the black community and get an African American on the city council. They succeeded with the election of Dr. William Hampton in 1951. Two years later, Hampton augmented his solid black support with enough white votes to put him at the top of the ticket in the first primary. He served another term but subsequently returned to his medical practice. Falkener was elected in 1959 and re-elected in 1961, but the elites on Benbow Road wanted a change in 1963. During his four years in office, Falkener had won some concessions from city hall. East Greensboro had a new firehouse, manned by black firemen, but detractors said he had lost touch with the community. As a result, he and a preferred candidate, J. T. Taylor, a retired Boy Scout executive, split the black vote in the municipal primary in 1963. Neither one placed high enough to win election in the at-large contest.

Despite assurances to Shirley that he would avoid politics, Henry Frye had started thinking about running for office as soon as he was free of the restrictions of his federal job. He was not as well known as Falkener, Taylor, or others who had been on the ballot, but he was no stranger in the community either. He had chaired the Greensboro Citizens Association and had performed other civic chores. His reputation was spotless and those who knew him found him thoughtful and thorough, but these same traits made him appear, to some, to be overly cautious. There were other bona fides. He was active in the A&T alumni organization, which set well with the academic crowd. Teenagers filled his Sunday school classroom at Providence Baptist Church where, despite his relative youth, he chaired the pulpit committee and that brought the Reverend Howard A. Chubbs to the church. Frye's appointment as a professor of law added to his résumé.

The Fryes were solidly middle class. They appeared to be prospering in their new home in Benbow Park, a comfortable suburban neighborhood with split-level residences built on a rolling section of land just east of Benbow Road. It was one of the first neighborhoods of its kind in east Greensboro. Yet, the family lived simply and without pretense. When Chubbs came to preach at Providence one Sunday before he accepted the call to Greensboro, he and his wife stayed overnight at the Frye home. As the Fryes were leaving for an evening engagement they couldn't avoid, Chubbs urged them to drive his car, a newer and shinier model than the one Henry and Shirley had parked in the driveway. "It was an old Chevrolet or something," Chubbs said. "I thought a lawyer ought to do better than that."[2]

The law office that Frye opened at 107 S. Dudley Street was one room, but sufficient for his abbreviated practice. Also in the building was Dr. W. L. T. Miller, an ally from his Citizens Association days. Miller was the man the insurgents at Precinct 8 put in as chair when they took over in 1960. Frye talked with Miller, and others, about finding a candidate for the legislature. Major S. High, who got his UNC law degree the year after Kenneth Lee, was a possibility. He had run and lost in 1964. Frye also started thinking about becoming a candidate.

One of the influential men Frye approached was Dr. B. W. Barnes. He was a dentist, a leader among A&T alumni, and a friend. Barnes had called on Frye in 1960 to aid in his granddaughter's bid to enter Gillespie Elementary, a lightly integrated former white school two blocks from her home. The school board had assigned her to all-black Bluford Elementary, which was more than a mile away. "Before I could get [a question] out of my mouth," Frye later recalled, "he said, 'Son, if you will run, I will raise the money for you.' After that, the only question was who else do I need to talk to."[3]

Frye set his sights as high as was reasonable for any black man in the mid–1960s. With the governor limited to one term and no veto power, the N.C. General Assembly was the most powerful legislative body in the nation.

Winning a legislative race was the necessary first step for any ambitious white man who dreamed of being governor, a congressman, or a U.S. senator. A legislative seat meant even more to African Americans. The last black legislators were five Republicans who had survived the white supremacy campaign mounted in 1898 by the Democratic Party when it regained control of the legislature and subsequently passed restrictive laws and constitutional amendments that had sidelined the black vote for more than half a century.[4] In 1966, it was folly to think a black candidate could be elected governor, or even win some down-ticket position such as commissioner of labor or insurance, but Frye believed it was time that blacks in North Carolina regained a voice in state government, as they had in Georgia the year before when Julian Bond was elected to that state's legislature.

By the time Frye's political plans made the newspapers, it appeared he might have competition in the black community. Falkener and High were said to be thinking about the race. When High was asked about Frye, he offered a hearty endorsement. Falkener was cool to the news, however. He said he would not run, but he declined to say if he would support Frye.[5] Neither filed for the race and Frye became the only African American among the nine candidates seeking nomination for six seats elected at large.

Political campaigns of the day were not long affairs. Frye announced his plans in late March with the primary election only sixty days away. Somehow, he had to squeeze a political campaign into a crowded weekday schedule where he was tied up fifty miles away in Durham for Monday through Thursday and his Fridays and Saturdays were needed to see his law clients. He devoted Sunday to his family and church.

Frye knew nothing about organizing a political campaign and neither did anyone else close at hand. A legislative race meant he would need votes from throughout the county, not just in Greensboro, where he was known. The other candidates included popular incumbents with ties to the party organization. Frye had none of that. His last political activity had been to help organize Precinct 8 in 1960.[6]

Working with what he had, Frye relied on advice from Barnes and an A&T faculty member, S. J. Shaw, who along with Barnes was a member of the influential Greensboro Men's Club, a selective organization that was well regarded on Benbow Road, but which had no practical political record. In the end, Shirley became his most tireless and enthusiastic worker, despite her misgivings about politics. She brought with her the contacts she had made through volunteer work at the YWCA and the Greensboro Community Fellowship. Both organizations provided access to politically active whites that might support her husband's candidacy.

For the most part, Frye followed the routine of appearances—school picnics, civic clubs, and a few newspaper and television interviews. The press gave him no special attention because of his race and lumped his responses to questions on popular political issues right in with the others. Frye was in favor of adopting daylight savings time and opposed to the death penalty, as were the others. He was the only Democrat who didn't state any outright opposition to liquor by the drink. He said the law should be studied, as should state financial aid to cities.

Campaign solicitation letters went out to blacks and whites. One made its way to Ceasar Cone, the gruff, plainspoken head of the Cone textile empire. Cone knew Frye from his volunteer work at the Hayes Taylor YMCA, with which the Cone family had a close connection. He called the young lawyer and asked him to stop by. "I went out and we started talking and had a nice conversation for a while and then he said something about the right-to-work law in North Carolina. I said, 'Well there is a so-called right to work law.' I explained what I thought were the good and bad points about it and he said, 'I can't support you. I can tell you that right now.' So I said, 'Thank you. I appreciate it. That is the way I feel about it.'"[7] (The right-to-work law prohibited unions from requiring membership of all workers in a plant that voted for representation. It was considered an effective firewall to union organization by manufacturers like Cone.)

All political campaigns were largely popularity contests, with candidates spreading their message through newspapers ads, campaign flyers, and personal contact. Frye's spending was modest — about a thousand dollars was raised — and the money went to pay for letters, posters, and a few small advertisements in the daily newspapers that appeared just before Election Day. On Sundays, he had invitations to speak at one, and sometimes two, churches. At the Poplar Grove AME Church on May 1, the Reverend M. L. Johnson turned the pulpit over to Frye immediately after the collection had been received. Frye told the congregation about the first time he tried to register to vote and said he wanted to do something about such devices that kept blacks off the rolls. The turnout for the primary election on May 28 was modest. Frye ran ahead of the pack in east Greensboro, but he placed seventh overall, about twelve hundred votes behind the next candidate.

"He was young," recalled Chubbs. "Nobody knew him that much. It was the time before the time. It was not time yet in the minds of the majority culture that they necessarily had to have black representation."[8] Years later, Shirley agreed. Nonetheless, she was sorely disheartened. She had put too much faith in her husband's solid reputation in the community and at the courthouse, where he was known for his sound legal work. One regret was that Henry refused to ingratiate himself to the elites on Benbow Road. He wasn't comfortable with self-promotion or shallow socializing. He had even asked Shirley to turn down an invitation to join the local chapter of The Links, a selective national organization of socially prominent black women.

Young African American mothers knew they had arrived when they were invited to join The Links. All in all, her determined efforts to overcome her husband's discomfort with putting himself on public display simply had not been enough. For a man with a deep interest in politics, he was, at best, a mediocre candidate.

Shirley had never believed she would assume such a prominent role in a political campaign. She disliked the criticism and pettiness associated with politics, not only because of her deep love and affection for Henry but because she was uncomfortable with social discord. Shirley did not like to hear complaints and gossip, and would deftly change the subject to deflect unwanted conversation. She couldn't always do that in a political setting. Henry told her to ignore the carping. "His response to me was, 'If you are not doing anything they are going to criticize you and if you are doing anything they are going to criticize you.' You just have to develop a thick skin. I learned to accept that."[9]

Even though Frye placed out of the running, he made an impression. A week after the May primary election, city council member Jack Elam proposed Frye as a replacement for William A. Folk, Jr., who had resigned from the council to campaign for a seat on the county's board of commissioners. Frye told a reporter who called to ask about Elam's bid on his behalf that he would take the job if it were offered, but he wouldn't campaign for it. Surprisingly, Elam's nomination drew a complaint from Ezell Blair, whose son had been one of the A&T students who had launched the lunch-counter sit-ins. Blair said the appointment should go to O. C. Stafford, one of the three unsuccessful black candidates in the municipal elections in 1965. Blair said Frye was not a choice "of the majority of the Negro community." The council dodged the issue and voted 4–2 to give the seat to Carson Bain, a prominent white businessman.[10] In the next municipal election, Bain led the city council balloting and became mayor.

A month later, a house seat became vacant when Governor Dan Moore appointed James G. Exum, Jr., to a new superior court judgeship. Frye was the most likely nominee to replace Exum, who had placed just ahead of him in the 1966 primary. The seat was left open; the legislature wasn't due to reconvene until after the next election. Nonetheless, naming Frye would have been a generous gesture had the party been inclined to acknowledge him. Apparently, none of the white leadership was ready to give that sort of a boost to a black candidate.

Frye had no doubt that he would try again in 1968. "I wasn't going to quit losing," he said.[11] Adjustments would have to be made, however. In the meantime, he turned to his work at the law school. He completed his career as a professor at the conclusion of the spring term in 1967, and began work on building up his law practice. Shirley was already into a new challenge. She left the school system to become the coordinator of the special education department at Bennett College in the fall of 1966, where Henry's old chemistry professor, Dr. Isaac Miller, had recently succeeded Dr. Willa Player as president.

Shirley had been teaching a methods class for special education teachers since she began work on her master's degree. At Bennett, she was working with young women — teachers-to-be — some of whom were beginning to chafe under Bennett's tradition as a finishing school for proper young ladies. Shirley was younger than most of her peers and she offered a sympathetic ear to the student complaints. Especially grating to her students was a required course called Family Life 101 where the lessons on how to manage a home and otherwise prepare for a life of genteel domesticity were to be learned. At one faculty meeting, Shirley presented the student objections to the course as a waste of time for young women who clearly saw their futures as being more than a loyal, unquestioning helpmate to a husband. Shirley's ideas got nowhere and some senior faculty members froze her out of future conversations, at least until her husband began winning elections.

Young black men and women, especially those who came from middle- and upper-class families, were experiencing liberation from the structured and socially proper world that held tight in the black community. Now they were hearing talk of "Black Power" challenges to the old order. The civil rights movement itself was undergoing a change that would drive whites from their jobs in the Student Nonviolent Coordinating Committee and produce the rise of angry voices of new leadership under men like Stokely Carmichael. In the fall of 1967, sociologist Kenneth Clarke delivered a paper at an academic gathering in Greensboro in which he said the black middle class, as well as white America, were under a threat. Both should heed the impatience and anger rising from poor blacks, especially those in the cities. The civil rights movement may have opened opportunities for those who could afford to live with the Fryes in neighborhoods like Benbow Park, but poor black Americans were no better off. Clark's message was underscored in the summer of 1967 when a race riot leveled block after block in the city of Detroit.[12]

The rising militancy among young blacks, and the growing attraction of whites to Alabama's segregationist governor George Wallace, meant that 1968 was going to be a very different kind of political year from what Henry Frye had experienced two years earlier. The mild-mannered 1966 contest was beginning to look like something from another era as the political stage was being set in North Carolina with a gubernatorial contest at the top of the ticket. The leading candidates in the Democratic primary came from the usual places. The erstwhile progressive in the race was Lieutenant Governor Robert W. Scott, the inheritor of the reputation of his father, W. Kerr Scott, the populist governor who had been elected twenty years earlier. The elder Scott was

best known for populist rhetoric and miles of farm-to-market roads built
during his administration. Opposing Scott was J. Melville Broughton, Jr., a
tall, lanky Raleigh lawyer whose father had been governor during World War
II. He had the backing of the state's conservative Democrats who had enjoyed
four comfortable years with Governor Dan Moore. The spoiler in the race
was Dr. Reginald Hawkins of Charlotte, an outspoken black dentist who had
proven to be even more of an irritant to the white establishment than Greensboro's Dr. George Simkins, Jr.

Hawkins had taken on the Charlotte school system, the state's white doctors and dentists, the YMCA, segregated hotels and restaurants, election officials, county health departments, and even the administrators of government
anti-poverty programs. He bore the scars for his battles; his house was
bombed in 1965. A voter registration drive he led added 15,000 voters to the
rolls but his methods got him in hot water with the county election board.
Licensed as a dentist and ordained as a Presbyterian minister, Hawkins was
irrepressible, independent, and likely to say almost anything. He promised
to shake things up. "God has called me for this day. I stay in contact with
Him," he said early in his campaign. "These plans could only come from
divine guidance. There is not going to be any 'white folks business' or 'white
folks politics' any more. There's going to be a cutting of the political and economic pie."[13]

A Hawkins victory was improbable and for that reason many blacks
believed he could do nothing more than sour the good will they might otherwise gain by throwing in with Scott or Broughton. Even those who approved
of Hawkins's motive — to get blacks more involved in politics— suggested he
would be better to run for lieutenant governor. Scott was the favorite among
African Americans, some of whom were old enough to remember his father's
response to black support after he was elected governor in 1948. A protracted
and angry debate broke out among black public officials meeting at Shaw
University in January 1968 over allowing Hawkins to speak to the group. He
was not invited.

Hawkins bulldozed ahead with a campaign managed by James Ferguson
II, an energetic young lawyer in Julius Chambers's firm in Charlotte. Hawkins
and his people were willing to gamble that if he could withhold the support
of the state's black voters from both Scott and Broughton, then neither would
gain a majority and Hawkins could broker black support in a run-off election.
He had seen that work in 1964 when segregationist candidate I. Beverly Lake
had helped swing the election in favor of Governor Moore. After Moore was
inaugurated, Lake became the governor's choice to fill a vacancy on the state
supreme court.

The number of blacks registered to vote was on the rise in North Carolina, thanks in part to the provisions of the 1965 Voting Rights Act, which

outlawed the literacy test in thirty-nine of the state's one hundred counties. About half of those eligible to vote were registered by 1968 and the number was slowly growing larger. The N.C. Voter Education Project based in Durham, and funded by the Southern Regional Council, was focusing much of its attention in the eastern part of the state where one of Frye's former law students, Eva Clayton, was mounting a congressional campaign. Hawkins claimed that of the estimated 300,000 blacks registered to vote, 200,000 would vote for him, and that was enough to swing an election.

In January 1968, Hawkins appeared at a campaign rally in Greensboro before a large crowd. He never failed to arouse his audience. He had a bottomless inventory of one-liners and audacious claims that guaranteed people would remember him. He liked his role as the spoiler, calling himself "the ink in the milk" of the Democratic primary, and he played around with talk about race that could put both blacks and whites on edge. On one occasion, he said, "I say to the people of North Carolina — and especially the white people — I am the best riot insurance." He held his crowd with his energy and audacity. It made no difference whether the day was hot or cold, Hawkins's ebony face would be glistening with sweat by the time he was through with his stump speech. He could swagger and stomp when he needed to, and he used language that no candidate, black or white, had ever attempted in public. At one point he called his campaign the "deniggerization" of North Carolina. "There's nothing wrong with being black," he said during one campaign stop with black businessmen. "Look at me. I'm beautiful, baby."

For all his bluster and entertainment value, Hawkins raised serious issues that the other candidates avoided. College students and some of the seasoned veterans of the state's small but energetic organized labor movement helped him with position papers and campaign research that produced one of the most progressive programs the state had seen since the gubernatorial campaign of a bona fide liberal named Ralph McDonald in 1936. Hawkins called for new taxes on cigarettes and said approval of the sale of liquor by the drink was a way to raise money to support a broader program of education. He was opposed to the state's right-to-work law and proposed tuition grants for college students. He supported an open housing law. While Scott and Broughton spoke often about the need for law and order in a troubled, racially torn society — a response to the riots of the year before — Hawkins scoffed and called their comments "bilge." "They never talked to me about equal administration of justice for black and white men. They never said why we don't have any black judges in North Carolina, why there are no convictions of Klansmen who burn crosses in our front yard."

Henry Frye was only vaguely aware of Hawkins when Hawkins launched his campaign for governor. In January 1968, Frye turned out to see who this man was, just like a number of other blacks in Greensboro. He was no more comfortable with the exotic rhetoric than he was with a preacher who counted on soaring phrases and amens to move a congregation, but after his first exposure Frye was sure of one thing. He was impressed with the way Hawkins energized a crowd, and Frye vowed to be on hand every time Hawkins was close by. The man could excite people like no other candidate around, and he hoped to gain from the exposure.

From the outset, Frye showed he had learned from his previous campaign. He got an earlier start and announced his intentions in February rather than late March. His prepared statement had some real meat in it. While he had not heard Kenneth Clarke when he was in Greensboro four months earlier, Frye spoke to Clarke's concerns about America's fractured society. He said that if he was elected his intention was to "bridge the differences between the haves and the have-nots." The real issue was not liquor-by-the-drink or crime, he said. "It is, I believe, the growing differences ... between those who enjoy the good things in life and those who for various reasons do not." He was in favor of recruiting high-wage industries—a dangerous commitment in a county whose largest employers ran textile mills—and he supported equal job opportunities for blacks. A few months earlier, Frye had made the newspapers by challenging a claim by the city attorney that equal housing couldn't be achieved through a local ordinance.[14]

Two years earlier, Frye was little known outside of east Greensboro. In the run-up to his second election he paid a call on David Morehead, the executive in charge of the Hayes Taylor YMCA. Over the years, Morehead had cultivated contacts in the white community, and he was eager to lend a hand. He asked Frye to get him a complete résumé that he could circulate among prominent white businessmen he knew. One of them was Ed Zane, a top executive at Burlington Industries, which was the city's leading corporate citizen. The exposure paid off there, and elsewhere. Before the campaign was over, a senior executive of Pilot Life Insurance Company invited Frye to visit the company's headquarters on a sprawling country-club campus south of the city where he escorted Frye from department to department to offer his endorsement.

"I suspect that Dave Morehead said to Zane that the business leadership didn't support him," Frye later recalled. "And he may have said, 'Well, they don't know him.'"[15]

Frye remained a very buttoned-down candidate, cautious in his manner and his public statements. He was usually turned out in a dark suit, white shirt, and silk tie, often with a matching pocket square. He wore close-cropped hair and was clean-shaven at a time when nearly all black men of his age wore some sort of facial hair and Afro hairstyles were in vogue. He didn't try to emulate the rousing style of Hawkins, but he regarded his campaign to be just as important, if not more so. Hawkins made noise; he planned to make a difference.

"I don't think anybody expected [Hawkins] to be the governor," Frye said many years later, "but he was saying things that got a lot of blacks excited and they would come to a rally to hear him and be motivated to go register and vote. Whereas my talking about let's do something about housing, and we need to do all this, black and white need to work together, didn't stir them up the way his message did."[16] Frye's natural reserve, his reticence with self-promotion, and a lack of fire in his message meant that he would, once again, be just another name in a field of eleven candidates competing for six slots. For the most part, this race was going to be a popularity contest, with each candidate looking out for himself.

In late March, Dr. Martin Luther King, Jr., announced that he would spend all of April 4 in a tour of the state to promote the Hawkins campaign. A caravan was to start in Charlotte, pass through Greensboro, Durham, Rocky Mount, and end that evening in Wilmington. There were a number of blacks on the ballots across the state, including Eva Clayton in the eastern part of the state. She was challenging veteran white incumbent L. H. Fountain in the state's Second Congressional District where North Carolina's last black member of congress, George H. White, had served until losing re-election in 1900. At the last minute, King cancelled the trip to return to Memphis, Tennessee, where he was leading a campaign in support of striking garbage workers. He was shot and killed there on April 8.

The news of King's death reached east Greensboro while a testimonial dinner for A&T President Dr. Lewis Dowdy was underway on the campus. As the evening event broke up around 10 P.M., a crowd of about two hundred fifty persons, mostly students, soon formed and a line of marchers reached downtown. Earlier in the day, the Greensboro Chamber of Commerce had elected Dowdy and three other businessmen, including Kenneth Lee, to the chamber's board of directors. The shift in sentiment among the white business leaders from its earlier line of resistance to breaking the race line was lost in the tumult of the days that followed King's death.

Initially, the response was muted, although a few store windows had been broken during the impromptu march downtown in the hours immediately after King's death. The next day, a Friday, there was a peaceful march into downtown following memorial services for King at A&T and Bennett. By Sunday, however, the city was under curfew after gunfire injured three city policemen. The shots were fired from the A&T campus, where students had been released early for the Easter recess, and National Guardsmen, who had been called in on Saturday, used tear gas and selective live fire in response. Campus buildings, and black businesses along Market Street, suffered in the exchange. The soldiers continued to patrol and the city remained under curfew into the following week. Years later, the Fryes remembered little of the turmoil that was centered on the A&T campus. Like many, many others, they felt a deep sense of loss in King's death and were uncertain what the future would bring as smoke from burning buildings settled over Washington, D.C., the scene of riots. Shirley turned her home into a refuge for a few Bennett College students who were afraid to remain on campus. She called the parents to let them know their daughters were safe.

King's death provided the impetus for Congress to send to President Lyndon Johnson a broad open housing bill that was designed to remove racial barriers to housing in America. Once the curfews in major North Carolina cities were lifted, and National Guardsmen were released from temporary duty, the spring political campaigns resumed with full intensity. Frye and his supporters were optimistic that 1968 would be different. They hoped the Hawkins campaign would produce a larger-than-average turnout of black voters, and Frye was encouraged by the inroads he had been able to make into the white community. His campaign treasurer, Dr. Miller, opened the mail one day and found a donation from Ceasar Cone, who had dismissed his candidacy two years earlier. Miller immediately called Frye and told him he was going to win the election.[17]

Frye had more time to campaign in 1968 than two years earlier, and that helped build momentum. So did wider recognition in the community. He made appearances through the county, even in rural precincts where he expected little support. One woman surprised him, however, when she told him of her devotion to George Wallace. His immediate thought was that this encounter was wasted when she told him, "You people need someone in there, too" and promised him her vote. In Gibsonville, a small textile town on the east side of the county, Frye would place fourth among the eleven contenders.

Frye's calm demeanor and moderate approach — he was not one to make campaign promises, about anything — was troubling to some black voters who expected more fire in his speeches. He once told a reporter that black friends told him, "Some times I have trouble telling whether you are white or Negro. Get into your tie and shirtsleeves."[18] His platform wasn't designed to impress those infatuated with black power or the rhetorical excess of Carmichael and H. Rap Brown, although he agreed with both men that African Americans must take charge of their own destiny. Instead, Frye said he was for higher teacher pay, bus transportation for city school children, and improved schools. It was not the kind of stuff to grab newspaper headlines. He said he was old enough to understand the issues, and young enough to do something about them. The only item on his agenda that suggested a racial agenda was his support for greater minority representation in Greensboro's government. He favored a change in the city charter to provide for election of council members from districts, which would improve the chances for election of black candidates, rather than the current system of at-large representation.

Shirley Frye organized college students to work in her husband's successful campaign for the state legislature in 1968 (courtesy Frye family).

As Election Day approached, Frye and those responsible for preparing a recommended ticket that would be distributed at black precincts faced a decision. The Hawkins campaign had become more than political theater. The combination of a lively candidate willing to say what a lot of blacks, young and old, were thinking, and a growing awareness of the utility of political power gave blacks more reason than ever to go to the polls. There was no question that Dr. George Simkins, Jr., who was the leader of the NAACP, and A&T professor Ralph Wooden, the head of the citizens association, would endorse Hawkins. But what about the other races?

Georgia State Representative Julian Bond, the first black elected to the legislature in his state, campaigned with legislative candidate Henry Frye in 1968. Bond urged Frye to capitalize on his own historic victory by going on a national speaking tour (courtesy Frye family).

In 1966, Simkins and Wooden had circulated a ticket that had included Frye and four white candidates for the legislature. The endorsement had helped the whites do well in the black precincts, but there was no corresponding return for Frye in white precincts, where he ran seventh or eighth. Some of these same incumbents were running in 1968 and there was strong sentiment to continue to support white candidates who listened to the black community. Having one or two sympathetic white friends in office was better than one sure thing, it was argued. On the other hand, if the endorsement two years earlier had named only Frye, which would have limited the total votes going to white candidates, then North Carolina might already have a black legislator.

Single-shot voting, as this option was called, had helped put the first black man on the Greensboro City Council in 1951, but it had fallen into disfavor. Many blacks were concerned about alienating white politicians, whom they considered friendly to their interests. Even Hawkins had voiced objections to single-shot voting. "It hasn't gained us a thing," he told the *Charlotte*

Observer in 1967.[19] Hawkins had never run for office in an at-large election, and he was discounting a tactic that scared some white politicians to death. The 1965 General Assembly had outlawed single-shot voting in some counties in eastern North Carolina, where blacks made up half or more of the population. In 1968, east Greensboro's new newspaper, the *Carolina Peacemaker*, didn't advocate single-shot voting by name, but in his weekly column publisher John Marshall Kilimanjaro urged blacks to "VOTE RIGHT," as he put it, capitalizing these words for emphasis.[20]

The slate makers in east Greensboro decided to take no chances in the May primary. On the Friday night before the primary election, the ticket was prepared and printed on a mimeograph machine on donated paper. Only one candidate — Henry Frye — had the groups' endorsement in the legislative races. The tactic worked. While Frye's total vote in the four Greensboro precincts where blacks made up the majority was largely unchanged from the 1966 primary, he led his opponents by nearly ten to one. At Precinct 5, on the A&T campus, Frye received 538 votes and the other eleven candidates got a combined total of 329 votes, out of a potential 2,200 votes that Frye's voters could have given other candidates. In Precinct 6, it was Frye with 697 votes and all others, 381. In Precinct 7, the final vote was 755 to 413, and in Precinct 8, which voted at Gillespie Elementary School, Frye still won a majority despite a higher number of white voters registered there.

Frye did better in white precincts than he had in 1966, but he still ran seventh or eighth in most of the white areas. In only five did he place among the top six. It was the 2,500-vote advantage he gained from voters in the predominantly black precincts that allowed him to finish in third place with 12,412 votes, a gain of 20 percent over his vote total in 1966.

Hawkins didn't realize his dream as a deal maker. Out of 800,000 votes cast in the Democratic Party primary, he received only 130,000, well short of the number he had claimed would give him a seat at the table to bargain with the white candidates. While Hawkins had made history with his campaign, the turnout of African Americans was disappointing. Even in Greensboro, only about 40 percent of the eligible black voters in key precincts even bothered to vote.[21] And some stopped there. Frye's share of the eligible black vote was 35 percent. As it turned out, Scott didn't need Hawkins to claim the Democratic Party nomination. The Broughton camp determined they couldn't overcome the Scott lead and conceded the election, saving the state from a second primary.

Frye's victory was a high honor for the folks in the Mineral Springs community, where Frye's widowed mother lived. When the people there learned about the outcome of the election, they immediately sent an invitation to the youngster they had known as Hen'rell to be the guest speaker at Community Day less than ten days after the election.

No matter how excited the homefolks were, Frye didn't have a ticket to Raleigh. He still had to survive the fall general election and being one of six Democratic Party nominees was no guarantee of victory. Guilford County had become a swing county in the 1960 elections as voters pulled away from the Democrats and began electing Republicans. The GOP leaders were moderate, Eisenhower Republicans who believed that they could appeal to black voters. One of the county's leading Republicans was William Osteen, who had received an endorsement from Kenneth Lee in his first legislative race. More importantly, the fall ballot would include the name of Elreta Alexander, who was the GOP nominee for district court judge. It was possible that Frye could end up like the black minister in Winston-Salem who won the Democratic Party nomination in 1966, only to lose in the fall.

Democrats in North Carolina were facing a troubling political season. The national party convention in Chicago was a disaster. Hubert Humphrey had won the presidential nomination at the cost of a battle in the streets between the young, mostly white, followers of Eugene McCarthy and the Chicago police. President Lyndon Johnson's support of civil rights legislation had produced plenty of disaffected Democrats in the South, where George Wallace was a popular third-party candidate for the presidency. The GOP gubernatorial nominee, Congressman Jim Gardner of Rocky Mount, was boldly making a play for Wallace Democrats in eastern North Carolina, where a combination of support for Nixon and Wallace was gnawing away at the Democratic Party's traditional base of support.

Henry Frye had his own concerns. He was caught between his quiet, middle-of-the-road approach to issues and African Americans who believed he was a poor substitute for the provocative rhetoric of Reginald Hawkins. At the same time, he couldn't afford to alienate white voters, or position himself as just a "Negro" candidate who was running to make a statement. Frye believed there was a place for the Hawkins-style candidate in politics, but that didn't get people elected. "You have people who stir up things and others who come behind and try to transform things," Frye said later. "In other words, the people doing the stirring up are not the ones to get the job done."[22]

Dr. Alvin Blount had picked Frye as a potential leader not long after he became involved in Greensboro affairs. He was impressed with his thoughtful approach to questions, challenges, and issues facing blacks. "I don't think you want to call it radical, moderate, conservative. I think you want to say he wanted to know the truth about things and let's see if we can work this thing out so everybody benefits.

"Many times, I think people weren't satisfied with this. People who are dissatisfied are all or none. Some of us take the position that at least we want to examine it. I think that is one of the things that impressed me about Henry and I think that won almost 100 percent support. I could trust him. If he took a stand on something he wasn't one way today and another way tomorrow. He did not change his ideas to satisfy anyone. He wanted to satisfy himself that whatever he was going to do was right."[23]

Frye steered clear of Hawkins's challenge to the racial makeup of the state's delegation to the Democratic National Convention. Only 10 of the 130 delegates were blacks and they were not rabble-rousers. Hawkins said there should be at least thirty blacks to reflect the racial makeup of party registration. In protest, he led a walkout of the state convention, but many of the 150 or so who followed him out of the hall later returned to their seats. His challenge didn't succeed in Chicago. Two of the governor's twenty-eight at-large appointees were from Greensboro. One was Lewis Dowdy from A&T and the other was L. R. Russell, who was a long-time paid poll worker who turned out votes in the black community for white candidates. Russell was one of those that the Simkins crowd had been trying to put out of business on Election Day.[24]

If Frye was bland, he was not lifeless. In mid-summer, he criticized the state department of conservation and development for not including an African American in a group of eight young women who had been hired as official hostesses in the new welcome centers that opened in early August along interstates 85 and 95. As mild as this sounded in the wake of the Hawkins campaign, whites let him know they didn't appreciate his comments. The narrow line he was attempting to walk was frustrating. "If I can't criticize something like that," he told a reporter, "I don't care if I lose. I'm not running to raise issues, I am running to win. But not at any cost."[25]

For Frye, the fall campaign shaped up as a repeat of the primary. Once again, the election would not turn on issues, but on name recognition and hardball politics. A&T's Dowdy saw to it that Frye had a platform at the Fall Convocation on the A&T campus where Frye urged students to vote. In his own remarks, Dowdy sounded like an apologist for the Democratic Party. He said he was sorry that the street battles at the Chicago convention had gotten more attention than the new role that blacks were playing in national politics.[26] In mid–October Frye was at the University of North Carolina at Greensboro for a campus visit by the exciting young black legislator from Georgia named Julian Bond. Earlier in the day, Frye had introduced him to a study group at Guilford College. During some private time together, Bond urged Frye to put his law practice on hold and join him on the public speaking circuit. Bond said his booking agent could keep him busy. "I was interested at first," Frye recalled. "He was speaking all over the country at these colleges. I guess he made good money. You don't have to have but one speech, and fit it in locally. That sort of turned me off."[27]

On the evening before the Tuesday election on November 5, the slate makers released their ballot and it did more than name the preferred candidates. Simkins and Wooden used their sample ballot to publish grievances against local Democrats that, in part, explained the variety of the selections they made. As expected, Frye was the only candidate endorsed in the state house race. The groups also endorsed the Democratic candidates for president and governor and most of the state races, but the similarity with past elections ended there. The ticket endorsed Republicans running against incumbent U.S. Senator Sam Ervin, Jr., as well as the longest serving Democrat in Raleigh, Secretary of State Thad Eure. Other Republicans on the list included a candidate for the board of county commissioners; state senate candidate Calvin Coolidge Murrow, a High Point furniture dealer; and, as expected, judicial candidate Elreta Alexander. In the sessions leading up to the final meeting, Frye had questioned the decision to favor so many Republicans. He was told: "This is not a branch of the Democratic Party."

On election night, Henry and Shirley, and their two sons, Henry Jr. who was nine, and seven-year-old Harlan, were in the campaign office they had opened on East Market Street in a building that once had been a state-run liquor store. It was equipped with a few desks and some folding chairs, and was decorated with campaign posters. Shirley had organized a phone bank of housewives and they had fielded calls from volunteers from around the county, not just east Greensboro. Gathered around them there, instead of at the Democratic Party headquarters downtown, were friends, neighbors, and a collection of students from A&T, Bennett, and UNC–Greensboro. A sign, hand-lettered in red and illuminated with Christmas tree lights, read, "Headquarters of Henry Frye." Election returns arrived over the small portable television and a radio.

Frye's victory was evident fairly early. Richard Nixon easily carried Guilford County, but he had no coattails to speak of. Frye and most of the Democratic candidates ran well almost everywhere. The single-shot support in the black precincts provided an extra measure of comfort for Frye, but he would have won without it. A Republican, Howard Coble, led the state house race and was followed by the county's most popular Democratic incumbent, Charles Phillips. Frye placed third, 5,000 votes ahead of the candidate in seventh place. Ironically, that was Democrat McNeill Smith, a liberal Democrat who would have voted with Frye on issues important to African Americans. In an editorial published a week later, the *Greensboro Record* called Smith a casualty of the black ticket's devotion to Frye.[28] Simkins had sent his message. Murrow, the Republican furniture man from High Point, won one of the senate seats, thanks to black support.

Before the night was over, Frye learned he was not just one of the first black legislators in North Carolina since 1899, but he would be the *only* African American in the upcoming session of the General Assembly. The other black legislative candidate, William Crawford of Winston-Salem, had lost his second bid by six votes.

The Fryes in the early 1970s with sons Harlan (left) and Henry Jr. at the front of their home on Drexmore Avenue in Greensboro (courtesy Frye family).

The Associated Press report of Frye's victory appeared in newspapers across the state as well as in Chicago, New York, Atlanta, and Washington, D.C., sometimes accompanied by a wholesome family photo of Shirley, Henry, and the two boys bent over a sheet of election returns. Shirley described his reaction to the election as nonchalant, but the photograph that appeared in the Greensboro paper the day after the election was one of a kind. Never before had the calm, reserved Henry Frye displayed such a broad, open, toothsome smile. A dozen years earlier, he had been denied the right to vote. On November 5, he was given a chance to do something about the insult he had suffered in Ellerbe.

8

Representative Henry Frye

As Representative Henry Frye waited for adjournment of the opening ceremonies of the 1969 General Assembly, he looked across the airy expanse of the house chamber and his mind fixed on one thought — more African Americans need to be sitting at the other 119 desks. For the time being, black North Carolinians had one member of the General Assembly, the first in seventy years. And while Guilford County had elected him, Frye would find that voters in his home district would have to share his time with African Americans from across the state who also claimed him as their own.

The worn wooden desks used by the last African American legislators were still in place at the old house chamber in the State Capitol, a copper-domed limestone pile in the familiar neo-classical style that stood just a block away. It had been home to the General Assembly's biennial sessions until 1963 and the opening of the State Legislative Building, the only hall in the nation designed exclusively for state legislative business. Those nineteenth-century black legislators were Republicans, not Democrats like Frye, and they stood no chance against the Democratic Party's determination in 1899 to drive them from office and see that black voters were permanently sidelined in public life.

Frye mounted no triumphant return on opening day, January 15, 1969. Rather, he greeted his peers modestly, thankful for the warm welcome he had received. He offered gracious assurances that he would be working hard at learning the legislative process. "I was pretty careful about what I did and what I said," he later recalled. His entourage included Shirley, their two sons, Henry's mother Pearl, his sister Ola Stringer, and the Reverend Howard A. Chubbs, their minister at Providence Baptist. Frye wore a pinstriped business suit with a white shirt and a club tie with a subdued pattern. The thin line of a white handkerchief square accented the breast pocket of his jacket. The only hint of ostentation was the new Cadillac he had parked in one of the spaces reserved for legislators. A fellow church member, businessman John L. Vines, had insisted he use the car. "It wasn't, would you like to use it? It was, you are going to drive down there in style."[1]

African Americans in Greensboro were proud that they had made history on Election Day, and curiosity about North Carolina's first black legislator in the twentieth century remained high more than two months later. The state's daily newspapers published accounts of his oath taking before Associate Justice William Bobbitt, who swore in members en masse. Newspapers carried photographs of Frye, who managed a friendly smile for the camera. They reported he had co-signed his first bill, a popular measure calling for a statewide Youth Council. The fascination with Frye within the press would fade. Blacks, on the other hand, had found a champion, albeit a mild-mannered one, and Frye already had a list of speaking engagements before African Americans who wanted to meet this phenomenon. In a week or two, he even had an invitation to speak at Harvard University's Kennedy School of Government.

Much of official Raleigh, including the new governor, Robert W. Scott, opened doors for the Fryes. Scott put the couple on his inaugural committee, a high honor for a freshman legislator. "There was practically no work to do and they treated you like royalty," Henry said. They enjoyed special accommodations at the inaugural ball as well as reserved seating at the inauguration and, later, on the reviewing stand for the parade with the justices of the supreme court, the Council of State, Democratic Party bigwigs, and other notables. A State Highway Patrol captain was their escort and drove them wherever they wished to go.[2] Shirley soon got a welcome note from the governor's wife, and that was followed by an invitation to the two of them for luncheon at the Executive Mansion.

House Speaker Earl Vaughn, a convivial lawyer from Eden, a textile town north of Greensboro in Rockingham County, filled Frye's requests for committee assignments. Among others, Vaughn gave him a seat on prime committees that would write the state's budget, update the banking laws, and handle legislation on education and public welfare. As a lawyer, Frye was virtually guaranteed a spot on one of the two house judiciary committees, but Vaughn also included him among the veterans he appointed to the important rules committee, a pinch point that would control the flow of legislation in the hectic closing days of the session.

The 1969 class of the house of representatives included a future governor and lieutenant governor as well as two congressmen-to-be, four future house speakers and others who would hold statewide office in the decade ahead. Frye was one of forty-six lawyers, and seated around him were businessmen, preachers, teachers, accountants, insurance agents, oil dealers, farmers, a banker or two, a retired admiral, and an undertaker. The only female was Nancy Chase, a native of Fremont, Shirley Frye's hometown. She was beginning her fourth term. With regular sessions only once every two years, the legislature took pride in its "amateur" status. Legislative compensation of $15 a day ran out after 120 days, so members usually tried to wrap things up as soon as possible. The rate of pay hadn't changed in a hundred years, but there was some talk of an adjustment for members of the 1971 session.

Frye used his $20 daily expense stipend to cover part of the cost for a room at Raleigh's Statler-Hilton Hotel. The Hotel Sir Walter in downtown had long been the legislators' home-away-from-home and some of the old war horses still spent their evenings in the deep sofas and overstuffed chairs of the Sir Walter lobby, smoking cigars and talking politics. The place was showing its age, however, and younger members, like Frye, were going else-where. Some members rented apartments, while the Hilton was a popular alternative.

The high-rise hotel was west of downtown, near the N.C. State University campus and a short walk from the Velvet Cloak Inn, a classier, and newer, rendition of the Sir Walter. A major attraction at the "Cloak" was the trucking lobby's hospitality room where members could enjoy a generous nightly feed with free booze. The head of the state's Motor Carriers Association said he never talked politics with his guests, but in the weeks ahead he hoped legis-lators would grant permission to put twin-trailers on the road. Velvet Cloak guests were automatically members of a private club where an honest mixed drink could be poured from liquor stored in a locker. (Liquor-by-the-drink was illegal in North Carolina but it was available by the bottle if you brought your own.) The arrangements at the less-expensive Hilton suited Frye's budget and his modest social habits. The management also allowed him to leave a spare suit hanging in the closet if the hotel wasn't going to be full over the weekend.

A legislator's schedule was jammed from the outset. Work began on Monday with a session at 8 P.M., so Frye had at least one weekday to practice law, conduct business, and take care of things at home. He was usually running behind when he left Greensboro in his brown Rambler station wagon — the Cadillac was for one-time use only — for the ninety-minute drive to Raleigh. Rushing to finish business one Monday afternoon soon after the session began, he got stopped for speeding on Greensboro's East Lee Street. He paid the citation without protest, although legislators enjoyed some immunity when traveling to and from their duties. Tuesdays, Wednesdays, and Thurs-days were filled with committee meetings and, of course, the daily session that began at noon and ran for an hour or two. Frye often didn't leave the legislative building until well after dark. On Friday morning, the house con-vened at ten in the morning and was usually done with business by noon, and Frye headed back to Greensboro. That left him Friday afternoons and Saturdays for legal work. Sundays now weren't entirely off limits for work because of the press of affairs.

Pauline Irving kept Frye's professional life organized. She was a secretary in the city school system when Frye hired her in the fall of 1966 to manage the cubbyhole of an office he rented on Dudley Street near the A&T campus. She had become an accomplished and indispensable assistant who kept him on top of his caseload of estates, wills, real estate closings, and other civil matters. When he got back to his law office on Friday, she was waiting with documents that needed a signature, phone numbers of clients who required his attention, and other business that could not wait. He couldn't have managed without her.

The firm was now Frye and Johnson. Frye had known Walter T. Johnson, Jr., since he was a teenager in his Sunday school class. Johnson had finished A&T in 1961 and was sitting on the stage at graduation when UNC President William Friday encouraged him to become one of the first black law students at Duke University. Johnson and Frye began talking about building a law firm while Johnson completed his military service as a lawyer in the air force. They started working together in the spring of 1968 with the two of them wrestling for space in the Dudley Street office. One of Johnson's first assignments was to help get his partner elected. By the time the legislature opened, they were talking about moving their offices to a building on Elm Street. Urban redevelopment had eliminated the thriving center of black commerce on Market Street, but that wasn't their only reason for seeking a downtown address. They wanted something other than a second-floor walkup. They eventually hired an architect to overhaul rooms on the eighth floor of the Southeastern Building, borrowing the money they needed to create a style comparable to what clients found at the nearby offices of white firms.[3]

For all the camaraderie of opening day, when it was over Henry Frye was still the only African American in the State Legislative Building who wasn't preparing meals in the members' cafeteria, cleaning the floors, or keeping the building's polished brass to a high shine. There were plenty of people in Raleigh who weren't pleased at the social changes forecast by his election. He didn't hear the comment of Chief Justice R. Hunt Parker who was seated three rows in front of Henry and Shirley on the parade stand at the inauguration. As a national guard unit from Halifax County passed by, Parker leaned over to Lieutenant Governor H. Patrick Taylor, Jr., whom he had just sworn in, and said, "Here are some real men. Their grandfathers fought at Appomattox and Gettysburg. Not a nigger in the crowd."[4] Frye would encounter vestiges of the state's racist and segregationist past during the coming years, with discrimination appearing in both bold and curious ways.

The seating in the house chambers was assigned by Secretary of State Thad Eure, who signed his official documents in green ink and called himself "the oldest rat in the Democratic barn." He had been in office since 1936 but he didn't punish Frye, despite the slight he had received at the hands of the Greensboro blacks, who had endorsed his Republican opponent in 1968. He gave Frye seat number 73. It was a convenient spot on the outside aisle just a few steps from the heavy wooden doors along the side of the house chamber. He sat immediately behind the chairman of the Guilford delegation, Representative Charles W. Phillips, a Democrat, whom all called "Mr. Charlie." Frye's seatmate was John Ridenour, a low-key lawyer and a Democrat who won election by a margin of thirty-three votes. In the rows to their rear were the two dozen or so Republican members, including the state party chairman (and future governor), James E. Holshouser, Jr., of Boone.

Legislators' offices lined the outside walls of the building's first and second floors. Those on the first floor opened onto one of four landscaped "garden courts," three of which had shallow pools, large stone planters, and bench seating for visitors. A handful of lobbyists, those who showed up daily, usually staked out the back left court where the chairs and tables served as overflow seating from the cafeteria open to members, their guests, and staff. Frye was in Room 1308, on the first floor in the front left quadrant. Since legislative service was considered part-time work, the architects had been told to stint on space. Committee chairmen were rewarded with a suite, in the building's interior, but the standard issue office was an eight-by-twelve-foot room with barely enough space for a desk, a high-backed office chair, seating for two visitors, and a wastebasket. Stained wood shelving hung on the walls. From his office window, Frye could look out onto the broad front plaza that featured a 28-foot terrazzo replica of the state seal embedded in front of the main entrance. On one side of him was Representative Gus Speros, a rollicking Greek who was a building contractor from Maxton, and on the other was Representative Joe Raynor of Fayetteville. His company supplied paint to auto repair shops in the southeastern part of the state. Both of them were Democrats, of course.

Frye found a few members from around the state that he had known before. Representative David Reid from Greenville was a law school classmate. Holshouser and Representative R. C. Soles also had been in the law school during his time there. For the most part, he was starting from scratch, and he didn't go far without his copy of a pocket-sized legislative directory published by Southern Bell Telephone Company. It included a photo of each member, his party affiliation, and contact information. Newcomers and visitors were lost without it. He also kept a copy of the house rulebook close at hand.

Throughout his life, Frye had worked hard to be prepared, and to consider all available information, before he made a decision. It was a character trait that some confused for excess caution. He planned to do his homework in Raleigh so he set out to read every bill that was introduced. (A modern record of 2,347 of them in 1969.) The piles of paper produced by the legislative process soon overwhelmed him and he fell back on the *Daily Bulletin* published by the Institute of Government. It carried a synopsis of each bill and with it he could separate the legislative wheat and chaff. If he found a bill that needed further attention, he pulled a complete copy and read it word for word. Some of the bills were innocuous enough — inviting the governor to speak, honoring a high school band, and the like — but there were others with simple titles that disguised legislation with more serious intent. One such bill created a school district in the town of Scotland Neck, deep in northeastern North Carolina. It was sent forward with little notice amid the backslapping and smiles that followed Governor Scott's evening address to the General Assembly a week into the session.

After fifteen years, whites in North Carolina were just coming to grips with the full impact of the *Brown v. Board* decision. School integration had been delayed by the adoption of "freedom-of-choice" plans that allowed school boards to continue to operate what amounted to dual systems. In the years since *Brown*, few, if any, whites asked to be enrolled in former black schools and few blacks — the Fryes were the exception — had asked to have their children assigned to white schools. As a result, 80 percent of the black students in the state still attended schools with their own race. Six months earlier, the respected head of the state's Good Neighbor Council told a group of teachers meeting in Raleigh that the time since *Brown* had been "a period of gradualism, circumvention and tokenism." David S. Coltrane's remarks came on the heels of the U.S. Supreme Court ruling in *Green v. County School Board of New Kent County* that freedom of choice was no longer acceptable as a plan for desegregation.[5] *New Kent County* would have dramatic consequences all across the South, but especially in Black Belt counties like Halifax, where the town of Scotland Neck was located. Blacks made up a majority of the county's population, and the decision meant the end to the all-white, or white-majority, schools. The Halifax County school board had already been informed by the U.S. Justice Department that freedom-of-choice would have to go.

The Scotland Neck bill, as it came to be called, was simple enough, as explained by its sponsor, Representative Thorne Gregory, one of Frye's fellow Democrats. The good folks of Scotland Neck, a community of fewer than three thousand residents, wanted to have their own school system, rather than be a part of the county school system. (There already were separate systems in Roanoke Rapids and Weldon, two larger municipalities in the county.) They were willing to tax themselves to support a school district that would serve all students who lived within the boundaries of the new district. The few blacks attending the Scotland Neck union school, with grades one through twelve, would continue as before, as long as students lived in the new district. Left unsaid were two salient facts. The county school system, of which Scotland Neck was a part, had a three-to-one majority of black students. In the new district, which roughly corresponded to the town limits of Scotland Neck, whites would outnumber blacks by four to one.

The legislative session had yet to settle into its regular rhythm when Gregory's bill came before the house education committee, where Frye was a member. On most measures that were filed as local bills, as this one was, members deferred to the sponsor and didn't meddle. That tradition should hold here, Gregory argued. This was a local affair and did not impact the lives of citizens elsewhere in the state. According to the terms outlined in the bill, the new Scotland Neck district would take over the existing county school building located in town and operate an independent system of less than a thousand students.

When Frye took his seat at the table in the committee room, he was still learning to navigate around the legislative building where the uniform appearance of interior hallways easily disoriented newcomers. The room was crowded, with eager visitors filling the chairs that lined the walls. All but one of those from Scotland Neck was white. Clearly, Frye could not support the bill, but before he said a word, he found others shared his misgivings, despite Gregory's saccharin assurances. The committee chair, Graham Tart, a former schoolteacher from Clinton, deep in eastern North Carolina, maintained neutrality, but he put the members on notice that Gregory's bill was more than a mere "local" measure. He called on the state superintendent of public instruction, A. Craig Phillips, who reminded the members that only two months earlier a governor's study of public schools had argued for consolidation of school districts rather than encourage the creation of more. It was a policy that Governor Scott had endorsed in the address he delivered the night the bill was introduced.

Eventually, Frye got his chance to question the printed premise of the bill — to increase financial support for a school in Scotland Neck — but he didn't confront the measure directly and challenge its racial implications, as some expected. Rather, he asked if town leaders had considered merging the county's existing three districts into one, so that the combined tax base could produce a stronger and better-funded school system for the entire county. Indeed, Halifax County was a poor area where financial support of education was half that of the state average. Moreover, the support of whites was dwindling as parents who could afford the cost were sending their children to newly created all-white private schools that some called "rebel-yell academies." "It's been considered for years," a former county school board member told the committee in response to Frye's question, "and nothing ever came of it."

Doubt over the legitimacy of the measure lingered with the committee vote. On a voice vote, the committee sent it to the house floor "without prejudice," one notch down from a "favorable report." Voting with Frye for an "unfavorable report" was a Republican, Representative James C. Johnson, Jr., a trial lawyer from Concord, a textile town near Charlotte. His determined questioning of Gregory and the Scotland Neck visitors rose to the level of a cross-examination. He didn't impugn anyone's motives, but the point of his interrogation was clear. Whites were using the state to establish a majority-white school and, if Scotland Neck could do that, other communities facing the same changes would follow. After the meeting, Johnson was quoted as saying what others believed was clearly the case. "The race issue is involved here."

The committee's neutral report did nothing to impede the bill. It easily passed the house by a vote of 82–27. Representative Perry Martin from neighboring Northampton County called any opposition an "affront" to Gregory. Half of the Republicans voted against the bill, as did committee chairman Tart, who had been a member of the study commission favoring consolidation of districts.[6] There were other "no" votes cast by members from Charlotte, Raleigh and Greensboro. Voting with Frye in the negative were Guilford legislators Charles W. Phillips, a retired school man; Republican Howard Coble; and Frye's seatmate, John Ridenour.

By the time Gregory's bill got to the senate, it was much more than another local bill. About two hundred people filled the auditorium in the legislative building one afternoon after Senator Martha Evans of Charlotte, the chair of the senate education committee, called for a public hearing, an extraordinary measure for local legislation. By now, blacks in Scotland Neck had found their voice and they showed up in strength. Some said they had not spoken out earlier on the advice of the principal of the all-black county school that stood just outside the town limits, whose principal owed his appointment as a trustee at nearby all-black Elizabeth City State Teacher's College to Gregory and who considered his silence a favor to his benefactor. The group's leading spokesman was a black physician from Weldon, Dr. Salter J. Cochran, who described the bill for what it was, "just another form ... to avoid school desegregation required by federal authorities."[7]

That may have been the case, but federal law was up against something stronger in the General Assembly. There it met Senator Julian Allsbrook, a Roanoke Rapids lawyer who easily filled the role of the defiant southern white segregationist. A legislator who had served intermittently since 1935, Allsbrook was a proud scholar of North Carolina history. He wrapped his arguments for the ambitions of tiny Scotland Neck in not one flag but two. His half-hour defense of local self-determination was founded on the virtues of freedom and liberty written two hundred years earlier when colonists from the plantations and farms of northeastern North Carolina had drafted the Halifax Resolves in 1776. Their call for independence from the king was of such moment in state history that the very date was inscribed on the state flag. He asked that the legislature do for Scotland Neck what it had done over the years for other communities that wanted to improve education. He held the podium for nearly half an hour.

The hearing provided a time and place for venting of feelings, but nothing more. The bill passed the senate by a vote of 30 to 14 with Guilford's legislators divided. Coolidge Murrow, the Republican endorsed by the black political committee, voted no. Hargrove Bowles, Jr., a Democrat who didn't get the committee's endorsement, voted for it. Six weeks later, the legislature approved an identical measure for the communities of Warrenton and Littleton–Lake Gaston in counties just north of Raleigh. Frye was more vocal this time, and he labeled the Warrenton bill for what it was. "You say the people want this bill," Frye said on the floor, directing his attention to one of the bill's sponsors. "Who are the people? Certainly the Negroes don't want the bill. And Negroes make up most of the county's population."[8]

The Scotland Neck bill helped define the role that Henry Frye intended to play in the legislature. He would make his positions clear, but he would pick his battles carefully, and his measured response on the school bills showed he wasn't one for grandstanding. He would use his vote and his voice to do what he believed he could do best: poke and prod the soft underbelly of state government that, at best, was indifferent to African Americans if not outright discriminatory. He believed he could accomplish more by questioning a state bureaucrat about the absence of blacks in his department than haranguing a bill that he was powerless to stop. He certainly wasn't keen on bootless challenges where he was defeated before he ever uttered a word. Neither was he going to fill out a stereotype. "I was interested in some things that were not just purely black or white." Of course, he voted against the Scotland Neck bill, and the one for Warrenton when it came to the floor. In reality, that was all a freshman legislator could do.

Frye had not been in Raleigh long before he discovered just how far his reputation had spread among African Americans in North Carolina. Many saw him as their representative, regardless of where they lived. Blacks telephoned his office, rather than that of their own legislator, to ask for help on local matters, and virtually every African American who entered the legislative building stopped first at Room 1308, which was only a few steps from the elevator that carried visitors to the third floor gallery. Frye was flattered by the attention, but he also was burdened with the lack of political sophistication that brought so many to his door. "They didn't know the name of their legislator," he said. "They had never had any real contact with him. Some would say, there isn't any use in me going down there and talking to him. I would say, 'How do you know? Isn't he up for re-election? Are you registered to vote?' I said, 'I can't work the whole state of North Carolina. I have to work for the people of Guilford County. I am going to take you to your legislator and you talk to him.' If I had a real legacy in my first years of the legislature, I think that may have been the most valuable one. I was introducing people to the system, and how it works, and giving them a little encouragement."[9]

The referrals served a dual purpose. His efforts to introduce citizens to their elected representatives helped Frye open conversations with colleagues on a level that was apart from the daily routine of lawmaking. White legislators were still trying to figure out who Henry Frye was. Most of them — and that meant the overwhelming majority who lived in small towns and rural communities— had never met an educated, thoughtful black man who wanted to talk about something besides racial injustice. By and large, the only black men and women that legislators knew were the hired help in their homes or on their farms, or unlettered preachers and undertakers, some of whom took their money every two years to haul voters to the polls on Election Day. Few, if any, had ever had any direct contact with a contentious, politically aware black man like Reginald Hawkins, but they had read enough about Hawkins to know that Frye was different. He was smart, confident, and articulate. He was "country regal," as his friend Howard Chubbs put it. "He creates a confidence in people that he is going to do what is right and you can count on him."[10]

In time, Frye discovered, members began paying attention to him when he rose from his desk to speak during a floor debate or when he posed a question in a committee room. In his thorough reading of bills he often discovered missing words or incorrect punctuation, or he flagged awkward phrasing that could later prove troublesome if the bill became law and was challenged in court. The amendments he sent forward to correct these oversights or the negligence of bill writers drew respect from those who might not otherwise have recognized his talent. Clearly, he was someone who took his responsibilities very, very seriously. These impressions later grew to deeper appreciation of Frye's ability and his value as an ally in later elections. "Sometimes, legislators would call me if they were running for reelection and ask me if I would do something on their behalf, say a word. Things like that. I would ask them, 'Who are the blacks who are supporting you?' I think that is one of the most helpful things I did. And I feel good about it."[11]

Frye had an agenda for his first term in the General Assembly and the hubbub over Scotland Neck was history when he rose on March 12 and sent forward a bill that he had been considering since long before he won election. It was an amendment to the state constitution that would remove the literacy requirements for voter registration, a provision that voters had approved in 1900 to limit black political participation. He had not made an issue of the literacy requirement during the campaign, although it figured in some of his speeches to black audiences who understood the hurt left by the insult he had endured a dozen years earlier. When the session began, Frye put in his request

for a bill from the attorney general's office, which provided bill-drafting services to members, and he waited for it to arrive. He sent the bill forward the
same day that the Reverend Chubbs delivered the invocation as the house
convened for business.

Frye was gaining his footing by the time he introduced his literacy bill.
The legislature had been in session for nearly two months and he was building
some relationships with legislators who asked for his support. He co-signed
a bill to lower the voting age to eighteen and another to provide free fishing
licenses for people over sixty-five. The Guilford County delegation met weekly
but was fumbling its biggest assignment, changes to the Greensboro city charter to provide for district election of council members. It was election season
back home and no one wanted to drop this bomb in the middle of campaigning. In early May, Jimmie Barber overcame east Greensboro's ability to defeat
itself. He was a lively part-time preacher and full-time director of student
housing at A&T, and called himself "Bowtie Barber," because of his choice
in neckwear. Barber survived a field of seven black candidates and was elected
to the council. It didn't right the situation for activists like Simkins, but it
was satisfying to finally have an African American in office after six years on
the outside. Frye kept the issue alive, and in early June the delegation's bill
passed. It allowed for a local initiative from citizens or the council to set an
election for changes to the charter.

In addition to growing confidence, Frye also had the assistance of a legislative aide, something quite rare in those days. She was Patricia Walters, a
senior pursuing a degree in sociology at Shaw University. One or two other
members drew on outside help and paid their wages from their own pockets.
Unless a legislator chaired a major committee and was assigned a full-time
clerk, all the rest relied on a secretarial pool of women who were outnumbered
five to one by the legislators they were expected to serve. Walters was paid by
the Voter Education Project in Durham that began working to enroll as many
black voters as possible after the passage of the 1965 Voting Rights Act.

The daily session was about to begin on April 4 and Frye was on the way
out of his office, headed for the house floor, when Walters stopped him and
asked what he planned to do to remember Dr. Martin Luther King, Jr., who
had been killed one year earlier. Despite his admiration of King, Frye needed
constant reminders like this; such details did not come naturally to him. He
stopped and asked for her suggestions. By the time he got to the house chamber he knew what he wanted to do. As the session wore on Frye left his seat
and quietly got the attention of Speaker Vaughn. He wanted the house to
adjourn in King's memory, Frye told Vaughn. The speaker agreed, but on one
condition; he didn't want Frye making a long speech. Frye agreed and Vaughn
told him to be ready at the proper time. The day's business was at the end
when Vaughn recognized Frye, who rose and in thirty words or less made his

motion as members gathered their papers to leave for the day. When Frye finished, Vaughn quickly called the question, asked for a voice vote, and the gavel was on its way down by the time members had time to consider what they had just done.

It was a small victory, but worth it, Frye thought, even though his colleagues were probably caught off guard by the speaker's speedy handling of the matter. Aside from the residual glow of inner satisfaction, he had all but dismissed the episode from his mind until he was on his way back to Greensboro later in the day. The radio in his Rambler was tuned to an AM station that broadcast reports on the day's legislative action when Frye heard his name, King's name, and adjournment all used in the same sentence. Throughout the weekend, his friends and neighbors stopped to tell him what a great job he was doing in Raleigh. Years later, he laughed and said, "And I bet a lot of them, before that, didn't even know the General Assembly was in session."

The only public response to Frye's proposed constitutional amendment

Governor Robert W. Scott put newly elected Representative Henry Frye on his inaugural committee photographed here on the stairway in the State Legislative Building. It was a rare honor for a freshman legislator (courtesy Adjutant General's Department, Public Affairs Section; photograph by SMJ J.L. McGee).

The first bill Frye wrote and introduced in the 1969 General Assembly called for an amendment to the state constitution to remove the literacy requirement for voting. It passed both houses but was not approved by the voters when put on the ballot in 1970 (courtesy Frye family).

came from Alex Brock, the director of the N.C. State Board of Elections. Brock was a holdover from the previous administration and a member of the conservative wing of the Democratic Party. He ran a clean shop and had a reputation for fairness, but he didn't take much to change. He all but called Frye's bill frivolous, telling a reporter the constitutional requirement that a voter be able to read and write any section of it in the English language was "simple and minimal," especially since the state spent 65 percent of its budget on education.[12] The literacy test wasn't used to discriminate against blacks, Brock said. A few days later, Frye challenged Brock's comments, saying, "If he would talk with some of the persons who have participated in registration drives, he would probably find it is a deterrent."[13]

The news cycle moved on, and Frye was perhaps the only legislator thinking about the bill that had been shipped off to the constitutional amendment committee chaired by Representative Ike Andrews. He was a likeable lawyer from the small Piedmont town of Siler City with political ambitions that would end with election to Congress. Frye believed Andrews was in his corner, but the chairman would still require cultivation. The eighteen other committee members were an odd lot of easterners, Republicans, and a liberal or two. The friendliest face was that of Wade Penny, a liberal Democrat from Durham, who had joined Frye in his opposition to the Scotland Neck bill. Frye hunted down each member of the committee to take his pulse on the bill and afterward put a plus or a minus beside his name in his Southern Bell directory.

The exercise was an education in the whims and follies of the legislative process. Frye discovered that the merits of a bill weren't always paramount and that not all business was conducted amid the stately grandeur of the house chamber with its deep red carpet, rich tapestries depicting the coats of arms of colonial lords, and soaring coffered ceiling tinged in gold. Instead, he learned, the fate of bills was often decided in various social venues that Frye largely ignored. He seldom attended the evening receptions hosted by a range of special interest groups, from the cosmetologists to the bankers' association. He was usually too busy trying to survive the daily flood of business to venture out for evening social events. Then again, he didn't appreciate the need to schmooze his colleagues any more than he had the elites on Benbow Road.

His naiveté eventually caught up with him. He was comparing notes with a colleague one day when he was told a commitment he had gotten probably wouldn't hold. "I said, 'What do you mean?' He said, 'Do you know who his roommate is?'" Frye confessed his ignorance that the man shared an apartment with one of the known opponents of the bill. "I didn't know who was rooming with who." Shirley would have catalogued that kind of detail and Henry discovered just how handicapped he was without her social antennae.

With two sons under ten, Shirley spent most of the session in Greensboro where she was winding down her teaching job at Bennett College. "I told people somebody had to take care of Henry's children," she said some years later. She put her plans for a doctorate on hold and became a den mother instead. The family crammed in as much time together over the weekends and always had Sunday dinner together, usually at the International House of Pancakes. During the meal, each boy was asked to speak his mind on whatever was bothering him. Henry compensated for his absence during the week with a Wednesday evening phone call when he talked only to Henry Jr. and Harlan. From time to time, when a babysitter was available and her schedule permitted, Shirley joined her husband in Raleigh.

By virtue of Henry's election, Shirley was invited into the Sir Walter Cabinet. It was a white-gloves-and-hat kind of group whose members included the wives of legislators and the wives and widows of top-level state officials. She was the first black member. Like their spouses, the ladies of the Sir Walter Cabinet had had little contact with African Americans and they weren't sure how to bring Shirley into the fold. A few singled her out for special attention to see that her introduction was as graceful as possible. She noticed early on that when she arrived for a meeting, usually a luncheon at the Sir Walter Hotel, someone always was on hand to greet her and shepherd her about the room. After this occurred a few times, Shirley responded. She thanked her escort and told her in her sweet but firm voice, "'I don't need a sponsor.' They were as happy as I was. It didn't happen again."[14]

It wasn't easy for the Fryes to move around Raleigh in 1969 without bumping into a way of life in Raleigh society that remained founded in the Old South, despite new federal laws, different voting habits, or the occasional intrusion of outsiders. That didn't bother Shirley, who had been managing racially mixed situations since she was a girl on the farm. She was bold enough and confident enough to make her own way, and she wasn't above setting things straight when she found that social graces and gentility disguised deeper feelings. She arrived at a program in the State Legislative Building one afternoon and was invited to sit with May Gordon Kellenberger of Greensboro, a woman who was a grand dame in the socially rich circles that supported the arts and historic preservation. When one of Mrs. Kellenberger's white friends approached to join her, she took notice of Shirley and then moved to another chair a distance away. Later, after the program had concluded, Shirley introduced herself to the woman, telling her that her father had been a sharecropper near the woman's hometown. "She said she was glad I came to speak to her because she had never met a black person on her level," Shirley recalled. "I told her that I was pleased to meet her and at some point I would like for her to meet my black friends who were above her level. I couldn't resist."

While his literacy bill rested in the pocket of the committee chairman, Henry was busy with other matters. He found himself in a tangle of competing interests in the banks and banking committee, which was working through a long-overdue revision of interest rates on home mortgages and business loans. The bankers said they couldn't live with the state-imposed 6 percent ceiling on home loans and needed higher rates if they were to make money available to growing families and businesses. The governor set off a fierce lobbying effort after his call for the state's first-ever tax on tobacco, a move that was considered heresy in some circles. Shirley's father was confident his son-in-law wouldn't ever approve of such a crazy thing. Frye's temper almost got the best of him when tobacco workers from Greensboro's Lorillard plant stood in his office and demanded an answer on how he was going to vote. Legislators also were angry about student protests that had disrupted the peace on college campuses and punitive measures popped up like daffodils in spring.

A crisis arose in Chapel Hill in late January after members of the Black Student Movement turned their discontent over the administration's response to its demands for greater recognition on campus into support for striking food-service workers who were demanding better pay and working conditions. Governor Scott sent highway patrol troopers to the campus and put a National Guard unit in Durham on alert. The protests at UNC carried over to the campuses in Greensboro, where students at A&T and the University of North Carolina at Greensboro gathered en masse to challenge the administration and lend aid to their own underpaid food workers. UNCG students appealed to Frye for help.

It was late March and the tempo of the General Assembly was increasing when a contingent from UNCG showed up at Frye's law office and asked him to negotiate a settlement for the workers. He had more than enough to do, but he succumbed to their pleas when they told him no one else would take their case. It was small wonder that they had trouble finding a lawyer. Neither the students nor the workers had any money, and the bargaining sessions involving the administration and the private catering firm that employed the striking workers could easily burn up hours of valuable time. "They told me that if I didn't do it, then folks weren't going to get their grievances resolved," Frye said. "They played to my ego; I took it on." He found himself in lengthy meetings that began over a weekend and dragged on long enough to prevent Frye from attending the legislative sessions until late Tuesday. Finally, the parties reached a settlement and the crisis passed. "I wish I hadn't gotten into that one," Frye said years later.[15]

The richest legislative vein for Frye to mine, if his service as an African American legislator was to mean anything, was found in the quiet, dull tedium of afternoon meetings of the appropriations subcommittee on health, welfare and institutional care. The group's task was to meet with directors of state agencies who arrived with stacks of documents to justify their budget requests and account for the money they had spent during the previous two years. Their departments ran the mental institutions, the state schools for the deaf and blind, and even a home for the widows and daughters of soldiers of the Confederacy. The agencies administered miserly welfare payments and the preventative health care available through county health departments. In many cases, the people these agencies served were poor and in need, and that included proportionately more African Americans than whites.

Frye studied the numbers in the three-inch-thick budget books that crowded each legislator's desk, but he wanted to know more about the operations of these departments that touched directly upon the lives of ordinary citizens. "I would ask what I thought was a simple question and I was surprised at the backing away from my question, just not answering my question. I would ask 'Where are you going?' and they would answer, 'Where are you coming from?' I didn't quit. I would just keep asking until I got the answer. That happened on several occasions. Some times I realized why: There were things they did not want to answer before the committee. I found out more stuff by asking questions than I could have done by researching myself if I had three or four researchers."[16]

Those who stood the examination of the committee heard from Frye on one subject for which they had never had to account for, in public, at least. As each agency passed through for review, Frye wanted to know how many African Americans were working in their departments. "They would talk and talk and finally, I would say how many in your leadership group are black. That would lead to a long discussion of why they didn't have any blacks." Indeed, there were few blacks working in state government, despite an effort more than five years earlier by Governor Terry Sanford to increase their numbers. In 1969, the ranking black official in state government was John R. Larkins, a sociologist, who had been a token representative in administrations for nearly twenty years. Among some blacks he was known as the "deputy for the colored." Larkins spent many of his years at a post in the welfare department. He was just before being reassigned by the governor to become an associate director of the probation commission. His desk was in a hallway, but that was an improvement from four years earlier, when he was segregated from his white colleagues. Larkins was a survivor who did not make waves.[17]

Frye was pushing into areas that whites would have preferred remained closed to examination. "In some very few cases, I would get a straight answer when I asked the question," Frye said. "We have no African Americans or Negroes. [Usually], it was always excuses and on and on. Some of them tried to defend themselves. Others would say we are looking at that and say we will make some changes down the road." If he had the opportunity, Frye wanted to make that sooner rather than later.[18]

He threatened to make an issue of state support for the Confederate Women's Home in Fayetteville, but decided to give it a pass. There were only a handful of residents, all ninety years old or older, and the numbers were small and dwindling. Some of his allies on the committee, members he respected, pulled him aside and asked him to drop his objections. "I said, well, OK. Let it go," Frye recalled. "I have got a lot of other things to work on. Why make a great big issue about something like that. Now if it had been getting ready to start, that would have been different."[19] (The home remained in service until 1981.)

Frye paid special attention to the two agencies supported by the state that operated well outside of any special attention by the General Assembly. Central Orphanage at Oxford, until a name change in 1965, was known as the Colored Orphanage of North Carolina. It was a companion institution to the Oxford Orphanage, which served white children. Both had been created in the nineteenth century as quasi-public agencies that received state funds but also drew support from racially separate Masonic orders. The Grand Lodge of North Carolina, A.F & A. M.—the white masons—established and owned the Oxford Orphanage, while the Prince Hall masons, whose members were African Americans, supported the Central Orphanage. Both institutions had received state money for more than a century, and over the years had shared in donations from various members of the Duke family in Durham. Looking closer at their finances of the two, however, Frye found that state aid to the Oxford Orphanage outstripped that for Central.

Frye didn't approach his examination of these institutions completely empty handed. The father of his law partner, Walter T. Johnson, was a trustee at Central Orphanage. He was a politically savvy leader, with broad contacts around the state that he had developed during his years with the New Farmers of America, and he had been instrumental in the merger during the mid–1960s of the New Farmers with the all-white Future Farmers of America. Johnson prepped Frye, who often knew the answers before he started asking questions. "I kept asking, how do you determine how much each one gets," Frye recalled. "It boiled down to we had no system or formula. It depended on whichever legislator was interested in it, or the people who came to present. I kept asking so many questions about it that the chairman said I am going to appoint a subcommittee to look into this and he appointed me chairman. We visited the orphanages to find out various things. Most of them were segregated. Some were very clear about it, while others said we have had no Negroes to apply." Before the end of the session, Frye's subcommittee developed a funding formula based on need, which boosted the annual subsidy to Central. It wasn't long before Central's director was spreading the word about that black legislator from Greensboro. "He said, 'That Frye boy over there, he came up here and the next year we got all kinds of money.'"

The session was nearing the end when Frye's bill to change the constitution eked its way out of the house committee, where it received the same weak endorsement as the Scotland Neck bill. It was reported "without prejudice." An unfavorable report would have been fatal. All the while that Frye was tending to his own bill he was involved in daily sessions with the banking committee, where he had become a swing vote between the high- and low-interest partisans. With the committee split almost evenly, Frye learned that a member dare not depart for a minute or two, even for a trip to the men's room, for fear the balance would swing the other way and a crucial vote be reversed. For the most part, Frye voted with the low-interest crowd, but in the end he helped shape a compromise on lending rates and other lending regulations. He didn't run into the same kind of shenanigans with the constitutional amendments committee, but it still required close attention.

He was learning politics in the raw. Nothing had prepared him for the hard-nosed bargaining that preceded the settlement of the tax issues. The governor had asked for a tax on cigarettes. A counter proposal was for a tax on soft drinks. The issue was joined and the legislature appeared deadlocked. Democrats locked themselves into a committee room, kicked out the reporters, and went at it among themselves. "That is where we settled it, in that caucus," Frye recalled. "I remember somebody from Wilmington who was close to the bottling industry. You would have thought he was going to have a heart attack to have a tax on soft drinks. That is where I saw politics work."[20]

Nothing that had gone before, or would follow in the 1969 General Assembly, was as important to Frye as the moment that the house clerk called his literacy bill for floor debate. He had prepared as carefully as he had for anything in his life. The lack of an affirmative endorsement from the committee was disappointing, but the opposition he faced in the committee was a valuable prelude to what to expect on the floor. One ready opponent was Representative Perry Martin, the Democrat with whom he had tangled on the Scotland Neck bill. Martin was a feisty bantam of a lawyer — he had won oratorical honors as an undergraduate at Wake Forest — and just a couple of years Frye's senior. He had been first elected to the state senate when he was twenty-four, and had returned for a couple of sessions. This was his first term in the house. Martin had challenged the bill in committee where he was a vice chairman and he came after the bill with full confidence that he could keep Frye from getting the three-fifths majority — or 72 votes — that was required for approval of a constitutional amendment. Allied with him in opposition was a Republican from Winston-Salem, Hamilton C. Horton, Jr., who spoke with precise diction and wore three-piece suits and a bowler. One reporter described him as looking like he was on an exchange program from the British Parliament.

Frye opened the debate with an argument in behalf of the broad constitutional principles involved with such a bill. His approach was dry, even clinical. He could as easily have been describing a client's obligations in a mortgage. The issue was clear for Frye: the literacy test created an inequity in law and was the product of a repressive era. Article VI, Section 4 of the constitution, required literacy of all voters but it was freighted with an extended exclusion of the requirement for turn-of-the-century whites who were given eight years to learn to read and write or it would apply to them as well. In the meantime, it guaranteed that African Americans would be tested immediately if they attempted to register. At the time of its approval by voters in 1900, more than 40 percent of all African Americans were illiterate.[21]

Frye argued that "there is no question that the purpose of it at the time was keeping the so-called illiterate Negro from registering to vote."[22] If he had needed further evidence, he could have quoted from a campaign speech by Governor Charles B. Aycock in 1900 as he championed this and other amendments to stifle black political participation. "Life and property and liberty from the mountains to the sea shall rest secure in the guardianship of the law," Aycock declared. "But to do this, we must disenfranchise the negro."[23]

Frye didn't bring Aycock into the fight but he did argue that the test presently was being administered unevenly across the state, with some voter registrars using it, while others did not. Meanwhile, in those locales where it was administered, illiterate whites and blacks were being disqualified from voting at the same time they were being required to pay taxes, were eligible to sign contracts they didn't understand, or obtain a driver's license. As he did when he appeared before the committee, Frye stuck to the broader application, and he waited for the rebuttal that was sure to come from Martin.

Martin was good on his feet. He relied on his experience as a legislator and as a district prosecutor. The bill was unnecessary, he said, and the provision was a simple and minimum requirement needed to safeguard the integrity of elections. Voters should cast their votes intelligently, he argued. Leave the constitution alone, he said. The literacy test had been upheld by the U.S. Supreme Court, and, he assured his colleagues, race had nothing to do with the requirement when it was added to the constitution. Certainly, it was being properly administered in the present day. It became law "without regard to race, creed or color."

Martin didn't appreciate the effectiveness of good timing that Frye had learned during those years on his college debate team. Frye waited for Martin to make his claim of racial neutrality and when he regained the floor, he nailed the door shut on the opposition's claims. Firmly, and with conviction founded in personal experience, Frye told the house about what had happened to him when he and Frederick Terry had attempted to register to vote that Saturday in Ellerbee. "I remember that day very well," he said. "It was my wedding day."

Frye may have had the votes he needed already, but once he recounted his own story, the opposition began to lose any advantage that may have remained. The bill had struggled to get to the floor, but now momentum for passage began growing. A Wake County legislator said his Wake Forest law class had been administered the literacy test and not a single student would have qualified to register. One of Martin's allies tried to help. Was there anything in the bill to prevent "morons" from voting, Representative Horton asked Frye? He said no. Then, Horton drew a mocking response from his own ranks. The Republican minority leader, Representative Charles Taylor, said, "If the constitution doesn't keep morons from running for office, why should it keep them from voting." At that point, Speaker Vaughn banged his gavel to add, "I assume the gentleman from Transylvania is speaking for himself."

When the roll was called, Frye had eleven votes to spare. All but five of the Republicans voted for it. The Democratic opposition was scattered. Frye's seatmate John Ridenour voted present. Shirley was on hand for the debate and was sitting in her husband's office after the vote in the house as legislators came by to compliment Frye on his success. She couldn't understand what she took as duplicity — legislators opposed to his bill who offered congratulations. She wanted Henry to explain why. That's the way the legislature works, he said. You argue your point, vote, and go on. Shirley told him women would never be able to do that. They take things too personally.[24]

Some of Frye's colleagues may have passed the bill out of the house sure that it wouldn't get through the senate, where it was sent to Julian Allsbrook's constitutional amendments committee. But, it had passed, for whatever reasons may have carried it through. Indeed, Frye was anxious about its future, and before he began working Allsbrook's committee members he called on Senator Ralph Scott, the governor's uncle. Ralph was a wily old bird whose country manner disguised a decidedly liberal streak. Nobody knew the legislature better. He had been in the senate from the early 1950s when his brother, W. Kerr Scott, was governor. Scott told Frye to pay a visit to Allsbrook and he even told him what the chairman would say. More important, however, he advised Frye not to press Allsbrook for a vote on his bill until he heard from him. Ten days later, just two weeks before the session was due to adjourn, Allsbrook's committee gave Frye's bill a favorable report. The senate took it up the next day and passed it with only one dissenting vote. Even those who spoke against the bill on the floor voted for it. (The only "no" came from a Wilson County senator who was representing a county board of election in a challenge filed under the 1965 Voting Rights Act by the U.S. Justice Department.)

Frye was never clear on why the mountain of opposition that had been seen for his bill in the Senate had disappeared almost overnight. A few days after the senate vote, the *News and Observer* reported that Senator Scott, Lieutenant Governor Taylor and some other supporters of Frye's bill won agreement from Allsbrook that he would give the bill clear sailing if supporters of a bill recalling North Carolina's endorsement in 1965 of a national constitutional convention didn't force their bill out of his committee.[25]

Frankly, Frye didn't care what magic Scott had performed. He also didn't bark when another bill that he had heavily invested in was allowed to wither and die in a senate committee. After introducing his literacy bill, he had submitted another that would have reinstated a clause in the Uniform Commercial Code that outlawed "unconscionable contracts." North Carolina had adopted the UCC, which was designed to streamline business transactions from state to state, but it had not included the contract provision. Frye believed consumers in North Carolina were disadvantaged by its absence.

Opposite, top: State Representative Henry Frye with Deborah Barnes (left) and Angelina Boulware. Legislators named teenagers as pages, and these two Greensboro girls were his first appointments during the 1969 General Assembly (courtesy Frye family). *Opposite, bottom:* Subsequent campaigns for re-election to legislature became easier after 1968. The Fryes were together at this 1972 fund-raiser held at Bennett College (courtesy Frye family).

None of Frye's elders in the legislature put it in plain English, but the freshman had been around long enough to know that he had been blessed with good fortune on his literacy test bill, but that wasn't going to happen twice. He let the consumer bill go without complaint.

Frye approached the end of the session with a deep sense of satisfaction. A Greensboro television reporter caught him at a weak moment and he expressed some doubt about running for a second term. He never seriously considered that, however. Frye had found a place for himself in the General Assembly. He wasn't leading a street march, or scorching whites for injustice. That wasn't what he was built for. Rather, he had secured a place at the table where he could actually get something done, even if it just began with more money for an orphanage at Oxford that was trying to overcome a century of neglect. He planned to be back in the house, where he could build on what he had learned in the late winter and spring of 1969.

Frye's careful, determined, and serious approach to his work won the respect of many in the house. They could see the workings of a keen mind, and they appreciated his penchant for wit and good humor. On the closing day, a legislator from the mountain foothills west of Charlotte praised Frye's work, and he was given a standing ovation. His colleagues genuinely liked Frye, who expressed his dry sense of humor in bits of short verse. There were many long sessions, when Frye struggled to remain alert, his mind numbed by repetitive arguments over some bit of legislation. To fight the boredom, he began writing bits of rhyme. It was something he had done for several years, though he usually used it to loosen up audiences who had invited him to speak. One day, in the midst of the tedium of the house session, he rose for a point of personal privilege and tried out a few lines on his colleagues, just to ease the tension. It worked and others came forth. By the end of the session members had begun to anticipate Frye's "poetry."

On closing day, Frye made the motion for adjournment with this:

> "We have appropriated money
> To operate the state;
> We have added a few taxes
> At a little higher rate.
> We have played around with day care
> And decided it should wait.
> We tried to repeal car inspections
> But decided it was too late.
> So now it is time to finish up
> And say to all goodbye,
> I'd like to make the motion
> That we adjourn *sine die*."

9

Greensboro National Bank

Just ten weeks into the 1969 legislative session, in early April, Henry Frye announced that he and a group of Greensboro investors, all of them African Americans, planned to open a bank in the city. Having fulfilled at least one of his ambitions, to win election to the General Assembly, Frye was driven with equal determination to make good on a dream of longer standing — a bank where customers could see African Americans making financial decisions about the future of their own community.

Henry had first floated his notion of a black-owned bank more than a dozen years earlier as he and Shirley drove to his uncle's home in the Virginia mountains on their honeymoon. He talked about it again when they were returning to Greensboro after he had earned his law degree. It came somewhere in the conversation between establishing his law practice and random musing about going to medical school. Shirley thought her husband was rushing things on both accounts. "I could not visualize somebody who had no money, no experience with a bank, wanting to organize a bank," she said. "He kept saying if you organize a bank you have somewhere that you can offer a person a job."[1]

For Frye, developing a bank was a cornerstone of his belief that racial justice went hand in hand with economic justice. While the growing discontent of young blacks acting out for news reporters and carrying their message to the streets captured the headlines, Frye believed that the people who would make a difference in his community were those who could provide jobs and capital for growing businesses.

He had to look no further than fifty miles away in Durham to see the impact of black enterprises. Frye was still setting up his law office when he drove to Durham to meet John Wheeler, the president of Mechanics and Farmers Bank, one of about a dozen black-owned banks in the nation. Mechanics and Farmers was one of the oldest and strongest of its kind. It was an outgrowth of the success of the nation's largest black-owned business, North Carolina Mutual Insurance Company. Together, these institutions gave substance to the title of "Black Wall Street" as it was applied to Parrish Street in Durham, where the two businesses had been headquartered since the beginning of the twentieth century.

John Hervey Wheeler was the man to see. In the 1960s, he was secure in his position of influence and power in this southern center of African American business, and his reputation extended well beyond Durham. He was a resolute political leader who carefully balanced his support for the street marches and student demonstrations that were considered "radical" behavior by some of Durham's black upper class, with the caution and fears of his neighbors that the demands of the marchers threatened the order of their relatively comfortable lives. Those who owned small businesses in Durham's black business district in Hayti knew that one day the marchers who passed by their stores on the way downtown to demand equal service at white establishments would some day no longer be stopping in to do business with them.[2]

Wheeler didn't bend to pressure, black or white. When the city's most powerful white banker demanded he curb the demonstrations, Wheeler responded by making sure marchers had a warm refuge in the lobby of his bank.[3] Frye approached Wheeler with some trepidation and he left his first encounter with Wheeler's advice that he forget about his dream and concentrate on his law practice. But he also left with a belief that he was also inspired by the sight of black folks working as tellers and loan officers, something he had never before experienced.

Despite Wheeler's unenthusiastic reception, the two men remained in touch. Wheeler was impressed enough with Frye to put him forward as his candidate when Attorney General Robert F. Kennedy was looking for an African American to appoint to the U.S. attorney's office in the latter part of 1962. Once Frye left government service, he revived his plans for a bank and Wheeler finally succumbed. "I think that once he realized that I was going to try it come hell or high water, he decided I was serious and said I believe I will help him," Frye later recalled.[4]

The goal still seemed unattainable. Frye was so short of ready cash at the time that he took the bus to Richmond, Virginia, for his initial visit to the regional office of the comptroller of the currency, where he introduced himself to bank regulators and retrieved the necessary papers for acquiring a charter. Frye wanted a national charter after he was advised that the state banking commission would never approve his application.

"I was afraid they would have made it very hard for us," Frye said of the state regulators. "I am sorry to have to say that, but that was the advice I got." Indeed, the state banking commission was controlled by bankers who were reluctant to give an edge to any competitor, black or white. The major state-chartered banks—Wachovia Bank and Trust and First Citizens—had no history of involvement in the black community, but adding another bank to the roster wasn't in their interest. Frye didn't even apply. "Everybody I talked to said you are wasting your time."

Black-owned banks had opened in the South after the Civil War but only a few survived the financial panics of the nineteenth century. At the time of Frye's trip to the former capital of the Confederacy, Richmond's Consolidated Bank and Trust Company was the oldest black-owned bank in the country. It had been organized by a fraternal organization in 1903 as St. Luke Penny Savings Bank. A woman, Maggie Walker, ran it and issued low-cost home mortgages to African Americans. Over the years, the bank extended its services and during the Depression absorbed two other black-owned banks.[5] Durham's Mechanics and Farmers, which was founded in 1908, also weathered the Depression and continued to grow with offices in Raleigh, Charlotte, and Winston-Salem. By the mid–1960s, twenty black-owned banks were in business nationwide; about half of them had opened after 1963.[6] Frye found that he was part of a trend. Not only were African American banks growing in number, they were accumulating deposits at a faster pace than other commercial banks.[7]

Frye's bank would not be Greensboro's only black-owned financial institution. Kenneth Lee's American Federal Savings and Loan Association had begun business in 1959, within days of Frye's graduation from law school. Lee was inspired to create American Federal after he ran into a form of redlining by Greensboro's bankers who refused to lend the money he needed to build a house on a large corner lot on Benbow Road. Lee had $35,000 of the $60,000 necessary for his stylish modern home that included an indoor swimming pool. But, he discovered that the bank's lending limit for any home built in east Greensboro was $13,500, regardless of the financial standing of the borrower, or the quality of the house he wanted to build. "Suppose something happened to you," Lee said he was told by one banker. "How many Nigras could afford house payments such as these and certainly no whites would locate in the area."[8]

Frye had first considered organizing a savings and loan, but once he learned of Lee's plans, he turned his attention to commercial banking and a business that would offer a full range of financial services to customers, not just home loans. He envisioned a place where African Americans could deal with someone like themselves who understood the difficulties of starting a business, or applying for their first loan, or who only had a few dollars a week to put into a savings account. The bank would be a showplace for east Greensboro where young people could see African Americans doing something other than manual labor. He wanted to recreate for others the image deeply imprinted on his own mind from that first visit to Mechanics and Farmers. It would come at a steep price. The federal banking officials told Frye he would need $300,000 in capital before his application for a charter could be considered. It was a daunting sum for a man whose annual take-home pay was a slim fraction of that.

There probably was no better candidate in east Greensboro to undertake such a challenge. Frye's reputation for honesty and integrity was unblemished. He was sober and hard working and a fixture at Providence Baptist Church. Frye had demonstrated his concern for moving the community forward as president of the Greensboro Citizens Association, a post he held for two years. He was known as someone who didn't grab attention for himself. Though he was considered cool and aloof by some in the community, his conservative nature was a sign of security to others. If African Americans had accumulated any wealth, they were careful about letting anyone know about it. Frye also was building a solid reputation in the city's corporate community through his work with the United Way and the community unity committee of the Chamber of Commerce where Hal Seiber, an old friend from his law school days, recruited Frye to help interest African Americans in the traditionally all-white organization.

Although Frye hoped the bank would be quickly adopted by east Greensboro, he envisioned it serving whites and blacks throughout Greensboro and becoming a source of local pride. The city's image as a financial center had suffered in 1960 when the city's locally owned banks had disappeared into the merger that created North Carolina National Bank, whose headquarters was in Charlotte. Gaining broad white support was a thin reed on which to lean, however. A city that had never embraced A&T, with its thousands of students and employees, was likely to have little more than idle curiosity about a small bank. Practically speaking, Frye would have to depend on east Greensboro, which was not known for its wealth. Businesses there were small, often run by the owner and his wife or another family member, and the number was small. In the mid–1960s, the city had moved headlong into urban renewal and eliminated seventy black-owned businesses from the traditional commercial center along East Market Street.[9] A huge postal facility now covered the dozen acres of land once occupied by beauty shops, clothing stores, cafes, and even churches, including the original site of Providence Baptist Church.

That few of these early entrepreneurs were able to relocate and resume business as before testified to the modest operating margins that had sustained them for years. The shops and small retail stores had produced enough income for the owners to buy a home, have a new car, and perhaps send their children to college, but there was never enough left over to allow for any accumulation of wealth that could be used to grow or expand. The relocation settlements they received from the city were based on current market values and, in most cases, the payments were for a few thousand dollars. That was barely enough to acquire a plot of land and certainly an insufficient sum to restart a business. Moreover, the future prospects for renewal of a thriving black business district were not promising. The social changes of recent years meant black customers could shop anywhere in the city and no longer were dependent on neighborhood stores. The suburban shopping centers were as alluring to black customers as they were to whites who had forsaken downtown retailers.

During his years in Greensboro, Frye had learned that one had to know where to look to find those who could help make his dream come true. Slowly he began making contacts and accumulating support, especially among A&T alumni. In his small group of enthusiastic investors were men who would never have found themselves on the board of a bank. One was James Burnett, who ran Sanitary Cleaners, a long-standing business where he welcomed his customers by their first name. Another was Ernest Canada, an A&T graduate and a home builder; his wife worked at A&T. W. Edward Jenkins was an architect while Durel G. Long was a dentist with a thriving practice in Greensboro and High Point. Dr. James E. Smith was the administrator at L. Richardson Memorial Hospital. Almo McCoy, from nearby Reidsville, was a vocational education teacher. His circumstances were more modest than the others, but Frye liked McCoy's spirit. He had never known an ag teacher who wouldn't get in with both hands and help someone complete a task.

Each of these men put up at least $10,000 to qualify as organizers. As the leader of the effort, Frye's investment was $2,500. The man who put in the largest amount, $30,000, was the Reverend Wyoming Wells, a presiding bishop of the N.C. Conference of the Church of God in Christ. He was a big man, with a broad open face and high forehead that flowed into a dusting of white hair. He had a voice that could roll out like thunder. Wells was in the third decade of a dynamic ministry in Greensboro for the predominantly black Pentecostal denomination. He had come to Greensboro from Pennsylvania in 1934 to take over a small church that grew rapidly under his charge, bolstered in part by a radio ministry he started in the 1940s and tent meetings he held on his way to establishing other churches in the area.[10] Frye had seen him about town and had even made some small donations to Wells, who solicited street-corner contributions for his missionary work. Frye had never considered him as a potential investor until Wells stopped in at Frye's Dudley Street office to ask about his plans. "Brother Frye," Wells said, "I hear you are organizing a bank. Is it too late to get in on it?" Frye assured him he was welcome to join, and told him of the minimum investment requirement. Wells was unfazed and tripled that amount by the time the bank opened. He became the bank's first chairman of the board.[11]

As Frye progressed with his plans, he depended heavily on advice from Wheeler, who passed along the names of contacts as well as some paying assignments. Their relationship had deepened with each year, particularly after Frye began handling the legal work for low-income housing developments, including one for Greensboro's Shiloh Baptist Church, which were financed through Mechanics and Farmers. When the National Bankers Association, the trade association that served America's black institutions, needed an update of its bylaws, Wheeler saw to it that the legal work went to Frye.

Even before the formal organizing got underway, Frye attended the annual meetings of the NBA. Later, whenever he traveled out of town he called ahead and made appointments with the presidents of black-owned banks, if one happened to be nearby. In the spring of 1969, when he was invited to speak at Harvard, he stopped in at Unity Bank in Boston, which was in its first year, where customers were greeted with a fountain of orange juice from which they could draw a cup while conducting their business. "I was real impressed with that," Frye said later. "The next thing I knew they were in trouble."[12] The lesson of costly frills like free refreshments was not lost on him.

Frye called on the president at Freedom National Bank in New York City, where the legendary ballplayer Jackie Robinson was one of the founders. The bank was organized on the same premise as Greensboro National, to serve customers in the black community, and some of the challenges were similar. Freedom National was only about three years old when Robinson visited Greensboro for an engagement at A&T. The school's president, Dr. Lewis Dowdy, saw to it that there was time in Robinson's schedule for him to talk with Frye and his investors. The evening turned into one that Shirley Frye would never forget.

She had prepared a coconut cake, which was one of her specialties, for Robinson's visit to her modest home on Drexmore. It wasn't until all of her guests had arrived, however, that she discovered Robinson was a diabetic. She not only had nothing to serve one of the most honored black figures in the twentieth century, but her cupboard didn't even include a sugar substitute as a sweetener for his coffee. She slipped out the back door and made a hasty trip to a grocery store to purchase Sweeteena.[13]

Frye's plans might have easily died aborning. Each time he returned to the comptroller's office in Richmond, the regulators raised the minimum requirements. The first threshold of $300,000 went up to $500,000, and by the spring of 1969 the requirement was for $700,000 in capital. "I didn't know where we were going to get it," Frye said later, "but I said we are going to do it." In addition, the organizers would have to have an experienced management team in place to gain approval. The two requirements worked in tandem with those Frye approached about either running the bank or investing in it. Bank executives he talked to about moving to Greensboro were reluctant to commit until they knew he had the capital, or a sound plan to acquire it. Meanwhile, potential investors held back until they knew who was going to be running the bank. Frye's efforts moved slowly as he tried to bring one or the other of the two requirements to a sufficient level of comfort. Two investors became impatient with his progress and pulled out.[14]

Finally, he began making some headway. Mechanics and Farmers bought some stock, as did North Carolina Mutual Insurance, where Frye was a newly elected member of the board of directors. Frye also discovered that Greensboro's white businesses were willing to help. North Carolina National Bank bought stock, as did the two insurance companies based in Greensboro. When he went to talk with executives at Southern Life Insurance Company he discovered they were willing to match the $30,000 put up by Jefferson Standard Life Insurance, the much larger company just up the street. "I went to Bo Carter at Southern Life and explained it to him," Frye recalled. "He said, 'How much did Jefferson buy?' and I told him. He said, 'Well, we've got a lot of people in this community and we'll take the same amount.' I was learning. I had thought of Southern Life as being this old small insurance company." Carter's response was totally unexpected. "You could have pushed me a little bit and I would have fallen out of my seat," Frye recalled. When he left Carter's office, he was sure that if Southern Life was willing to take a chance on Greensboro National then he was on his way.[15]

The fence straddlers waiting for word on the bank's management finally unlimbered their checkbooks after Frye convinced Vernard Henley, a vice president at Consolidated Bank in Richmond, to take a chance on Greensboro National. Henley was in the top tier of management at the Richmond bank and well grounded in the business. He was comfortable enough with Frye's financial commitments that he agreed to let his name be included in an initial offering circular that came out in January 1971. Frye was listed as the president, but Henley was executive vice president and the man who Greensboro National's investors planned on handling the day-to-day business of the bank.[16]

In February 1971, Frye and his organizers held a community meeting in east Greensboro to talk about their plans and to introduce the bank's leadership. Frye announced that Henley would be in Greensboro by the end of March to prepare for the formal opening, scheduled for later in the year. Then the bottom fell out. Shortly after that meeting, Henley drove to Greensboro and told Frye that Consolidated had made him such a strong offer to remain in Richmond that he could not afford to leave. (He ultimately became CEO and board chairman.) On Henley's previous visits to Greensboro, the two men had ended their sessions with a meal at Frye's home. On this visit, even after Henry had invited him to stay for dinner, Shirley was so angry that she refused to have him in the house.[17]

"I tell you," Frye said years later, "it was a sad time around here." All of the printed materials carrying Henley's name had to be recalled, and Frye was left with finding a replacement immediately if plans were to remain on track for the opening. The organizers already had selected a site for the bank on a prominent corner midway between the A&T campus and downtown.

Plans were in place to erect a $200,000 building on land reclaimed during urban renewal at the corner of East Market Street and a new dual-lane thoroughfare named in honor of broadcaster Edward R. Murrow, who was born in Guilford County. Frye was in no position to resume what surely would be a lengthy search of a replacement for Henley; he was well into the work of the 1971 General Assembly. He had run for a second term and had led the ticket in the general election in November 1970. His briefcase was stuffed with legislative matters that needed review, but now he also had to find a new bank president.

Losing Henley threatened to derail the entire affair. Frye had already taken an inventory of the available talent, and there were few candidates that he didn't already know and whom he already had rejected in favor of Henley. Indeed, this list was a short one. While African Americans were beginning to show up on loan platforms of the major banks, there were few black bankers who had been on the job long enough to run an entire operation. Frye needed a man familiar with the ins and outs of lending, but also someone who was experienced in the operations side that handled the details of individual transactions. Frye had worked out an arrangement for Greensboro National's junior officers to undergo training at Mechanics and Farmers, but the bank regulators and his investors were going to require an experienced banker as president. "I said I am not going to give up on this thing," Frye said. "That was when I went and talked with Tom Storrs. I told him what my problem was and he came up with the answer."

Thomas I. Storrs was executive vice president and the second in command at North Carolina National Bank under the bank's founding CEO, Addison Reese. Storrs was trained as an economist and had a Ph.D. from Harvard. He had joined the bank as executive vice president just as it was organized, after years with the Federal Reserve. Reese assigned him to Greensboro during an awkward period in the 1960s when NCNB maintained a fiction of having two headquarters, one in Charlotte and one in Greensboro. It was an effort to placate the Greensboro shareholders who had lost their hometown banks in the merger. In 1971, Storrs was Reese's heir apparent and had already begun to take on additional responsibilities. He would subsequently move to Charlotte and launch the interstate expansion of NCNB, which later would become Bank of America. Old friends called him "Buddy," but to subordinates he was known as a steely administrator who focused on results. They called him the "ice man."[18]

Storrs knew Frye and liked the way he operated. Some time earlier, Frye had come to him with a concern about a touchy racial situation within the bank's offices in Greensboro. Storrs investigated, found Frye's report was correct, and dealt swiftly to resolve the problem. He was grateful that Frye had contacted him privately about a situation that would have become an embarrassment if he had complained publicly.[19] As Frye's plans for Greensboro National began to come together, NCNB had taken notice. A new bank was going to need the kind of back-office support for handling deposits, shifting money around accounts, and other services that a large operation like NCNB could offer for a fee. When Frye came to Storrs for advice on finding a replacement for Henley, Storrs provided a solution for that as well.

One of the senior vice presidents in NCNB's Greensboro office was about to retire, Storrs told Frye. He was James H. Witherspoon, who was a tough-minded banker with a strong background in operations. He had been one of Neil VanStory's chief lieutenants at Security National before that bank disappeared into NCNB and Witherspoon had taken on regional responsibilities during his years with the new bank. He was white, but he possessed the qualifications that Frye needed to satisfy regulators and investors. Storrs was agreeable to waiving any non-compete requirements that usually went with retirement packages if Witherspoon wanted to work with Greensboro National.

Witherspoon accepted the offer and in May 1971, a new offering circular introduced him to prospective shareholders as the bank's vice president along with another new name. Frye also recruited William J. Pickens, an African American, away from Chemical National Bank in New York City. Prior to that he had worked at Freedom National. He dispatched Pickens to complete a training program under Wheeler's supervision at Mechanics and Farmers while Witherspoon operated behind the scenes. When Pickens returned to Greensboro, he would be the public face of Greensboro National. The arrangement was not what Frye had hoped for, but it was the only solution.

The banking market had changed since Frye had first envisioned his enterprise. Following the passage of civil rights laws in the mid–1960s, American businesses had begun to discover a new market of African American customers who they earlier had largely ignored. Green power was beginning to trump white and black power. The year before Frye announced plans for Greensboro National Bank, NCNB had launched a major initiative to recruit black customers in Charlotte. There, the bank's city executive, Luther Hodges, Jr., hired a Durham native, William Clement, Jr., the son of one of the top officers at North Carolina Mutual, and assigned him to find new commercial customers for NCNB. Hodges also overcame objections from Mechanics and Farmers and opened a NCNB branch right in the middle of Charlotte's black community on Beatties Ford Road, where Wheeler's bank had long been the area's sole provider of financial services. "We want to be more responsive to the community," Hodges said at the time. "This is a more aggressive approach. The Negro community is saying that no one is listening, that no one is hearing them and we're going out and trying to do this."[20] In Greensboro, Storrs had reassigned an African American who was working in the bank's back-office as a teller in the bank's main office on Elm Street. It was a small step, done without fanfare. Storrs watched cautiously as white customers accepted the change without complaint.

Storrs wanted Frye's bank to succeed, even though its offices would be near NCNB's busy branch office on Bessemer Avenue, at the northern boundary of the A&T campus. It was a busy place on payday at the huge Lorillard plant in east Greensboro. On occasion, the line of customers waiting to do business spilled out the front door. The branch manager was a young civic-minded Jaycee named Jim Melvin who had been elected to the city council during Frye's first term in the General Assembly. On the days the eagle flew at Lorillard, Melvin had to put on extra tellers to accommodate customers, about a third of who were African Americans.[21]

Melvin was a hustler and doing his best to sign up customers from among the business owners in east Greensboro when he got word from Storrs to limit his efforts. "We were told to do everything you can to help this bank," Melvin

Henry Frye (left) opened the temporary offices of Greensboro National Bank in 1971 next to its permanent location at the edge of Greensboro's black community. The bank's executive vice president, William J. Pickens (with microphone), spoke to a crowd that gathered in the gravel lot, as did the bank's chairman of the board, Bishop Wyoming Wells (center) (© *Greensboro News and Record*, all rights reserved, photograph by Dave Nicholson).

said some years later. The word was: "Don't do any recruiting from that neighborhood." Melvin supported Frye's efforts personally. He bought a few shares of stock in Greensboro National and later opened a savings account there. He was on hand on November 3, 1971, when the bank opened for business with as much fanfare as Frye, his board, and east Greensboro could muster.

The National Bankers Association honored Frye in 1983 with its top honor, the R. R. Wright Award, which was presented at its annual meeting in Tulsa, Oklahoma. The award is named for one of the association's founders, a businessman and educator in the early years of the twentieth century (courtesy Frye family).

By the time Greensboro National greeted its first customer, Melvin had become the city's mayor and was present for the ribbon cutting. "This is truly a great day in the community," Melvin told a crowd gathered around the front door. "I think the financial institutions in this community are totally dedicated to quality and the betterment of life. I'm sure this bank will be a leader in that field. Now, let's get on with the depositing of money."[22] Standing with him, holding the ceremonial scissors, was the bank's chairman, Bishop Wyoming Wells. Together, they pushed open the doors to the bank's temporary quarters, an eleven-hundred-square-foot temporary building with an aluminum overhang at the entrance.

Wells was joined at the front by John Wheeler, who recalled for the crowd Frye's early visits to his office. He said the new bank was good for the community because it made competitors work harder for the business of African Americans. A&T's Lewis Dowdy and Bennett's president, Dr. Isaac Miller, also were part of a program that drew about one hundred fifty people to the flat graveled parking lot beside the site where construction was to begin on a permanent building in about thirty days. The crowd included older businessmen in conservative attire as well as young men and women in bushy Afros. (Frye's nod to fashion was a new mustache that was broad in the middle and tapered to a fine point at the edge of his mouth. It was a style favored by Dr. Martin Luther King, Jr., among others.)

At the time it opened, Greensboro National was one of twenty-nine minority-owned banks in the United States, and challenges abounded both on the east side of the railroad tracks in Greensboro, and beyond. GNB would face increasing competition from white banks, and the business that the organizers hoped to realize in the black community would grow slowly. Frye had encountered skeptics all along. Some older folks recalled a black-run credit union that had failed some years earlier. He knew customers would have to be cultivated, and part of the bank's public relations program included classes on financial management in an effort to reach his neighbors who had little or no experience with banks. As he was leaving the ceremonies on opening day, an elderly woman approached Frye and he asked if she would be opening an account. No, she told him, she wouldn't be a customer, at least not for the present. Her money wouldn't be safe in that flimsy building Frye called a bank. Recalling the encounter some time later, Frye said, "She thought we kept her money in there."

Construction on the permanent building began in early December, and Frye's schedule only grew more complicated. In addition to bringing in business and overseeing the fledgling operations inside the bank, he had to keep abreast of construction. The board of directors had planned to hire a minority-owned general contractor but, to their dismay, they found there was none available that could secure the sufficient bonding capacity to undertake a building of that size. The board — which meant Frye — became the general contractor with bank director Ernest R. Canada, a homebuilder, supervising construction details as the clerk of the works.

Tucked inside a pocket in Frye's suit coat a day or two after the opening-day ceremonies was a political circular that he had received announcing plans by Reginald Hawkins to run for governor again in 1972. Frye used the back of the form letter to scribble notes from a busy day: negotiations over the cost of steel for the new building, a $75,000 certificate of deposit that cashier Bill Pickens was expecting to issue, a speech at a luncheon club where he planned to announce the time and date of the groundbreaking. In many respects, the letter and the notes were a metaphor for Frye's life. During the past two years he had juggled the demands of his business and professional life, both of which were dear to him, with the ever-present tug of politics.

It had not been easy. Time remained ever precious. Frye's legislative work had continued beyond the close of the 1969 session when he was named to a commission that was revising state laws governing cities and counties. It was mind-numbing work as the Local Government Commission slogged through a jumble of laws. Sessions were held on weekends, keeping Frye away from his church and his family. He also was appointed to a commission charged with developing minimum standards for law enforcement officers in the state. This group was examining issues that were vitally important to the black community. African Americans had long been excluded from jobs that allowed them to carry a badge, and they often had been on the rough end of treatment from politically appointed deputy sheriffs whose only qualification for their job was their size and brutality. Both of the legislative assignments offered a unique opportunity for Frye: no black man had ever sat at the table making decisions on a broader array of policy that affected the daily lives of African Americans. It was an assignment he could not, and would not, ignore.

Despite the demands on his time, Frye had never questioned that he'd seek a second term. He began his re-election campaign in the spring of 1970 with an event at an east Greensboro supper club that attracted more than three hundred blacks and whites for a ten-dollar-per-plate dinner. Virginia state Senator L. Douglas Wilder, the commonwealth's first black legislator in modern time, was announced as the principal speaker, but travel problems prevented his timely arrival. (Twenty years later, Wilder would be the first African American elected governor of Virginia.) Frye's supporters were enthusiastic and voters didn't seem to mind that Frye had given his support to Governor Scott's tax package, which included the state's first levy on cigarettes. Frye wasn't sure his father-in-law was as forgiving.

Throughout the 1970 campaign season, east Greensboro struggled with issues and events that cut deep into the fabric of the community. It began in the spring of 1969, just as the legislative session was ending, with protests at

the all-black Dudley High School that spilled into the streets and onto the
N.C. A&T State University campus. Subsequent testimony at a hearing into
a tumultuous time by the U.S. Civil Rights Commission revealed a wide rift
between Dudley's teachers, for whom order and discipline was to be accepted
without question, and young students who challenged rules limiting their
dress and political behavior.[23]

Overlying it all was white Greensboro's heavy-handed response to the
troubles that the school flap inspired. What had begun as a disputed student
council election ended with snipers and gunfire that left an A&T student dead
and an early-morning assault by National Guard troops on Scott Hall, the
dormitory where Frye had lived as a senior. Even Governor Scott was shaken
by the damage to the residence hall and the threat to innocent lives brought
on by the might of the Guard. "They lied to me," Scott told the trustees at
Winston-Salem State University a short time after the incident as he spoke
of the Guard's assault. He was deeply apologetic and said of A&T's president,
Dr. Lewis Dowdy, whose authority on campus he had ignored, "I've hurt a
good man."[24]

The deadly incident further encouraged the militancy that was rising
among young African Americans, many of whom had been too young to participate in the civil rights marches of the early 1960s. One of the most active
organizers was Nelson Johnson, an A&T graduate who had remained in
Greensboro after graduation to create the Greensboro Association of Poor
People, a community organizing effort in east Greensboro. He and others
drew on the energy and idealism of younger students like Deborah Barnes,
who was then in high school. "They used to have protests all the time," Barnes
recalled. "It was all about protests in those days. Garbage workers, we'd be
like rent-a-protestor. We'd go by after school and say, you need somebody to
protest, I am with you. It was a very hip, wonderful thing to do. You felt all
engaged."[25]

Barnes's parents were close friends of the Fryes. Her grandfather, a dentist, had been something of a mentor for Henry. The Barnes family enjoyed
a solid middle-class life in Benbow Park and Deborah hid her involvement
with Johnson from her parents. "That was worse than smoking dope. I would
say I am going to Kathy Webb's house to do homework. Parents had a fit, to
some degree, about our big old Afros. You wouldn't want to say something,
like talk about the pigs. That was not appropriate language, and it was all
about being appropriate. You could be political. They expected you to be
political, but you had to be appropriate with it."

The black separatism preached by Johnson disturbed many in east
Greensboro, especially the Fryes. His rhetoric discounted virtually everything
that Henry and Shirley believed was right and necessary to change conditions
for African Americans. Real change, lasting change, was impossible if African

Americans boycotted the system and ignored opportunities to be part of the decision-making process. That is why Henry was so determined to attend every one of the meetings on the legislative commissions on which he served. If he was absent, so was a point of view that he and others had worked very hard to have heard. For Frye, the questions facing the state and the nation cut across racial lines. The larger issues were a matter of justice, not simply race, and it was not enough to make noise and challenge the white establishment. In Greensboro, his firm took the case of sanitation workers, most of whom were African Americans, who were bargaining for better pay, but he also represented the city's firemen — most of whom were white — when they pressed their own demands for higher wages. At the request of some in the community, he also intervened with Governor Scott to help arrange for Johnson's early release from state prison following his conviction on charges rising out of the troubles at A&T in 1969.

The general election in 1970 was a different kind of contest from what Frye had known two years earlier. This time he campaigned with fellow Democrats and ran as part of a ticket with the other white incumbents. When Simkins and others announced their preferred ticket for voters in Greensboro black precincts, they didn't promote a single-shot for Frye, because, Simkins said, Frye didn't need it. He got a boost from the black precincts, of course, where he ran better than the white Democrats, but he did well all across the county. Frye led the ticket. The previous frontrunner, Charles Phillips, came in a thousand votes behind him.[26]

Frye's constitutional amendment to eliminate the literacy test that he had diligently maneuvered through the General Assembly did not fare as well. The change failed to win approval of a majority of the voters, although a handful of largely procedural changes to the constitution passed. Six weeks later, however, the U.S. Supreme Court ruled literacy tests, such as the one used in North Carolina, were unconstitutional. Frye said he was disappointed that his amendment hadn't passed, but neither he nor anyone else had done anything to educate voters about it. The Fryes had attended the N.C. Bar Association meeting the year before, where he was scheduled to make a pitch for the association's endorsement of the measure. The family had to leave before Henry got his chance to speak.

Frye returned to his old seat in the state house when the 1971 General Assembly convened in mid–January. This time, he was not the only African American in legislature. A Baptist preacher from Robeson County, the Reverend Joy Johnson, joined him in the house. A few years older than Frye, Johnson was of medium height with a slight build. He made up for his size with a pulpit-style of oratory that could brace to attention any legislators who nodded off during the proceedings. Johnson was blunt and pugnacious. Speaking to a group of African Americans gathered for the NAACP's Freedom

Day meeting later in the session, he said, "We must force the white man to do right. If the donkey is hesitant and balks, and the elephant is afraid, grab an ear." He also admonished blacks for selling their votes "for a drink and fifty cents."[27]

The Legislative Building was now familiar territory for Frye. Other incumbents, especially those legislators with whom he had spent weekends poring over proposed changes in municipal and county laws, or revamping hiring and training standards for lawmen, knew him well. In addition to his legislative assignments, Governor Scott had put him on a Democratic Party study commission whose job was to open party affairs to minorities, women, and young people. The hearings on proposed changes had been held all across the state and further expanded his exposure. As the bills began coming to the floor, Frye displayed more confidence and found himself at the forefront of issues that he had supported two years earlier, but on which he had figured less prominently in the debate. He led an unsuccessful effort to abolish the death penalty but he was on the winning side with a bill to reduce the voting age to eighteen. He continued to nudge bureaucrats and state agency heads to increase their hiring of African Americans. Even Benjamin Swalin, the director of the N.C. Symphony, got a letter from Frye inquiring about the racial composition of his players.[28] With Johnson close at hand, Frye could hand off some of the watchdog work—checking bills that might have racial implications—that had kept him tied down two years earlier.

There was a new political awareness among African Americans in the state. Richard Nixon's Republicans had devised a new strategy in 1968 to cripple the Democratic Party's hold on the South. While much was made of Nixon's appeal to whites in the South, the Republicans also were courting black voters. The first White House appointment of a North Carolinian came in January 1969 when Robert J. Brown, an African American, was named a special assistant to the president. Brown was a former High Point police officer turned public relations consultant. He was well known among textile executives for his work in their behalf to discourage union activity in their plants. The president picked him to lead a new initiative to boost minority businesses. His appointment came as a surprise to North Carolina Republicans, who had no black representation in the state party leadership.[29]

Prior to Nixon's election, Durham's Floyd McKissick, the former head of the CORE, the student-led organization that had buttressed the sit-in demonstrations in Greensboro, left CORE and the Democratic Party to register as a Republican and endorse the Nixon's candidacy. McKissick subsequently landed $25 million in commitments from the U.S. Department of Housing and Urban Development to support the creation of Soul City, a new town to be designed by and built for African Americans in Warren County, North Carolina. The initial site was 1,800 acres of farmland alongside Interstate 85 just south of the Virginia line that had once been worked by slaves. McKissick said Soul City would grow and thrive into a multi-racial community of nearly 20,000 within two decades. His name began appearing on partisan literature that was circulated among African American.

Frye had no patience with Republicans, but he believed Democrats would have to do better than they had in the past. For years, white politicians and the white press had regarded black voters as a simple-minded monolithic block of voters that could be bought, sold, and manipulated on Election Day. All a candidate had to do was touch base with a handful of poll workers in each community whose allegiance went to the highest bidder. The outlay for unscrupulous poll workers had even become a line item in a candidate's campaign budget. This remained a fact of life in cities like Greensboro and Durham where citizens' groups had tried to break the cycle and get voters to exercise more independence. Buying votes was easy when there were only whites on the ballot; it made little difference to the average black voter who got elected. As a result, it was easier to make a few bucks than to sort out the names on Election Day, if one bothered to vote at all. When Henry Frye decided to run for the legislature he told Shirley that there would be no money changing hands on his behalf.[30]

The Hawkins campaign in 1968, Frye's success in the General Assembly, and the 1969 election of Howard Lee as mayor of Chapel Hill — he was the first African American elected to lead a majority-white city in the South — awakened politically aware African Americans to possibilities that they had only dreamed about before. By the time the 1972 elections rolled around, the political landscape was beginning to look a little different.

No one — black or white — had expected Hawkins to win, but victory was not the objective, according to Hawkins's campaign manager, James Ferguson. Many years later, Ferguson said what was important was inspiring confidence. "Blacks had a hard time bringing themselves to believe that a black candidate could be taken seriously by whites," Ferguson said.[31] Hawkins had challenged blacks to question the status quo, and his campaign had aroused young men like Howard Lee to consider their own prospects. While Hawkins was not universally accepted as the man who would lead blacks to the political promised land, his campaign had, for the first time, established political connections among African Americans that crossed county lines and focused attention on the potential strength of black voters like never before.

Hawkins's political activity had not ended with the 1968 elections. In August 1969, he called a statewide meeting in Raleigh that drew several hundred politically active blacks. He turned the podium over to Frye, Lee, and others who had broken through the barriers of old, including Eva Clayton, who had challenged an incumbent white congressman when African Americans in the district could not find a man who was willing to run.[32]

The meeting serviced Hawkins's need to keep his name in the public discussion — he planned another run for governor in 1972 — but at the same time the session was a boost to the missionary work he had done. Many of those attending simply didn't know one another. Despite the proximity of Greensboro and Chapel Hill, Lee and Frye had been strangers until a few weeks prior. The two had met almost coincidentally after one of Lee's Chapel Hill friends suggested he should go to Raleigh to meet the legislative leadership before the session adjourned.

Later in the year, Frye organized a meeting of black elected officials, and a new group emerged that was called the N.C. Black Caucus. There was considerable overlap between the two, but Frye said those in public office needed to put some distance between themselves and the caucus. "We tried to keep them separate because some of us who were elected officials thought some of the people in the Black Caucus didn't really understand some things," Frye said some time later. "I don't remember specifics. The folks who were not elected officials would take positions sometimes that those of us who were elected officials said, 'That won't work. You can't do it that way.' And they would say, 'Why not?' That was the biggest thing. Our approach was a little different."[33]

Frye welcomed the company of other elected officials. They helped field the calls of African Americans from all parts of the state who assumed that Frye could solve their problems since he was in public office. Now, when Frye got a call about a situation in the Sandhills, he could contact Felton Capel, the mayor of Southern Pines, or he could relay a caller to Lee who could check out a complaint related to municipal government. Many of the pleas for help came out of precincts in eastern North Carolina, where blacks had long been denied easy access to the political system. "I began to learn about people down there, some white and some black, that I could call on," Frye said. "I made a lot of telephone calls. Some times it worked and some times it didn't. But, having that network was key." What was taking place reminded him of the practice of Frye and other black lawyers who usually phoned ahead for advice before traveling into unfamiliar territory to take care of business. "If I were going to Wilmington, for example, I would call the black lawyer the day before and tell him I was coming down there and what I was coming for to see if he had any suggestions about what to do and what not to do. If you didn't, you might get yourself into a problem."[34]

White politicians were beginning to take notice. Governor Scott had run on a "law and order" platform in 1968 when racial tensions were high in the wake of the riots that burned Washington, D.C., following the murder of Dr. Martin Luther King, Jr. In Scott's first year in office, he had responded with force to demonstrations by black students at Chapel Hill and at A&T. The long-suffering governor's "liaison" to the black community remained John

R. Larkins, but he was buried in a secondary government job. Scott had appointed John H. Baker, Jr., of Raleigh, a recently retired pro football player and son of an influential black politician in Raleigh, to the state parole commission.

Late in 1971, as the governor was approaching his final year in office, he appointed Sammie Chess, an African American lawyer from High Point and a one-time business partner of the Republicans' Robert Brown, to a four-year appointment as a special judge on the superior court bench. Scott had earlier named Clifton Johnson of Charlotte to a district court judgeship, but Scott's appointment of Chess was the one that made headlines across the state. Never before had a black man been put in a position where he could deprive a white man of his liberty and property in any county in the state. "At that period, a superior court judge was God," Chess said some years later. "To put that kind of authority in the hands of a black person at that point in history took a lot of courage."[35]

Scott and Chess were not strangers. Chess served on the State Board of Higher Education, which Scott chaired, where he was the representative of the historically black Winston-Salem State University. Coincidentally, Chess's wife was from a rural community in Alamance County that was not far from the governor's home at Haw River, where Scotts had been farmers since the nineteenth century. The two men were together at a board of higher education meeting early in 1971 when Chess passed along a request from the Southeastern Lawyers Association — a group of black lawyers in the Carolinas and Virginia — who wanted a meeting with Scott. He told the governor they wished to talk about judicial appointments, a subject Hawkins had raised in his 1968 campaign.

In early spring, Chess arrived at the governor's office along with Greensboro's Kenneth Lee and Harvey Beech of Kinston, the first black graduates of the UNC law school; attorney Earl Whitted of Goldsboro; and Julius Chambers and James Ferguson from Charlotte. Chess opened the conversation by saying they weren't there to trade votes or capitalize on past support in exchange for an appointment of an African American to the bench. "This is not quid pro quo," Chess later recalled telling Scott. "There are a lot of reasons why you ought to do this. I am going to mention one: You ought to do it because it is the right thing to do."

None in the group was looking for the job for himself, Chess told the governor. "Knowing each one, I know that not one wants to be a judge," Chess said he told Scott. "They are all superb advocates. They wouldn't want to change their advocacy role for a judgeship. But I said to them, this is bigger than each of you and you therefore must not think about how it would impact you personally, but think of the greater good for the greater number." They left the governor with a commitment for an appointment in the near future.

Kenneth Lee followed up the meeting with a letter that included a list of candidates for the governor to consider. The names agreed upon by the delegation included Beech and Chess, as well as Clifton Johnson; Richard Erwin, a Winston-Salem attorney whom President Jimmy Carter later would appoint to the U.S. district court bench; and William G. Pearson III, a younger cousin of Durham's Conrad Pearson, who at one time was the leading NAACP attorney in the state. "We have not considered any individual's desire to serve and our recommendations are based solely upon our opinions of the qualifications which we consider essential to the judiciary of North Carolina, and the possession of these qualifications by the individual attorneys."[36]

Chess was surprised when the governor's legal counsel, Fred Morrison, called to tell him the governor wanted him to take the job. Chess backpedaled, and argued that he didn't want to leave his law practice. Morrison then reminded him of his own words during the delegation's session with Scott. Any man nominated for the job would have to sacrifice for "a big blow for equality and crack the ice for equality." Chess finally agreed. When he later got the telephone call from Scott, he said the governor's confidence was unreserved. His only concern was how a black judge would be received in some courthouses around the state. Chess later recalled that during his four years on the bench he never encountered disrespect for himself or his position. "[Chess] did a good job," Henry Frye said years later. "He changed things in some of the courthouses just by showing up. He reminded some of the lawyers that we were going to treat everybody the same."

Of those on the delegation's list, Chess was the most logical choice. Scott knew him and had had an opportunity to take a measure of his judgment at the higher education board meetings. Chess perhaps was more acceptable politically than others on the list. He had handled civil rights cases — virtually every black lawyer in the state had at one time — but Chess's profile was not nearly as high as those of Chambers, Ferguson, and even Pearson. Charlotte and Mecklenburg County were still in an uproar over federal court ordered cross-town busing that grew out of Chambers pressing a lawsuit to desegregate the local school system. Scott would have enraged a large portion of North Carolina if he had put an "NAACP" lawyer on the bench.

"I was at the meeting when we talked about [the meeting with Scott]," Frye said later, but he had ruled himself out as a potential candidate. Even if he weren't involved with starting a new bank, he believed it did not make sense to trade one political achievement — his seat in the house — for another, especially since there was no guarantee that Scott would appoint an African American to take his place, or that a black successor could win election to a full term. The Chess appointment suited Frye just fine, although he said Chess took considerable ribbing from his colleagues for setting up a meeting with the governor and then taking home the appointment himself.[37]

It was apparent early in the 1972 political season that, for some, it would be one of those watershed years after which the old rules would no longer apply and outcomes would never be easy to predict. For Frye the campaign season followed the pattern that had proved successful for him two years earlier. He kicked off his bid for a third term with another ten-dollar-a-plate dinner. This year his speaker for the evening was C. Delores Tucker, an African American woman who was the secretary of state in Pennsylvania. Henry and Shirley took nothing for granted, but Frye remained one of the most popular political figures in Guilford County. His success in the primary was never really in doubt.

That was not the case in the Democratic Party's gubernatorial primary. Most of the attention was on the two leading candidates, Lieutenant Governor H. Patrick Taylor, Jr., from Wadesboro and state Senator Hargrove Bowles, a Greensboro businessman. Both men had ties to the more liberal side of the state party organization, personified by former governor Terry Sanford, although Taylor was often cast as the more conservative of the two. Much of that image arose from his personal style. He was a country lawyer who had a wry wit, liked to tell stories drawn from his days in court and in the legislature, and spoke with a "broken-toned nasal drawl, punctuated with ain'ts and I-do-declares."[38] Sanford had depended on Taylor and Bowles during his term as governor, although when he asked for Bowles's help he was pretty sure he was a Republican, because of his mansion overlooking a fairway at the Greensboro Country Club. Bowles raised the money Sanford needed to win the election, and then joined his administration in Raleigh, where he helped the governor integrate the state's parks without incident. Bowles was a happy warrior of a candidate who armed himself with an optimistic outlook and a broad smile.[39]

The race issue had divided the state in 1960 when Sanford beat an unabashed segregationist, I. Beverly Lake, in the Democratic Party primary. The question a decade earlier had been "if" black students should go to school with whites. The incendiary question now was "how" black and whites would end up in classrooms together. Politicians from President Nixon down to outraged parents running for the school board were capitalizing on white anger over desegregation plans that included court-ordered busing. To the credit of both Bowles and Taylor, neither tried to gain an advantage in this fight. Taylor dismissed the busing issue early, saying the governor should not do anything to defy the law.[40]

For Taylor and for Bowles, the wild card was Reginald Hawkins. This time, Hawkins's splinter effort was complicated by the candidacy of labor leader Wilbur Hobby of Durham, the head of the state's AFL-CIO. He joined the race with a slogan of "Keep The Big Boys Honest," one he borrowed from Henry Howell, an unsuccessful independent candidate for governor in Virginia in 1971. Four years earlier, Hawkins had tried to build a campaign around a coalition of blacks and working-class whites. Hobby drained Hawkins's support from organized labor, as modest an effort as it was. As a result, the Hawkins campaign was virtually a one-man show that struggled for attention.

Hawkins even found he wasn't the automatic favorite of African Americans, especially those who were young and angry. Early in the campaign, the 48-year-old dentist was confronted by a student at N.C. Central University. The young man was wearing a Fu Manchu mustache and goatee, and he met Hawkins with a stare and a challenge: "Let's you and me be practical about it. You can't win so why should I waste my time and energy on you." Hawkins brushed off the incident and told a reporter traveling with him, "They were trying to see if they could shake me."[41] Black voters would stand with him, he said, and leave him with that bargaining chip that he planned to use when the leading white candidates squared off in a second primary.

The old standard about black unity was growing weak, however. Four years of talking, organizing, and electing blacks to office had undermined the dictum that black voters must stand together, or suffer from internal divisions that would dilute their power. Now, there were black candidates running for public office that understood the new dynamics and were learning how to work their way around a student wearing a mustache and a stare and older blacks who worried about upsetting the status quo.

Mayor Howard Lee launched a congressional campaign that carried him from his base in Chapel Hill — and energized black militants on the college campus — deep into eastern North Carolina. "Even though I may have disagreed with Stokely Carmichael it was not acceptable for me to go out and trash him," said Lee some years later. "The black community was divided along those lines. There were those who thought he walked on water and there were those who thought he was devil reincarnate. You had to be careful with that."[42] A year earlier, Shaw University in Raleigh had illustrated the divide when it gave honorary degrees to Carmichael as well as a centrist politician like Frye.

At the same time, Lee confronted the old politics of ward heelers that greeted him with their hand out. "We knew, for example, that there were people in the black community who took money from white leaders to influence the black vote in a given election, even if a black was running," Lee said. "These people were there. We knew they were there and none of us ever felt we could call them out, or we didn't call them out. Those were the kinds of behind the scenes problems that were really worrisome to black politicians."

The wisecracking Hawkins chose his words more carefully in 1972. He retained a knack for alliterative phrasing — he called himself the candidate of the "oppressed, suppressed, compressed and damned" — but he found it hard to deal with criticism that came his way from African Americans, according to one report. One newspaper reported an encounter this way: "'My campaign is not a civil rights march,'" he blurted during one conversation with a supporter, meaning he has turned to "politics, not protest."

The 1972 campaign season really didn't need any more players to become interesting, but the conversation grew even livelier after Congresswoman Shirley Chisholm of New York launched her bid for the Democratic Party's presidential nomination. She chose the North Carolina presidential primary as one in which to spend time. It was as quixotic an effort as was Hawkins's gubernatorial bid, but she captured the imagination and attention of African Americans in a special way. She was scheduled for an appearance on the A&T campus that Frye attended.

"I knew she didn't stand a chance, period," he said some years later. "In fact, I had decided not to get really involved in it. I knew it wasn't going to get anywhere. I told somebody that I am not going, I don't have time. And then, for some reason, I changed my mind. When they introduced her and she stood up and said, 'I am Shirley Chisholm, the congresswoman from the state of New York and I am running for president of United States,' it felt good just to hear her say it. I said, 'I sure am glad I came to this.' It was almost like a religious experience. I felt as good listening to her, almost, as I did hearing Martin Luther King preach at his church. I thought, one of these days we are going to have a black who has a chance to win."

The impact of her campaign in North Carolina fell most heavily upon Terry Sanford, who had become president of Duke University the year before. He had joined the Democratic presidential contest early in the year with hopes of defeating former Alabama governor George Wallace in the state's new presidential primary and then going on to the party's national convention as a new leader from the South. In the end, Sanford trailed Wallace by a hundred thousand votes. Even if Sanford had won Chisholm's 61,000 votes, Wallace was the runaway favorite, despite the fact that he was recovering from crippling gunshot wounds after an assassination attempt a month earlier.

Bowles and Taylor were set for a second primary, with Bowles the leader in the first round of voting. Four years earlier, Hawkins had been cheated of his chance to broker black support because the primary contest was settled on the first ballot. This time, however, he was finding it harder to be the man to speak for African Americans. Now, there were others with as much or more influence in political affairs. Operating under new rules, the Democratic Party required a seat at the table for women, blacks, and young voters. Howard Lee had been elected as a party vice chairman.

"I really think we were starting to see more overt process of prominent black leaders growing up," Lee said. "Up to that point, if you watched the process, the leadership acted more out of emotion. Just as when I was growing up in the early days, we gave the Republican Party credit for freeing the slaves. Therefore, my family, and all of us voted for the Republican Party because we wanted to reward them for freeing the slaves. It was emotion. When John Kennedy came in, and all the shifting started to the Democratic Party, it was emotional. We began to see the Republican Party as devil reincarnate.

"[In 1972], we started to see people breaking off into little groups. It was a growing up process. Even I was starting to ask questions. What is in the best long-term interest of the broader community? You also saw prominent blacks beginning to look at the broader voting population and say, this cannot just be black, I cannot just be a black flag bearer. I have got to be much broader than that and rise above that kind of emotionalism."

Lee was one of dozens invited by Julius Chambers to meet at St. Joseph AME church in Durham to consider their next move. Prior to the meeting, small groups had been organized to interview Taylor and Bowles. These delegates were to make their report at the May 20 meeting. Then, on the morning of the meeting, while most of those planning to attend were driving to Durham, Hawkins called the Associated Press in Raleigh and released a statement that declared his support for Taylor. The meeting convened as scheduled — some were handed copies of Hawkins's endorsement statement as they arrived — but any chance at unity had evaporated with Hawkins's unilateral action. Rex Harris, a Fayetteville businessman, was still bitter several days later when he told a reporter, "He wrote us off just like a white writes me off."[43]

Bowles and Taylor scrambled in the following days to make the best of the situation. Some of Hawkins's supporters signed on with Taylor, who had the most to gain from the confusion. While Harris was angry with Hawkins, he gave his support to Taylor. He said Bowles had refused to commit to appointing blacks to high-profile positions in his administration. The Taylor camp approached Howard Lee with an offer to generously fund a get-out-the-vote effort among black voters. Lee's support would have been important. His congressional race was unsuccessful, but he had created a relatively strong organization among black voters from Durham in the Piedmont to Wilson in the eastern part of the state. "I was offered a lot of money to participate in the Taylor campaign. I felt insulted," he recalled. "They were going to give me money to spread around in the black community. I was going to go out and underwrite the GOTV [get out the vote] process; he was in effect buying us off. I wasn't the only one that was going to do that." He endorsed Bowles, and some of his key workers did the same.

The runoff election was Hawkins's last hurrah. Bowles easily overwhelmed Taylor in the June election. Hawkins could not even deliver in his own hometown. Out of eleven precincts in Mecklenburg County with large registration of African American voters, Taylor carried less than half. The election was the end of Hawkins's political career.

Frye had declared himself for Bowles from the beginning. Harris's irritation that Bowles wouldn't commit to specific appointments didn't bother him. "He is the first candidate that I ever gave $100 to," Frye said. "I remember he had something [a fundraising event] way out in the country and I managed to scrape up $100 and that was big money for me. I worked hard for him." Bowles had reciprocated and was one of the early investors in Greensboro National Bank. The two trusted one another. Bowles's commitment to deal fairly was good enough. "It was for me," Frye said, "but it wasn't good enough for a lot of folks. They didn't trust politicians. I thought he would be the best thing for North Carolina."[44]

Bowles approached the fall campaign with supreme confidence. He had the money to buy wave after wave of television advertising that was the foundation of the state's first modern media campaign. His campaign's pollster, Walter DeVries, coordinated television messages with what he was learning from the data accumulated in waves of telephone polling. Bowles distanced himself from the party's presidential candidate, George McGovern, and didn't bother to attend the national convention in Miami. It didn't help. Slowly, and steadily, his lead over Republican James Holshouser began to fade. Holshouser was an experienced state legislator and state party chairman and his youthful, "aw shucks" image provided a striking contrast to Bowles's slick media package.

Holshouser looked like he had just graduated from law school, even though he had finished a year or two after Frye in the early 1960s. He was on a ticket that featured a popular incumbent president, Richard Nixon, and a former television commentator named Jesse Helms who was running for the state's open seat in the U.S. Senate. Helms was a different brand of Republican from Holshouser. He was new to the party, like many of the Democrats who had defected in the 1960s. His reputation was built on ridicule of civil rights and downright racist commentary that had been broadcast nightly on Raleigh's WRAL-TV. Holshouser's base was with the moderates and fiscal conservatives, old-line Republicans in the state's western Piedmont and mountains who fondly remembered the Eisenhower administration.

Though Helms was anathema to blacks, Holshouser began a quiet courtship of African American leaders. Solicitous Republicans were a unique phenomenon for blacks. In 1968, the Hawkins campaign had approached Jim Gardner, the Republican gubernatorial candidate, to talk about an appeal to African Americans. Gardner had refused in rather rough language. Gardner said he'd rather have the support of George Wallace's supporters than an endorsement from Hawkins.[45] By the fall of 1972, Holshouser had a few disaffected Democrats like Rex Harris actively promoting his candidacy. Holshouser extended the hand through one of his white supporters from Fayetteville who approached Harris and told him Holshouser wanted to meet.

Harris said he was just back from an angry confrontation with Bowles, who had refused to commit to appointing blacks to major positions, when Holshouser's emissary David Jones called. "David came to me and said, 'Rex, this governor will appoint African Americans on every board there is. I have talked with him and he wants to meet with you.' So I went and met with him." Harris set up a meeting with others from the Black Caucus where Harris said Holshouser told them, "'Whether I get a black vote or not, I am going to be fair with this politics. I will do just as much if I get only one black vote, and it is yours.' That impressed me. We never did go over anything he would do." In the fall, Holshouser met with black political committees wherever he could, including the group headed by Greensboro's Simkins.[46]

Holshouser later recalled that meeting. "I told them, and I told a group that Rex got together in Fayetteville, that whether I got any black votes or not, I thought that whoever was governor owed it to the state to have an administration in which everybody in the state could look and see some people like themselves."[47]

The fall elections were a disaster for the Democrats. Nixon carried the state, Helms was elected to the Senate, and Holshouser became North Carolina's first Republican governor in the twentieth century. Decades later, Hawkins and Harris were convinced that inroads that Holshouser made among black voters made the difference in the outcome of the election.[48] Returns in black precincts in Charlotte, Hawkins's home territory, didn't show any shift to Republicans, however.[49] Others attributed Bowles's loss to the popularity of Richard Nixon and the failure by the Bowles campaign to reconcile intra-party differences with Democrats who had voted for his opponent in the spring primary.[50]

Holshouser made good on his commitment. It took Governor Scott nearly four years to name an African American to lead a department of state government. He installed James M. Page as head of juvenile corrections in May 1972. Within weeks of taking office, Holshouser appointed Larnie Horton, a black college president, as his assistant for minority affairs and gave him an office near his own. He picked a Durham educator as the state's new commissioner of social services. She became the second highest-ranking woman in state government. Later, Harris would become a member of the state highway board.

In early March, the governor's wife, Pat, was in Greensboro for the opening of the permanent quarters of Greensboro National Bank.

10

Working on the Inside

Early in their marriage, Shirley Frye resolved that her most important job, aside from raising children, was to give complete support to her husband in everything that he did. Over the years, that meant rising at 4 A.M. to prepare breakfast before he headed off to law school and, later, even subordinating her career ambitions to his advancement in political office. In time, however, she succeeded so well as her husband's partner that by the mid–1970s Shirley had created her own record of civic participation.

Governor Bob Scott asked her to help plan the state's new kindergarten program, her presidency of the Greensboro Young Women's Christian Association in 1971 led to membership on the Y's national board of directors, and the city's United Way called on her to chair board committees at the same time she was helping parents of children in the Greensboro public schools navigate the difficult days of school desegregation. In 1973, she received an award for outstanding community service from the city's chamber of commerce.

Shirley's emergence in civic affairs was unlike Henry's historic election to the legislature. She had steadily built a reputation for getting things done with grace, patience, and charm. Her accomplishments in civic life would make her a much sought-after candidate for boards of foundations and educational institutions well beyond the boundaries of Greensboro and one of the most influential women in North Carolina. She even co-chaired the 1988 gubernatorial campaign of Democrat Bob Jordan.

Virtually every assignment she accepted along the way was calibrated by how it would affect her husband, and their family. In 1969, with Henry in Raleigh for legislative sessions six months out of every twenty-four, she set aside her own plans to pursue a doctorate in education in order to be available for their two boys, Henry Jr. and his younger brother, Harlan, especially when family time was in short supply. "The best thing I could do," she said years later, "was be sure our children were developing into the kind of human beings we wanted them to be and in order to do that I needed to be there with them. I told people, 'Somebody had to raise Henry's children.'" In order to make things work, the two constructed a balance in their lives that served both of their interests. "I have been allowed to just be me. Henry has accepted that," she said. "I said, 'OK, let me see what I can do.'"

What she could do with gracious aplomb, especially in the early years, was bridge the racial divide as Greensboro institutions sought to move beyond the past. Shirley knew the hurt of segregation, but, like her husband, she had been raised in the blurry world of rural race relations where contact with whites, rare in urban areas, was a part of daily life. Her family's nearest neighbors were white. Black and white workers shared lunch in the field and drank from the same dipper in the water pail. On schooldays and Sundays, whites and blacks went their own way, but she was a teenager and a student at A&T before she discovered that movie theaters had separate entrances. What she brought with her from her childhood, and her Christian upbringing, was a quality that she cultivated and developed in later years: a firm conviction that people were people. She operated on one basic tenet: "I treat people like I want to be treated."

Shirley pushed at the door whenever she could, beginning in the late 1950s. Scouts in her troop attended integrated activities. A few years later, when her husband was cloistered by the restrictions of his federal job, she was the one who became an officer in the city's most prominent bi-racial group, the Greensboro Community Fellowship. She recruited children for a demonstration pre-school program for white and black children. She volunteered at the YWCA and was invited to join the board of directors. In late 1969, five fellow board members, all of them white, called on her and asked if she would complete the term of a president who was leaving her post early to spend time with a husband entering retirement.

As her civic profile expanded, Shirley's picture began appearing in the local newspapers. On one day, she was with the governor's wife, on another she was welcoming a visitor to the YWCA. As the press discovered the accomplishments of black women and began writing features about them, Shirley was often on a reporter's call list. Some accused her of being an opportunist, and riding her husband's celebrity. Shirley was savvy enough to know that her recognition was due to her race, gender, political position or a combination of all three. "I was used in a lot of things," she said many years later. "I don't mind being used when I know that I am being used. It doesn't bother me to go some place and be the only African American. They had the Sir Walter Cabinet [in Raleigh] and I didn't change my behavior. I don't know how to pretend." But it wasn't about resume building. When the women's auxiliary of the Greensboro Bar invited her to join, after ignoring wives of black lawyers for more than six years after her husband was admitted to membership, she told them she didn't have time for a group that only had a social agenda.[1]

The YWCA job tested her talents, her patience, and her people skills, but a decade of teaching emotionally disturbed children was good preparation for the challenges she found there. She had just returned from the YWCA's national convention in 1970, where eliminating racism was the top agenda item, when she was confronted by two white local board members who told her that merging the programs for whites and blacks was not going to happen in Greensboro. She deftly handled that dustup, only to find, a short time later, that she was being accused of racism by two former white staff members who had been dismissed when their jobs were eliminated. They took their complaints to the newspaper, and a reporter called Shirley for a comment. The reporter closed her conversation with an unprofessional aside that in light of the accusations she'd have to rethink her vote for Henry Frye in the next election. Shirley was mad, hurt, and looking for solace. She called her husband.

"He said, 'If you can't stand the grease get out of the kitchen.' I was so angry — I was so angry with Henry — I didn't know what to do. It caused me to stop crying. I took a shower. I went down to the newspaper office and went to [Editor] Bill Snider's office — walked right past his secretary — and I told him the whole story. He said 'Shirley I will take care of it.'

"I was expecting Henry to solve a problem for me. He gave me the kind of medicine I needed. From that point on nobody has had to fight my battles for me. It was a good lesson. Oftentimes, whether it is your spouse, or someone close to you, who cares for you, tough love is very important. And that is what he gave me."[2]

Staff members from the national YWCA who worked closely with Shirley during the transition took note of her considerable skills. When her presidency ended with the successful opening of a new YWCA facility in downtown Greensboro, she was asked to become a member of the board of directors of the national YWCA. She had thought she was only a nominee, and reasoned that a nobody from Greensboro clearly was not a contender, only to discover there was only one slate of candidates. Her service proved to be a stimulating experience, one heightened by the introduction to scores of women whose politics, backgrounds, and lifestyles were unlike anything she had known in Greensboro. Her mentors on the board were Mrs. Laurance Rockefeller — whose husband was the grandson of the founder of Standard Oil Co. — and Mrs. Rockefeller's sister, Edith Hitchcock. Another fellow board member was Sarah Belk Gambrell of Charlotte, the daughter of Belk Stores founder William Henry Belk. Another's husband would be elected the mayor of Honolulu.

Her years on the board coincided with an era when women were seeking, and gaining, leadership roles in business, the professions, and public life. Shirley became one of the trainers in a YWCA program sponsored by the American Management Association. It was designed to cultivate and assist women seeking to participate in civic affairs. The program sharpened her own skills in working with groups and running meetings. "That is where my M. O. comes from," she said. "I believe in starting on time. If a meeting is scheduled for four o'clock, I start. It was unfair to the others to be sitting in place waiting for the meeting to start." It also introduced her to new experiences, such as one that occurred at a gathering of women in the Midwest. "I was teaching a session on communications and I was talking about looking a person straight in the eye, giving a firm handshake. A tall woman, a Native American, stood up and said, 'That is disrespectful in our culture. You don't look at a person straight in the eye.' It was a learning experience for me because you know mother and daddy always said you look a person straight in the eye. Don't give them any of those flimsy handshakes."

As exciting as YWCA work was, Shirley was anxious and feeling guilty about her service since the Y board meetings were held on weekends. Early on, she and Henry had agreed that Saturdays and Sundays were family time, especially after church when they and the boys talked about the joys and concerns of the previous week over a meal at the International House of Pancakes. "I broke the pact," she said. Henry wasn't pleased with her being away or traveling alone to New York City. She was just as uncomfortable leaving everyone behind. Finally, she told her husband that she didn't sleep well while away and she needed him to accompany her. He brought work along and their anxiety was relieved. "It was a win-win for both of us," she said. "Of course, we always had competent people to keep our children."

In the process, Henry learned something about his wife. "I would make sure I would have Henry waiting [after a meeting]. Most of my life I had been standing around waiting on him so I wanted him to have that experience," she confessed some years later. "So I would be among the last coming out, and I would always say, 'Have you met my husband?' All the other times he was saying, 'Have you met my wife?' He needed to get that kind of experience. He was always the star and he needed to know there were other stars."

Shirley's work at the YWCA expanded from year to year. She chaired the program and budget committee, was elected vice president in 1982, and chaired the national convention in 1985. Her work put her in touch with other outstanding black women from around the country, including Dr. Dorothy Height, president of the National Council of Negro Women for forty years. "She is the only person I know who can sleep during a meeting, wake up, and ask an intelligent question," she said. Mrs. Height knitted a cap for Shirley. In 1984, the YWCA named her Woman of the Year. She received the same honor from the National Council of Negro Women in 1986.

While Shirley's YWCA work carried her throughout the United States, Henry met an exhausting weekly schedule at home. On most weekdays, he began each morning at Greensboro National Bank. He arrived before the doors opened for business, reviewed the transactions from the day before, and usually huddled with the chief operating officer about any pressing matters. He then headed to the eighth floor of the Southeastern Building and the offices of his law firm that in 1972 became Frye, Johnson and Barbee. Pauline Irving, his assistant at his law office, kept his schedule. She made sure he was prepared for the rest of the day.

Henry Frye had visions of the firm developing a substantial personal injury practice, which, he discovered, wasn't enhanced by his legislative service. While visiting in the hospital at one point, a neighbor told him he had planned to ask Frye to handle his injured son's claim against an insurance company, but was sure a busy state representative wouldn't have time for it. In fact, the firm ended up handling a variety of clients. "I was looking for rich corporate clients," he said years later, stifling a laugh, "but I never did get any."

Henry concentrated on civil matters; he was considered the firm's best negotiator. He also developed a clientele among non-profits, and built on his earlier work for churches and groups that were developing low-income housing. Walter Johnson was the firm's litigator. He had begun his career as an assistant district attorney, a first for the county, and he knew his way around the criminal courts. From time to time, both men worked with business clients and assisted in the establishment of a few minority-owned enterprises. One of them, a warehouse business, helped an enterprising African American Greensboro businessman, Ralph Shelton, on his way to financial success.

Ronald Barbee was six to ten years younger than his partners. He began as the utility infielder but, in time, developed his own client list. He also handled the legal work for the bank. Barbee was the top graduate of N.C. Central Law School in 1971 and had accepted a job in the tax division at the U.S. Department of Justice in Washington when Frye asked him to come to Greensboro to talk. Barbee liked what he heard, especially the prospects of making partner within a year. He and his wife cancelled the lease on their apartment in Washington and moved to Greensboro.[3]

Barbee had counted on the senior men as mentors, but learned quickly there was little time for that. He took his oath with eighteen other young lawyers and headed to the courthouse vault to perform searches on property titles, along with more than half of the other neophytes. Nonetheless, he wasn't disappointed with his choice and learned to adapt. One day not long after he arrived, Johnson was delayed out of town and dispatched Barbee to superior court with instructions to get a continuance in a murder trial. Barbee made apologies for his absent partner, and petitioned for more time, but the judge was unmoved. Barbee was ordered to be ready for trial at two o'clock. He hustled to the jail to meet Johnson's client, a man whose freedom now was his responsibility. When the case was called in the afternoon — fortunately at three o'clock or later, rather than two— Barbee succeeded in delaying the trial until the next morning, when Johnson relieved him of temporary duty.

Barbee also accompanied Frye to Salisbury, a thriving mid-sized textile town about fifty miles south of Greensboro, where Frye had developed a portfolio of clients disputing condemnation claims by the city's redevelopment commission. Frye was reluctant to take on business so far away, but he had accepted his first case after a minister pleaded with him to help a church member who claimed she couldn't find satisfactory representation in Salisbury. "It started with this lady who was about eighty-some years old," Frye said years later. "She came out of her house one day and there were these surveyors measuring around her house. She got her shotgun and ran them away. And so they filed condemnation and she said they weren't going to take her house."

Frye was able to forestall outright eviction, aided in part by information forwarded to him by his client's daughter, who was an employee of the U.S. Department of Housing and Urban Development in Washington. When the commission's attorney would cite a provision in the law in aid of the taking, Frye would respond with a reference to regulations that hadn't made it through the bureaucratic pipeline to the local level. "I said, 'Have you read regulation so and so that was revised last week?' He said 'What is that?' He had to contact D.C. to get the regulation. I was ready for him, every time he came along." Frye's client finally agreed to the relocation of her home. "Then the word got around that I was doing a good job and I must have had ten or twelve clients down there. Most of them were interested in the money; the houses they were in were all beat up. I became pretty well known down there as being a great lawyer."[4]

Frye's strength was negotiating settlements. His calm demeanor, serious intent, and attention to detail all came into play. Barbee was impressed with his sense of honor, and eagerness to find a solution that satisfied everyone. "He is very conservative," Barbee said. "He has always been conservative. He would have made a good Republican. He wouldn't make waves. I admired him for the kind of person he was. I never heard him say anything bad about anybody. He is the only lawyer I know that would give money back. He had a lot of common sense."

One of the firm's largest fees during the mid–1970s came out of a case that Frye settled following months of legwork by Barbee, who traveled to Oklahoma, Texas, Colorado, Maryland, and Washington, D.C., to interview witnesses and gather documents. At issue was the distribution of a large estate of a widow in Maryland who had died without a will. Competing sets of heirs claimed a share of an estate fattened by oil wealth. Frye negotiated a settlement and secured a $250,000 fee for the firm, but Barbee wasn't entirely pleased. "I had this case in the bag," he said. "The facts and the law were on my side." The firm's share should have been twice what was paid, he said, because one side had what he believed was a doctored birth certificate. "I think he did it because he saw dollar signs and didn't want to [take a] risk."

Frye took extraordinary steps to avoid controversy, or provide fodder for gossips. The purchase of the Frye's home on Benbow Road was an example. The house belonged to Bishop Wyoming Wells, the pastor who was the first chair of the bank's board of directors who came to admire Frye's private and public success. After his death in 1976, the bishop's widow called Shirley and asked her to come to look at the large, ranch-style home built on a corner lot on Benbow Road. It was "her" home, Mrs. Wells told Shirley, if they wanted it. She said the bishop would be disappointed if it was sold to anyone else.

Henry and Shirley talked about what to do. The house was more spacious than their split level on Drexmore, with plenty of room on a lower level that opened onto a patio in the steeply sloped lot. Shirley liked the generous layout of the rooms. They were large enough to accommodate family gatherings. In addition, Providence Baptist Church was only a block away on Tuscaloosa Street. She and Henry talked about moving out of east Greensboro, into a predominantly white neighborhood where new homes were going up, but the conversation was not a long one. Henry said that he wasn't going to leave the people who had been responsible for his political and professional success. Harlan, their youngest son, was eager for his parents to buy the Wells home. The Benbow address would admit him to Grimsley High School, where most of his buddies from a YMCA basketball league attended.

Family interests came first with Henry and Shirley. Weekends were time together, even to the extreme. One Saturday the four went shopping for a particular style of basketball shoes for the boys. They couldn't be found in Greensboro, so the four drove to Richmond, Virginia, where it was said a store had them in stock. It didn't. After the four-hour drive, and still no shoes, they went on to Washington, D.C., where they finally found the shoes. They broke up the monotony of the return trip by stopping to bowl in one town and play basketball on an empty court in another.[5]

Every Sunday all four were seated on a pew near the front of Providence Baptist Church. Henry Jr. would later fulfill the dream his grandmother had for his father. He would become a preacher, after serving first as a superior court judge. One of young Henry's early appearances in the pulpit was to read a selection of scripture. He had never seen a Bible that had some of the text printed in bold face type. Not knowing any different, he placed special emphasis on them. It got the congregation talking about what a good preacher he would be.

The Fryes decided to buy the house, but only after Henry put his offer at $20,000 above the asking price, because he believed the appraisal was too low. "I said, 'Henry you are crazy,'" recalled Barbee, who did the title work on the transaction. "'Why would you want to do that?' He said he did not want to give the appearance that he had taken advantage of his association with somebody. He bought that house for $90,000. Notwithstanding, some people were saying he had taken advantage of somebody. That really upset me."

The law firm never made wealthy men out of Frye or Johnson or Barbee. "It was successful, by our standards," Frye said. "It was never lucrative, but it afforded us a living and we got to do a lot of things. We were doing community work, Walter, and I and Ron."[6] In 1971, the Greensboro City Council appointed Johnson to the city school board, where he ultimately became chairman. It was a non-partisan job, but he was as steady a Democrat as Frye. Johnson's wife, Yvonne, was one of Shirley's protégés. She was a volunteer with the YWCA and became the first African American member of the Junior League in Greensboro. Years later, she would be elected mayor of Greensboro.

Democratic Party politics was the norm, but the partners and their spouses were in Washington, D.C., on January 20, 1972, for a dinner honoring High Point's Robert J. Brown, who was leaving his post as President Richard Nixon's point man on minority business. The event was billed as a fundraiser for various non-profits, including the Sickle Cell Anemia Fund and the United Negro College Fund, but the political overtones were inevitable. U.S. Commerce Secretary Maurice Stans, the Nixon campaign's chief moneyman, was the emcee. While Sammy Davis, Jr., entertained, Johnson noticed a stir in the crowd. Shortly afterward, the president made a surprise appearance. As the president made his way to the front, he passed by the Frye, Johnson, and Barbee table. "Ron was sitting on the aisle side of table so he got to shake Nixon's hand," Johnson said. Later in the year, Barbee began working with disaffected Democrats on behalf of North Carolina's Republican candidate for governor, Jim Holshouser. "One day, we had an office meeting, and they said it doesn't make any sense for everybody to be Democrat," Barbee recalled. "Somebody's got to be a Republican. They looked at me." In 1976, Holshouser, the state's first Republican governor in the twentieth century, appointed Barbee to the superior court bench. It was the same appointment that Governor Scott had extended to Sammie Chess. Barbee held court for four years and returned to the law firm in 1980.[7]

The law firm was Frye's top priority. The law was what he had trained for and the firm provided the livelihood that sustained his family. Nonetheless, Greensboro National Bank was a constant companion and occupied his attention during the early years of steady but slow growth. At the end of the first year, deposits had grown to about $3 million, and the bank showed a profit at the end of 1972. The return was modest—four cents per share—and could have easily been wiped out by the default of a couple of car loans, but the bank was making a difference. "Several hundred black men and women, for the first time in their lives, now own stock in a commercial bank," Frye said in early 1973. "Now they have a stake in the economy, in a substantial way that has direct meaning to them."[8]

Greensboro National's new building opened on the last day of February in 1973, as a celebration of achievement for African Americans, especially those who shared A&T as their alma mater. The tellers for the city's only black-owned bank moved from the trailers standing in a graveled lot into a stylish, modern building fashioned out of cast stone that was designed by W. Edward Jenkins, a graduate of A&T. He was one of the bank's directors and known for buildings on A&T and Bennett campuses. The day's celebrated speaker was another A&T man, an Air Force ROTC graduate like Frye. Just sixteen days earlier, Major Norman A. McDaniel had arrived in the United States after spending six years in a Vietnamese prison. He stood before the crowd gathered in front of the building, seeming a bit dazed by the sights and sounds. He looked out on a streetscape reconfigured by urban renewal since he had left the city in 1959 and invoked God's blessing on all. "Your faces are beautiful. Your smiles are wonderful," he said. The upcoming issue of *Time* magazine would describe McDaniel as a "Gibraltar of Guts" who had worked with other prisoners in the "Hanoi Hilton" to construct a Bible from memory.[9]

Frye arranged McDaniel's appearance through his college buddy, David McElveen, who was then an air force colonel with his own Viet Nam record. It was quite a coup, one that the city's leaders almost pulled out from under Frye. McDaniel spent more time touring Greensboro with the mayor and speaking to the chamber of commerce than he did at the bank.

Pat Holshouser, the governor's wife, was another guest of honor; she cut the ribbon opening the new building. She knew both of the Fryes, especially Shirley. Their husbands both stayed at the Raleigh Hilton during the legislative session and their rooms were directly across from one another on the first floor. Frye's overlooked the hotel pool, so Pat Holshouser and Shirley Frye could sit in the cool of the hotel room while they kept an eye on their children as they played in the water. The governor was barely six weeks into his term and had his hands full with a testy legislature filled with Democrats, virtually all of whom seemed intent on making him uncomfortable. Frye liked Holshouser, and had sent him a note after the election that wished him well, but noted, "I especially disliked your busing ad." Holshouser didn't take it personally and asked his wife to attend the ceremonies since he was tied up in Raleigh. Years later, the former governor said, "This is one where you have known somebody, and you knew they were good people. It was a pretty bold step. It is the kind of thing that you have a duty to yourself, to show the flag, and say that this is a good thing."[10]

Indeed, Frye believed that simply getting the bank up and running was an affirmation of the future for African Americans. "I was surprised at some of the people who bought shares in the bank who really didn't know anything about banking and who wanted to be part of something progressive," Frye said. "That was one of the things that impressed me. They were ordinary folks who would never invest in anything, but they wanted to be a part of it."[11]

Frye, his board of directors, and his investors were counting on strong community support and no small amount of black pride to move Greensboro National forward. Robert Brown's consulting firm in High Point offered a proposal for advertising and promotion for the move to the new building that read: "The idea of black self-determination and economic community control appeals to all segments of the black community. The black bank, being the primary agent of self-determination and economic community control, should have an overall theme that encompasses self-determination, economic community control and strong banking services."[12]

Greensboro National's annual reports showed steady progress over the next few years. Deposits doubled to near $6 million by 1976 and were almost at $9.5 million by 1978, when the bank posted a profit of $1.02 a share and declared a dividend of 30 cents a share, up from the quarter a share paid the year before. The progress lagged behind Frye's ambitions. Unfortunately, a local stand for the advancement of black economic progress was lost on many potential customers in east Greensboro.

Each increase was hard won. "We tried to take everybody as a customer," Frye said later. "Anybody who walked in for an account, if they had ten dollars we opened an account. Other banks required a little more than that." Everyman banking raised Greensboro National's costs, while larger banks picked off the fatter customers and even made a run at some of Greensboro National's directors. "They got ten, twelve, or fifteen [customers] who were making good money and they said, 'What are you getting at your present bank? We can do better than that. And if you need money, we can lend you a million dollars if you need it.'"

Indeed, the bank's modest size was a problem. Greensboro National couldn't compete with the lending capacity of Wachovia, NCNB, or First Union, the leading banks on Elm Street, whose marketing was becoming more inclusive. Regulators monitored loan agreements and called Frye and the loan committee on some of their decisions. Conservative lending, and a cap on what they could put out to any one borrower, discouraged large customers from doing business with Greensboro National. As result, the bank handled a lot of smaller accounts with customers demanding the same attention as large depositors. "It is really rough," Frye said, "when you are trying to do something on a small scale and you are having to do everything that the big ones have to do on the big scale. People coming in and depositing $500 a month and thinking they have got the big account."[13]

Frye faced one frustration after another. The board asked A&T Chancellor Dr. Lewis Dowdy to become a director in 1973, only to have to accept his resignation a year later when the UNC General Administration ruled

A&T's bank account at Greensboro National created a conflict of interest. "They said, either he has to go or we couldn't have the account," Frye said. Meanwhile, Dowdy's bosses allowed his peers at other institutions to enjoy similar appointments at larger banks because they were members of "advisory boards" that didn't set policy. On another occasion, Frye got word from the state treasurer's office that money deposited by a paving contractor that was required to be set aside until a job was complete could not remain at Greensboro National because the bank didn't have a trust department. Frye said he called state Treasurer Harlan Boyles and told him: "You don't need trust departments for this kind of account. 'Henry,' he said, 'you know I agree with you and I'll change it.' If I had not been a lawyer I probably wouldn't have known the difference between a trust and escrow account."

Frye was especially disappointed that many of those he had counted on as steady customers— politically and socially aware academics from the A&T community—could not be persuaded to leave the major banks and move to Greensboro National. "They had their own accounts at other banks and they were treating them well. Why move? I thought that our being right here that they'd say, 'Oh, yeh, let's go on over there.'" The bank had about a fourth of the available business, by Frye's rough estimate.

The suspicious nature of many in the east Greensboro community was a persistent problem, said Robert Chiles, who joined the bank as vice president and chief operating officer in 1978. "The most curious reason that I got from many professionals, doctors and lawyers, people who had encouraged Henry and his group to start this thing, was that they were afraid that our employees would see their business and talk about their business outside of the bank. I would say, 'If you are able to prove to me that any employee in this bank would go out and talk about your business, there is no question that proof of that would mean they would be fired.' We ran a professional, confidential bank just as any other bank."[14]

The problems faced by Greensboro National weren't limited to east Greensboro. When Nathan Garrett opened his accounting practice in the 1960s in Durham, where black businesses were more robust and longstanding, he ran into the same attitude there. "There weren't a lot of black professionals. I am a CPA and if I am at a party and [a client] says, 'I made so much money last year. Ask Nate.' Nate would not say a damn word. That is not something you can do as a professional. I don't think a lot of people in the black community had had experience with true professionals."[15]

Chiles joined the bank nine years after Greensboro National had opened for business, as the board of directors made changes in management. Earlier, they had asked Frye to consider devoting full time to the bank operations after the departure of Chiles' predecessor, William Pickens. Frye said he would give it a try but quickly discovered that he simply wasn't cut out to be a banker. "I went down there and I stayed two or three days and I said I am not going to be happy doing this. It is just too much of a headache to spend my life down here doing something I don't like doing. I enjoy practicing law," he said. "I didn't know the difference between those things you had to look at and those you didn't. I didn't know that. I might have had a heart attack." Frye called Chiles and hired him to run the bank.

Aside from cultural problems, Greensboro National's slow growth may have been a result of the changes taking place in east Greensboro. The bank's location at the edge of downtown, in an area marked for urban renewal, looked promising in the years when city planners were envisioning an overhaul of blighted areas, replacing dilapidated buildings and aging commercial areas with new businesses. In 1971, when the bank was trying to establish itself in the community, the city had demolished about a thousand homes and businesses in the Warnersville neighborhood, just south of downtown, and was clearing a 108-acre area near Bennett College, which was virtually at the bank's front door. The overhaul of East Market Street had already removed buildings that had once been the home to seventy black-owned businesses. In its place was a huge postal facility that covered several acres. Planners offered designs of what these urban renewal areas could become, and, in fact, a few other professional offices had opened in the vicinity of the bank's building. J. Kenneth Lee's American Federal Savings and Loan was just across the street along with some offices for doctors. East Market Street would never regain its earlier standing as a commercial center, however, and retail businesses would struggle to get a toehold for the next forty years.[16]

The city's entire central business district was suffering from the flight of retail businesses to the suburbs. This relocation began in the mid–1960s and accelerated in the years that followed. City leaders seemed helpless to do anything about it. "I think we have come to the point that if downtown Greensboro is going to make it, we're going to have to start doing it pretty quick," Mayor Jim Melvin said in 1971.[17] Melvin led the city council into innovative efforts to overhaul Elm Street, including the creation of an urban mall, but nothing seemed to work. Shoppers were in love with the relative convenience of shopping malls, free parking, and the freshness of new stores. Once the major department chains closed their downtown stores, the smaller shops and stores along Elm Street eventually disappeared. By the mid– to late–1970s, Elm Street was virtually empty. A few black-owned clothing stores and wig shops arrived to fill the void, but the makeshift signage and ethnic merchandise only emphasized the transition that had taken place.

Greensboro was like cities elsewhere in North Carolina and across the nation; it was struggling to fit a tired model of commerce into a new era where many citizens considered the city center to be a relic of the past. The change in business coincided with rising pressure from African Americans for a greater voice in local affairs. Their answer was the creation of districts, or wards, for municipal elections where voters in a particular area could focus their voting power. As ward elections came to Raleigh and Charlotte, the Greensboro white establishment held on to its at-large system and would be the last major municipality to overhaul its electoral process.

Henry Frye had participated in the ward debate in the early years, and during his first term had offered some legislative measures in an effort to move along the process of change. There was a limit to what he could do, however, and still respond to issues that required his attention in Raleigh. As the campaign for a change in Greensboro's election process progressed, he left the issue to George Simkins and others back home and worked where he thought he could do the most good.

By the mid–1970s, the number of blacks in the General Assembly had grown from two to five. Representative Mickey Michaux, Jr., of Durham was elected in 1973 and Senators Fred Alexander of Charlotte and John W. Winters of Raleigh were seated in 1975, when a fourth black house member, Richard Erwin of Winston-Salem, was sworn in. Frye remained the elder statesman, but not in any formal organization. Even after Erwin joined the "black caucus," as it were, they only had four out of the 120 votes in the house. They played on their own individual skills to get things done. "When there were three of us, we tried to run a game on folks in the legislature," recalled Michaux. "Joy Johnson was the firebrand; he was a preacher. I was a rebel, and Henry was the conciliator. We hit that thing from those three areas and got to be right successful."[18]

In the 1973 session they succeeded in winning almost unanimous support for a bill that appropriated a million dollars for research and treatment of sickle cell anemia, an inherited condition that afflicts non-whites, but then they ran into trouble from an unexpected quarter. The bill sailed through the house, with endorsements from state health officials, and was in a senate committee when Michaux got a call from the management of North Carolina Mutual Life Insurance Company in Durham. North Carolina Mutual's executives were offended that they had not been allowed to be heard on a provision that protected from discrimination those who carried the sickle cell genes. Michaux said he was told, "If we had known about it we would have been over there and opposed it." Michaux had the bill recalled, hearings were scheduled in the house, and then it was approved again with a larger majority than before.

They got nowhere with a controversial measure that would have expanded the legal rights of renters in dealing with landlords. At the time, the relationship was governed by English common law, which was tilted in favor of property owners. Tenants faced evictions if they complained about unsafe conditions and virtually had no standing in court to force landlords to provide clean, decent housing. The standard was *caveat emptor*, or "buyer beware," said Ted Fillette, the head of the Legal Aid office in Charlotte, which had filed a number of lawsuits in aid of renters.[19]

The issue was freighted with seething resentment among the poor, especially African Americans, whose housing remained in poor repair while they had little or no legal standing to force landlords to make improvements. In 1973, Frye sponsored a comprehensive landlord-tenant bill to establish responsibilities of landlords and provide legal remedies for proper maintenance of rental housing. The bill did not reach the floor until March of the following year as part an extended session that was prompted by the Democratic majority to keep a close watch on the state's first Republican governor. During the interim, the bill had been amended and massaged in long committee sessions. On March 12, it got to the floor, where it was whittled down to nothing by opponents, who then killed it.

Some of the stiffest opposition arose from legislators representing farming interests in lightly populated counties, many of which did not have even basic building codes or housing ordinances that were becoming common in major cities. These areas operated on what Frye called a version of old English law founded in the good nature of the landlord. "Our landlord-tenant law is still feudalism from England," Frye recalled. "Basically the landlord is in control. That was it. If you call [a problem] to his attention, he'll take care of it. They said, "You don't need [this law].""[20]

After the loss in 1974, the three black members of the house returned in the 1975 session and teamed up with legislators from urban areas, including Representatives Louise Brennan from Charlotte and Wade Smith, a Raleigh trial lawyer, on a bill that was less comprehensive but which struck at the heart of the issue. Their bill established an implied warranty by landlords that their property was habitable and offered protection from eviction to tenants who complained about unsafe or uninhabitable housing. After several hours of debate, this bill, too, failed to gain a majority of votes.

Michaux and Frye were standing just outside the house chamber after they had watched opponents dismantle their bill that had taken more than a year of work. "I just wish some of these guys in there could live in one of these homes," Michaux told Frye. Unlike Frye, who buried his emotions, Michaux was visibly angry. Was the bill "too liberal," a reporter asked him? "Yes, I think that's probably it." Michaux added, "Yeh, it's too liberal a piece of legislation because it promotes fairness and decency. It would prevent you from letting people live in hovels."[21]

Frye took up the matter again in the 1977 session at the request of Fillette, who provided research and backup. Fillette said, some years later, "The good thing about Henry was that he was smart and he was kind and he was fairly well-respected and he had been appointed chairman of the judiciary committee by Carl Stewart, the speaker of the house. I think he realized that it was very difficult. He knew that two-thirds of the people in the legislature were probably landlords, but he realized that this was probably the single most important thing for African-American families in the state that he could deal with."

That session was loaded with hot topics. Ratification of the Equal Rights Amendment was on the table and this mobilized women's groups at the local level. "Many of those groups wanted to get the Landlord-Tenant Bill passed," Fillette recalled, "because most of the tenants that were low-income were female. So we would end up getting a lot of support from the political caucuses at the county level." He said Frye and others also found some leverage in a statewide mixed drinks law. When the trading was done, the bill emerged from the house by a slim margin. It appeared dead in the senate, said Fillette, until Lieutenant Governor Jimmy Green was visited by a lobbyist for the American Association of Retired People. "She came out and said, 'He's going to get the bill out.' I said, 'How in the world is he going to get the bill out?' She says, 'Well, I had to explain to Mr. Green that if he didn't get the bill out, I was going to have to go on my TV program this Sunday and explain how he didn't care about the housing for any of the elderly people in this state.' The bill came out of the committee the next day and it passed. It was truly amazing." The Residential Agreements Act became law.

The black legislators didn't move in lockstep. In the closing days of the extended session in 1974, Joy Johnson had urged Frye to join him in supporting Representative Jimmy Green, a conservative easterner, for speaker of the house in the 1975 session. Johnson lived near Green's home county of Bladen and had endorsed him in his race against Representative Carl Stewart, a progressive Democrat from Gaston County near Charlotte. Frye favored Stewart over Green and remained faithful to his commitment. When Green was elected speaker and he organized the committees for the 1975 session, it was Johnson who got the chairmanship, not Frye. Stewart was elected speaker for the 1977 and 1979 sessions, the first to serve to successive terms, and he named Frye chairman of one of the house judiciary committees, a prime appointment.

Michaux liked to cause a stir. He came from a privileged background and had spent his final year of high school at Charlotte Hawkins Brown's Palmer Institute, where he saw her correct Governor Gregg Cherry over his pronunciation of the word Negro. "She stopped him in the middle of a speech. She said, Governor, no disrespect, but she hit him on the knee. What did I just hit? You hit my knee. What does a tree do to get that tall? Can you put the two of them together? Your knee, and grow. And you have got it right. And he did." One of his classmates was Martin Luther King's brother, and he had brought the Reverend King to speak in Durham just before King became a national figure. "It was right at the end of the Montgomery bus boycott. He loved my mother's cooking. He would put his feet under that table and chow down."

Like Frye, Michaux had ended up on the wrong side in the speaker's election and Green took him off the appropriations committee and gave him a seat on finance and the house manufacturing and labor committee. In a bootless gesture, designed to pull the lion's tail, he introduced a bill repealing the state's right-to-work law, a measure held dear by employers who saw it was a deterrent to unions. "He knew I was going to do it," Michaux said. "And he loaded that [committee] with everybody who could call you everything but a child of God. I just accepted it and went on."

Michaux said, "We were called 'super niggers' by the members. You just don't get elected to legislature; you have to have something up here. And they believed black folks just didn't have it up there. I heard the term. They'd get in their cups and start talking and you'd overhear them in their conversation. It was not used in the derogatory sense. They respected the fact that we were there and able to get things done."

Frye carefully picked issues that would occupy his time and attention. In 1971, he had made a frontal assault on the death penalty. He worked his bill for abolition of capital punishment as hard as he had his bill banning the literacy test two years earlier. His bill would have substituted life in prison for those convicted of first-degree murder, first-degree burglary, arson, or rape in cases where a jury doesn't recommend mercy. At the time, eleven men and one woman — a seventeen year old when she killed a Rocky Mount grocer — were on death row. Frye had the support of Governor Scott, former governor Terry Sanford (who was in office at the time of the last execution in 1961), the lieutenant governor, the state attorney general, the state Jaycees, and the North Carolina Council of Churches.

Odds of passage remained long. Similar bills had failed before Frye got to the General Assembly and his efforts in 1969 had been in vain. Nonetheless, he was optimistic as he headed into the 1971 session. He didn't do any better than those who had preceded him, however. His colleague Joy Johnson's heated rhetoric — he tied the death penalty to victims of poverty and racism — angered conservatives, but they weren't going to vote for the bill anyway. Frye's bill failed, 65 to 46.[22]

The loss hurt. "A few people who told me they would vote for the bill ended up voting the other way," Frye told a reporter who stopped by his office after the session. "What really made the difference were those who told me they were undecided. With about two exceptions, every one of them ended up voting against it." While he talked, a fellow member stopped by to say, "You accomplished a lot even though you lost. Really you did." Asked what he accomplished, Frye told the reporter, "I don't know. Why don't you go ask him that question?" He made other attempts to remove the death penalty; all failed.

Frye's victories more often came in the negotiations that took place off the house floor, sitting in a committee room where the decisions were made. That was where Frye could be most effective. His one vote in an evenly divided committee could count for far more than the ones he cast on the floor. Moreover, none of the white legislators sitting with him came to the task with the same agenda born from experiences of being left on the outside looking in. This was particularly true as the state wrestled with reorganization of higher education in 1971.

Frye was a member of the house committee on higher education. His paramount concern was insuring representation of African Americans on a new governing board that would run all of the state institutions. Greensboro was home to two state universities, A&T and the University of North Carolina at Greensboro. During his years in Raleigh, Frye focused his attention on how historically black institutions like A&T would fare. He reasoned that UNCG with its broad constituency of graduates had many champions, but black institutions had never had a voice or a seat at the table when plans were being made on their behalf. He had seen that at North Carolina Central's law school, and on the A&T campus, whose administrators were still treated like step-children by some in the General Assembly.

The historically black campuses had only recently escaped total control by the white establishment. The chair of A&T's board of trustees was a white man until Governor Bob Scott named John S. Stewart of Durham to the job in 1969. Frye was concerned that those constructing a new governing board had made no provision for black representation, which threatened to perpetuate the imbalance. As the bill was going into its final form, Frye held out for a guarantee that blacks would be appointed to seven seats on the 32-member board. Some of those he considered legislative allies tried to talk him out of his position, arguing that any guarantee of seats could turn into a limit. "They were saying, 'Let's not put that in there and work to see that that will happen.' I said, 'I can't count on that.' Back then, you had better put something in there." The final bill not only guaranteed representation on the governing board for African Americans, but also for women and Republicans.

Frye played a similar role two years later when the legislature was considering the creation of a four-year medical school for East Carolina University in Greenville. He rejected entreaties from the university administration in Chapel Hill, which opposed building a second medical school in the state, and supported funding for the medical school after supporters agreed to make special efforts to recruit African American students. Thirty years later, Frye was recognized by the Old North State Medical Society for his efforts, which the society said helped bring more black doctors to eastern North Carolina.

The creation of the consolidated university system was just the beginning. Larger threats to A&T's future loomed in the mid–1970s as the UNC general administration engaged in a long-running battle with the U.S. Department of Health, Education and Welfare over the desegregation of the state system. The greatest fear of the five historically black institutions was that their interests would be ignored, and the schools that had given hope and opportunity to many young African Americans like Henry and Shirley Frye would eventually be absorbed into the white institutions. One of Henry and Shirley's classmates, Velma Speight-Buford, was the president of the A&T alumni, and she attended a meeting where she heard UNC President William Friday raise that possibility. "He said, 'We may not be able to keep all five,'" Buford later recalled. "I said, 'Dr. Friday, my name is Velma Speight. I represent A&T. You must be talking about the other four because we will be here."[23]

There were also recurring reports of a possible merger of A&T with UNCG. The two campuses were a five-minute drive from one another, with one on the west side of the downtown and the other to the east, and they shared many of the same courses, including specialized schools for training nurses. Frye and others believed that should a merger come, then A&T would suffer in much the same way that black elementary and secondary schools had during the desegregation of other public schools. They would be closed and any semblance of black educational traditions would be gone. "There were statements to the effect to close a lot of schools and at the top of the list were the black schools," Frye said. "We didn't want that. We felt that we would get the short end of the stick."[24]

As was his style, Frye did not take a lead role in the fight. He remained close to all sides in an ongoing legal battle that would last nearly a decade. He met regularly with a group called the N.C. Alumni and Friends Coalition, which was organized to promote the interest of the black schools. A&T, the largest of these schools, took a commanding role, with Speight-Buford at the forefront. She had lost none of the fire and spirit she had exhibited when she was an undergraduate with the Fryes. Frye also remained in touch with Julius Chambers, who was one of the original members of the university's board of governors. Chambers resigned after he was elected president of the NAACP Legal Defense and Education Fund, which had brought suit to force HEW action against the university system.

Frye used what leverage he could apply in the General Assembly, where he and Michaux brought pressure on the administration at every opportunity. Their goal was to not only maintain the black schools, but to increase funding and make them attractive institutions to whites as well as blacks. "We had to fight pretty hard to insure that historically black schools got what they needed," Frye said. "We fought for all of them."

On April 4, 1979, Frye introduced a resolution that called for a state investment of $30 million in the historically black schools. "I think it would be a sign to HEW that the state is committed to bringing these schools up to the others (the 11 white universities)," Frye told a reporter. Before the month was out, the board of governors approved spending $40 million to upgrade the historically black schools.[25]

Frye and his colleagues in the General Assembly, and the coalition of alumni, could argue for their schools in ways that the appointed chancellors could not. They were bold, outspoken, and aggressive, traits that were just not in the job description of the African Americans appointed to head these institutions, such as A&T's Dr. Lewis Dowdy. "You didn't [speak out] and you always turned some money back," Speight-Buford said, referring to earlier years when chancellors enhanced their standing by scrimping on programs so they could prove their good stewardship. "The A&T alumni got named as being radicals. We were saying we don't have enough money to run institution, why are we going to send some back? We nearly killed Dr. Dowdy. Our plans were more ambitious. We were asking for, I guess you could say, the world. Why not? We wanted all of the programs that all of the other schools had. We were not astute enough at that time to say, if we want this, maybe you ought to drop this. We wanted to keep everything. We didn't want to lose anything.

"We gained the respect of the entire system, the legislature, and we got programs that we don't believe we would have ever had," she said. "We believe we are responsible for A&T beginning to have Ph.D. programs. We were responsible for broadening the scope of A&T."

Frye's role was important, Speight-Buford said. "In his own way, in his unassuming way, he [has] a way of getting to people, he did that very effectively. He will be sitting down with you, asking you questions, about something totally different from what he wants to talk to you about. He wants to find out where your head is. If your head is in the right place, he is going to come back to you and talk to you about what he wanted to talk to you before. I am not a diplomat. He is a diplomat in a sense that he reads people well. He always knows when it is time to strike. That is a skill that a lot of people don't have."

Moments of high legislative drama were separated by long periods of numbing tedium. Frye was attentive to his duties and was in his seat during the daily sessions. His colleagues came to depend on Frye to relieve their boredom with his extemporaneous bits of rhyme and poetry. When N.C. State University basketball All-American David Thompson visited the house chamber in 1973, Frye fashioned a piece of rhyme that closed: "I know that others counseled him well/and his choice of schools was free/but I wish that had been real smart/and gone to A&T."

Two years later, in 1975, he and other supporters of the Equal Rights Amendment lost for the second time, in part because of members who had promised to support the bill changed their minds by the time the roll was called. Members of the senate sent roses to the house, in a gesture of support to opponents. Frye couldn't pass up the moment and wrote that the roses "were funny and sweet/but to the losers who went down to defeat/it was not so funny coming twice in a row/with would-be supporters ending up voting 'No!'"

The political landscape was changing in the late 1970s, especially for African Americans. James B. Hunt, elected governor in 1976, included African Americans in his administration like no other Democrat before him. Former Chapel Hill Mayor Howard Lee was appointed to a cabinet post and the governor picked Ben Ruffin, who had led civil rights demonstrations in Durham in the 1960s, as an advisor in his office. Hunt also appointed blacks to the superior court, as Scott and Holshouser had done, and named Charles Becton, a member of the Chambers law firm in Charlotte, to the state court of appeals. Frye's law partner, Walter Johnson, left Greensboro to become chairman of the state parole board.

Frye had been in the state house for a decade by the time the 1979 session came to a close. Voters were likely to continue electing him to the job — he regularly led the ticket — but he was beginning to tire of the job. He said he had become "paranoid" and had begun to wonder if those who asked for his attention really had something else in mind. He had gone about as far as he could in the house, at least for the time being. His consideration of the speaker's job was fleeting. (The house wouldn't elect an African American as speaker until 1991.) If he was to run for higher office, it would be for governor or lieutenant governor, but that seemed distant, if not remote. In order to find a new challenge, and a new environment, Frye opted to run for the state senate in 1980, rather than return to the house.

For the first time in many years, Frye did not lead the ticket. A Republican, Walter Cockerham, got 2,600 more votes than he did. Some of that margin came from black voters who now received sample ballots from competing black organizations in Greensboro. One list was produced by the NAACP and the Greensboro Citizens Association, which were run by George Simkins and the old-line black political leadership. The new Progressive Committee, an upstart organization run by Herman Gist, wasn't the first to challenge Simkins's group, but it was one of the most aggressive and public. Gist came from an old Greensboro family which had once run the Magnolia Hotel, a popular spot in the days of segregated accommodations for African American musicians when they booked dances or performances at local nightspots.

While Simkins had endorsed Republicans in the past, Gist put more of them on his ballot. He told a reporter they were more "accessible" than their white competitors. Cockerham got the nod from the Progressive Committee, but not from Simkins's group.[26]

Cockerham was a product of the new Republican Party that was influenced less by the moderates who had helped elected James E. Holshouser and more by the conservatives who had returned Jesse Helms to the U.S. Senate in 1978. Two years later, Helms's candidate for president, Ronald Reagan, easily carried the state over incumbent Jimmy Carter, who had won North Carolina's electoral votes in 1976. No Democratic presidential candidate would again carry North Carolina until 2008. The Helms political organization also prevailed in the U.S. Senate race. Incumbent Robert Morgan, elected in the wake of Watergate in 1974, was turned out and replaced by John East, a professor from East Carolina University in Greenville. Closer to home, Henry Frye's personal hero, Richardson Preyer of Greensboro, lost re-election to the U.S. House to another conservative Republican, businessman Gene Johnston.

Frye returned to Raleigh as a state senator just as Hunt took the oath as the first governor in state history to be elected to a second term. Hunt had won handily over his Republican opponent, I. Beverly Lake, Jr., a former Democrat from Raleigh who had recently ended a term in the state senate. Lake's campaign was run by the Helms political organization, but the national issues that had aroused voters to support Jesse Helms didn't benefit Lake. The contest never developed into a close race. Hunt won going away.

Frye's principal contact in the governor's office was Ben Ruffin. He had come up through the civil rights movement, had led street marches and worked as a community organizer in Durham. He now appeared smartly dressed in coat and tie but he approached his role with a different and more aggressive spirit than John R. Larkins, who had helped Hunt for a time before retiring from state government.

Frye was as busy as ever. The bank occupied his time as he looked for ways to broaden its base and boost its growth. New directors were added, including Alex Spears, who was white and ran Lorillard Tobacco Company, whose plant was on Greensboro's east side. Frye said he brought more discipline and focused energy to the bank's operations, even though Spears's pointed questions at board meetings would make Frye uncomfortable. "I had the highest respect for him," Frye said. "He said we needed a planning session and he was in charge. He embarrassed me almost in asking so many questions. What do you want the bank to be? Do you want to do this? Do you want to do that? I almost got mad with him he asked me so many questions in front of everybody. He was just a valuable person."[27]

Frye turned over the presidency of the bank to Chiles in 1981 as his own state responsibilities were increasing. Near the end of the 1981 legislative session, Hunt appointed Frye to the state Advisory Budget Commission, a powerful board that had never before had an African American as a member. Greensboro's leadership spoke to Frye's standing at home by including him on a list of those who make things happen. A *Greensboro Daily News* survey ranked Frye in the top ten of "Who Runs Greensboro," right behind Roger Soles, the chairman and CEO of Jefferson-Pilot Corporation.[28]

Service in the state senate did not deliver the satisfaction that Frye had hoped. He was impatient with the upper chamber's clubby nature and missed the rough and tumble of the floor debate that had been part of his experience in the house. After one term, he had decided to leave the legislature and tend to his affairs in Greensboro. The bank needed attention; an expansion to a branch office was not going as planned. His law firm also could stand some work. His old friend Thomas Ross, a superior court judge and active Democrat, also was tugging at his sleeve to run for Congress and retake the seat the party had lost to Republican Gene Johnston in 1980.

"I decided to go home and stay home. I wanted to practice law, build up my law firm, and, frankly make money and get myself in decent financial condition," Frye said. "I wanted to pay off my credit cards, so if I decided to run for something I would not have to depend on the campaign to pay my living expenses. I was hoping that the opportunity to do something else didn't come up before I got [too old]." Frye sat out the 1982 election. It was the first time in sixteen years that his name wasn't on the ballot.[29]

"Doing something else," as Frye described it, included a statewide race, possibly for governor. Perhaps not in 1984, when Hunt would leave office, but later. In the meantime, he considered running for a council of state position. The office of secretary of state looked good. Frye was in his early fifties, and even if he waited until 1988 or even 1992, he would not have been too old. Another option was presented, tentatively, by Governor Hunt. In the middle of 1982, Hunt talked to Frye about a seat on the state supreme court when he called to tell Frye that he was appointing appeals court Judge Harry Martin of Asheville to an open seat. Hunt made no promises about the future; the purpose of the call was to let Frye know his name was on his list if another vacancy occurred.

In August 1982, the N.C. Association of Minority Public Officials, the group that Frye had helped organize a decade earlier, rented the Raleigh Civic Center for a luncheon to honor Frye. Eight hundred people turned out. It was part tribute, part political rally, and part revival meeting. The four-hour event opened with the African American anthem hymn, James Weldon Johnson's "Lift Every Voice and Sing." The crowd included party leaders, educators, legislators, and African Americans in business, religion, and the law. The governor introduced Frye and teased him about sizing up the mansion during a recent visit for a formal reception. Frye was forthright about his

Black elected officials from across the state turned out in 1982 to honor Senator Henry Frye. Seated on the dais with him was Governor Jim Hunt. Another attendee was H. M. "Mickey" Michaux of Durham (middle), who was in the state house with Frye in the early 1970s and later served as U.S. attorney in the district where Frye broke the color line in 1963 (courtesy Frye family).

plans. He might seek statewide office some time later. For the time being, he said, he told the black elected officials, whose numbers had swollen considerably since the early days a dozen years earlier, "Will North Carolina move forward or backward in the years to come? The answer, folks, is in your hands."

When asked, Frye was coy about a possible appointment to the supreme court, which was being talked about in Raleigh. By 1980, African Americans had made gains elsewhere in government, but the supreme court remained the domain of whites. Ruffin was pushing from inside the governor's office to change that. In early January 1983, Ruffin called Frye to tell him another vacancy might be coming on the supreme court. "When the governor calls," Frye said Ruffin told him, "'You have got to accept it.' He said, 'You are the person to get it. Now, don't be talking about you don't want to do it, you have to go practice law or you have whatever.'" It was 1962 and John Wheeler all over again. Earlier he had turned down a seat on the state court of appeals when his name showed up on Hunt's short list. Ruffin wasn't going to lose this opportunity and pressed Frye hard for a solid answer. "He kept trying to get me to commit. I said, well I'd give it serious…. He said, 'Now, Henry, I ain't talking about no serious thought.' That was the way Ben Ruffin was."[30]

Frye was truly conflicted. He had already told Ruffin he wasn't interested in appointment to the trial bench, or even to the state court of appeals. However, the supreme court was another matter. There had never been an African American on the state's highest court.

Hunt's call came in late January 1983. He offered the appointment to Frye and asked for an answer by breakfast the next morning. Frye polled his family. All urged him to take it, but he had questions. The money wasn't all that attractive — an associate justice was paid $57,000 at the time — and he would have to mount a statewide campaign for a full term in less than two years. The opportunity to become the state's first African American justice was just too great to ignore. "I really had no interest in being on the supreme court," he said, "but it was sort of like the U.S. attorney situation. It was the kind of thing that you just couldn't turn down."

Frye called the governor the next morning and told him he would accept. Hunt's announcement that Frye would be joining the court on February 3, 1983, came later in the day.

11

The Court

On February 3, 1983, Henry E. Frye took the oath of office and began his service as the first African American associate justice of the N.C. Supreme Court. The ceremony was held in the wood-paneled courtroom beneath the portraits of former chief justices, including the commanding full-length image of Thomas Ruffin, a nineteenth-century jurist whom Harvard Law Dean Roscoe Pound called one of the ten greatest jurists in American history. In 1829, Ruffin also wrote the opinion in *North Carolina v. Mann*, which established the absolute right of a master over a slave.[1]

Frye arrived that morning with a host of friends and family members, including his mother, Pearl, who was a bit dizzy over the high honor that had come to her family. On hand to give the invocation was the Reverend Howard A. Chubbs, the family's pastor from Providence Baptist Church. Shirley Frye held three Bibles upon which her husband rested his left hand as he raised his right to take the oath from Chief Justice Joseph Branch. Governor James B. Hunt attended the ceremony, as did the rest of official Raleigh. Court Clerk Gregory Wallace said the number packed into the hall was comparable to the turnout eight years earlier when Susie Sharp took her oath as the state's first female chief justice.[2]

Attorney General Rufus Edmisten introduced Frye to the court. The governor sat facing his appointee, pleased that he had made history with his selection. "It was something I wanted to do, not something I had to do," the governor later told a reporter. He said he watched the proceedings with thoughts of Frye's rise from humble beginnings and the barriers he had overcome throughout his life. "How unfair it has been that black people had no opportunity to become part of this court for so much of our history."[3]

Once installed, Frye retired to a conference room where the court's messenger, a black man named William Person, helped him into his new robe. Frye reappeared to accept the congratulations of those on hand. A while later, as the crowd dispersed, a photographer gathered the justices around Frye, who was seated in the middle of the group, for a formal portrait. The arrangement broke all manner of court traditions; the walls wore photographs of

earlier courts, all of which featured the chief justice seated front and center with the associate justices seated or standing about in order of their seniority. Frye's colleagues indulged the new man and no one admonished the photographer, who knew nothing of such rules.

The weight of history hung heavily over the court and accompanied the new associate justice in no small measure. His appointment as the first of his race was not something that he wished to dwell upon, at least not publicly. "It's one of those things I hope now we can get away from and start playing it down," he told a reporter. He was humbled by all the commotion, but, at the same time, he was equally proud of his part in set-

After Henry Frye took his oath as the first African American on the state supreme court, he was helped into his robes by William Person, the court's messenger (© Greensboro *News & Record*, all rights reserved).

ting another milestone in state history. A few African Americans wore the robes at other levels of the North Carolina judiciary, but none had ever sat where he did, where tenure and political good fortune could lead to his heading one of the three branches of state government. Frye was deeply conscious that in a little more than a dozen years he had gone from being one voice among 120 in the state house, to one of fifty in the state senate, to one of seven making decisions on issues that touched the lives of all of the citizens in North Carolina.

Opposite, top: Henry Frye was sworn in as an associate justice of the N.C. Supreme Court in February 1983 with his wife, Shirley, holding three Bibles (courtesy Frye family). *Opposite, bottom:* Henry Frye's mother, Pearl Frye, attended the ceremony. His father saw him sworn in as an assistant U.S. attorney in 1963, but died a few years later (courtesy Frye family).

Members of the supreme court are customarily photographed with the associate justices seated around the chief justice in the center. An out-of-town photographer didn't know about this tradition when he posed Henry Frye with his colleagues in 1983. Standing from left to right are Associate Justices Harry Martin, Burley Mitchell, James G. Exum, Jr., Louis Meyer II, Chief Justice Joe Branch, and Associate Justice J. William Copeland (courtesy Frye family).

At the time, the supreme court occupied the entire third floor of the Justice Building that stood on Raleigh's Morgan Street, across from the southeast corner of Capitol Square anchored by the State Capitol. Depression-era money from the federal government had helped the state pay for a structure that came in standard-issue government limestone with heavy brass-framed doors at the entrance and touches of art deco in the courtroom. The building's interior had changed little in the forty-plus years since the official dedication by Chief Justice Walter P. Stacy in 1940, who, at the time, called the courtroom the "sanctuary for the brooding spirit of the law."[4] The tall windows in the courtroom offered a postcard view of the Capitol surrounded by monuments and huge oaks and maples. The senior justices, with offices on that north side of the building, could enjoy this soothing scene. The windows in Frye's quarters on the south side of the corridor presented a view of the brick wall of a neighboring building. Pigeons roosted on the windowsills over a narrow alley-way. One of Frye's predecessors had used a similar spot in his chambers to cool his late-afternoon beer during the winter months.[5]

Frye inherited the standard state government office furnishings that had been left behind by the previous occupant, Associate Justice J. Philip Carlton, whom Frye was replacing. There was a large desk, a couple of straight chairs for visitors, and a bookcase along the wall that was filled with the decisions of the court written since its founding in 1818. Fluorescent fixtures hung from the ceilings. Each justice did have a private lavatory. The office, and an ante-room, opened onto a long corridor that was paved in polished marble and partially covered by a worn, black, rubber runner that reached from end to end. Portraits of former associate justices lined the walls. The spare furnishings and understated accessories reflected the court's reputation for being tight with the state's money. Chief Justice Branch, who had come to the post less than four years earlier, had only recently been convinced to purchase a copy machine. There were no computers. Secretaries used typewriters to produce opinions, drafts of opinions, bench briefs, court memos, and correspondence. Before the arrival of the copier, Frye, as the junior justice, would have received the barely legible sixth carbon copy of documents that circulated among the justices.

The office had recently been given a thorough cleaning, thanks to Lisa Marie Nieman, Frye's law clerk. She had been hired by Carlton and was staying on. When she learned about Frye's appointment, she looked in on the empty office and discovered it was littered with paper and had accumulated an impressive layer of dust. She went to the basement of the Justice Building, found the cleaning staff — all of them African Americans — and asked them to prepare it for the arrival of the state's first black justice. She later heard another justice marvel at their thorough work, saying he had never had been able to get such good service.[6]

Pauline Irving, Frye's assistant from his law firm, arrived a few days ahead of the swearing-in ceremony to organize her boss's office. "You and I are going to Raleigh," he had told her when he broke the news of his appointment a few weeks earlier. She wasn't so sure, at first, but she agreed that he probably couldn't get along without her. She had married a preacher since first coming to work for Frye in 1966 and one of the churches he served was in Raleigh. By the time attorney Frye became Justice Frye, she had his chambers open and ready for business. Irving would soon impress the other justices, the clerks, and court officials as a devoted, protective, and competent assistant. Not the least of her duties was keeping track of all of his guests, whose names often slipped his mind. He didn't readily catalogue such trivia.[7]

Frye was joining a court that was known for its allegiance to tradition, conservative rulings, and insular habits. The justices carefully avoided publicly participating in the partisan life of a capital city despite the fact that all but two owed their seats to political appointments, as well as their legal abilities. Associate Justices James G. Exum, Jr., and J. William Copeland had arrived anew after winning election to office. The chief justice had managed the gubernatorial campaign of Dan K. Moore before he took the veil. The justices seemed to consider it bad form even to acknowledge that they were responsible to the voters, largely because rules of judicial ethics precluded them from stating little more than their name and age when they were on the stump. All were independently elected Democrats and for most of the twentieth century, each was all but assured re-election until retirement was enforced at age 72. That would all change during Frye's years on the court.

The court heard a full range of issues and had to accept any case not receiving a majority opinion in the court of appeals. The rulings affected the conduct of business, the rights of workers, constitutional issues, and decisions of regulatory bodies. All of the cases involving capital punishment came directly to the court. The death cases weighed heavily on the justices and accounted for about half of the docket. The court's opinions occasionally made headline news, but the justices never spoke for attribution to reporters, whose principal contact was limited to the clerk's office, which put out a call when opinions were released. Aside from their appearances at official functions, the justices were seldom seen by those outside the close-knit fraternity of justices, their clerks, and the court's official staff. Passersby would comment on the midday parade they formed while walking together down the Fayetteville Street Mall on their way to lunch.

Joe Branch had been named chief justice in 1979, upon the retirement of Susie Sharp, the state's first female justice. There had been a bit of a stir among court insiders ahead of Branch's appointment when the word out of Governor Hunt's office was that he might not follow the court's tradition of elevating the senior associate to chief. "Some thought it ought to be automatic, but I didn't believe that," Hunt said some years later. It was said he preferred a younger candidate who would shake up the place. "I satisfied myself that Joe Branch would be the best person."[8] Branch was quiet, steady, and a son of eastern North Carolina. He was the fourth chief justice from the tiny town of Enfield, as unique a historic footnote as any. He was almost avuncular with his warm smile, broad shoulders, and full head of gray hair. Frye found him friendly and welcoming, and he joined in the admiration that Branch enjoyed from his colleagues. Frye believed Branch brought "common sense" to the law. While the chief was slow to break with judicial precedent, he believed that what the court had created it could also change. When Branch suggested in deliberations that a case might warrant such attention, his colleagues took notice.[9]

The court's senior associate, James G. Exum, Jr., of Greensboro, was the man who had finished less than a thousand votes ahead of Frye in his first legislative race in 1966, thus edging him out of a ballot position in the fall. At the close of the 1967 legislative session Governor Moore appointed him to the superior court bench even though Exum had supported Moore's opponent for governor. Exum was thirty-one years old at the time. He was elected to the supreme court in 1974, winning a seat that came open due to the retirement of Justice Carlisle Higgins. Exum was a Morehead Scholar at the University of North Carolina at Chapel Hill and a Root-Tilden Scholar at New York University School of Law. He enjoyed free-wheeling debate over the foundations and finer points of the law. Exum also rode a motorcycle and, soon after arriving at the court, was admonished by Associate Justice J. Frank Huskins to get his hair cut. At the time, Exum was more than twenty years younger than his colleagues. Some years after he left the court, Exum discovered that he was a direct descendant of Chief Justice Thomas Ruffin.[10]

Associate Justice J. William Copeland was another easterner, from the town of Murfreesboro. He, too, was a former trial judge and had been on the ballot with Exum in 1974. Copeland had served Governor Terry Sanford as his legislative counsel in 1961 when he helped the governor pushed through a sales tax on food to pay for his education program. Sanford had rewarded him with a superior court judgeship. Copeland favored the habits of a networking politician. Frye noticed early on that Copeland often sought a family or political connection each time someone's name was mentioned.

The remaining three associate justices were more recent Hunt appointees. Louis B. Meyer II was from the governor's hometown of Wilson. He had served as a city attorney and had represented municipalities that operated their own electric power systems. Meyer was close to the chief justice, who had co-signed notes that had allowed him to enter Wake Forest University, both as an undergraduate and a law student. Hunt's appointment came in 1981. In 1960, Meyer and Exum had served together as law clerks— Exum with Justice Emery Denny and Meyer with Justice R. Hunt Parker. Another of the governor's picks in 1981 was Burley Mitchell. He had known Hunt since they were teenagers. All of Mitchell's legal career had been in state service, first in the attorney general's office, then as the prosecutor in Wake County, and later, through a Hunt appointment, as a member of the court of appeals. He left that court to join the governor's cabinet as secretary of crime control and public safety before Hunt appointed him to the supreme court a little more than a year before Frye arrived.

One of the first of Frye's colleagues to drop into his office for a chat was Harry Martin, whose office was next door. He was from Asheville, and the only justice from west of Greensboro. Martin finished the University of North Carolina on a music scholarship and got his law degree from Harvard right after World War II. Governor Sanford gave him his first judicial appointment.

Governor Hunt put him on the court of appeals before elevating him to the supreme court. Unlike some of Martin's stiff-necked predecessors, his sense of humor pervaded his everyday life. One of his opinions from the court of appeals began, "This is a case about dogs. As dogs do not often appear in the courts, it is perhaps not inappropriate to write a few words about them." A social and legal history of dogs continued for eight pages.[11] Martin had joined the court about six months earlier than Frye and was pleased to hand off the title of junior justice to his new colleague.

The first thing that Frye noticed about life on the third floor was the absence of contact with the wide variety of people that had been a part of his day throughout his adult life. Before joining the court, he had endured the sleeve tugging of constituents that came with being a legislator and the constant attention to customers' needs that went into running a bank. He had seen clients daily at his law firm, was active in his church, and Shirley's busy schedule included appearances at public functions. Over the years, Pauline Irving had become expert at managing his time and regulating interruptions from phone calls or drop-in visitors. After a week or two on the third floor, he told Mrs. Irving to stop screening his calls. "I was ready for some conversation," he recalled. "I would be around there for a whole week and the only person who would call would be Shirley. As much as I like to talk to her, it was a big change."[12]

Despite the upheaval that the appointment brought to his personal life, it came at as good a time as any. The Fryes were on the verge of becoming empty nesters. Henry Jr. had a degree from the University of North Carolina at Chapel Hill and was working as a probation officer in Durham, just twenty-five miles away, and contemplating law school. Harlan was finishing his undergraduate studies at A&T. The new job did not require the Fryes to leave their home on Benbow Road; residence in Raleigh was not a requirement to serve on the bench. Fifty years earlier, former justice Sam J. Ervin, Jr., had listened to oral arguments and attended conferences in Raleigh and then returned home to Morganton to write his opinions and send them off to the court in the mail.[13] Henry had grown accustomed to the Raleigh commute and living out of temporary quarters during his years in the legislature. When he came to the court, he stayed with a friend at first and then leased an apartment. He usually drove home on the weekends. Shirley joined him in Raleigh whenever she could fit it into her very busy schedule.

Shirley wasn't going to leave her job. She was securely installed as an assistant vice chancellor for development at A&T, a position that made full use of her skills as an enthusiastic booster, organizer, and fundraiser. It also played on her deep love for the institution. She had accepted the appointment in 1977 when the school was beginning to move into a new, bolder era as it tried to shake free of its paternalistic past. A&T had never before organized any efforts to raise large sums for special projects or expansion of its academic program. Rather, school administrators had waited on legislative handouts and an occasional windfall to begin something new. Shirley was just the kind of ambassador that A&T needed to present itself to a broader community, especially among Greensboro's business leaders. She was not shy about asking for money. It was also a job that established her as more than Henry Frye's wife. Her representation of A&T showcased her talents as a community leader.

One of her early projects had been to raise money for a new football stadium. The campaign was successful, in part, because of an initial visit Shirley paid to Joseph M. Bryan. He was one of Greensboro's wealthiest businessmen and had a gruff exterior that discouraged most of his casual callers. At their first meeting, she immediately asked him about the large marlins mounted on his office wall. "I said, 'Mr. Bryan did you catch these marlins?' I don't know how I knew what they were. I just said it. He said, 'You are the first woman to come in here who knew what they were.' He said, 'Why should I give to A&T?' I said, 'Because I asked.'" Bryan made an initial gift of $80,000, about 10 percent of the total needed, as well as other donations that came later to help the school complete the campaign. A few years later, when Bryan organized his own foundation, he asked Shirley to become a founding board member and accept a lifetime membership to the board of directors.[14]

The governor had pushed Henry for a quick decision because the court was just before entering its spring session. When the day for oral arguments arrived, the clerk called his "oyez" and Frye, as the junior justice, entered the courtroom behind all of his colleagues and took his seat on the end of the bench nearest the window. When Sam Ervin, Jr., occupied that same seat in 1949, Associate Justice A.A.F. Seawell leaned over and told him, "You can look out the window and watch the squirrels running up and down the trees on the Capitol grounds, and ignore the nuts who argue cases before us."[15] Frye noted the cars passing by but was more concerned about the noise generated by street construction that made it hard for him to hear what was being said in court.

The deep expanse of the courtroom opened out before the seven justices seated on the raised dais. A bank of waist-high bookcases holding the court's decisions—the "Brown Books"—separated them from the tables for lawyers representing the opposing sides. Overhead were chandeliers of buffed aluminum and discs of glass that had been stylish when Frye was a youngster. Leather-covered armchairs could seat an audience of about seventy-five spectators. Thomas Ruffin's portrait loomed behind the justices, framed by two tall columns of polished wood with ionic caps. The court's clock, a tall floor model in a case of dark carved wood, purchased in 1875, stood just inside the entrance to the courtroom on Frye's far right.

When Frye arrived at the court, he was more accustomed to Raleigh and its grand halls of government than when he arrived in 1969 as a wide-eyed and nervous freshman legislator. Years later, he said he didn't recall any flush of imagery similar to that which had come over him on that first day in the state house. In fact, there had been little time for reflection; he became immersed in his work as soon as he put on his robe. When all the arguments for the cases set for the day had been heard, the justices returned to the conference room and immediately began deliberations. Tradition called for the junior justice to speak first in conference.

Throughout his career as a lawyer, during his years in the legislature, and on the boards and commissions where he had served, Frye was the one who sat quietly through the debate, gathered his thoughts, and then, when others had exhausted their arguments, he would speak. Now, he didn't have that luxury. He was the one who would have to begin the discussion. The tradition was based on the premise that by speaking first, the junior justice wouldn't be intimidated by the senior men and conform his opinion to theirs. Frye also learned it was his duty to answer the door, if there was a knock from the outside, and handle all of the routine paperwork.

All in all, the experience on his first day was a bit unnerving. Frye had never done anything halfway, and he was determined to be prepared and avoid lapses that would embarrass. He had read and reread the briefs from the opposing sides, and he had reviewed the bench briefs (a summary of the issues and the law) prepared by his law clerk, but he had taken an extra step and gone back to the trial transcript to answer questions that arose. Whatever he said that day apparently didn't leave his colleagues questioning the governor's decision to name Frye to their court. He acquitted himself well enough to lay the foundation for a respect for his thoroughness, his thoughtful consideration, and his reasoned judgment that would grow with each session.

The court's work was carried out on paper. The corpus of a case arrived in the dense annotated paragraphs of the briefs from the opposing sides. Since the court did not limit the verbosity of lawyers, some of their briefs could run on for hundreds of pages. A justice's clerk (each had one when Frye arrived) would prepare an abbreviated summary of the case and, if asked, would offer an opinion for consideration. The entire file could be quite large. At the same time, the justices communicated through typed memoranda, and when a justice had completed a draft of an opinion it was circulated to the others for comment. Pauline Irving had completed the draft of her boss's first opinion and the messenger was delivering copies to the justices when Frye's neighbor, Harry Martin, walked past her into Frye's office carrying his copy. It was littered with edits, marked in red ink.

"I read it and it was bad," Martin said many years later. "It was Henry's first. It was a little short opinion. I ran in there to Henry's office and I said, 'Tell the messenger to pick up this opinion, right now.' He said, 'What are you talking about?' I said, 'I want to talk with you about this opinion. This opinion is terrible, it won't do. I don't want all the other justices reading it. Get him to pick up it up.'

"He said, 'Well, all right.' He was irritated. I was flat out talking to him, like the truth," Martin said. "He had it picked up and brought it back in. He and I worked on it for a day or two and got it all fixed like it ought to have been. I don't remember anything at all about the case. It went back out and everybody agreed to it."[16]

Martin's intrusion into his chambers had caught Frye off guard. It took a minute or two for him to realize that Martin wasn't trying to change the outcome of the court's vote, or pull rank, but to help the new man provide a more coherent and better-reasoned argument for the decision that had been agreed upon. "He said, 'You can make whatever changes you want to,'" Frye recalled. "It is your opinion and whatever you want to do is fine, but I think you ought to take another look at it." It was the beginning of a long friendship. Martin became one of his closest advisors during the nearly ten years they served together.[17]

When Frye took his oath in February 1983 he was not only beginning his service as a justice of the court, it was also the first day of a political campaign. He would have to win election to a full term in the coming year if he were to remain on the court beyond December 31, 1984. Judicial races had not attracted much attention since a decade earlier when Susie Sharp was running for chief justice, and her Republican opponent in the fall was a fire extinguisher salesman who didn't have a law degree. In the aftermath of that embarrassment, the legislature restricted the candidacy for judgeships to attorneys. In 1984, the political tides were running against Democrats, and a popular incumbent Republican president, Ronald Reagan, would be on the ballot.

Frye would have to work to keep his seat, and dive right back into a political campaign, something he had hoped to stay away from for a few years when he left the state senate. He would have the support of the Democratic Party, whose leaders, like Hunt, were eager to have an African American on the ballot in the fall. It would still require time away from what Frye considered his most important assignment, doing a good job on the court. "At the time," Frye said, "I wanted to win, but I wasn't hung up on it. I wasn't going to let the campaign interfere with my work. If I lost that election, I was going to come on back and practice law, which I enjoyed doing."

Judicial candidates were limited in what they could say and do in a political campaign. It was permissible to talk about personal qualities that might attract support from voters— a family man, regular church member, honesty, integrity, professional qualifications— but talking about specific issues that might come before the court was prohibited. Frye wasn't even sure whether an incumbent could endorse fellow Democrats. He had long been conscious of ethical campaigning and he took his new obligations under the Code of Judicial Conduct seriously. With little to say to arouse a crowd, he fell back on his knack for spontaneous poetry and used that to gain the attention of those gathered for a campaign rally or political event.

"People would be so interested in the poem they didn't pay much attention," Frye said. "Here I could say a few things in poetry that I might have had a problem with. For example, one of the big things was could a judge say support the Democratic ticket? The only way you could do it was based on qualifications. You couldn't say support them because they are Democrats. I fixed it up in my poem somehow that the best qualified were the Democrats. Somewhere in that poem, somebody would find something to laugh about."

Frye had been a popular candidate in Guilford County, and his name was familiar to many African Americans around the state, but he was not well known among the general voting population. He would have to mount a statewide campaign, something quite new, and he would need help. Early on, he got a call and pledge of support from Sam Johnson, a Raleigh lawyer and a colleague from his days in the state house. Johnson was well regarded in legislative circles and had developed many contacts around the state through his service as the chief assistant to Lieutenant Governor Jimmy Green. In Johnson, Frye got an able and conscientious campaign advisor and one who knew his way around the state, especially eastern North Carolina. He became the co-chair of the campaign along with Ruth B. Jones, a retired teacher from Rocky Mount, and Jim Morgan, a High Point lawyer with whom Frye had served in the General Assembly. An old friend, Harold Webb, who had a post in the state personnel department, ran the campaign office in Raleigh.

Much to his chagrin, Frye drew a challenger in the Democratic Party primary. He was Raymond Mason Taylor, a conservative Democrat who had been one year behind Frye in law school at Chapel Hill. He served as the supreme court marshal and librarian for thirteen years before U.S. Senator Jesse Helms, a Republican, nominated him as the librarian of Congress. He didn't get the job but he enjoyed Helms's support for another federal job. He was named superintendent of documents in 1982. After he announced, Taylor discounted his ties to Helms and the Republicans. He said he was following a tradition of challenging the court's junior justice on his first election.[18]

Taylor's candidacy didn't sit well with the governor. A few weeks before the election, Hunt broke with tradition of staying out of primary contests and publicly endorsed Frye. He had done it once before, in 1978, after he had appointed another African American, Richard Erwin, to the state court of appeals. "I appointed him about December and the minute I appointed him, or shortly thereafter, this white person said he was running against him. He was running against him for one reason. He was African American. I got out there and put all my troops behind him and he wouldn't have won if we hadn't have done it," Hunt said. "I didn't get involved again until Henry's race came along. Listen. What are you in it for: To help people and to create a fair society, full and equal opportunities. You have a team, a political organization to help you win and help others win, too. Those were two times when it was the right thing to do and the necessary thing to do."[19]

Taylor gathered some support from endorsements in the eastern part of the state, but Frye won more than 60 percent of the vote in a busy, hard-fought party primary season in other races. Hunt was leaving office and Democrats were backed up, waiting in line, for the chance to succeed him. Republicans also were energized and they were looking forward to being on the ballot with President Reagan in the fall. Frye campaigned at party events in the fall, but scant attention was paid to him or his Republican opponent, Clarence C. Boyan of High Point. On election night, Frye grew increasingly anxious as another sweeping Republican victory was becoming apparent. In the end, Reagan carried North Carolina and voters elected Congressman James G. Martin of Charlotte as the state's second Republican governor in the twentieth century. Fortunately for Frye, the voters' enthusiasm for Republicans didn't extend deep enough to upset the Democrats in the judicial races. Frye won election to a full eight-year term with more than a million voters on his side.

For years, justices who were approaching the end of their terms would often consider early retirement, which enabled the governor to appoint a successor rather than leave an open seat to be filled directly from the ballot. This precluded Election Day surprises and also enabled the court, or at least the retiring justice, to have some influence on his replacement. All of this maneuvering began to take on more partisan significance with the election, in 1972, of James E. Holshouser as the state's first Republican governor in the twentieth century. Associate Justice Carlisle Higgins and Chief Justice William Bobbitt, both of who were nearing retirement age and whose terms would expire in two years, were caught by surprise with Holshouser's election, along with the rest of the state. There were post-election conversations with out-going Democratic Governor Bob Scott on the future of their seats, which would become vacant during Holshouser's term, but the two stayed in place rather than give the new governor the opportunity to appoint their successors. As it turned out, Democratic replacements were elected over Republican opponents in 1974.

Democrats were more prepared in 1984. A month before Governor Martin took his oath of office, Associate Justice Copeland announced his retirement (he had been reelected to a full eight-year term in 1982). Hunt appointed Court of Appeals Chief Judge Earl Vaughn, the speaker of the state house during Frye's first term, as his replacement. Vaughn was sworn in and wearing a new robe before Christmas. The move robbed Martin of an early appointment.

Seven months later, however, Vaughn announced he was leaving the court because of poor health. Vaughn's departure allowed Martin to appoint the first Republican associate justice to serve since Democrats had tried to rid the court of Republicans in 1901 when Chief Justice David M. Furches and Associate Justice Robert M. Douglas, both Republicans, were impeached. Democrats in the state house were angry at the court's attempt to overturn the white supremacy laws passed by the Democratic majority in the 1899 General Assembly. They brought charges alleging that the two had exceeded their authority by ordering the state to pay the wages of a shellfish inspector, an expense that had been denied by the legislature. The senate failed to convict. A former governor, Democrat Thomas J. Jarvis, defended the justices at trial. Furches and Douglas continued in office but lost re-election to Democrats in 1902.

The governor's choice was Rhoda Billings, a Wake Forest University law professor. In 1968, she had been elected as a district court judge in Forsyth County. More recently, she had taken leave from her teaching duties to accept a Martin appointment as chair of the parole commission. She had barely settled into her new office when Martin called to offer her the supreme court appointment. One of the reasons the governor gave in support of his selection was her willingness to mount a vigorous election campaign. She would have to defend her seat in the fall election of 1986, fourteen months away.

Billings and her husband, Donald, also an attorney, were lifelong Republicans. Donald had known Governor Holshouser as a teenager in Boone and had served as Governor Martin's campaign manager in Forsyth County in 1984. Rhoda's father had served in the General Assembly. She was considered an able lawyer and had previously served on the state's criminal code commission. The governor said gender had not played a role in his selection. In fact, Billings said some years later, there was a very short list of Republican lawyers willing to upend a law practice and take a supreme court appointment on the chance they might survive what appeared to be almost certain defeat at the polls. No Republican in the twentieth century had ever won a statewide judicial race.[20]

Partisan differences were set aside once Billings took her oath and began work in an office on the east end of the third floor corridor. The court had no record of taking sharp departures from the past and her one vote wasn't going to change history. In fact, when Chief Justice R. Hunt Parker was running the court just twenty years earlier, he took pride in his defense of precedent.[21] Billings would have little opportunity to strike a blow for Republicans, even if she wanted to. She usually found herself in agreement with the majority of her colleagues and took on her share of the load in writing opinions. She later described her acceptance as warm and friendly. In conference, as the first to speak, she oftentimes reverted to her experience as a law professor, where she presented a review of the law from many jurisdictions. It was a style that sometimes left the chief justice muttering in complaint to Justice Harry Martin as they left their conference to return to their chambers. "Joe and I were walking down the hall and he said, 'If that woman doesn't quit lecturing us on what the law is, I don't know what I am going to do,'" Martin recalled. "She kept on. It was just in her. She was a teacher, and she was just teaching."[22]

Billings was only doing what every newcomer did: establish credibility. She had taught criminal procedure and was making use of her scholarship. She believed she was just bringing what she knew to bear on the cases at hand. "At the time I was on the court, most of our cases were criminal and dealt with the most serious offenses, first-degree rape and murder," she later said. "I had taught criminal procedure so I was well versed in all those things through my teaching."[23]

Branch wasn't ready to be lectured on the law after nearly twenty years on the court, with five of those years as chief justice, which included managing the operation of the state's entire judicial system. "As junior justice, she got to speak first and boy she would lay things out there, almost like teaching her class," said Frye. "Some of [the other justices] didn't appreciate that too much. But we still got along. We all went to lunch together."[24]

Martin's appointment of Billings was a political bonus, but only a prelude to a battle that would turn bitterly partisan and challenge the traditions of the court itself. This transformation was set in motion in late spring of 1986 when Branch called on the governor to inform him of his plans to retire on September 1. He told the governor about the court's tradition of naming the senior associate as chief. This was not a partisan habit, Branch explained, but one that had evolved to preclude any political jockeying among the associates when the position came open. Branch left his meeting believing that the governor would honor the tradition and that Exum, as the senior associate, would be his successor.[25]

Branch's pending retirement was well known in late June when he appeared before the N.C. Bar Association and put the governor on the spot, telling those attending the association's annual gathering that Martin should appoint Exum. The governor confirmed to reporters that he and Branch had talked, but he declined to endorse Branch's plan to elevate Exum. His response was similar to that of Governor Hunt seven years earlier. "I would rather take time to reflect on it and be sure that the decision is the appropriate one," he said.[26]

The governor's statement made it clear to Branch that while he may have understood that the path of succession was a tradition of the court since 1878 and had nothing to do with politics, Martin saw it differently. It was a tradition, Martin agreed, many years later, but "their tradition was that only Democrats were supposed to be chief justice. So, I didn't follow that one."[27]

While the Democrats fumed — Branch believed he had been betrayed — the governor and Billings talked about the options. She was the most likely candidate, but a reluctant one. She understood the criticism that would come if the governor named her, the court's junior justice with less than a year of experience, to run the court system. In preparation for the anticipated campaign to stay on as associate justice, she had lined up an impressive array of endorsements, from Republicans and Democrats. Clearly, the governor believed that Exum, with his liberal reputation, would not do, but the next senior justice, Louis B. Meyer II, was considered to be more conservative. The governor's former legislative counsel, I. Beverly Lake, Jr., then sitting as a superior court judge, argued Meyer's case to the governor.

"I said if you want to do what is best for the court, and what is politically smart, and what is best for Rhoda, you will not put her in that position," Lake later recalled. "She will be immediately challenged and she will lose. The best thing for her and for the court is to appoint Louis Meyer as chief justice. You will immediately show the General Assembly that you are nonpartisan. It will do a lot for you, it would do a tremendous amount of good to the court, and it will save Rhoda."[28]

Martin was not persuaded. He wanted to make a partisan statement and when he could find no other Republican of sufficient standing in the profession to accept an appointment for a position that he might hold until the next election, which was less than ninety days away, he continued to pressure Billings.

Exum did not wait for the governor to announce his decision. In anticipation of a political campaign in the fall, either as Martin's appointee or not, he secured the nomination as a candidate for chief justice from the executive committee of the state Democratic Party. He wrote Martin in late July to say he would retire September 1, or he would remain if he were appointed chief justice. Exum offered the retirement option because he did not want to be deciding cases while in a political contest with a fellow justice.[29]

Martin announced his appointment of Billings in late July, soon after he heard from Exum. The two never did talk, which produced a retort from Exum, who told a reporter, "We're both grown men, and we could have sat down and talked about his concerns." At Billings's swearing-in ceremony in September, the governor called "unseemly" Exum's decision to retire, instead of resign, "while he campaigns and his successor will do the work of the court [during] a very heavy schedule in September and October."[30] It was just the beginning of a political fight that would end with both Republicans and Democrats talking about changing the way the state's judiciary was selected.

With all the shuffling about, the governor ended up with not just one judicial vacancy, but three. Billings became chief justice, and he appointed Francis Parker of Charlotte to fill her term while he chose Robert Browning of Greenville to fill Exum's term. He got one more in the mix. With Exum's retirement, Willis Whichard, a Democrat, resigned his seat on the court of appeals and filed as a candidate to succeed Exum. The governor named Robert Orr, a young Asheville Republican, to replace Whichard. There was some history in all of this. Parker, a 63-year-old Republican, was the son of U.S. Appeals Court Judge John J. Parker, the Republican candidate for North Carolina governor in 1920 whom President Herbert Hoover later nominated to the U.S. Supreme Court. His nomination was rejected in the Senate by a vote of 41 to 39. He went on to become one of the best-known jurists in the state and was chief judge of the Fourth Circuit Court of Appeals at the time of his death in 1958.

North Carolina Democrats were eager to recover from the head knocking they had received in 1984, while Republicans wanted to show that Martin's election demonstrated the ascendancy of the Republican Party in North Carolina. Leading the campaign for the Democrats was Lieutenant Governor Robert Jordan, who had his own ambitions to challenge Martin in 1988. At the top of the ticket was former governor Terry Sanford. He was a candidate for the U.S. Senate against former congressman James T. Broyhill. He had won the Republican primary to succeed incumbent John East but was appointed to the job in July after East committed suicide, an event that added even more tumult to what had already been a busy summer for the governor.

The Sanford-Broyhill race captured most of the attention of voters, but Republicans, led by former governor Holshouser, organized the Citizens for a Conservative Court and added some fire to the judicial races. The CCC warned that the election of Exum and the other Democrats would tilt the court to the left. "I think, assuming the general perception that Exum is much more liberal, he could cause a shift in the court," Holshouser was quoted as saying. "We saw that with the [Earl] Warren Court in Washington that an activist court could write the law just as easily as the legislature and could change the direction of the state."[31] The CCC focused their campaign on death penalty cases, and claimed that Exum had "voted against the death penalty" in 43 of 49 cases since 1977. Exum responded that he had voted to affirm death sentences in 35 of 112 cases he had heard since joining the court in 1975.

The intensity of the campaign drew former chief justice Joe Branch from retirement. He took to campaigning on Exum's behalf. "I'm back to being a Democrat," Branch said. "I was on the court with most of these people. I think they're good, strong, experienced judges and I think that's good for the continuity of the court."[32] Meanwhile, representatives of the CCC preceded Exum to various counties where the court had decided a death case of local interest to say that Exum had dissented in the case or voted for new trial. "When the bar found out what the CCC was doing," Exum said, "they dispatched lawyers to courthouse steps where these people were speaking and came to my defense as a judge. Saying, yes, Justice Exum may have dissented in this case, but that is not the question. Why did he dissent and these are the reasons? We think he had good reasons for what he did. I remember one in Charlotte where Ozzie Ayscue appeared and deflected some of that."[33]

The tone of the race was speeding downhill when Billings called upon the Holshouser-led group to discontinue what she called "personal attacks." She told a Durham luncheon group that "it is not appropriate" for the CCC to make an issue of Exum's personal opposition to the death penalty.[34] Some years later, Billings said the group's efforts interfered with her campaign. "It is always difficult to have an uncontrolled group trying to run your campaign," she said. "This was done without my knowledge and without my consent. I had no control over it and it did create great deal of animosity in some quarters that I thought was unfortunate. It didn't help me. It did create a view of the court as being more partisan than I certainly would have wanted it to be viewed."

In fact, both Billings and Exum were highly regarded within the legal profession. Her colleagues on the bench, while prohibited from taking sides publicly, had agreed among themselves that they wouldn't oppose her reelection as an associate. "The Democrats, including Exum, had decided that we were going to support her for reelection [as associate justice] and had gotten pretty broad support for that so that she was not going to have a big problem," Frye recalled.[35] That bi-partisanship evaporated when she became chief justice. "Of course that never got published," Billings said later. "I changed opponents—certainly the stature and friendship that a lot of those people had for Exum meant they would not chose me over him. It was a matter of changes in position and changing opponents."

The Republicans didn't have a Reagan or a Helms on the ballot in 1986 and Democrats rebounded from their losses two years earlier. Sanford was elected to the Senate and all of the Republican judicial candidates lost. Exum became chief justice and the court added two new members, Willis Whichard and John Webb, as associate justices. Because of the turnover in the court's membership, and the interference from the fall campaign, a handful of cases were reheard in late 1986 and 1987.

After the election, Billings urged the General Assembly to consider changing the way the state's judges were selected. She preferred a system of merit selection, which had been the way most members of the appellate bench had secured their jobs since they had been first appointed to the position before being required to submit to the voters. "Simply because the system has worked in the past doesn't mean that it is going to work in the same way in the future," she said.

12

In Chambers

Four years before Henry Frye joined the N.C. Supreme Court, Michael Meiselman and his younger brother, Ira, could not come to terms over the management of the business enterprises they had inherited from their father. Unable to resolve the matter, Michael sued Ira for a fair-value settlement of his share of the business where he was a minority shareholder. In the spring of 1983, *Meiselman v. Meiselman* reached the court.

Meiselman was one of the cases called for oral arguments on Frye's first session on the bench. The issues were complicated and the law left much to be interpreted on the rights of minority shareholders in closely held corporations in North Carolina. Something about the case intrigued Frye, the only justice on the bench with any practical business experience. It may have been his high regard for small investors like those who had given him $100 or $200 for shares in Greensboro National Bank, and were willing to take a chance with him and the other organizers. On a much deeper level, however, it may have been the fact that African Americans had always been "minority shareholders" in the Great American Enterprise and had long been told their limits by the majority. Whatever the reason, when it came time to choose cases on which to write an opinion, Frye enthusiastically picked *Meiselman*.

His colleagues were happy for him to have it. In fact, some of them later ribbed him about his choice. The complexity of the case, and the research that would be required to write an opinion, meant that it was one they were unlikely to select, certainly not on the first round, so there was no need for Frye to take it as his first choice. In conference, case selection is like a game of poker, and with each trip around the table the decisions become a bit tougher. Frye's colleagues wouldn't have thought any less of him, as the new man, if he had chosen something much easier in an early round, such as one of the *per curiam* decisions. These were unanimous decisions that were called "cripples."[1] These cases required little more than a signature, leaving a little extra time for the golf course. The fact of the matter was that Frye was so green, he hadn't learned he probably would have ended up with *Meiselman*, anyhow.[2]

Cases are chosen in conference, a private session attended by only the seven members of the court, with the justice who had the last pick at the previous session waiting for the others before taking a turn. The last case on the table is called "Hobson's Choice," as it is no choice at all. Most likely on that day, Frye would have gotten Hobson's by exercising a lower pick, but freshman jitters got the best of him. He wanted *Meiselman*, and asked for it right away, along with three others that would require considerable effort and research.

The facts in *Meiselman* were pretty straightforward. The younger brother owned a majority interest and he had complied with the boilerplate legal obligations due minority stockholders, such as keeping them informed about decisions, notice of meetings, and that sort of thing. Michael Meiselman said that wasn't sufficient protection for his interests, and he wanted out of the business, but the law was unclear on how that should take place. Thus, the legal journey had begun in 1979. As Burley Mitchell, then an associate and later chief justice, later put it, *Meiselman* "was one of those situations where the road had run out. The existing law, well, we had reached the end of the trail."[3] Frye felt the same way. The last word dealing with the issues such as those contained in the suit had been written by his predecessors on the court in the 1920s. Over the years, the appreciation of the standing of minority shareholders in private, closely held corporations had changed, leaving North Carolina statutes insufficient to resolve issues like those raised in *Meiselman*.

"I had studied the briefs," Frye said some years later, "and the more I read the more I felt like there is something that is not right in there and I am going to see if I can find out what it is. It was something to write. Good gracious alive, the statute was not clear. They had not been brought up to date."[4]

Frye took up the challenge to establish clear and equitable standards and procedures for the trial courts to use in governing internal disputes where minority shareholders could be held virtual captives. "We all knew there had to be some limitations," Mitchell said. "It was desirable that there be, and it was probably what the legislature had intended but the extent of them was not spelled out." This was not judicial activism, Mitchell insisted. "There is a narrow category where the gap has to be filled. You have a case before you," the former chief justice said, "you don't do like the ancient kings of Israel and just call it. That is what he was doing in *Meiselman*, setting forth the rules that would prevail."

It is rare that a justice on a state supreme court has the opportunity to write something that might be called a "landmark decision," and even more of an occasion when it arises in a justice's first session. But this happened with *Meiselman*. Long after Frye left the bench, lawyers helping clients establish corporations in North Carolina had better know something about the decision Frye wrote and that was subsequently adopted unanimously by the court. More than likely, they learned about *Meiselman* in classes on corporate law, especially if they attended law school in North Carolina. If their client's enterprise would be incorporated under North Carolina law, then the majority shareholders would have to pay careful attention to minority interests. Otherwise, they might want to file their incorporation papers in the state of Delaware, where the rules weren't quite so confining.

The case proved to be something of a surprise for Frye. He had not come to the court to change society, but to serve the calling of the law, which had always been his first love. He had always believed the practice of law included a component of public service. He didn't have an agenda, like the one he carried with him to the General Assembly in 1969. There was no litmus test for cases that would attract his attention. Rather, he approached his work with "a forward-thinking, free energy," as one of his early law clerks, Kenneth Lewis, described it.[5] He joined the court with enthusiasm, recalled Lisa Nieman, his clerk in that first term. "He not only rose to challenges, he welcomed them," she said. "It was really refreshing."

His love of the law, especially business law, was evident in the way he approached cases. He threw open the door to research and dug deeply. In *Meiselman*, for example, Nieman said, "He wanted to know what the best and brightest thought about this area." As the opinions went through the drafts he asked his clerks to examine his thinking, and he challenged theirs, as he brought them into the decision-making process. The 347 decisions and 75 dissents that carried his name during his eighteen years on the court were always his own, but he and his clerks moved slowly and carefully through the language of each one, reviewing every word, sometimes reading the drafts aloud as they sat at his desk. Frye insisted on clarity of language, as well as sound legal reasoning, in anything that came from his office.

The numbers of decisions written by Frye and the other justices don't adequately reflect the intensity of the court's work. In North Carolina, the supreme court is a "warm court," in the judicial vernacular.[6] Every justice has read the briefs in a case before it is heard in oral arguments, unlike the British system where judges wait to hear from attorneys from opposing sides. In addition to their own review, North Carolina justices usually carry into court with them a summary of each case that has been prepared by their law clerks. The familiarity with the case leads to some give and take as the justices pose questions to opposing counsel. The exchanges are generally polite and don't feature the abrupt interruptions that characterize oral arguments at the U.S. Supreme Court. Justices are respectful of the limited time given each side to present its case, and attorneys were mindful of the attention span of the justices before them. Former chief justice I. Beverly Lake, Jr., who joined the court in the 1990s, had a case before the court in the early 1970s and recalled keeping an eye on a pencil that Chief Justice R. Hunt Parker held at the ready. "He'd listen to you a few minutes and then tap, tap, tap with a pencil and he'd say, 'All right Mr. Lake I think we have your point.' That was the end of it." Lawyers could continue, but at their peril.[7]

Parker was an austere fellow who intimidated others with his lack of humor. He didn't tolerate levity, unless he himself made an attempt at a joke. Then, Lake said, Parker expected at least a smile. The atmosphere on the third floor of the Justice Buildings was a bit more relaxed by the time Frye arrived a decade later. Chief Justice Branch had a sense of humor, enjoyed telling stories, and he was not above passing commentary to his colleagues as the attorneys droned on before him. One day, Justice Harry Martin said the justices were listening to an attorney from Florida who appeared wearing an expensive suit, a shirt of blinding whiteness, and "the most dazzling gold cuff links the court had seen in some time." Branch scribbled a note and passed it down the bench. It read: "This fellow did not get here on any chicken truck, did he?"[8]

Frye usually made up his mind about a case after reading the briefs, but he did not discount the oral arguments. Any questions he raised in open court were to establish points of law, or to clarify an issue. "Almost always I would have some question about something. I would write that down on my bench briefs," Frye said. He said attorneys often tried to interpret a justice's opinion on a case based on questions. That was a mistake he learned in his years at the U.S. attorney's office. He thought he had won a suit for the federal government based on a judge's questions only to find when the decision was filed that the judge was firmly opposed to the government's position.

Oral arguments continued through the morning without a break until midday. The session then resumed after lunch. When the last case of the day had been heard, the justices began their conference with that case at the top of the agenda. The ensuing discussion could last only a few minutes for each case or continue for an hour or two. It was at this conference of "first impression" that a tentative vote would be taken and cases selected for writing.

There is no place in state government, other than the conference room of the supreme court, where debate over a citizen's life, liberty, and property is cloaked in such secrecy. Only the justices who shape the outcome of the court's decisions are present, and there are no recordings of the deliberations. Justices hold to the sanctity of these private sessions long after they leave the court. The most that outsiders can learn is a general description.

The debate can be as routine as "conversation over a cup of coffee," said former justice Willis Whichard, who served with Frye. "I had a friend who said something is an 'obviosity.' There is no such word, but you knew what he meant. It was an obviosity that this case ought to be affirmed, and you quickly passed by those. But, then you could then spend two hours on something."[9]

Occasionally, tempers would flare, said former Justice Harry Martin. "I remember one time, I am not going to say names, but two justices got into a shouting match in conference. One of them jumped up out of his chair and went out in the hall. Exum was chief. We just sat there. After a while, I said, 'Chief Justice, if it is all right with you I will go out there and find him and bring him back. I went out and as I was getting ready to turn left, he came walking back. I said, 'Come on, let's go on back in here.' He said, 'You go ahead, I will be in there in just a minute.' In a few minutes he came back in. There wasn't any more shouting or carrying on."[10]

Frye was unfailingly courteous and dispassionate in conference, his colleagues said. "He was not usually the first one to speak," recalled Whichard. "He was not one to speak the most adamantly or vociferously, but when he weighed in everybody listened. I would say, when he could, he attempted to be a conciliator. He was always happy if we could pull together around a contentious matter. He was the calm voice of reason, making Isaiah's plea to come down and reason together."

The seven knew one another well, or would soon, after a newcomer arrived. "These people were not only colleagues," said Exum. "They were friends. They were people you enjoyed being with after hours." Each had a perspective of the world that was shaped by life experiences, legal training, and a professional life. When Frye joined the court, four of his colleagues—Chief Justice Branch and associate justices Martin, Copeland, and Exum—had each spent nearly twenty years on the bench. Exum, Copeland, and Martin were former superior court judges. It was the job of the chief justice to supervise the assignments of the superior court bench, and he knew the judges well. As a result, there was considerable empathy for the challenges that trial judges faced, and these three backed them up whenever possible. "You had to have pretty clear evidence to overrule a trial judge," Frye recalled. "[Branch] wouldn't say he had abused his discretion. He would say he made a mistake of law." Justice Mitchell had spent most of his entire career as a lawyer for the government, first for the attorney general and later as the district attorney for Wake County. During much of his career, Justice Meyer had been involved in municipal law and had handled legal matters for a group of municipalities that ran their own electric power distribution systems. "A journeyman lawyer's lawyer," Mitchell said of Meyer. "He was down in the trenches, and knew how you get things done." Meyer and Frye often disagreed, but Frye liked the mental and legal challenges that Meyer raised in his conference arguments.

"Sometimes, Louis Meyer and I were on opposite sides," Frye said. "I didn't understand his thinking and he didn't understand mine. So if we had an issue, where I knew how he felt on it, and thought he was completely wrong, sometimes I would quote what he had said previously. So why isn't that controlling in this case? I knew why it wasn't controlling, but I wanted to hear the answer, to see if he could convince me. Sometimes I would phrase it before he got a chance to lecture on it."

Mitchell also had a personal history not often found attached to a supreme court justice. He was a high school dropout who had some scrapes with the law as a youngster. He got to college late, entering after four years in the navy as an enlisted man. He then whizzed through N.C. State University, got his law degree at Chapel Hill, and went to work for N.C. Attorney General Robert Morgan. Mitchell's temper could rise in conference. He once told Frye that if he had been required to face the challenges of African Americans during the era of segregation, "I think instead of being with the moderates I would have been with Malcolm X or some real radicals."[11]

Frye's professional portfolio was broader than most of his colleagues. He had been a businessman, and as a banker he had reviewed loans of those

The justices of the supreme court turned out for a day's work in aid of a Habitat for Humanity homeowner in Greensboro in the early 1990s. Standing with the homeowner are (left to right) Associate Justices Willis Whichard, John Webb, Louis Meyer, Henry Frye, Harry Martin, Chief Justice James G. Exum, Jr., and Associate Justice Burley Mitchell, Jr. (courtesy Frye family).

Around the table in the conference room of the court are (seated left) Associate Justices I. Beverly Lake, Jr., and (seated right) Louis Meyer, and standing (left to right) are Associate Justices Burley Mitchell, Jr., John Webb, Willis Whichard, Henry Frye, and Chief Justice James G. Exum, Jr. (courtesy North Carolina Supreme Court Historical Society).

starting small businesses or families buying a first home. During the early years of his legal career, he had represented criminal defendants before settling into representation in civil matters, handling wills and estates, and the like. Until Whichard arrived, Frye was the only justice with broad legislative experience and knew, first hand, what went into the writing of laws. Like Frye, Whichard also had served in the state house and senate. Frye also had grown up in a segregated world where African Americans were frustrated and humiliated at will by whites. No other member of the court had been called upon to explain to his child why a vendor wouldn't sell him an ice cream cone because of the color of his skin.

Frye was not one to talk freely about his personal life, especially those incidents peculiar to his experiences in a segregated society. He would more easily relate the broader tale of a childhood in a large family, in a small farm house on the outskirts of town, where everyone was expected to work from

Justice Henry Frye began his work with tutoring children in the mid–1980s with his visit to a classroom at Bessemer Elementary School in Greensboro, where he read to a group of first graders (© Greensboro *News & Record*, all rights reserved, photograph by Joseph Rodriguez).

"can't to can't" ("can't see until you can't see," as his father would say). That was part in his repertoire. By the time he got to the court, his story about being refused in his first attempt to register to vote was well known. According to those who sat with him in conference, however, he did not bring the racial dimensions of his life into the discussion. It was probably unnecessary under the circumstances. "Certainly, there were times when he spoke and he was speaking from that experience," recalled Whichard. "But he wouldn't say, 'Well, I experienced so and so in such and such a time in such and such a situation.' He would say, 'Well, we know that such and such is going on.'"[12]

"It could be the simplest little things," Mitchell said. "I remember one time we were talking about the practicalities of law enforcement officers asking questions and whether they could be overburdened. I remember saying it doesn't make any difference what kind of warnings they put out there if they had sent someone to my house when I was a kid, my mother would have told me, 'Now you answer whatever they ask you.'

"Then Henry popped up, and this is where you see a distinction in background. He said, 'Well, my mother would have never thought that I had any right to do anything else. She wouldn't have known you had any choice.' That is the practicality that the guys, [U.S. Supreme Court Chief Justice] Earl Warren and those guys up there, didn't have any access to. They not only didn't have any blacks, they didn't have anybody from the street level."

Associate Justice Robert Orr was a Republican who served with Frye in the 1990s. "We all take our personal experiences and it plays upon how we view things," Orr said. "He was not overtly filling a segment of the court that none of the other justices could fill. Everybody fully respected Henry. If he had something to say, you listened to him. You might not always agree. It was always reasoned and modulated. You never looked at Henry as the black member of the supreme court. Henry was Henry Frye with all of the background and skills and experiences that you would want to see in a justice answering tough questions."[13]

Assessing the impact of the first African American justice on the court's decision-making process some years later, U.S. Appeals Court Judge James A. Wynn, Jr., said Frye's presence on the court was "enormous," but not measurable. Wynn, an African American, served on the state court of appeals and briefly, in 1998, joined Frye on the supreme court. "What you don't know, and you can't gauge, was his influence on the decisions written by other justices. I can tell you that at times it was enormous. For instance, his service in the legislature alone commanded some deference. Who knows what he said that may have affected decisions that he did not author. Or who knows what influence he asserted because he had grown up in Ellerbe, and denied the right to vote. When his life-long experiences would aid the decision-making process, Henry Frye spoke up and he no doubt made other justices think deeper about the impact of their opinions. So his influence on the court was immeasurable from that perspective."[14]

By the 1980s, there were few cases brought to state courts that dealt directly with the civil rights of African Americans. The lawsuits that had integrated schools, opened employment, and removed racial barriers to public accommodations and housing came through the federal courts. Questions about the rights of minorities were more likely to arise in a case like *Meiselman*, which had nothing to do with race. An exception was capital cases, which retained the stain of unequal application as Frye had argued during his years in the legislature when he had tried, without success, to remove the death penalty from North Carolina law. During his arguments on the floor of the house, he stated his beliefs that the death penalty fell most often on the poor and on blacks, who received a different level of justice from whites and those with money who could hire the best representation.

When Frye joined the court, it had been more than twenty years since the last execution in North Carolina. In 1972, the U.S. Supreme Court had invalidated the death penalty in states where, as in North Carolina, the trial judge or the jury could decide, unhindered by established procedures, on whether the guilty received death or life imprisonment. The General Assembly reinstated the death penalty in 1974 and made it mandatory for the crimes of murder and, later, first-degree rape. The Court overturned that law in 1976. A new law, covering first-degree murder only, was enacted in 1977 and established a procedure for two phases in a trial involving capital murder. The first phase determined guilt or innocence and, in the second, the jury was to consider punishment. That was where a jury determined whether a guilty party would get life or be put to death, based on mitigating and aggravating circumstances. Appeals of death cases went directly to the supreme court. In the 1980s, they accounted for about 40 percent of the court's work.

Frye understood that as a justice he had to put aside his personal opposition to capital punishment. He was no longer a legislator, where he shaped state policy. His job now was to see that the law was fairly and equitably applied, regardless of his beliefs. "My question in each case," he said, "was did the person get the benefit of the law — the constitutional and procedural protections and things like that — did he get the benefit of that. If he did, uphold it."[15]

The atmosphere on the third floor changed when death cases were before the court. "I will never forget how death penalty cases felt," recalled Kenneth Lewis, one of Frye's early clerks. "The courtroom had an air of solemnity that was different from the normal level of solemnity. A life was in the balance here." Another of Frye's clerks, Donna Rascoe, said she felt "almost a different intellectual energy" as she and the clerks for the other justices pored over the briefs.[16] Those were the days when Shirley Frye made it a point to spend as much time as she could with her husband in Raleigh. "I knew it was difficult," she said. "I just wanted to be there if he needed some tea or coffee. It would affect him personally."

Appeals in capital cases usually raised multiple questions of possible error at the trial stage. Defense lawyers presented everything they could think of to avoid being criticized for sloppy performance, which led to lengthy briefs. Frye and his clerks reviewed each case in detail. Some involved horrific crimes and the files included more than cold legal arguments of the opposing sides. The visual evidence could be very disturbing. Rascoe was older than most of her fellow clerks, having worked for nine years as a teacher before entering law school, and she asked to be excused from studying the photographs of the victim in one case. "I remember going to him and saying I really don't want to have to go look at pictures," she said. "He said that was fine. He would take care of it. I felt bad, but I did not want to see those pictures. The descriptions were bad enough."

Rascoe shared Frye's objections to the death penalty. "In doing the brief and report to him, I was almost always proposing to him there was room for error or there were errors. I remember him talking to me about what I was presenting, but [he said] that we could not let them all go. Which was wonderful for him to be teaching and attentive and respectful of the law, no matter that we might have strong feelings in that area."

Death cases were on the docket during Frye's first session, but he did not write a dissent until his second year, when he was joined by Exum in *State v. Maynard*. Frye did not disagree with the conviction of Angus Maynard for the murder of a man Maynard believed was going to testify against him in a burglary case. Frye was troubled that the court had allowed the full reading of indictments from a completely unrelated case that contained errors during the sentencing phase. "Accordingly," Frye wrote, "I am not prepared to say that the combined effect of the erroneously admitted testimony and the prosecutor's improper argument based thereon were not sufficient to tip the scales in the minds of the jurors between life imprisonment and death for this defendant." Governor Martin later commuted Maynard's sentence to life in prison. He died in the Central Prison hospital in June 2006.

Frye said he had no trouble doing his duty as a judge, but these cases required extra care since the penalty was irreversible. "Death cases gave me more trouble than any other," Frye said some years later. "Whether you have the death penalty or don't have it is a legislative matter. In each case, the question was did the trial court follow the law. If you are going to take a man's life then you ought to do it in accordance with the law. Where there is any serious doubt in which that has been done, then I couldn't uphold it. Give him a new trial. It didn't make any difference if the guy was a Sunday school teacher or a serial killer. That made it hard, sometimes, with such terrible people, but you have to make sure it was in accordance with the law."

Over his eighteen years, Frye heard five hundred thirteen death cases. He dissented in thirty and wrote a dissent in twenty-four more. "Henry probably dissented beyond the norm in death penalty cases," recalled Whichard, "but while he opposed the death penalty personally he could do his job. I will say there were people on the court who were strongly pro-death penalty and strongly anti-death penalty and some with ambivalence, but I never knew anybody on that court not to take it very seriously regardless of what their personal view of what the policy should be."

Exum was the only other justice who had publicly declared his opposition to the death penalty. He did not believe it was good public policy, but he respected his oath and his obligation to uphold the law. "I have the duty to enforce the law as declared by the legislature," he said during his campaign in 1986, "and I don't think capital punishment is in any way unconstitutional."[17] After the legislature set up the two-part process in death cases, Exum and Frye continued to question the fairness. They argued in dissents that it was unfair to require all the jurors to agree that a mitigating circumstance should be allowed.

Whichard and Frye were on opposite sides in 1988 when the court considered the case of Dock McKoy, Jr., who had been convicted of killing an Anson County sheriff's deputy who was trying to coax McKoy, drunk and armed with a shotgun, out of his house. The court voted 4–3 in *State v. McKoy*, with Whichard writing the opinion upholding McKoy's sentence of death. Frye, Martin, and Exum wrote dissents. The case abounded with issues, including McKoy's competence, a "confession" made in a police van hauling him through the night to Raleigh, and the proportionality of the sentence. The one that caught the eye of the U.S. Supreme Court when the case was heard there was the procedure used in the sentencing phase. North Carolina required the jury to agree unanimously on admitting to consideration aggravating and mitigating circumstances.

While *McKoy* was making its way to the state supreme court, the U.S. Supreme Court heard a case from Maryland, a state that used a similar procedure. The court reversed the Maryland death sentence because jurors may have thought they could not consider mitigating circumstances that did not have unanimous agreement. In essence, the Court ruled, one holdout on the jury who refused to agree to a mitigating factor should not prevent it from being considered. Justice Thurgood Marshall wrote the opinion vacating McKoy's death sentence and sent the case back to North Carolina for a re-sentencing hearing. The result was a flood of appeals from many of the eighty-six men and two women on death row with McKoy in 1989 seeking review of their cases to determine if similar errors had occurred.

McKoy was re-sentenced and given a life term. He was ninety-one years old when he died in prison in 2004. The U.S. Court's decision in *McKoy* prompted a flurry of legal filings to the state court, which was asked to take another look in cases decided before the federal decision. Between 1990 and 1994, the state court overturned about 80 percent of the death penalty cases and imposed a life term or called for new trials or sentencing hearings. Most of the changes were a result of *McKoy*.[18]

Racial prejudice and the stereotypes of black men as predators were on Frye's mind in a case involving Ronald Junior Cotton, an African American who had been convicted of rape and burglary in 1987. Cotton was serving a term of life in prison, plus fifty-four years, when his appeal reached the court in 1991. The majority of the court upheld the conviction, while Frye disagreed, writing that the identification of Cotton by the white rape victim was suspect. In addition, the trial court had been wrong in allowing Cotton's employer to testify that Cotton had joked around with two white co-workers who were about the same age and race as the victim. The state court of appeals and the majority of the supreme court held this testimony was "irrelevant" to the outcome of the trial. Frye wrote that he agreed with Appeals Judge Clifton Johnson, his former law student at N.C. Central, that the error was not harmless "because the evidence of defendant's guilt ... is not so overwhelming as to remove a reasonable possibility that if this testimony had not come in, a different result would have been reached at trial."

Talking about the case years later, Frye said the racial implications in the case were inescapable. "I said you have a black man charged with raping a white girl, and they said he messed with white girls mostly, you can't say that is harmless, if it is error. As far as I am concerned it made a difference with the jury."

Cotton remained in prison for another four years until new attorneys took up his case, arranged for DNA testing of evidence, and found that the samples taken during the investigation matched a man who, at the time of Cotton's trial, had told another inmate that he had committed the crimes. The trial judge had excluded the jailhouse confession. Faced with the new DNA evidence, all charges against Cotton were dismissed and he was released in May 1995 after spending ten and a half years in prison. Cotton's story and the wrenching confession of the woman who misidentified him were later told in the book *Picking Cotton: Our Memoir of Injustice and Redemption.*

Over the years, justices tended to develop areas of special interest. Frye became the court's specialist in automobile liability insurance, an area of the law that he found jumbled and confusing due to years of adjustments and amendments made by the General Assembly. "He liked uninsured and under-insured motorist cases," recalled Seth Cohen, a clerk in 1991. Like several of Frye's clerks, the law was a second career for Cohen. He was a newspaper reporter before entering law school. "He loved stacking and unstacking. It is kind of subtle law. Say, you have three cars, and for some reason you have more than one policy. You have three insurance policies. You have a wreck in car A. Can you stack those up? The law was complicated. It was not clear you could do it."[19]

Frye's legislative experience was replayed in a case involving the land-lord-tenant law that had been part of his agenda in the General Assembly. The court decided that a renter who had been harassed by his landlord, in a so-called "self-help eviction," was entitled to treble damages under a section of the law that had been rewritten by the legislature in 1981, the last year that Frye served in the General Assembly. The changes adopted in 1981 didn't pre-clude tenants from seeking damages available under common law, Frye wrote.

On at least one occasion, Frye's instincts about a case produced a reversal of the tentative vote taken during the first-impression conference held at the conclusion of oral arguments. That vote had been 6 to 1, with Frye the holdout for a unanimous decision. "The one I remember when I knew the rest of them were all wrong had to do with interest rates. The statute that passed the leg-islature didn't say what it meant," Frye recalled. "[The case] was a petition for discretionary review from the court of appeals. Whoever had it recom-mended that we deny it. I asked that we not act, but hold up until I could look at legislative history. I said I just don't believe that the legislature meant what the court said it did. I looked everything up, wrote a memo to the rest of court saying why we ought to take the case, and what the result ought to be if we took it. We took the case and there was a split vote, even then. I was on the losing side. Somebody wrote an opinion affirming what had been pre-

viously decided and I wrote almost a stinging dissent and I circulated it. The
majority of the court went with mine. I just knew. It didn't make sense."

Frye's clerks were impressed with the care that he devoted to his work
and with his ability to find the humanity in a case involving cold, dry legal
opinions. He brought that to the discussions with his law clerks, most of
whom were over-achieving legal scholars. Their academic records demonstrated their ability to research the law — they had been doing little else for
three years — but they had no experience in how the law applied in the real
world. That was what attracted Kenneth Lewis, a Harvard graduate, to his
door. "He had this wealth of practical experience representing ordinary folks,
a broad personal background, as a lawyer in private practice," recalled Lewis,
who worked with Frye in 1986. "He really sought to try to understand the
cases from the eyes of the people involved. He tried to see that the law was
applied in a way that took into account the practical realities of people."

One such case involved the application of common law protections for
employers wishing to discharge workers without cause. *Amos v. Oakdale Knit-
ting Mills*, a 1992 case, challenged the doctrine of "at-will employment." The
plaintiffs were employees in Surry County whose employer told them they
would be required to work for less than the state minimum wage in order to
keep their jobs. The opinion followed a case two years earlier (*Coman v.
Thomas Manufacturing Co.*) in which the court held that a truck driver could
not be fired after refusing to violate federal transportation regulations. In
Amos, Frye and a unanimous court found that "firing an employee for refusing
to work for less than the statutory minimum wage violates the public policy
of North Carolina." The case reaffirmed the earlier decision, and Frye was
emphatic about the court's ruling.

"To repeat," he wrote in *Amos*, "our discussion of bad faith discharge in
Coman was *dicta*. The issue in *Coman* was whether to adopt a public policy
exception to the employment-at-will doctrine. We did."

Opinions that came from Frye's office not only had to be thoroughly
researched, and annotated, but he tested the clarity, and the tone, of the language. Frye did not indulge in flowery prose or head off into lectures on legal
history, as his friend Harry Martin did on occasion. His opinions were written
in clear declarative sentences that were free of ambiguity. They also had to
"sound" as well as they "read."

"If I had done a first draft of a document, he would sit with me and read
the opinion word for word, out loud," recalled Alan Woodlief, who clerked
with Frye in 1994 and later joined the administration at Elon University
School of Law in Greensboro. "Usually it was him reading. I generally had a
habit of reading to myself. He confirmed that was a good thing. I tell my students now, does it take time? Yes. Does it make you uncomfortable? You hear
what doesn't sound good. There is no better way to tell if something is well

written than to read it." Frye's concentration on the work remained with Woodlief for years. "This associate justice was going to painstaking detail to make sure that it was not only technically right, but it read well. This was going to be in the 'Brown books.' People are going to be quoting this, citing this."[20]

Respect for the rules of grammar and proper construction of a sentence took Frye back to his days in Ellerbe when Mrs. Hilda Easterling was grading his papers, teaching him the fundamentals of the English language, and pushing him to read some of the classics. His school may have been poor in resources, but it was rich in talent and determination of the teachers who met the students there each day. Mrs. Easterling didn't know where a Henry Frye would be in adulthood, but she was going to be sure he was prepared. "He is a poet and seemed very invested in the English language," said former clerk Beth Smoot, "especially when it was a very controversial opinion, or one that was not unanimous. It had his name on it. That was what he was very aware of. I wouldn't call him a perfectionist, because it wasn't problematic. It was just in terms of duty. It was important to the parties and he was going to get it right. Sometimes it was painstaking, because it was line by line."[21]

He also honored another lesson learned from his parents, such as respect for the dignity and feelings of others. Lisa Nieman and her boss were reviewing an opinion during Frye's first months on the court when she described a lawyer's argument as "meritless." On hearing her comment, "He pricked up his ears. He said, 'It is really not meritless, is it?' I said, 'Why isn't it?' He said, 'Well the fact that case is here and we are listening to it means it is not totally without merit.' He said, 'You know that term is kind of harsh.' He told me to think about how a lawyer would react and feel upon reading an opinion that said one of his arguments was meritless. Wouldn't that make you feel kind of bad to be on the receiving end of it?' I have never used that term since. It is cruel for one lawyer to say that to another. It is dismissive."

"I had never met, then or since, anyone who treated other people, particularly lawyers, with as much genuine respect and dignity," Nieman said.

During his nearly twenty years on the court, Frye hired more than two dozen clerks. They came from a variety of law schools and many had other work experience before they became lawyers. The high quality of clerks that he took on from law schools that had not been represented in the court before caught the eye of his colleagues. "I would ask Henry, how did you get this guy," said Justice Martin. "He told me about going to North Carolina Central Law School. He says there are a lot of people over there at Central who could be at Chapel Hill if they wanted to, but they prefer to go to a basically black school."

Frye looked for clerks who had excelled in the classroom and whose reputations were impeccable. Before making an offer, he called references like former teachers, even those who had taught his candidates in high school. And he read carefully their writing samples and legal handiwork submitted with their applications. One candidate arrived to find that Frye had taken his pen to one of the briefs she had submitted with her application. "He had gone through it, considered it, and analyzed it," recalled Rascoe. "He pointed out two or three things that could be improved."

Just as Governor Hunt had given him an opportunity to serve as the state's first black associate justice, Frye wanted to open the door to young black lawyers and graduates of schools who had often been overlooked for opportunities at that level. His first hire was an African American, Alexis C. Pearce, a Wake Forest University law graduate. In his second year, he hired Kathryn DeAngelo, a former West Virginia schoolteacher who was white and a graduate of North Carolina Central. "She had the best grades," Frye said. "I was looking for a black clerk and she wasn't black. But among those I interviewed, she was the best. I needed help."

Clerks lived on subsistence wages. Life was tough, especially with college bills to pay, but the jobs were coveted nonetheless. "Think about this," said Lewis. "The year before you are in law school. You are reading these cases and thinking about the law. Then you are reading cases and helping a judge deliberate on these cases and assist in writing of these opinions. That is pretty heady stuff. You start off at the top. You get to work closely and intimately with someone who has lived a very accomplished life professionally. They are asking you your opinion from your vast experience of twenty-five years of life.

"He would say, tell me your view about this. He would bring you inside his mind to see, here is how I am thinking about this case. What do you think about that? It was a rare opportunity to work with someone at that level with matters as serious as a supreme court decision. You have insight into how decisions are made. You have a base of actual knowledge about that."

Frye was a role model, especially for African Americans. Ken McNeely, a Charlotte native with a law degree from Howard University, said, "He became the perfect model for me as a lawyer and just a person of sensitivity and thoughtfulness. I immediately thought this is a person from whom I could learn a lot, not just about the law, but life. I thought, this is a perfect mentor."[22] Twenty years after he left the court for private practice, McNeely was the president of AT&T's California operations. His first job was at Moore and Van Allen in Charlotte, a firm that had also hired Lewis a couple of years earlier. "He said Ken, you really have to stay in North Carolina because you are really needed in North Carolina. We have to start to integrate these large law firms. You are the right person to do it. I went with Moore and Van Allen, one of the largest firms in the state. Ken Lewis was in their Raleigh office."

Reginald T. Shuford was a law student at the University of North Carolina in 1990 when he met Frye during a visit to Chapel Hill. Shuford was from Wilmington and was the first in his family to attend college. They met during a brief encounter at the law school, where Frye mentioned that he had yet to hire a UNC graduate. Shuford made up his mind to remedy that. "There were very few role models of successful black lawyers, let alone judges in my life," Shuford said. He applied for the clerkship and reminded Frye during his job interview of their earlier meeting. "He remembered that." Shuford got the job, along with a classmate, Seth Cohen.[23]

"It was sort of like a foursome, Seth and I and Justice Frye and Mrs. [Pauline] Irving," said Shuford. "We would talk with him about issues. I learned to be a better writer, to be careful about detail, and to be mindful of myself in the public. He was like, you all are a reflection of me and my office. I expect you to represent me well." Shuford later became a senior staff attorney for the American Civil Liberties Union, where he became specialist in racial profiling cases, before moving to San Francisco, where he became director of law and policy for the Equal Justice Society. Cohen entered private practice in Greensboro.

The clerks often became members of a justice's extended family. In Frye's case, some traveled with him when he had a speaking engagement out of town. They became his opponents in vigorous games of table tennis, and joined him when he went bowling. They had his respect for integrity and honesty, a strong work ethic, and a sense of humor. He never expressed anger and "great googlely mooglely" was the closest he came to uttering an expletive. Donna Rascoe, who went into private practice in Raleigh, remembered a quote Frye said he borrowed from a brother — "I'm doing the best I can with what I got and I ain't got much."

His quiet, humble nature was compelling. "To meet him you wouldn't know that he is the first in so many ways in North Carolina," said Lisa Nieman. "He never came across that way. Just so utterly respectful, just treats with dignity every person he ever met. And he did it in such a way, he was very kind."

Frye didn't flaunt his position. One day — Shirley Frye wasn't sure what year — she and her husband were returning to Raleigh from a state Bar association meeting when a state highway patrolman pulled them over. Henry was driving his wife's car, not his own, which carried a special license plate identifying him as a member of the court. "I don't know if he was speeding or what. Henry never challenges. If they say he was speeding, he'll say how fast was I going. I didn't know I was going that fast." As requested, Henry joined the trooper in the front seat of his car.

"The patrolman was writing the ticket," Shirley said, "and he asked, where did he work? In Raleigh. What do you do? I am in the legal profession.

What do you do? I am on the supreme court. And he said, why didn't you tell me? I didn't think it was necessary. He said I have already started writing the ticket. Henry didn't say anything. When he got ready to go, he shook Henry's hand."

In 1992, Justice Harry Martin left the court, a casualty of the state's mandatory retirement age of 72. He filed a lawsuit and challenged the legislature's mandate. "It's a matter of competitiveness and ability, rather than age," Martin told the *Associated Press*, calling the limit arbitrary. "I mean, if the legislature has got the authority to set it at age 72, they can set it at 50 if they want to."[24] His friend and ally in decisions for the past decade, Chief Justice Exum, wrote the court's unanimous opinion upholding the age limit. Frye had joined Martin in several of his major decisions, including two cases that had helped revive the state constitution as a protector of individual rights, but felt compelled to vote against him here.

Justice Martin left early in the year and Governor Jim Martin appointed I. Beverly Lake, Jr., in his place. Lake would serve for less than a year, however, losing to Democrat Sarah Parker in the subsequent fall election when voters chose her to serve the balance of Martin's term. The Republican Party under Martin had paid close attention to the judicial races and the 1992 race was another step in a campaign to relieve the Democrats of the dominance of the court, which they had enjoyed for nearly one hundred years. In 1994, Lake and Appeals Court Judge Robert Orr won seats on the court, defeating incumbent Sarah Parker and Jim Fuller, a Democrat who had unseated incumbent Louis B. Meyer in the spring party primary.

Chief Justice Exum had announced plans to retire at the end of the year. During his eight years as chief, Exum had modernized the court, bringing computers and other technology to bear on the internal operations of the judicial system. He had appeared three times before the General Assembly to give a report on the state of the judiciary. His predecessors in the job had been content to remain clear of the legislature, even to the point of depriving the court of funding for necessary equipment and supplies. One of Exum's greatest concerns was how judges came to the bench. He had been the object of a mean-spirited campaign in 1986 that attempted to make his election a referendum on the death penalty, and the experience was not lost on him. Exum had called the popular election of judges "a black cloud on the horizon of the judiciary," and both he and former Chief Justice Rhoda Billings had called for another way. His efforts to produce an alternative process had gone nowhere. In 2010 he co-chaired a state Bar association committee that came up with a non-partisan plan for the selection of judges who would then face a retention election if they remained beyond their first term.[25]

At the time of Exum's retirement in December 1994, four more years remained in his term. Governor Jim Hunt, who had been elected to an unprecedented third term in 1992, followed the court tradition and named the most senior justice, his old friend Burley Mitchell, as Exum's successor. As a result, Mitchell's seat became vacant and Hunt chose Parker to remain on the court as Mitchell's replacement. She took her seat at the conference table along with Lake, the man who had just defeated her in the general election. It was just the beginning of the development of a partisan court that held implications for its future.

13

Chief Justice

In the fall of 1992, Associate Justices Henry Frye and Burley Mitchell ran unopposed for re-election to eight-year terms on the N.C. supreme court. It would be the last time in the appellate court races that the Republican Party would allow that to happen. During the final decade of the twentieth century, the state judiciary would be called into play in more partisan contests than had been seen for nearly one hundred years, and the door would close on an era of one-party control.

While James G. Martin was governor the Republicans had broken into the last stronghold of the Democratic Party, the state's judiciary, first with the appointment of Rhoda Billings as associate justice in 1985 and later with the election, in 1988, of a feisty young lawyer named Robert Orr to the state court of appeals. Orr's election proved a Republican could win a statewide judicial race and, in 1990, emboldened by Orr's success, the party fielded a full slate of candidates, including the races for chief justice and two seats held by incumbent associate justices.

It was a historic election year. Most of the attention in the fall campaign was on the race for the U.S. Senate between Democrat Harvey Gantt and the man who was the state's best-known Republican, the incumbent Jesse Helms. Gantt was an architect, a former two-term mayor of Charlotte, and an African American who had broken the color line at Clemson University in the 1960s. His career had been much like Frye's. He had carved out a reputation as a competent professional who found success in the mainstream of white commerce and politics in Charlotte. Helms was a former television commentator who had greeted the civil rights movement with ridicule, and worse. Since election to his first term in 1972, Helms had consistently pulled the state Republican Party to the right as he taunted liberals and kept his political base afire with attacks on homosexuals and tangential racial issues like the Martin Luther King, Jr., holiday, while he wrapped himself in the flag and small-town virtues. He had defeated all comers, including Governor Jim Hunt in 1984, and Hunt was considered the most electable Democrat around.

The Gantt-Helms race was seen as metaphor for the shifting politics of a southern state. Liberal and moderate Democrats, and African Americans, rallied behind Gantt, who had won a party primary against white opponents. There was talk that a new progressive coalition could finally overcome the Republican who led the state party away from its traditional moderate base and created a bastion of support for the conservative political cause and its champion Ronald Reagan.

Gantt pulled close to Helms late in the campaign, but a wave of negative advertising, tainted with racial overtones, appeared in the final days and Helms walked away with his fourth victory. The contest generated attention all across the nation and North Carolina voters responded with the highest Election Day turnout in recent memory. Sixty-five percent of the electorate voted in Charlotte, compared to 45 percent in previous elections. Hundreds of people were standing in line at closing time. That was true elsewhere and Democrats in Durham and Greensboro got judges to order polling stations to remain open beyond the normal closing time to accommodate those waiting in line.

Helms's political coattails had never been especially long. He wasn't really a party man, although he was pleased to lend his political organization to Republicans he favored. Nonetheless, the large turnout, and the uncertainty of the shifting landscape, made for anxiety on election night among judicial candidates like incumbent Chief Justice James G. Exum, Jr., and Associate Justices Willis Whichard and John Webb. They won, but I. Beverly Lake, Jr., came within a handful of votes of unseating Webb. None of the Republicans on the ballot won. Lake and others called foul and challenged the results coming out of the counties where polls had been allowed to remain open beyond the appointed hour. They said the extra hours had not been allowed at precincts where Republicans held an edge.

Eighteen months later, in February 1992, Lake became an associate justice by virtue of an appointment by Governor Martin, who named him to fill the vacancy created by Harry Martin's retirement. Lake campaigned to retain the seat in the fall general election, the one in which Frye and Mitchell ran unopposed, but he was defeated by Appeals Court Judge Sarah Parker, a Democrat who had filed to run against him.

With Lake's defeat, Orr was once again the lone Republican on the appellate bench. He was from Hendersonville, in the mountains, and came from the party's moderate wing. Governor Martin had appointed him to the court of appeals in 1986. In 1988, he made history with his successful race and a campaign that broke from the script created two years earlier when the rump group, Citizens for a Conservative Court, had tried to make the death penalty *the* issue in the judicial races. Orr knew that politics could have hard edges, but he had campaigned differently from other Republicans. He tried to create a broader appeal. More importantly, he sought, and got, the support of organized black political groups, like the influential Durham Committee on the Affairs of Black People. He also met with newspaper editorial writers and secured endorsements.

"The theme of that [1986] race, was, we are the conservatives, they are the liberals. Beat your chest, talk about how conservative you were," Orr said one day long after he left the bench. "My whole strategy involved finding Democrat-leaning institutions and organizations and trying to get their endorsements. Of course, this drove Jack Hawke, the party chairman, absolutely crazy. I'd announce the North Carolina Association of Educators endorses me. I'd announce the trial academy. He said, 'What are you doing. This is crazy.' I said, 'Jack this is the only way you are going to win when you only have $55,000 [to spend on a statewide race].' The party was never comfortable with that strategy because it ran against the grain."[1]

After his election, the governor signed Orr's judicial commission for eight years, the term set by the constitution. That wasn't right, a Democrat challenger argued in a 1992 lawsuit contending that Orr was elected to serve the balance of an unexpired term, not for a full eight years, and should have to run again. The supreme court agreed. Orr won his second statewide race that year.

All in all, until Orr came along, Republican lawyers saw the state's judiciary as a closed shop where they were not allowed. The system for the election of judges had always favored the Democrats, who had long held the edge in down-ballot races that required candidates to campaign from one end of the state to the other. "With all due respect to my Democratic friends," Orr said, "the mindset was 'Hey we like you, but Republicans don't have any right to be on the bench.'"

The judiciary had been harder for Republicans to crack than it had been for African Americans. By the early 1990s, Frye was the only African American on the supreme court, but there were two African Americans on the court of appeals and three others had been on that bench and then left. Richard Ervin, the first African American on the state court of appeals, had gone on to serve as a U.S. district judge. The two sitting judges were Clifton Johnson and James A. Wynn, Jr., who had defeated Allyson Duncan, a Republican whom Martin had appointed to the court in 1990 to replace Democrat Charles Becton. (In 2003, Duncan became the first African American to be elected president of the N.C. Bar Association. That was the same year her nomination to the Fourth Circuit U.S. Court of Appeals was confirmed by the U.S. Senate. In a curious turn, Wynn would later join her on the appeals court in 2011 under appointment by President Barack Obama.)

Governor Martin's interest in breaking the Democratic Party's hold on the state judiciary coincided with the partisan battles taking place in Washington over the confirmation of President Ronald Reagan's Supreme Court nominees. With the Senate's rejection of Robert Bork, a Reagan nominee, in 1987, and the bitter and protracted confirmation hearings over President George H. W. Bush's nomination of Clarence Thomas in 1991, the composition of the nation's judiciary had become a political event where nominees were being measured not only by their professional qualifications but by their perceived attitudes on hot-button issues such as abortion. Governor Martin himself had introduced the theme in North Carolina when he had asked voters in 1986 to make the conservative choice and vote Republican. The drumbeat had continued on into the early 1990s and was attracting more and more attention from voters.[2]

The payoff for Republican efforts finally came in the fall of 1994. The results of the general election were an upending event for the Democrats with voters excited by a national Republican campaign against President Bill Clinton's health care plan and partisan rhetoric accented by congressional scandals. In that election, North Carolina Republicans doubled their congressional representation to eight, leaving Democrats in the minority with four seats. For the first time in the twentieth century, Republicans won a majority of the seats in the state house of representatives— enough to elect a speaker — and picked up thirteen seats in the state senate. Orr and Lake won full eight-year terms on the supreme court. For the first time in the state's history, Republicans on the supreme court would not have to defend their seats at the next election.[3]

Orr had precipitated the 1994 success by declaring his candidacy for the court in 1993, almost in a fit of pique. The incident arose when he was told that speaking to a group of Republican lawyers, who called themselves the Lincoln Forum, about running for office was a violation of the Code of Judicial Conduct. His colleague on the court of appeals, Clifton Johnson, who chaired the state Judicial Standards Commission, had questioned the propriety of his appearance before the group. Orr argued that the Lincoln Forum was no different from gatherings of women lawyers, black lawyers, or trial lawyers, but he did not want to risk a complaint. "Finally, I said, 'Cliff, I am correct that if I am a candidate for political office, I can speak at a political event.' He said, 'Yes.' Well consider me a candidate for the supreme court. I had no intention of running for supreme court [before that time]. I wasn't even sure who was up at the time, but it just irritated me so badly, and 1992 had left such a bad taste in my mouth, I just said, 'OK, if you guys want to mess with me I will run.'"

Orr subsequently talked Lake into joining him on the ballot. Lake was reluctant, having run and lost two statewide campaigns already. He was on hand, however, when Orr formally announced his campaign. Standing at the back of the room, a reporter asked Lake, "'Aren't you glad you are not going through it this time?' I said, 'Well, I am not so sure I am. I like what Orr is saying and he made a lot of sense and I am going to go back to office and think about this thing. I might change my mind.'" He did and filed as a candidate against Sarah Parker, the Democrat who had beaten him two years earlier.[4] Voters were single-minded in their rejection of Democrats in 1994, even in the judicial races. Orr and Lake received decisive majorities with vote totals that were within 150 votes of each other.

Changes that had come to the supreme court over the years had always been slow, almost imperceptible. If there were ever a noticeable and dramatic shift in the life of the court, however, it came in 1995. And it was not just the arrival of two Republican justices. The events of 1994, both with Republicans and among the Democratic membership of the court, created circumstances that would shift what had been considered a moderate to conservative court, with a reputed "liberal" as chief justice, to a more conservative body with not only new membership, but new leadership.

Early in 1994, Chief Justice Exum had announced his plans to retire at the end of the year. By tradition, Louis B. Meyer, the senior associate, would have been his successor. That spring, however, Meyer lost a primary election to challenger Jim Fuller, largely due to opposition from the trial bar, which was unhappy with Meyer's conservative voting record. He had a tendency to support the defendants in civil actions, said his old friend Jim Exum. Even Burley Mitchell, whom Meyer found to be an ally in his dissents in criminal cases, said the same thing. "I don't know anybody who knew Louis personally and didn't like him. But if you read his opinions, you would think he was Dracula. They were really draconian."[5]

With Meyer no longer on the court, the senior associate was Mitchell. Governor Jim Hunt, who had won an unprecedented third term in 1992, named Mitchell chief justice on December 12, 1994, as Exum prepared his exit after twenty years on the court. Cognizant of the apparent trend among voters to look for judges who were tough on crime, the governor said at the time of the appointment: "Burley Mitchell understands how important it is to keep dangerous criminals behind bars." Once again, the court's new chief justice warned that partisan politics was interfering with the work of the court. The electioneering required in the fall of 1994 had left the court behind in its work, Mitchell said.[6]

Mitchell took office in early January. Aside from Lake and Orr — the Republicans — Mitchell's court included Frye, Whichard, Webb, and Parker. Though Lake had defeated Parker in November, Governor Hunt appointed her to replace Mitchell, who would fill the balance of Exum's term. The revolving door of justices was still turning.

Some writers observed that the court would be more conservative than it had been under Exum. The definition of "conservative" at that time meant the court tended to side more with prosecutors and had a pro-business tilt.

In fact, the dynamics of the court were far more complex than that. The court no longer had Exum as chief, but it also did not have Meyer as an associate justice. The measure of conservatism most often used during Exum's administration — rulings involving the death penalty — was even less valid than it had been before. Between 1990 and 1993 the court had upheld the death penalty in only 12 percent of the cases it heard, but most of those were appeals for rehearing that had been filed in the wake of *McKoy*. Once those appeals had been exhausted, the court returned to its normal rhythm. From July 1993 to the end of 1994, the death penalty had been upheld nearly 70 percent of the time.[7]

The court was so backlogged with cases when Mitchell became chief justice that he opened the first week of work with five consecutive days of sessions. Twenty-seven cases were heard with oral arguments running well into the afternoon, with no break for lunch. "Burley didn't believe in taking breaks," Orr recalled. "If you needed to go to the men's room, you had better make a mad dash in between [cases]. He wasn't going to take a recess. We would go until two or two-thirty in the afternoon, sitting there just straight on, no break for lunch or anything, not until all arguments were heard." Mitchell may have been bounced from the U.S. Marine Corps when the service found he was underage at the time of his enlistment, but he was there long enough to learn how to be a demanding drill sergeant.[8]

Just as Mitchell was assuming the leadership of the court, in January 1995, a case involving a group of students from the southeastern corner of the state was just before being heard in superior court in Wake County. Its official title fills more than half of a standard-sized sheet of paper; it came to be known as *Leandro* because the names of Kathleen M. Leandro and her son, Robert, were the first in a list of sixteen parents or guardians suing for equalization of education funding in North Carolina. Supported by the boards of education in their home counties, and reinforced by more plaintiffs in other parts of the state, the suit alleged that a shortage of funds in low-wealth counties shortchanged students faced with sorry school buildings, inadequate supplies and instructional material, and low-paid teachers while students in high-wealth districts fared much better. The result was an inferior and unequal education that perpetuated a cycle of poverty. The plaintiffs argued that the state of North Carolina and the state board of education were failing to meet a constitutional obligation to "the privilege of education, and it is the duty of the state to guard and maintain that right."[9]

The N.C. Supreme Court, like others around the country, had begun to see more cases where attorneys relied more on the state constitution rather than the federal document. The shift had begun in the mid–1980s. Shortly after Associate Justice Harry Martin retired, he updated a history of the court. In his review of the court's more recent years, Martin highlighted three cases that illustrated the renewed interest in the state constitution. He called them the "three Cs." One was *State v. Robert Lee Carter,* in which the court held that the taking of a blood sample without a search warrant, but under another type of court order, did not meet state constitutional standards for search and seizure. In another case, *State v. Cofield,* five justices agreed that excluding an African American as jury foreman was unconstitutional under the state and federal documents. Finally, in *Dr. Alvis L. Corum v. University of North Carolina,* the court reaffirmed Corum's right of free speech under the state constitution.

Martin had become so interested in the state constitution that he had begun teaching a course on it at the UNC Law School. He believed that state constitutions, some of which predated the federal constitution, gave "the people of the individual states greater protection of their individual rights because of the way people live in the different states." Once these cases got to the courts, the state constitution came alive again. "The courts are not self-starters," he said in 1988. "We have to be cranked, and unless the lawyers raise state constitutional grounds, they're not before us."[10]

Leandro delivered a case that would have a profound impact on the state's educational system. Henry Frye took notice of it as it was making its way through the judicial system. In 1996, the court of appeals ruled in favor of the state and said the constitution provided a right to access to education but did not include any guarantee for the quality of education that students would find in the classroom. "What I remember," Frye said some years later, "was when the court of appeals decided the case and said in effect that the constitution doesn't really guarantee you anything. All of us, when we read it in the paper, said that can't be right. It has got to mean more than what the court of appeals said it did. Of course, the question is how much does it mean. That was really when I got interested in it. Some of the others had been following it. We said we have got to see what we can do about this thing."

Every chair in the courtroom was filled when the case was called by the supreme court. By that time, *Leandro* had attracted attention from attorneys representing school systems across the state, public interest groups associated with the public schools, including those in poor counties, as well as the American Civil Liberties Union, Legal Services of North Carolina, and the Eastern North Carolina Chamber of Commerce. When arguments ended later that afternoon and the justices had retreated to their conference room, Frye was eager to take the case and write the court's opinion. The case touched him to the core; he had experienced a world of unequal school funding and neglect that stifled lives and curtailed promising futures. It had been apparent in his youth in Ellerbe when his high school principal, S.B.T. Easterling, struggled to find decent books, adequate space for his classrooms, and school buses with engines that could be counted on to start early in the morning.

The consensus for supporting the plaintiffs' arguments was strong within the conference. There was no question that the quality of education varied widely from county to county, all across the state. The problems were not just within the five counties that were part of the lawsuit. At the same time, the members of the court realized that if they did speak to the issue and compel the legislature to come up with a remedy, the message should be clear and unmistakable. Frye didn't ask for the case when he had a chance. Rather, he left the opinion for Chief Justice Mitchell to write. There was agreement that while unanimity was important, so was a decision written by the chief justice.[11]

"We said the constitution has got to mean something and so what does it mean," Frye recalled. "We not only interpreted the statute but we had to decide how to get something done. One of the things we wanted to do was to push the legislature to do something. But in trying to tell another branch of government, especially a more powerful branch, what they needed to do was a pretty serious thing. It reminded some of us, me in particular, of [U.S. Chief Justice] John Marshall and his first major case where he was trying to say what had to be done without ordering the person to do it. In this case, if we had ordered [the legislators to provide more funding], they would have said go jump in the lake somewhere. The question was how to write it to get the legislature to do something and keep with it. We thought a unanimous opinion, or close to a unanimous opinion, written by the chief justice, would have come close to getting that done."

Buried in Mitchell's experience were years of defending the state's school laws. He was a young lawyer in the state attorney general's office in the late 1960s and early 1970s when he had represented the state school superintendent and the state board of education in suits involving school desegregation. At times, he had even argued against the intrusion of the federal courts in the state's school business. Now, he was on the other side as he prepared an order for the state supreme court that would affect years of public school financing and reshape the public schools by judicial fiat.

Sitting in his office many years later, with windows overlooking Fayetteville Street and the Justice Building where he struggled with *Leandro*, Mitchell said, "The first brief I ever signed in the Supreme Court of the United States was in a case, *Rodriquez v. San Antonio Independent School District*. [The question was] does the U.S. Constitution guarantee the right to public education? I was on brief with all the attorneys general who sided with Texas and said there wasn't such a right. We won there. Here I am now, towards the end of my court career, and out pops up the same issue, but under a different constitution. Our constitution says there is a right to a free public education. It is in there. If it is there, it has got to mean something. It was a simple opinion to write but it took me some months to get everybody in harness, everybody except Bob Orr. If there is not a quantitative aspect to it, it is a meaningless right.

"It is a once-in-every-other-generation type of case," he said. "It was not a new right, but it had never been acknowledged. The court of appeals had decided there wasn't such a right. Basically, they had decided you had to have some shed to open up, and let the kids in for so many hours a day, but it doesn't have to have any content. That's stated broad for effect, but it is accurate. That was it."[12]

Mitchell's first draft was edited word by word by the other six justices. He referred to prior court decisions, one dating to 1917, in which the court had held there is a qualitative standard for public education. Later provisions enacted by the General Assembly reinforced that requirement under the law. The difficult issue was not the constitutional promise of the state to provide good education, one that provides "academic and vocational skills to enable the student to compete on an equal basis with others in further formal education or gainful employment in contemporary society," but how to implement such a decision. The copies of Mitchell's handiwork made the rounds of the offices and his colleagues chewed over the draft for weeks. He failed to win unanimity. Justice Orr wanted the court to go further and require equal funding for each district. To Mitchell, that didn't sound practical.

"Orr wrote a dissent," Mitchell said. "He said, 'Yeh, there is such a right but I would go further and say every school district must have the same amount of money.' I had background he didn't have, I had dealt with all these school boards, and I knew it was going to be hard enough not to have it be entirely some measure by money. I went to great pains in that opinion to say we are not talking about money here, but educational result. You have got to show that your kids are given the opportunity for a sound basic education. The best way to show that is some of them are getting money. At that point, the Topeka schools, that school district was spending more per capita than any other district in the country and its performance was still falling. What Bob wanted, well it was simplistic in my mind."

Years later, Orr was steadfast in his position. "The big issue there, and I still can't believe Henry didn't join me on this, was that equality of funding. Burley was hell bent that we were not going down the equal funding road. We all felt there was the constitutional right, but how do you articulate it. The plaintiffs, that was their primary argument, there is this equal opportunity provision in the state constitution that requires that the state to equalize the disparity of funding in high-wealth and low-wealth counties. Burley was not going there. I dissented on that."

Frye tried to find a way to bring Orr along to the majority, but without success. "In other states, courts were ordering legislatures to do all sorts of things," Frye said, "and courts were taking over the schools in various parts of the country. Burley, in particular, said that is not working. We have got to find another way to get the same thing done. Largely it was his strategy to lay out what it means and then get it back to a trial judge. He wanted to write it in such a way that the legislature and the governor would try to get some money. That was the strategy. He and I and some others thought that we have got to get the legislature to see that this ought to be done. Of course the governor could use his persuasion."

Frye was sympathetic to Orr's position. "So we had to avoid saying the amount of money that each school got had to be exactly the same thing," Frye said. "The words had to be very carefully chosen to do that. When Burley wrote a draft, it wasn't just adopted. We all had criticisms of it. And we came to something that we thought all of us could live with, I think, except for Orr. He wanted to go further. I wanted to go further, but I didn't know quite how far. I figured I couldn't force it anyway. The more dissenting opinions you have in a case the more confusing the law is." Frye joined the majority.[13]

Mitchell put the implementation of the court's order in the hands of Superior Court Judge Howard Manning, who was known as a no-nonsense judge. A Republican, Manning had opposed former Chief Justice Exum in his bid for re-election in 1990. Mitchell had been through the experience of *Brown* and didn't want his court's decision to hang flapping in the breeze like the Warren Court's work in 1954. "Just writing that opinion didn't get it done," Mitchell said. "We went through 'all deliberate speed,' opinion after opinion out of the Supreme Court to get it. I knew what it was and I knew it was going to take a lot more follow-up, which is why I assigned Howard Manning to it."

The case was still in Manning's court more than a dozen years later.

Leandro never became infected with partisanship. It was an issue that touched schools all across the state. Frye said the introduction of Republicans Lake and Orr occurred without incident. In fact, Frye found himself siding with Orr in more cases than he had expected. The young Republican — he was finishing law school when Frye was halfway through his legislative career — had arrived at the court with a black law clerk and became the only other justice who regularly hired African Americans. After a few months of working together, Orr said any anxiety over their party labels faded into the woodwork.

"I think that after a while Henry gained sufficient confidence in me," Orr recalled. "One of the sort of tangential issues was that none of the other white judges ever hired black clerks. When I came to supreme court I had already had two black law clerks and brought a third with me. I taught at North Carolina Central. Henry knew that I had received endorsement with his groups. He felt comfortable with me. [But] it was still hard to get rid of the R by your name."

Frye and Orr ended up on the same side in a number of cases, including a high-profile lawsuit that arose out of the deaths in 1991 of twenty-five workers at the Imperial Foods Products plant in Hamlet, a small Richmond County town and former railway stop not far from Ellerbe. State investigators determined that the needless loss of life was due to plant exits that were locked and an inadequate fire suppression system. The state labor department issued eighty-three citations under the Occupational Safety and Health Act of North Carolina — whose creation had passed through a committee chaired by Frye in the legislature in 1971— and the plant's owner subsequently pleaded guilty to involuntary manslaughter.[14]

Injured survivors, and the families of those who were killed, sued state officials who they claimed had failed to do their jobs to protect workers under the "public duty doctrine." Justice Whichard wrote the opinion that reversed a court of appeals decision allowing the plaintiffs' suit against the state. Orr and Frye disagreed with the majority, which held that the state was not liable for the deaths and injuries.

"I voted with him," Frye said. "We were both in the minority." He did not join in Orr's written dissent because he believed the language was too intemperate. "I had to get him to tone it down some but he never did tone it down as much as I wanted him to. He felt strongly about that thing. He started off calling them all sorts of names and I said, 'You can't do that. This is something that is going to last for a hundred years. You have got to tone it down.' I generally agreed with him but the language that he was using was what I did not like.

"I didn't think much of the public duty doctrine anyway," Frye said. "I thought they ought to figure a way to pay those people something."

Orr said, "Henry and I fought it for the next three years. Every time a case came up on the public duty doctrine, Henry and I were in there whittling away, trying to reverse what they had done. Does that make me a liberal or a conservative? I'd say it was conservative that the other side pulled this theory out of a case that had no relation. That was one of the more interesting ones we teamed up on."

Orr was soon to have company, as the political complexion of the country took a dramatic turn. In 1998, Justice Whichard, a Democrat, retired from the court to become dean of the Campbell University Law School, and Court of Appeals Judge Mark Martin, a Republican, was elected to his seat. Justice John Webb reached the mandatory retirement age in 1998 and Governor Hunt appointed state Appeals Court Judge James A. Wynn, Jr., to his seat. But, Wynn lost election to the remainder of Webb's term to Republican George L. Wainwright. Thus, Mitchell's re-election to the court in 1996 now amounted to an important political footnote for the state. He would be the last white male Democrat elected to the supreme court for at least fifteen years.

Thus, when the court convened in 1999, Mitchell presided over the state's first supreme court with a Republican majority in modern history. Not long into the year, he let Frye know of his plans to retire on his thirtieth anniversary of state service. As the senior associate justice, Frye was in line to be his successor. He told Frye: "I have got my time in and I am working for nothing. If I am going to go out and do something else, I am still a pretty sellable commodity. If I wait ten or twelve years I may not be. I said I am going to go ask the governor and see if I retire, and will he appoint you because I would really like to be a part of making that history. If it is not you, it may be another decade or so before someone else comes up through the chairs."[15] (On retirement from state service, Mitchell became head of the appellate division of one of the state's largest law firms, Womble Carlyle Sandridge and Rice.)

Frye was ready when the governor called this time. "The governor said, 'Burley is going to retire and I want to appoint you.' At that time I didn't have to think about it. I had already thought about it. I wasn't going to turn that down. When he called me to go on court I wasn't sure I wanted to go on the court. But when he called with chief justice, I said, 'Yes sir.' I said, 'Governor, when do you want to do it?'"[16]

The date the governor chose to make his announcement, August 2, 1999, came right in the midst of a judicial conference that Frye was due to attend in Williamsburg, Virginia. Hunt was undeterred. He told Frye to continue with his plans, but to be ready to leave in the middle of the day for a helicopter ride to Raleigh. The governor's air service picked up Henry and Shirley and flew them Raleigh where a highway patrol detail drove them to the State Capitol where Governor Hunt made the formal announcement in the old house chamber, the hall where Henry had served as a student legislator in 1952.

Once again Frye was surrounded by his family as the governor announced his historic appointment. Sixteen years earlier, when he joined the court, there had been a possibility that Frye would some day lead one of the three branches of government. Now, political good fortune, and unexpected events along the way, had turned the possibility into a reality. "His very accomplishments have proven that you can rise to the top," the governor said, "no matter how small or how rural the town where you grew up."

Henry and Shirley Frye were still wobbly from the rushed trip to Raleigh. He beamed and a wide grin spread across his face as the governor talked. Frye was flanked by his wife, his son Harlan, and three grandchildren. His eldest son, Henry Jr., was absent. A superior court judge, he was holding court elsewhere in the state. Frye had little to say other than to thank the governor for the high honor. "This is a good way to cap my judicial career," he told a reporter from his hometown newspaper.[17] Shirley's eyes were filled with tears. "I thought about how hard he had worked and how hard he has been committed to this system. North Carolina has been good to us." All around the room were African Americans who held high-profile state jobs. Included in the audience were other judicial officers, a cabinet secretary, legislators, the chair of the board of governors of the University of North Carolina, and Colonel Richard W. Holden, the commander of the State Highway Patrol. In 1969, Henry Frye was in his first term in the state House when Holden was sworn in as a cadet in the first patrol class that accepted African Americans.

The governor recognized the changes that had taken place. "Henry Frye laid the ground work for this progress. This is the man that we announce today. As he becomes the first African American as chief justice, he will lead the courts into the next century. He has helped to build our schools, and build our people and given them full and frequent opportunity."

A month later, on September 7, 1999, Frye took the oath as chief justice in the courtroom of the N.C. Supreme Court. Every seat was filled and guests stood along the walls. The Frye family sat on the front row, along with the governor and his wife. Those who couldn't be accommodated there watched a telecast of the proceedings from the sanctuary of the First Baptist Church and the auditorium of the N.C. Department of Transportation. Frye made a point of thanking his hosts at First Baptist, an African American congregation on Wilmington Street, which had never before been given such as honor. The family's old friend from Providence Baptist Church in Greensboro, the Reverend Howard Chubbs, had been on hand for every similar occasion since Henry began his political career. He delivered the invocation this time as well, standing squarely in front of the life-size portrait of the nineteenth-century jurist Thomas Ruffin that hung behind the bench.

Chubbs was expansive in an invocation of more than four minutes. He took especial note of the importance of the day for North Carolina's African American citizens. "The history and significance of this occasion speaks loudly to this nation. That the descendant of those who were once considered commercial property and less than human, the son of poor, but honest and proud parents, who has been denied the right to vote after having served his country as an officer in her armed forces, has been asked to lead and become chief justice of this state's highest court, and to be the last to occupy it in this century and the first in a new century, we realize is unquestionably historic and we are grateful that you have allowed our eyes to see it."

Indeed, it was historic. A hundred years earlier, the 1899 General Assembly, which included the last African Americans to serve there until Frye arrived in 1969, had approved constitutional amendments that would marginalize African Americans from public life. Among the changes was a literacy requirement for voting. This and the other Jim Crow provision were approved in the election of 1900.

Shirley took her place beside her husband, holding a Bible in her hand, as Associate Justice Sarah Parker administered the oath to the state's twenty-fifth leader of the high court. With the ceremony complete, Chief Justice Henry E. Frye took his seat in the center of the bench, with future chief justices Parker and I. Beverly Lake, Jr., seated on either side. It was a profoundly moving occasion for a man who usually concealed his emotions. For Frye, a broad, toothy smile was an exception. Tears dropped from his eyes as he recalled his parents, teachers and others, and especially his wife, Shirley, who all had inspired and encouraged him along the way. "I didn't get here by myself," he said. "My mother and father told us not to give up when going gets tough.

"The English language has an abundance of words and expressions, suitable to every occasion, I suppose," he said. "Nevertheless I have searched, without success, for the appropriate words to fully express my own feelings today. I am awed." As he was concluding his brief remarks, his oldest granddaughter wiped a tear from the eye of her father, Henry Frye, Jr., now a superior court judge. The elder Frye said, "Thank you for helping North Carolina live up to its motto."[18]

In deciding cases, the vote of the chief justice carried the same weight as that of his colleagues, but the chief justice was the one responsible for the operation of the state's court system, from the tired and tattered quarters on the

Justice Henry Frye, with his granddaughter Whitney and the Reverend Howard Chubbs of Greensboro (right) at announcement of Frye's appointment as chief justice in August 1999. Standing in the middle is Theodis Black, state secretary of corrections (photograph courtesy State Archives of North Carolina and Scott Sharpe — newsobserver.com).

third floor of the Justice Building to the district courts holding forth in the furthermost county courthouse where citizens answered traffic citations. As the head of one of the three branches of government, the reach of the chief justice was considerable. He was responsible for employees of the court at work in every courthouse across the state. In his care was a budget of more than $324 million, but it was less than 3 percent of all state government spending.

The supreme court's offices had at least been given a good cleaning and some refurbishment when Frye took over. Mitchell had been asked to do what he could to refurbish the place after a justice asked one of the messengers how long a window air conditioner bearing a worn "out of order" sign had been in that condition. "Since I've been here judge," he was told. In the early 1990s, a study commission had recommended a new building to house the court, but those plans had been shelved for budget reasons. Instead, the windows in the Justice Building were washed and a new sign was erected out front.

Other African Americans followed Henry Frye to the supreme court. Among them were Associate Justice James A. Wynn, Jr. (left), who later became a member of the Fourth Circuit U.S. Court of Appeals, and Associate Justice G. K. Butterfield, who was elected to the U.S. House of Representatives (courtesy Frye family).

Frye and Pauline Irving moved into the chief's office on the northwest corner. The windows overlooked Fayetteville Street on one side and the grounds of the State Capitol on the other. As chief, he rated three law clerks, one more than the rest of the court. Also reporting to him were Thomas Ross, the director of the administrative officer of the courts, and Ross's assistant director, an African American named Thomas I. Hilliard. Ross was an old friend and Frye had convinced him to leave the superior court bench to take the job. The two shared deep mutual respect. Ross had chosen Frye to administer his oath of office when he became a judge. "If it had not been Henry I am not sure I would have [taken the job as administrative officer]," Ross said. "It turned out to be great experience for me."[19]

As chief justice, Frye set the pace of the court's work, and he ran the conferences. He had heavy administrative duties, but the chief was expected to share in the writing of opinions. The new responsibilities didn't come as a surprise. When Mitchell was chief justice, he would often pass off an administrative task to Frye. In the face of the challenges, the new chief justice remained upbeat, enthusiastic, and a source for the unexpected. One day he appeared at a conference reciting a short rhyme that he had learned years before from an elevator operator who had worked at the federal building in Greensboro when he was in the U.S. attorney's office. It went "Good morning, good morning, fine morning this morning/If every morning was as fine as this morning, every morning would be a fine morning." The rhythm and verse held fast in Justice Orr's mind more than a decade later.

The heavy lifting in the office was the administration of the court system. All the personnel matters crossed his desk, from the appointment of a court librarian to the assignment of superior court judges. The chief justice also appointed the chief judges for the district courts. Dealing with personnel matters from one end of the state to the other was a challenge.

Frye sent Hilliard out regularly to get acquainted. "Every county had people who were leaders, some of them dictators," Frye said. "He would go around and see who's who, and what's what. So if something came up in an area, he would already know who to call, or who to see when he got there. In some cases, the best place was to start with the sheriff. In others, it was to avoid the sheriff. In some cases, it was the clerk of court. In others, it was some senior lawyer. If you have a problem you talk to them first, to know who to avoid."[20]

Hilliard's reception varied from county to county. Some courthouses hadn't seen a visitor from the administrative office in years. When Hilliard, a middle-aged black man, showed up unannounced, and asked to see the judge, he often was greeted with indifference. "Until they got my card I was a nobody," he said. "Just a black guy in suit, with a briefcase, a lawyer." Once they understood his business, he would draw a crowd. "All of a sudden a judge would appear, the sheriff would appear, the clerk would appear, and I'd have an audience." Everyone wanted to know why he had stopped in.[21]

Frye knew his time as chief justice might be limited, but he wanted to know about the problems in the court system. As chief justice, it was his responsibility to speak for the judiciary, and to advocate for more financial support, if that was needed, or adjustments in the system that might require legislative action. Midway through 2000, he and Ross reported that the overall budget for court operations was declining. First-year attorneys were making more than some district court judges, the cost of indigent representation was climbing, and there was a steadily growing demand for interpreters for defendants who did not speak English. These problems troubled Frye, and at the same time he devoted attention to them, he worried that he was not carrying his share of the caseload. "I had plans to do a lot of things, but I was trying to take time to campaign, write opinions, and probably should have followed some advice from others who said, 'Henry you don't have to write every opinion until after the election.'"

On the day that Governor Hunt announced Frye's appointment as chief justice, the chairman of the N.C. Republican Party, Bill Cobey, told reporters that Republicans would have an opposing candidate on the ballot in 2000. It was quite likely that that candidate would be one of the four Republicans who sat around the conference table in the court's chambers to hash out decisions on cases. Partisanship was never apparent in the conference discussions, but the election that was only fourteen months away was never entirely out of mind, either.

Frye did not have the same level of comfort with his Republican brethren as he had when the court was composed entirely of Democrats. He and Louis Meyer seldom saw eye to eye on cases. Yet, when it came to his re-election to the court in 1994, he offered his support. Asked about it by his clerk at the time, Frye said, "Well, he is a Democrat."[22] The party label had meant something to Frye when he was a young man, and it remained a meaningful label as he became older.

It was not that he believed the Republicans were making decisions based on partisanship, but the party distinctions disturbed the collegiality. "It affected it some. I am sure. In the back of your mind you are thinking, why is he taking that position? Before, we seldom asked that question because we knew a person well enough to know which way he was going to vote." Frye was just getting used to Lake and Orr when two more Republicans joined the court in 1999.

Because of his uneasiness, Frye brought some relatively minor administrative questions to the entire court in order to head off any potential conflict. "The librarian retired during that period. I appointed the assistant librarian. Before I told him I was going to do it, I checked with the rest of the court. Some of [these decisions] I may have had authority to do on my own, but you have a court and you don't know how they feel about things. If you have a problem, you deal with it before you act." It was a consensus-building style that Frye had used for more than forty years.

The Republicans began recruiting a candidate to oppose Frye. They wanted someone who would be a credible challenger and, they hoped, one with campaign experience. Justices Lake and Orr were two most likely candidates. Orr took himself out of consideration early. He told party leaders he would not be comfortable running against Frye, for whom he had genuine affection and admiration. He also was troubled by the prospect of sitting justices running against one another.[23]

Lake and Frye had worked together on drafting opinions and they had played one or two rounds of golf together, even though there had been a bit of unease at first. Lake's name preceded him to the bench. His father had run for governor in 1960 as the segregationist candidate and the elder Lake maintained his beliefs about racial separation until his death.[24] His son never exhibited similar attitudes. He was affable and friendly, with a self-effacing wit, and could even be a bit shy, despite his years in politics. He also was not eager to create a political scene, which was what the media would make of a race between the son of I. Beverly Lake and an African American, especially an African American with a statewide reputation and following like Henry Frye.

"I never felt a cold knot like the one that came in my stomach when it was first suggested that I run for chief justice against Henry Frye," Lake said some years later. "I rejected it out of hand and they kept coming back, and coming back. I got more and more opposed to it."[25] He didn't expect to win in a presidential year when Democrats often had an edge in state races. Yet, if he lost, he told himself, at least he would still be on the court. "But when I made up my mind that I would do it, I walked down the hall—Henry was in the chief's office and it was at other end. It was one of the hardest things I ever did. He saw me outside and said, 'Come in Beverly,' and as soon as I walked in, he said, 'Well they talked you into it.' I said, 'Yeh.' I said I will do everything I can to make it the best, easiest, and friendliest campaign that you and I have ever been through."

Both Frye and Lake had declared their intentions by January. Frye depended on the help of his old legislative ally, Raleigh lawyer Sam Johnson, to put together his campaign. Lake's effort was launched with a Raleigh fundraiser chaired by former Governor James Holshouser, the man behind the Citizens for a Conservative Court campaign that had made the death penalty the issue in 1986.

The race for chief justice was indeed a gentleman's campaign. Lake even spoke on Frye's behalf when the chief justice didn't appear at a meeting of the trial lawyers held in Myrtle Beach that year. Frye honored the NAACP's call for a boycott of South Carolina conventions issued in a dispute over the use of the Confederate battle flag on the grounds of the state capitol. Lake promoted his friendship with Frye to the point that newspapers began writing about the two being golfing buddies, which was a bit of a stretch. When Lake was campaigning, he also became "Bev" Lake, a much friendlier version of his full name. This adjustment also created the impression among some voters that he was a woman, a misconception compounded by the name of the Democratic Party's candidate for lieutenant governor, Beverly, or "Bev," Perdue.

Frye mounted a full campaign and raised nearly a million dollars to underwrite an effort that included all the elements necessary for a statewide race. He campaigned whenever he could find time. At night, Hilliard volunteered his time to drive Frye to campaign events. He would pull the chief's ice-blue Lincoln Continental around to the front of the Justice Building, pick up his boss, and the two would head out to a political rally. Frye would nap or prepare his remarks. Often, in order to meet a schedule, Hilliard had to push the accelerator to the floor. "He would say, 'Thomas, you have a lead foot,'" Hilliard said. More than once a highway patrol trooper pulled alongside the car bearing a license plate with J-1, saw who was in the front seat, and then escorted the car into town.

Frye was very popular wherever he appeared, especially with black audiences eager to meet an African American of such prominence and high stature. "He was Barack Obama before Barack Obama," Hilliard said. Frye talked about the court system and reassured audiences of its fairness for all people. "He felt like his position allowed him to advance the cause of making sure that everybody received equal justice under the law. Most folks were enamored just to see him. You know, a black chief justice in North Carolina. It was almost a spectacle in lot of places. Folks felt proud and wanted to shake his hand. When we hit full campaign mode, it was tough getting him in and out of those places."

The Republicans fielded a full slate of judicial candidates and they stuck to a script that hewed to a conservative line. "We're telling [voters] we will interpret the law as it's written, not as we wish it were," Republican Paul Stam, of Apex in Wake County and a candidate for the court of appeals, told a reporter in the fall.[26] The judicial races were overshadowed by vigorous campaigns for governor, lieutenant governor, and for president. George W. Bush, the Republicans' presidential candidate, was considered the heavy favorite in the state. This time, it was believed he would bring a lot of other Republicans into office with him.

The old issues emerged. In news articles about the race of chief justice, voters were told Lake favored the death penalty while Frye remained opposed to it. Their individual beliefs had not made a difference in the court's overall record, but the facts were brushed aside. In 2000, the court had reversed only one of the eighteen death cases that it had reviewed. Both Frye and Lake said their personal feelings did not enter into their decisions. A pro-business lobbying group, called the N.C. Forum for Research and Economic Education, also injected a side story on the court's decisions related to business. Neither Lake nor Frye was the most conservative, according to this measure. It was Associate Justice Sarah Parker, a Democrat.[27]

A week or two before the election, Frye put in a call to a pollster who was working for another Democratic candidate. The Frye campaign had not commissioned its own poll, but his fellow Democrat had agreed to include a few questions about the race for chief justice. "I remember calling him one night, maybe Saturday, and I said tell me what you are finding out. He said, 'She is leading you,' and I said, 'Wait a minute, she who?' And he said, 'Bev Lake.' I said, 'Bev Lake? That is not a she, that's a man.' At that point, I told several people close to me that I believe we are going to lose this election."

The numbers relayed to Frye were turning up in other polling as well. Some urged Frye to solicit more campaign contributions so he could buy more advertising. He refused, and even sent back some money when the collections neared a million dollars. Frye didn't want to be known as the candidate who had spent that much to get elected to the court. The Lake campaign gained an edge in the closing weeks with a fund-raising letter that went to more than 80,000 state retirees. It reminded them that when Lake was a Superior Court judge he had ruled in their favor in a lawsuit reversing a legislative decision to tax state employee retirement benefits. In 1995, a similar case was filed as a class action. When it reached the supreme court, Lake wrote the opinion reversing the legislative action. Frye concurred in part of Lake's decision, and dissented in part. Frye's supporters objected and Lake criticized the Frye campaign for a fund-raising letter that was accompanied by endorsements from former chief justices Mitchell and Exum, both of whom had business before the court in their new roles as private attorneys.[28]

Frye pulled closer to Lake than what had been forecast in earlier predictions, but he could not overcome what turned out to be a swell of support for Republicans. He lost the election by a relatively slim margin of 77,000 votes.

The only bright spot in the aftermath was that in order to become chief justice, Lake had to relinquish his seat as associate justice. Appointed in his place by the newly elected governor, Mike Easley, a Democrat, was G. K. Butterfield of Wilson. Butterfield was an African American and the son of a prominent and politically active family. His father, a dentist, had served on the Wilson city council in the 1950s, one of the first twentieth-century African Americans to be elected to public office in eastern North Carolina.

Thirty years earlier, on inauguration day in 1969, Butterfield was awaiting his call to report to the army. He had spent the summer in Washington, D.C., where he had worked with civil rights leaders Ralph Abernathy and

Jesse Jackson in Resurrection City, an effort to raise national awareness of the plight of the poor and disadvantaged that had withered and died following the assassination of The Reverend Dr. Martin Luther King, Jr.

"I went to the inaugural parade," he said. "I am on Fayetteville Street in Raleigh looking for Henry Frye and here comes Henry Frye in a convertible car sitting in the back seat waving to the crowd. In January 1969, that was a big deal. I stood there on Fayetteville Street and watched him go by. I really didn't know Henry Frye then, but I knew of him."[29]

14

Making a Difference

As election night had worn on and the prospects dimmed for Henry Frye's election as chief justice, the Fryes thanked the friends and campaign workers gathered with them at a Raleigh hotel, with Henry consoling those who found it difficult to face the results. When the room cleared, they headed back to their room and by the time Shirley had finished her shower, Henry was sound asleep. The defeat hurt — and would continue to sting for years to come — but he wasn't going to dwell on it.

There were some who made much of the historical baggage attached to this particular contest. The Lake name was so closely identified with North Carolina's Jim Crow past that it was impossible to ignore the potential for Frye's skin color to be a deciding factor. That is too simplistic an answer. The majority of the voters who gave the new chief justice the winning margin in 2000 were not likely to have even heard of the elder I. Beverly Lake who had been on the ballot forty years earlier. "Bev" Lake of the twenty-first century was not elected by voters in eastern North Carolina, who joyfully embraced his father's defense of segregation in 1960, but by the new Republican majorities elsewhere in the state. In just the four counties clustered around the metropolitan center of Charlotte, voters gave Lake huge margins and accounted for more than half of Frye's deficit.

The election turned out just as the Republicans had hoped. They put a familiar candidate at the top of their judicial ticket — Lake had run three statewide campaigns in the last twenty years (once for governor and twice for the court) — and they made good on a concerted effort to organize support for the judicial races. There was another Democrat on the ballot with Frye: incumbent Associate Justice Franklin Freeman, and he lost by an even wider margin to his Republican opponent, Robert Edmunds.

The 2000 election was a difficult end to Henry Frye's career in public life, but he had no second thoughts as he headed back to Greensboro. He could have stayed on the court, through appointment to the seat Lake vacated to become chief justice, but remaining as the senior associate had no appeal. "Two or three people talked to me about it," Frye said with a rare tinge of bitterness in his voice. "One of them said I owed it to the party to do it. That upset me. I said, 'I don't owe the party a thing. The party is the one who let me down in this election, even in Guilford County.' We barely won in Guilford County. I admit I owed a lot to them, but I am not going to stay there and spend most of my time trying to help Lake be chief justice. And I wasn't going to stay and not be a part of it. I am sure he would have wanted to appoint me to this committee and do this and do that. I wouldn't have felt comfortable not doing it, but I wouldn't have felt comfortable doing it."

Frye joined the court in an era when former justices actually retired from professional and political life. In the 1990s, chief justices James Exum, Jr., and Burley Mitchell had established a different pattern. Exum left the court and returned to Greensboro for Smith Moore Smith Schell and Hunter (later Smith Moore Leatherwood), the firm where he had begun his legal career in 1961. When Mitchell retired, he moved across Fayetteville Street to the Raleigh offices of Womble Carlyle Sandridge and Rice, a firm that later added the name of Governor Jim Hunt on its letterhead. Frye had various offers, but the one he liked the most was from an established Greensboro firm, Brooks Pierce McLendon Humphrey and Leonard. It traced its founding to 1897.

"They said you tell us what you want to do and that is what you can do. So I said, OK," Frye recalled. The other firms that had come to talk to him had asked about areas of the law in which he wished to specialize. Brooks Pierce presented him with an open field. He asked to be named "of counsel," a designation conferred on senior associates who don't have regular assigned duties or areas of specialty. "Being of counsel is you do what you want to do," he said. The firm didn't have anyone in such a relationship, but it quickly conferred the designation on Frye.

In the coming years, Frye devoted his time to alternative dispute resolution, such as mediation and arbitration, and appellate advocacy. He taught a course in state government at N.C. A&T. From time to time, he pulled his robe from the closet and administered the oath of office to former clerks as their careers progressed to judicial posts. Community groups asked him to lend a hand with their causes. Ed Winslow, the managing partner at Brooks Pierce, said, "We just sort of bask in the glow of whatever he's involved in."

The glow was substantial. During his eighteen years on the court, Frye had refused to accept all but one honor that he was asked to receive. The exception was the brotherhood citation from the Greensboro chapter of the National Conference of Christians and Jews, which was conferred on Henry and Shirley together. That one, given in 1991, met his approval because it fell within Henry's narrow definition of ethical responsibility for a sitting justice.

Once he left the court, the tributes poured forth. The University of North Carolina presented him with the William R. Davie award in 2002; he received the N.C. Bar Association's Liberty Bell Award in 2004 and the John J. Parker

Award, its most prestigious honor, in 2007. In addition, Henry picked up honorary degrees at Fayetteville State University (2000), East Carolina University (2001), the University of North Carolina at Asheville (2003), Florida Memorial College (2004), and the University of North Carolina at Greensboro, an honor he shared with Shirley in 2006. The state Democratic Party renamed its summer fund-raising dinner in his behalf in 2009, linking him with iconic leaders and former governors Terry Sanford and Jim Hunt. The N.C. Press Association declared him its "North Carolinian of the Year" in 2011. There were others, including Father of the Year by the American Diabetes Association. He continued to get requests for speaking engagements. In 2011, the people of his hometown in Richmond County filled an auditorium at the school in Ellerbe — on the same campus that excluded blacks when he was a youngster — to hear the town's most famous former citizen applaud the town on the occasion of its centennial. Later, he and Shirley wandered through a new museum on American heritage that had just opened. A photograph of Frye was the only one that showed a black man in something other than work clothes. Just above and to the left of his picture is an image of pickers gathered in a pack house of an area peach orchard.

Of the honors that Frye had received over the years, none pleased him more than the R. R. Wright Award from the National Bankers Association. That had come in 1983, just as he went on the court. Creation of Greensboro National Bank remained a deep source of pride. In the early years, it had helped small businesses in east Greensboro and it offered African Americans an institution in which to invest. Throughout the 1970s, stockholders received modest dividends and the bank expanded its reach with a branch office on the south side of the city that was opened in 1981. Then, the bank began facing tough times. The economic downturn of the 1980s raised Greensboro National's loan losses and reduced its profits. The branch office was closed in 1988. The bank never fully recovered and in 1984 was merged with Mutual Community Savings Bank of Durham. It eventually became part of Mechanics and Farmers Bank of Durham.

When the bank was struggling in the late 1980s, it was under close management by federal regulators. Frye had severed his ties in 1983, remaining only a stockholder, but he considered leaving the court to see if he could turn things around, although he was uncertain he could have made a difference at that point. With deep disappointment, he watched Greensboro National disappear into the merger at a purchase price that, at best, returned the investment of the original shareholders. "It hurt me a lot," Frye said some years later. "I thought about coming back and seeing what I could do." Years later, Shirley said, "If there was any sour note in his life, I think that was it. He takes things in stride. In the long run, he says his goals were met." For more than two decades, African Americans had a commercial bank in Greensboro.

Meanwhile, Shirley's career continued to unfold. Her husband's eleva-
tion to the court released her into a wide range of civic and public involve-
ment. In 1986 she had become a member of the board of trustees of Blue
Cross–Blue Shield of North Carolina, the state's largest health insurer, and
by the early 1990s she was a director of three major foundations— Joseph M.
Bryan in Greensboro, GlaxoSmithKline in the Triangle, and Z. Smith
Reynolds in Winston-Salem. She was on the board of the Greensboro United
Way as well as arts and community organizations, from the Eastern Music
Festival in Greensboro to the Wake Forest University radio station WFDD.
She was the first African American trustee at Blue Cross–Blue Shield of North
Carolina and served for sixteen years, through a period of transition in health
care and a bruising political battle over the Blue Cross–Blue Shield corporate
organization. During her time on the board, she chaired the governance,
audit, personnel, and compensation committees.

Jane Smith Patterson was already on the Reynolds Foundation board
when Shirley became a member in 1994. "Coming from eastern North Carolina I really identified with her. First and foremost she is a woman. I was the
first woman elected as county chair of the Democratic Party in North Car-

As a member of the judiciary, former chief justice Henry Frye administered the
oath of office to his son, Henry Frye, Jr. (left), after he was elected to the state superior court, and to his granddaughter, Judge Frye's daughter Whitney, when she
became a lawyer in 2011 (photograph by Norris Greenlea, courtesy Frye family).

olina. It was a tough time for women. For her, she had it particularly tough. She had a husband who was already out front, and she had to take somewhat of a back seat because she was raising kids. She moved in ways to try to pull people together."

In 1988, she volunteered to manage the staff of Lieutenant Governor Robert Jordan's campaign for governor. Jordan, a moderate-to-liberal Democrat from a small town not far from Ellerbe, had served with Henry in the state senate before he was elected lieutenant governor in 1984. Shirley had been involved in her husband's campaign in 1984, but her work for Jordan was something new. She already had accepted Jordan's offer when her husband said he would ask the other members of the court if they had any objection to her political work. She told Henry that when the court allowed her to write opinions, she would ask them for permission to volunteer in a political campaign.

Jordan lost to Republican James G. Martin and Shirley returned to academic work as director of planned giving for Bennett College. In 1992, she found a job that would prove the most satisfying of all when Colleen Brown, the general manager of WFMY-TV in Greensboro, convinced her to manage the station's community affairs program. Brown had been in Greensboro for only a few months when she first encountered Shirley at a United Way board meeting. She was impressed. "Everywhere I went in the community, there was Shirley," Brown recalled. "I started moving in the direction of hiring a public affairs director who really resonated with the community and could connect the dots to what we stood for and what we could do with the community. Everybody volunteered Shirley as the person I should talk to."

Shirley refused Brown's first offer of a job. As a teenager she had dreamed of succeeding Pauline Frederick in broadcast news, but working at a television station was no longer on her list. She had never been attracted to the limelight, and certainly not in that industry. Brown explained that a working knowledge of broadcasting was not a prerequisite. "I was looking for the equivalent of Mrs. mayor, or Mr. mayor, someone who could get things done. She far exceeded my expectations. She was such a caring individual and then Henry came along with her." Brown insisted they meet, and Shirley discovered an opportunity to continue much of what she was doing in civic projects, but this time with all the resources of a major corporation and the creative talents of a television station at her disposal.

"I enjoyed that more than any job I had ever had," Shirley said. "It was the first time I had an opportunity to use what I call my creative juices. All of the resources you needed were there for you. You could visualize this sort of thing and feed it to the graphics department or the marketing department." Unlike some stations that supported only one organization's work in the community, Frye looked for ways to bring many groups and individuals together. Deborah Hooper, Brown's successor as WFMY's general manager, endorsed

Shirley's creative efforts. "We said wait a minute, what are greatest needs in this community? What can we do to create a project that will go beyond what we could have done with a single project and serve a greater need that is truly across this 15-county area?"

One of Shirley's first projects was "Food For Families." It enlisted the aid of volunteers, such as the Boy Scouts, to work alongside individuals to put canned goods and other food on the shelves of area food pantries. A later effort called "Tools For Schools" produced school supplies for children who needed them to start the school year. She continued "2 Those Who Care," a program that recognized community volunteers and boosted to record levels the amount of money from sponsors that the station then donated to a selected non-profit organization each year.

Her success drew notice from the executives of the Gannett Company, the station's corporate parent. Hooper was in a high-level budget meeting one year when a top Gannett financial officer questioned the amount set aside for WFMY-TV's community projects. Hooper said his boss spoke up immediately. "The CEO of Gannett broadcasting said, 'You know what, I will let you call Shirley and ask her about that, otherwise we are going to move on,'" Hooper recalled. "He had ultimate trust that she knew the resources that were needed to do that project in the way it needed to be done and nothing more needed to be said."

After Shirley was promoted to vice president, Hooper would leave her in charge of the station when she was away for an extended period. Most of the routine continued uninterrupted, but one night Shirley was called on to explain to viewers how an unedited and far more vivid version of a movie ended up on the air. She was caught unaware that the station had aired the R-rated version until she got a phone call from the news director. At 11 o'clock, she was facing the cameras to apologize for the error that had sent images and language considered unsuitable for a general audience into the homes of viewers. "Stations can be fined for things like that," Hooper said. "Shirley was doing her best to protect the station and address the concerns of the viewers."

What had begun as a short-term assignment — something Shirley later joked she accepted to ward off dementia — didn't end until a decade later. She retired from WFMY-TV in 2002. Her calendar continued to be full, however. She was asked to chair the board of trustees of the N.C. School of Science and Math in Durham and managed the difficult task of finding a new chancellor. She also chaired the board of Guilford Technical Community College. In 2011, she became a trustee of High Point University.

The lives of Henry and Shirley Frye spanned the most transformational era of the twentieth century. Born and raised in the days of Jim Crow segregation, they would later stand with the governor of North Carolina as Henry raised his hand to take his oath as chief justice of the state supreme court, the head of one of the state's three branches of government. Nothing that they and their talented classmates could have imagined while sitting on the steps of a dormitory on the A&T campus a year before the U.S. Supreme Court decided *Brown* would compare to the future that eventually unfolded for them both.

At the time, there was reason to believe that the end of segregation was near and a new day was ahead. Had they not already experienced healthy interaction with whites in the student legislature where one's college in the legislative alliances that arose during three days of mock law making amounted to more than whether one was white or black? Would not change come soon in North Carolina, with its reputation as a progressive outlier among the states of the Old South, thanks to the liberalizing influences of university president Frank Porter Graham's Chapel Hill? Hadn't Thurgood Marshall's legal challenges opened the UNC law school to African Americans? Wouldn't public schools be next?

At the time, however, the state labored under the influence of a defense of the status quo that inhabited the social, political and economic life of the state. So while young African Americans could dream, and see faint rays of hope, they still had to contend with the reality of the closed doors that confronted them at virtually every turn. Companies still interviewed "colored" applicants on days when whites were not in the room. As they sat and talked, the prospects for careers in something other than teaching and preaching were dim. As a result, many of Frye's classmates took their dreams and fulfilled them elsewhere, rather than seeing their ambitions proscribed and limited at home. Henry and Shirley Frye remained in North Carolina and in the years to come helped reshape the state, beginning with the slow and halting transition of the 1960s and the protests and demonstrations that shook the foundations of both white and black communities.

For the civil rights movement to succeed, an array of talent and determination was necessary for the overhaul of society that would eventually transpire. It required people of personal courage like the four A&T students who took a seat at that lunch counter in Greensboro. Their determination emboldened young and old to put their safety and comfort on the line when they stepped out to join marches and demonstrations that challenged the status quo. It also required the support and efforts of those behind the front lines who were willing to invest themselves in the slow, steady, chipping away at an unjust system. It required both the seen and unseen for all to realize new opportunities that African Americans had been dreaming about for generations.

In later years, Henry Frye would be called a civil rights leader. It was not a label that he subscribed to, or even easily accepted. Neither he nor Shirley spent their time, day in and day out, focused on organizing African Americans to push back the wall of segregation and discrimination that separated them from the full benefits of society. Instead, they bent themselves to the task in their own ways, using their talents to bridge the divide in a calm and civil demonstration of good will and openness. Neither had the desire to lead the parade, but they made sure that anyone who wanted to be part of it would be included.

Frye's steady and deliberative style suited his personality and reflected lessons learned as a youngster from his mother, who talked about the benefits of honey over vinegar in catching flies. If that didn't work, he also could rely on the example of his father, who made his way with strength and dignity that didn't bend in adversity. Frye didn't try to capture headlines and even seemed embarrassed by publicity. The court had been a suitable venue for him to perform public service. Efforts to pursue a statewide campaign probably would never have been as satisfying. Instead, he applied his talents as a lawyer to work within the system and brought a new perspective to decisions in Raleigh.

Frye was in the vanguard of what soon became a growing number of black elected officials in the state. He and others, such as Mayor Howard Lee of Chapel Hill, the first African American elected to lead a predominantly white southern city, established the first real political network of African Americans. They shared ideas, offered mutual support, and began to gain sufficient mass to become an effective force beyond their own communities. More African Americans joined Frye in the General Assembly. Among them was H. M. Michaux, Jr., of Durham, who later became the U.S. attorney in the same office where Frye had broken the color line more than a dozen years earlier. Richard Erwin of Winston-Salem, another legislator, became a U.S. District Court judge. One of Frye's former law students, Clifton Johnson, went on the state court of appeals. "A lot of people get their foot in the door and they are just happy to be there and they don't open it wider for anybody else," said former appeals court Judge Charles Becton. "He slammed that door wide open, as opposed to closed, and made it possible for others."

In time, architect Harvey Gantt was twice elected the mayor of Charlotte, the state's largest city. Dan Blue of Raleigh, an African American who began his legal career in the 1970s, was chosen speaker of the state House of Representatives. African Americans had been appointed in the cabinets of governors, and Mel Watt of Charlotte, G. K. Butterfield of Wilson, and Eva Clayton of Warrenton were elected to Congress. African Americans wore robes at all levels of the state judiciary, including Frye's own son, Henry Jr. Son Harlan was employed in state government where the African Americans made up more than a third of the workforce. When Harlan was born, the only African Americans to be found in state government were cleaning the offices and manning the elevators of state office buildings.

Some might argue that Henry Frye was an accident of history. If he had lost that election in 1968, he would have been just another casualty in the efforts of black North Carolinians to achieve legislative office. But he won that election and proved to be the right person to integrate an institution whose members had proudly defended segregation and denigrated the rights of African Americans without regret. He was dignified, smart, and the forensic match for any courthouse orator. The important thing about 1968 was that it was Henry Frye who was elected. He prepared the way for others who followed, as he did on the state supreme court.

"As black lawyers we would talk about what Henry was doing there," said Becton, long an admirer. "But I knew intuitively that his being there changed the conversation. Just being in the room, there is a chance for compromise. I have always felt that the best way to effect change was from within. If you can get elected to the legislature and start working your magic and if you are as charismatic as Henry is, as warm and friendly and outgoing, and as right as Henry is, you can effect changes."

In the summer of 2012, Henry and Shirley Frye traveled to Greenville, North Carolina, to see the medical school of East Carolina University admit its newest class. One of the new students was Endya Frye, the youngest daughter of their son Henry, who, like her grandfather, had earned her undergraduate degree in biology at A&T. The ECU Medical School was just aborning in the early 1970s, the child of the politics of higher education. Arrayed against one another were the considerable heft of the University of North Carolina and the regional universities, of which ECU was one. As the balance shifted to and fro, an unaligned member like Frye found an opportunity to bend the arc a little closer to equality. Before the bill granting $15 million for the start of the new medical school emerged from committee, Frye had inserted a provision requiring ECU to actively recruit African Americans for enrollment.

Henry Frye made a difference in North Carolina in ways difficult to measure. But the life of the state was different in the summer of 2012 because a half-century earlier he decided to remind North Carolinians of the state's motto. His literacy amendment was a bold gesture, but more often than not he employed ways as subtle as one amendment that spoke to broader opportunities for African Americans long before Endya Frye was even born, and long before her grandfather's eyes swelled with tears of pride as he and Shirley heard Endya's name entered on the student rolls.

Chapter Notes

Chapter 1

1. Henry E. Frye, January 28, 2009. (Unless otherwise indicated, interviews with Henry and Shirley Frye were conducted by the author.)
2. Author interview with Ola Frye Stringer, June 24, 2009.
3. Author interview with Sheridan and Shirley Easterling, November 14, 2009.
4. Frank Daniel McLeod, "A Survey of the Public School Facilities for Negroes in Richmond County," master's thesis, 1948, North Carolina Collection, University of North Carolina at Chapel Hill.
5. Ibid.
6. Henry E. Frye, January 28, 2009.
7. *Public Papers and Letters of Cameron Morrison*, edited by D. L. Corbitt, Edwards and Broughton Company, 1927, p. xxiii.
8. Henry E. Frye, November 5, 2009.
9. Henry E. Frye, February 4, 2009.
10. Henry E. Frye, November 5, 2009.
11. Voter registration records, Richmond County Board of Elections.
12. Tom Hanchett, "Beacons for Black Education in the American South," http://www.historysouth.org/rosenwaldhome.html; and Tom Hanchett, "Rosenwald School and Black Education in North Carolina," *North Carolina Historical Review*, Vol. 65, No. 4, October 1988.
13. Easterling, November 14, 2009.
14. McLeod, master's thesis.
15. Ray Gavins, "The NAACP in North Carolina During the Age of Segregation," in *The Civil Rights Movement*, Jack E. Davis, editor, Blackwell Publishers, 2001.

Chapter 2

1. Henry E. Frye, February 4, 2009.
2. Albert W. Spruill, *Great Recollections from Aggieland*, Whitehead Printing Company, Wilmington, N.C., 1964, p. 86.
3. W. T. Gibbs, *History of the N.C. A&T College*, William C. Brown Co., 1966, p. 158.

4. Author interview with Lucille Piggott, August 13, 2009.
5. Carrye Hil Kelley, "Profiles of Five Administrators," *Bulletin of the Agricultural and Technical College*, August 1964.
6. Lucille Piggott, August 13, 2009.
7. "A&T Reports Woman's Quota for Fall Teachers," *Greensboro Daily News*, September 14, 1949; and "Governor Scott Speaks," *The A&T Register*, July 1950.
8. Author interview with Velma Speight-Buford, June 20, 2009.
9. Donald W. Wyatt, "This Be Their Destiny," University Archives, F.D. Bluford Library, N.C. A&T University.
10. Ralph Johns, "Buzzin' With Cuzzin', *The Future Outlook*, September 3, 1949.
11. Henry E. Frye, January 14, 2010.
12. Author interviews with Velma Speight-Buford and David McElveen, June 22, 2009; and James Bridgett, August 18, 2009.
13. "A&T Amateur Thespians Give Superb Performance," *The A&T Register*, December 1949.
14. *The A&T Register*, December 1950.
15. Shirley Frye, June 29, 2009.
16. Ola Stringer interview; and author interview with Henry Frye, February 12, 2009.
17. Lawrence Otis Graham, *Our Kind of People*, HarperCollins Publishers, 2000, p. 85.
18. *The A&T Register*, January 1952.
19. "Student Legislature Meets," *The Carolinian*, November 24, 1945.
20. Velma Speight-Buford, July 20, 2009.
21. William Chafe, *Civilities and Civil Rights*, Oxford University Press, 1980, p. 22.
22. Lucille Piggott, August 13, 2009.
23. Flora Bryant Brown, "NAACP Sponsored Sit-ins By Howard University Students in Washington, D.C., 1943–1944," *Journal of Negro History*, Vol. 85, No. 4 (Autumn, 2000), pp. 274–286.
24. Jeffrey Crow, Paul Escott, Flora Hatley, *A History of African Americans in North Carolina*, Crow, N.C. Division of Archives and His-

tory, N.C. Department of Cultural Resources, Raleigh, p. 192.

25. Mary Frances Berry, "'Reckless Eye-balling': The Matt Ingram Case and the Denial of African American Sexual Freedom," *Journal of African-American History*, Vol. 93, No. 2, Spring 2008, p. 223.

26. Lucille Piggott, August 13, 2009.

27. N.C. Newbold, *Five North Carolina Negro Educators*, Chapel Hill: University of North Carolina Press, 1939, p. 50.

28. Burke Davis, "Deputies Prevent Violence at Nonsegregated Services," *Greensboro Daily News*, June 1, 1953.

29. Associated Press, "Shaw Graduates Hear Legislator," *Greensboro Daily News*, June 2, 1953.

Chapter 3

1. Shirley Frye, February 8, 2010.

2. Jacob Hay, "City Takes Court Ruling on Segregation Calmly," *Greensboro Daily News*, May 18, 1954.

3. Notes on interview with D. Edward Hudgins by William Chafe, July 6, 1972, William Henry Chafe Oral History Collection, Duke University.

4. "City Compliance on Segregation to be Studied," *Greensboro Daily News*, May 19, 1954.

5. "Residential Lines Seen as Affecting any Student Shift," *Greensboro Record*, May 19, 1954.

6. Howard Covington, Jr., and Marion A. Ellis, *Terry Sanford: Politics, Progress, and Outrageous Ambition*, Duke University Press, 1999, p. 134.

7. Arthur Johnsey, "School Segregation Banned," *Greensboro Daily News*, May 18, 1954.

8. "Armed Services Hailed in Ike's Charlotte Talk," *Greensboro Daily News*, May 19, 1954.

9. "Jaycees Endorse Board Stand on Segregation," *Greensboro Daily News*, May 21, 1954.

10. "County School Board Holds up Decision on Segregation," *Greensboro Record*, May 29, 1954

11. Shirley Frye, February 8, 2010.

12. Shirley Frye, July 6, 2009.

13. Shirley Frye, February 8, 2010.

14. Ibid.

15. Shirley Frye, June 29, 2009.

16. Henry E. Frye, February 19, 2009.

17. Ola Stringer, June 24, 2009

18. Henry Frye, February 19, 2009.

19. Henry E. Frye, April 31, 2010.

20. Henry E. Frye, October 2, 2010.

21. Henry E. Frye, April 2, 2009.

22. Henry E. Frye, January 14, 2010.

23. Shirley Frye, June 29, 2009.

24. Ibid.

25. Henry E. Frye, January 14, 2010.

26. "UNC Studies Applications of 11 Negroes," *Greensboro Daily News*, May 29, 1959.

27. Author interview with J. Kenneth Lee, March 3, 2009.

28. Winona Lee Fletcher, editor, *My Way: Memoirs of J. Kenneth Lee, Esq.*, Outskirts Press, Denver, Colorado, 2008, p. 12.

29. Author interview with Frederick Terry, August 5, 2009.

30. Henry Frye, February 26, 2009.

31. Richmond County Board of Elections.

32. Shirley Frye, June 29, 2009.

Chapter 4

1. Dick Murphy, "A Student," *Daily Tar Heel*, September 29, 1951.

2. "Groups Act on Segregation; Davis Calls Special Session," *Daily Tar Heel*, October 2, 1951.

3. Kenneth Lee, March 3, 2009; "No Rooms On Campus Four Basements Used," September 20, 1951, *Daily Tar Heel*; and interview with Harvey Beech by Anita Foye, September 25, 1996, J-0075, in the Southern Oral History Program Collection #4007, Southern Historical Collection, Wilson Library, University of North Carolina at Chapel Hill.

4. "Fowler Says Students are For Segregation," *Daily Tar Heel*, September 15, 1955; and "UNC Campus is Used for Civil Rights Filming," *Daily Tar Heel*, September 21, 1956.

5. Shirley Frye, February 9, 2010; and Henry E. Frye, March 10, 2010.

6. Henry E. Frye, February 26, 2009.

7. John W. Wertheimer, *Law and Society in the South: A History of North Carolina Court Cases*, University of Kentucky Press, 2009, p. 147.

8. Henry E. Frye, November 5, 2009.

9. Henry E. Frye, March 5, 2009.

10. Henry E. Frye, February 12, 2009.

11. Henry E. Frye, March 19, 2009.

12. Author interview with Robert Blum, August 20, 2009.

13. Henry E. Frye, March 5, 2009.

14. Howard E. Covington, Jr., and Marion A. Ellis, *Terry Sanford, Politics, Progress, and Outrageous Ambitions*, Duke University Press, 2000, p. 166.

15. Shirley Frye, July 6, 2009.

16. Shirley Frye, February 9, 2010.

17. Shirley Frye, July 6, 2009.

18. Taylor Branch, *Parting the Waters*, Simon and Schuster, 1988, p. 213–214.

19. The Papers of Martin Luther King, Jr., Clayborn Carson, senior editor, Vol. IV, Symbol of the Movement, University of California Press, 2000. Chronology.

20. *Parting the Waters*, pp. 75–76.

21. Martin Luther King, Jr., sermon, July 14, 1957, The Papers of Martin Luther King, Jr.

22. Henry E. Frye, March 10, 2010.

23. *North Carolina Law Review*, Vol. 36, 1957.

24. *North Carolina Law Review*, Vol. 37, 1958.

25. Author interview with Dan Pollitt, August 5, 2009.

26. Dan Pollitt interview. See also, "Taking Liberties, Dan Pollitt Unfashionably Defends Free Speech, Nude Dancing, The Works," *North Carolina Independent*, March 15, 2000.

27. Associated Press, "Seawell Defends N.C. School Laws, *Charlotte Observer*, April 12, 1959; and author interview with Henry E. Frye, March 31, 2010.

28. Dan Pollitt, August 5, 2009.

29. National Bar Association Hall of Fame, http://www.nationalbar.org/news/hallof-fame04.shtml.

30. Dan Pollitt, August 5, 2009.

31. *North Carolina Law Review*, Vol. 39, 1959.

32. Henry E. Frye, March 9, 2010.

33. L.R. Varser testimony, *Epps et al. v. Carmichael et al.*, 93 F. Supp. 327 (M.D. NC 1950).

34. Henry E. Frye, March 5, 2009.

Chapter 5

1. Author interview with Dr. Alvin Blount, March 8, 2010.

2. Henry E. Frye, March 19, 2009.

3. Interview with Elreta Alexander Ralston by Anna Barbara Perez, February 18, 1993, and March 4, 1993, J-0018, in the Southern Oral History Program Collection #4007, Southern Historical Collection, Wilson Library, University of North Carolina at Chapel Hill.

4. Author interview with Walter Johnson, Jr., July 15, 2009.

5. Interview with J. Kenneth Lee by Eugene C. Pfaff, 1980, Greensboro Voices Collection, Item 1.10.540, Jackson Library, University of North Carolina at Greensboro; and author interview with Kenneth Lee, March 3, 2009.

6. Shirley Frye , July 6, 2009.

7. Interview with Ezell Blair, Jr., by Robert Penn Warren, March 4, 1963, in *Who Speaks for the Negro?*, Alexander Heard Library, Vanderbilt University.

8. Dr. Alvin Blount, March 8, 2010.

9. Interview with Hobart Jarrett by Eugene C. Pfaff, 1980, Greensboro Voices Collection, Item 1.10.532, Jackson Library, University of North Carolina at Greensboro.

10. Notes from interview with Dr. Edwin R. Edmonds by William H. Chafe, William Henry Chafe Oral History Collection, Special Collections, Perkins Library, Duke University.

11. Pfaff interview with Jarrett.

12. Henry E. Frye, March 10, 2010.

13. "Part of Plight of Negro Laid to Poor Voting," *Greensboro Record*, April 4, 1960.

14. Henry E. Frye, March 10, 2010.

15. Newspaper advertisement for Lake campaign, *Greensboro Record*, May 18, 1960.

16. "NAACP Plots Strife, State Told," *Greensboro Record*, April 12, 1960.

17. Charlie Hamilton, "He's Too Busy to Keep Up His Golf Game," *Greensboro Record*, May 27, 1960.

18. Shirley Frye, July 6, 2009.

19. Bruce Jolly, "N.C. Negroes Seen Leaning to GOP, *Greensboro Daily News*, Nov. 5, 1960.

20. Pfaff interview with Jarrett.

21. Henry E. Frye, March 31, 2010.

22. Author interview with the Reverend Lorenzo Lynch, July 27, 2009.

23. Bruce Lambert, "Warmoth T. Gibbs, 101, Educator Who Backed Civil Rights Protests," *New York Times*, April 23, 1993.

24. Henry E. Frye, April 9, 2009.

25. Henry E. Frye, March 31, 2010.

26. Henry E. Frye, March 19, 2009.

27. P. Preston Reynolds, "Hospitals and Civil Rights, 1945–1963: The Case of *Simkins v. Moses H. Cone Memorial Hospital*," Annals of Internal Medicine, Vol. 126, No. 11, June 1, 1997.

28. Interview with George C. Simkins, Jr., by Karen Kruse Thomas, April 6, 1997, R-0018, in the Southern Oral History Program Collection #4007, Southern Historical Collection, Wilson Library, University of North Carolina at Chapel Hill.

29. Henry E. Frye, March 31, 2010.

30. Jim Schlosser, "Supreme Court Seat Another First for Henry E. Frye," *Greensboro Daily News*, January 13, 1983.

31. Brandt Ayers, "Justice Dept. Officials Consider Placing Negroes in N.C. District Courts," *News and Observer*, November 30, 1962.

32. "Ervin Uses Humor, Acting to Hold Floor in Senate," *Greensboro Daily News*, March 24, 1962.

33. "Local Negro Approved For Post," *Greensboro Daily News*, November 23, 1962.

34. Memo, "Pat to Senator Ervin," October 17, 1962, papers of Sam J. Ervin, Jr., Southern Historical Collection, Wilson Library, University of North Carolina at Chapel Hill.

35. Howard E. Covington, Jr., and Marion A. Ellis, *Terry Sanford: Politics, Progress, and Outrageous Ambition*, Duke University Press, 1999, p. 291.

36. "Ellerbe Negro Lands Big Job," *Rockingham Post-Dispatch*, November 29, 1962.

37. Ola Stringer, June 24, 2009.

Chapter 6

1. "Arguments are Heard on Pupil Assignments," *Greensboro Daily News*, May 2, 1963.

2. "Demonstrators March Again, 287 Arrested," *Greensboro Daily News*, May 19, 1963; and "Adults Warned to be Prepared to Go to Jail," *Greensboro Daily News*, May 20, 1963.

3. Shirley Frye, July 6, 2009.

4. Author interview with Melvin Swann, July 16, 2009.

5. Interview of Henry E. Frye with Amy E. Boening, February 18 and 26, 1992, C-0091, in the Southern Oral History Program Collection #4007, Southern Historical Collection, Wilson Library, University of North Carolina at Chapel Hill; and Shirley Frye interview, July 6, 2009.

6. Memorandum, The Director to The Files, May 20, 1963, Papers of Governor Terry Sanford, State Archives, Raleigh, N.C., and Henry E. Frye, April 2, 2009.

7. Charles Hamilton, "He's Too Busy to Keep Up His Golf Game," *Greensboro Record*, May 27, 1960.

8. Author interview with Roy G. Hall, Jr., June 17, 2009.

9. "Naming of Negro to Post Called Unprecedented," *Greensboro Daily News*, November 24, 1963.

10. "Attorney Takes Oath of Office," *Greensboro Daily News*, January 13, 1963.

11. Henry E. Frye, April 2, 2009.

12. Henry E. Frye, March 10, 2010.

13. Henry E. Frye, April 2, 2009.

14. Author's interview with Harper J. Elam III, August 12, 2002.

15. Interview of John and Betsy Taylor by William Chafe, July 7, 1973, William Henry Chafe Oral History Collection, Special Collections, Perkins Library, Duke University and Shirley Frye, September 9, 2009.

16. "Pro-integrationist Signers Sought," *Greensboro Daily News*, May 19, 1963.

17. Shirley Frye, September 9, 2009.

18. Author interview with Kikuko Imamura, December 11, 2009.

19. Henry E. Frye, March 10, 2010; and Roy G. Hall, Jr., June 17, 2009.

20. Author interview with Julius Chambers, October 5, 2009.

21. Henry E. Frye, March 31, 2010.

22. Shirley Frye, September 9, 2009.

23. Author interview with Deborah Barnes, June 22, 2010.

24. Shirley Frye, September 9, 2009.

25. Daniel Pollitt, August 5, 2009.

26. Author interview with H. M. Michaux, Jr., September 14, 2009.

27. "Chronicle of Black Lawyers in North Carolina," Vol. 2, Civil Rights Pioneers: 1950–1970, N.C. Association of Black Lawyers, October 1984.

28. H. M. Michaux, Jr., September 14, 2009.

29. Dwayne Walls, "They Knew Why Plea Had Failed," *Charlotte Observer*, December 15, 1966.

30. Daniel Pollitt, August 5, 2009.

31. Author interview with E. Osborne Ayscue, February 23, 2010.

32. Henry E. Frye, March 10, 2010.

Chapter 7

1. Dwayne Walls, "Negroes Gain Power Leverage in Local Elections," *Charlotte Observer*, June 24, 1967.

2. Author interview with the Reverend Howard A. Chubbs, May 27, 2009.

3. Henry E. Frye, April 9, 2009.

4. Benjamin R. Justeen, *George Henry White, An Even Chance in the Race of Life*, Louisiana State University Press, 2001, p. 248.

5. "Frye Enters State House Race," *Greensboro Daily News*, March 30, 1966.

6. Henry E. Frye, May 26, 2010.

7. Henry E. Frye, April 9, 2009.

8. The Reverend Howard Chubbs, May 27, 2009.

9. Shirley Frye, June 29, 2010.

10. "Frye Would Take City Council Post," *Greensboro Daily News*, June 2, 1966.

11. Henry E. Frye, October 2, 2010.

12. Kenneth Clarke, "The Present Dilemma of the Negro," *Journal of Negro History*, Vol. 53, No. 1, January 1968, p. 1.

13. Paul Jablow, "In Hawkins Camp There Was Hope for Change," *Charlotte Observer*, August 21, 1968.

14. "Greensboro Lawyer Enters House Race," *High Point Enterprise*, March 29, 1966.

15. Henry E. Frye, April 9, 2009.

16. Henry E. Frye, May 26, 2010.

17. Henry E. Frye, April 9, 2009.

18. Paul Jablow, "I Don't Have Hawkins Now...," *Charlotte Observer*, August 24, 1968.

19. Dwayne Walls, "Negroes Gain Power Leverage in Local Elections, *Charlotte Observer*, June 24, 1967.

20. John Marshall Kilmanjaro, "The Other Side of the Tracks," *Carolina Peacemaker*, April 27, 1968.

21. Undated "Proposal for Pilot Project in Citizenship Education," Greensboro Branch, NAACP, Henry E. Frye Files.

22. Henry E. Frye, May 26, 2010.

23. Dr. Alvin Blount, March 8, 2010.

24. Arthur Johnsey, "Ruling is Protested by Negro Delegates," *Greensboro Daily News*, June 7, 1968.

25. Paul Jablow, "I Don't Have Hawkins Now...," *Charlotte Observer*, August 24, 1968.

26. Frank Pleasants, "Avoid 'Trap,' Warns A&T's Dowdy," *Greensboro Record*, October 1, 1968.

27. Henry E. Frye, July 14, 2010.

28. "An Emphasis Too Harsh in a Message Repeated," *Greensboro Record*, November 11, 1968.

Chapter 8

1. Henry E. Frye, June 25, 2009.

2. Henry E. Frye, July 14, 2010.

3. Author interview with Walter Johnson, Jr., July 15, 2009.

4. H. Patrick Taylor, *Fourth Down and Goal to Go*, Ivy House Publishing Group, Raleigh, N.C., 2005, Page 75.

5. "N.C. School Integration Has Been Slow—Coltrane," *Charlotte Observer*, August 24, 1968.

6. "School Bid Ok'd in House Reading," *Charlotte Observer*, February 12, 1968.

7. Howard Covington, "Faced with 80% Negro Schools, Scotland Neck Has a Big Fear," *Charlotte Observer*, February 23, 1969; and Howard Covington, "Negroes Say School Bill Benefits Racists," *Charlotte Observer*, February 20, 1969.

8. "N.C. House Tentatively OKs Separate Warrenton Schools," *Greensboro Record*, May 2, 1969.

9. Henry E. Frye, June 25, 2009.

10. The Reverend Howard Chubbs, May 27, 2009.

11. Henry E. Frye, June 25, 2009.

12. "Voter Literacy Test Supported by Brock," *Greensboro Daily News*, March 18, 1969.

13. Jim Schlosser, "Frye Rebuts Brock," *Greensboro Record*, March 25, 1969.

14. Shirley Frye, September 9, 2009.

15. Henry E. Frye, July 29, 2010; and Alan Whiteleather, "Strike Negotiators Report Progress," *Greensboro Daily News*, April 1, 1969.

16. Henry E. Frye, June 25, 2009.

17. Author interview with Nathan Garrett, Dec. 6, 2010.

18. Henry E. Frye, June 25, 2009.

19. Henry E. Frye, December 3, 2010.

20. Henry E. Frye, July 14, 2010.

21. Huntington Hobbs, *North Carolina, Economic and Social*, UNC Press, 1930, p. 267.

22. Noel Yancy, "House Backs Ban of Literacy Test," *News and Observer*, June 11, 1969.

23. Archibald Henderson, *North Carolina, the Old North State and the New*, The Lewis Publishing Company, Chicago, 1941, Vol. II, p. 432; and R.D.W. Connor and Clarence Poe, *The Life and Speeches of Charles Brantley Aycock*, Garden City, N.Y., Doubleday, Page and Company, pp. 218–219.

24. Shirley Frye, September 9, 2009.

25. "Under the Dome," *News and Observer*, June 25, 1969.

Chapter 9

1. Shirley Frye, June 29, 2009.

2. Nathan Garrett, December 5, 2010.

3. Author interview with Ben Ruffin, February 14, 2001.

4. Henry E. Frye, March 12, 2009.

5. Charles Gerena, "Opening the Vault," *Region Focus*, Federal Reserve Bank of Richmond, Spring 2007.

6. "Minority-owned Banks in Existence as of January 1974," National Bankers Association.

7. Andrew F. Brimmer, Board of Governors of the Federal Reserve System, Washington, D.C., July 31, 1971.

8. Winona Lee Fletcher, editor, *No Way, Memoirs of J. Kenneth Lee, Esq.*, Outskirts Press, Denver, Colorado, p. 21.

9. Otis Hairston, Jr., *Black America Series: Greensboro, North Carolina*, Arcadia Publishing Co., Charleston, S.C., 2003.

10. Sherrod DuPree, *African American Holiness Pentecostal Movement: An Annotated Bibliography*, Religious Information Systems, Vol. 4, Garland Reference Library of Social Science, 1996.

11. Henry E. Frye, March 12, 2009.

12. Henry E. Frye, December 3, 2010.

13. Shirley Frye, June 29, 2009.

14. Henry E. Frye, December 3, 2010.

15. Henry E. Frye, March 12, 2009.

16. "New Bank Officials to Meet With Public," *Greensboro Daily News*, February 18, 1971.

17. Shirley Frye, June 29, 2009.

18. Author interview with Jim Melvin, October 19, 2010.

19. Author interview Thomas I. Storrs, November 2, 2010.

20. Author interview with Luther Hodges, Jr., November 1, 2010.

21. Jim Melvin, October 19, 2010.

22. Peter Leo, "Black-backed Bank in Business," *Greensboro Record*, November 2, 1971.

23. Jo Spivey, "SAC Asked to Push Death Probe," *Greensboro Record*, April 8, 1970.

24. Author interview with Sammie Chess, June 8, 2010.

25. Deborah Barnes, June 22, 2010.

26. Jim Schlosser, "Supreme Court Seat Another First for Henry Frye," *Greensboro Daily News*, January 13, 1983.

27. Bob Ashley, "Black Politics, Not Separatism Stressed," *Raleigh Times*, June 14, 1971.

28. Henry E. Frye to Benjamin Swalin, September 9, 1969, Henry Frye correspondence files made available to the author.

29. Author interview with Gene Anderson, November 5, 2010.

30. Shirley Frye, January 11, 2011.

31. Author interview with James S. Ferguson, November 8, 2010.

32. Author interview with Milton Fitch, Jr., October 19, 2010.

33. Henry E. Frye, January 11, 2011.

34. Henry E. Frye, December 3, 2010.

35. Sammie Chess, June 8, 2010.

36. Kenneth Lee to Governor Robert W. Scott, May 24, 1971, Papers of Governor Robert W. Scott, State Archives, Raleigh, N.C.

37. Henry E. Frye, May 26, 2010.

38. Howard Covington, "Taylor a Southern Will Rogers," *Charlotte Observer*, December 20, 1971.

39. Howard Covington and Marion Ellis, *Terry Sanford: Politics, Progress, and Outrageous Ambition*, Duke University Press, 1999, p. 200.

40. H. Patrick Taylor, *Fourth Down and Goal to Go*, p. 35.

41. Howard Covington, "To Beat 'Em, Join 'Em, Says Hawkins," *Charlotte Observer*, December 16, 1971.

42. Howard Lee, August 12, 2010.

43. Howard E. Covington and Larry Tarleton, "Hawkins Splits Black Voters," *Charlotte Observer*, May 28, 1972.

44. Henry E. Frye, January 11, 2011.

45. Author interview with Milton Fitch, Jr., October 19, 2010.

46. Author interview with Rex Harris, November 18, 2010

47. Author interview with James E. Holshouser, July 29, 2010.

48. Rex Harris interview with author; and interview of Reginald Hawkins by Joseph Mosnier, June 5, 1995, Southern Oral History Program, in the Southern Historical Collection Manuscripts Department, Wilson Library, the University of North Carolina at Chapel Hill.

49. "Precinct Data in State Races," *Charlotte Observer*, November 8, 1972.

50. Howard Lee, August 12, 2010.

Chapter 10

1. Shirley Frye, September 9, 2009.

2. Shirley Frye, June 29, 2009.

3. Author interview with Ronald Barbee, September 10, 2009.

4. Henry E. Frye, April 2, 2009.

5. Author interview with Henry E. Frye, Jr., October 13, 2010.

6. Henry E. Frye, July 29, 2010.

7. Walter Johnson, July 15, 2009.

8. Annual Reports of Greensboro National Bank, Henry Frye papers.

9. "Black Bank 'Doing Well,'" *Greensboro*

Record, March 1, 1973; and "POWs: The Saintly and the Sadists," *Time*, March 12, 1973.

10. James E. Holshouser, July 29, 2010.

11. Henry Frye, February 28, 2010.

12. "A Program to Provide Advertising, Public and Community Relations and a Program of Deposit Solicitation," B&C Associates, Inc., Henry Frye papers made available to author.

13. Henry E. Frye, August 6, 2009.

14. Author interview with Robert Chiles, August 19, 2009.

15. Nathan Garrett, December 5, 2010.

16. Jim Schlosser, "City's Slum Blight Disappearing," *Greensboro Record*, October. 13, 1971, and Otis Hairston, Jr., *Greensboro, NC (Black America Series)*, Arcadia Publishing Co., Charleston, S.C., 2003, p. 59.

17. Jack Scism, "Downtown Greensboro: The Future of a City," *Greensboro Daily News*, November 21, 1971.

18. H. M. Michaux, Jr., September 14, 2009.

19. Interview of Ted Fillette by Sarah Thuesen, April 11, 2006, U-0185, Southern Oral History Program, in the Southern Historical Collection Manuscripts Department, Wilson Library, the University of North Carolina at Chapel Hill.

20. Henry Frye, February 28, 2011.

21. Jim Schlosser, "House Rejects Landlord-tenant Bill," *Greensboro Record*, March 13, 1974.

22. Jack Aulis, "Nineteen House Votes Kill Capital Punishment Repeal," *News and Observer*, April 22, 1971.

23. Velma Speight-Buford, August 12, 2009.

24. Henry Frye, February 28, 2011.

25. Jim Schlosser, "Frye's Resolution Would Upgrade A&T," *Greensboro Record*, April 5, 1979; and William Link, *William Friday: Power, Purpose and American Higher Education*, UNC Press, 1995, p. 198.

26. Scott Shane, "Blacks Get Suggestions On Voting," *Greensboro Daily News*, November 1, 1980.

27. Henry E. Frye, August 6, 2009.

28. Jack Scism, "Who Runs Greensboro," *Greensboro Daily News*, September 6, 1980.

29. Henry E. Frye, August 20, 2009.

30. Ibid.

Chapter 11

1. Martin Brinkley, *Supreme Court of North Carolina: A Brief History*, www.aoc.state.nc.us/copyright/sc/facts.html; and James A. Wynn, *Thomas Ruffin and the Perils of Public Homage: State v. Mann: Judicial Choice or Judicial Duty*, N.C. Law Review, March 2009.

2. Chuck Alston, "Frye Takes High Court Oath," *Greensboro Daily News*, February 4, 1983.

3. A. L. May, "Henry Frye Becomes First Black to Sit on the N.C. Supreme Court," *News and Observer*, February 4, 1983.

4. 218 N.C. Reports, 788, "Acceptance of Chambers in the Justice Building," September 4, 1940.

5. Anna R. Hayes, *Without Precedent: The Life of Susie Sharp*, UNC Press, Chapel Hill, N.C., 2008, p. 256.

6. Author interview with Lisa Marie Nieman, April 13, 2011.

7. Author interview with Pauline Irving, September 3, 2009.

8. Author interview with James B. Hunt, Jr., September 29, 2009; and *Without Precedent: The Life of Susie Sharp*, p. 419.

9. Henry E. Frye, August 20, 2009.

10. Author interview with James G. Exum, Jr., August 7, 2009.

11. James G. Exum, Jr., presentation address of the portrait of Harry C. Martin, December 6, 2000, N.C. supreme court.

12. Henry E. Frye, January 11, 2011.

13. Karl Campbell, *Senator Sam Ervin, Last of the Founding Fathers*, UNC Press, Chapel Hill, N.C., 2007, p. 81.

14. Shirley Frye, September 15, 2010.

15. Campbell, *Senator Sam Ervin, Last of the Founding Fathers*, p. 77.

16. Author interview with Harry Martin, August 21, 2009.

17. Henry E. Frye, August 20, 2009.

18. "Supreme Court Race Enlivened by Hunt Action," *News and Observer*, May 5, 1984.

19. James B. Hunt, September 29, 2009.

20. Author interview with Rhoda Billings, March 25, 2011.

21. Hayes, *Without Precedent*, p. 258.

22. Harry Martin, August 21, 2009.

23. Rhoda Billings, March 25, 2011.

24. Henry E. Frye, March 17, 2011.

25. Harry Martin, August 21, 2009; and author interview with James G. Martin, May 25, 2010.

26. Associated Press, "Branch: Tradition Dictates Successor as Chief Justice," *Charlotte Observer*, June 22, 1986.

27. James G. Martin, May 25, 2010.

28. Author interview with I. Beverly Lake, Jr., August 26, 2009.

29. James G. Exum, Jr., August 7, 2009.

30. Tim Funk, "High Court Races Put in Spotlight," *Charlotte Observer*, August 1, 1986.

31. Pam Kelley, "Respected Foes Vie for N.C. Chief Justice, *Charlotte Observer*, October 2, 1986.

32. Pam Kelley and Jim Morrill, "Former Justice Free to Politick," *Charlotte Observer*, September 19, 1986.

33. James G. Exum, Jr., April 13, 2011.

34. Tim Funk, "Billings Disavows Attacks on Exum, *Charlotte Observer*, October 2, 1986.

35. Henry E. Frye, August 20, 2009.

Chapter 12

1. Harry Martin, August 21, 2009.

2. Author interview with Burley Mitchell, September 1, 2009.

3. Ibid.

4. Henry Frye, March 17, 2011.

5. Author interview with Kenneth Lewis, March 15, 2011.

6. Author interview with Willis P. Whichard, August 26, 2009.

7. I. Beverly Lake, Jr., August 26, 2009.

8. Harry Martin, *History of NC Supreme Court, N.C. Reports*, Vol. 355; also author interview with Harry Martin, August 21, 2009.

9. Willis Whichard, August 26, 2009.

10. Harry Martin, August 21, 2009.

11. Burley Mitchell, September 1, 2009.

12. Willis Whichard, August 26, 2009.

13. Author interview with Robert Orr, September 8, 2009.

14. Author interview with James Wynn, February 23, 2011.

15. Henry Frye, August 29, 2009.

16. Kenneth Lewis, March 15, 2011; and author interview with Donna Rascoe, March 29, 2011.

17. Don Pride, "Exum Court Stronger, More Progressive?" *Charlotte Observer*, December 12, 1987.

18. Foon Rhee, "Chief Justice to Retire: Mitchell Likely to Succeed Him," *Charlotte Observer*, July 29, 1994.

19. Author interview with Seth Cohen, August 27, 2009.

20. Author interview with Alan Woodlief, March 14, 2011.

21. Author interview with Beth Smoot, March 18, 2011.

22. Author interview with Kenneth McNeely, March 28, 2011.

23. Author interview with Reginald Shuford, March 22, 2011.

24. Associated Press, "Respected Justice Leaving Court at 72, Not by Choice," *Charlotte Observer*, January 7, 1992.

25. James G. Exum, Jr., August 7, 2009.

Chapter 13

1. Robert Orr, September 8, 2009.

2. Pam Kelley, "GOP's Shot at Judgeships May be Best in Decades," *Charlotte Observer*, October 26, 1986.

3. Rob Christensen, *The Paradox of Tar*

Heel Politics, University of North Carolina Press, p. 257.

4. I. Beverly Lake, Jr., August 26, 2009.

5. James G. Exum, April 13, 2011; and Burley Mitchell, September 1, 2009.

6. Foon Rhee, "Mitchell Appointed to Lead N.C. Supreme Court," *Charlotte Observer*, December 13, 1994.

7. Foon Rhee, "New Era, New Tone for N.C. High Court," *Charlotte Observer*, January 9, 1995.

8. Robert Orr, September 8, 2009.

9. *Leandro v. State of North Carolina* 346 NC 336 (179PA96) 07/24/1997.

10. Katherine White, "North Carolina's Constitution Comes of Age," *North Carolina Insight*, N.C. Center for Public Policy Research, March 1988, p. 118.

11. Henry E. Frye, September 9, 2009.

12. Burley Mitchell, September 1, 2009.

13. Henry E. Frye, April 25, 2010.

14. John Drescher, "Fireball Kills 25 Plant Workers," *Charlotte Observer*, September 4, 1991.

15. Burley Mitchell, September 1, 2009.

16. Henry Frye, April 25, 2011.

17. Eric Dyer and Paula Christian, "Frye Named Court's Chief Justice," *News and Record*, August 3, 1999.

18. Anna Griffin, "The Source: Public Life in the Carolinas," *Charlotte Observer*, September 12, 1999.

19. Author interview with Thomas Ross, June 28, 2009.

20. Henry E. Frye, April 25, 2011.

21. Author interview with Thomas Hilliard, May 26, 2011.

22. Seth Cohen, August 27, 2009.

23. Robert Orr, September 8, 2009.

24. Pat Taylor, *Fourth Down and Goal to Go*, p. 252.

25. I. Beverly Lake, Jr., August 26, 2009.

26. Matthew Eisley, "With Voters," *News and Observer*, November 4, 2000.

27. Matthew Eisley, "Death-penalty Reversals Plummet," *News and Observer*, September 16, 2000; and "On Business Matters, High Court Judge to be Fair," *News and Observer*, September 12, 2000.

28. Matthew Eisley, "Fund-raising Letter Stirs Race for Chief Justice," *News and Observer*, October 15, 2000.

29. Author interview with G. K. Butterfield, February 5, 2011.

Bibliography

Manuscript Collections

Chapel Hill, North Carolina: University of North Carolina Archives, Gordon Gray Papers and William Aycock Papers.

Charlotte, North Carolina: UNC–Charlotte, J. Murrey Atkins Library Special Collections, Fred Alexander Papers.

Greensboro, North Carolina: UNC–Greensboro, Jackson Library Special Collections, William A. Link Papers; Greensboro Voices Collection and N.C. A&T State University F.D. Bluford Library, University Archives, the George Simkins Collection.

Raleigh, North Carolina: North Carolina Department of Archives and History, Papers of U.S. Senator Sam J. Ervin, Jr.; Official Papers of Governor James E. Holshouser, Jr.; Official Papers of Governor Terry Sanford; Official Papers of Governor Robert W. Scott.

Interviews by the Author

Anderson, Gene, October 28, 2010
Ayscue, E. Osborne, March 10, 2010
Barbee, Ron, September 10, 2009
Barnes, Deborah, June 22, 2010
Becton, Charles, September 21, 2009
Billings, Rhoda, March 25, 2011
Blount, Alvin, March 8, 2010
Bluethenthal, Joanne, September 18, 2009
Blum, Robert, August 20, 2009
Bridgett, James, August 18, 2009
Brown, Colleen, June 17, 2011
Brown, Lane, February 24, 2010
Butterfield, G. K., February 5, 2011
Chambers, Julius, October 5, 2009

Chess, Sammie, June 8, 2010
Chiles, Robert, August 19, 2009
Chubbs, Howard, May 27, 2009
Cohen, Seth, August 27, 2009
D'Angelo, Katheryn, March 14, 2011
Eagles, Sid, February 23, 2011
Easterling, Sheridan, December 12, 2009
Easterling, Shirley, December 12, 2009
Evans, George, February 24, 2009
Exum, James G., April 13, 2011
Ferguson, James, November 8, 2010
Fitch, Milton, Jr., October 29, 2010
Frye, Harlan, September 9, 2009
Frye, Henry, January 28, 2009; February 4, 12, 19 and 26, 2009; March 5, 12, 19, 2009; April 2 and 9, 2009; May 28, 2009; June 3, 18 and 25, 2009; August 6 and 20, 2009; September 3, 2009; October 2, 2009; November 5, 2009; December 18, 2009; January 14, 2010; March 5, 10 and 31, 2010; April 31, 2010; May 26, 2010; July 14 and 29, 2010; December 3, 2010; January 11, 2011; February 28, 2011; March 17, 2011; and April 25, 2011
Frye, Henry, Jr., October 13, 2009
Frye, Shirley, June 29, 2009; July 6 and 9, 2009; September 9 and 15, 2009; February 9, 2010; June 8, 2010; December 7, 2010; March 3, 2011; and June 1, 2011
Garrett, Nathan, December 5, 2009
Hall, Roy G., Jr., June 17, 2009
Harris, Rex, November 18, 2010
Hilliard, Thomas, May 26, 2011
Holshouser, James, Jr., July 29, 2010
Hooper, Deborah, June 17, 2011
Horton, Larnie, October 1, 2010
Hunt, James B., September 29, 2009
Imamura, Kikuko, December 7, 2009
Irving, Pauline, September 3, 2009

269

Johnson, Sam, July 13, 2010
Jordan, Robert, April 12, 2011
Kilmanjaro, John Marshall, August 28, 2009
Lake, I. Beverly, Jr., August 26, 2009
Lambeth, Thomas, June 15, 2011
Lee, Howard, August 12, 2010
Lee, J. Kenneth, March 3, 2009
Lewis, Ken, March 15, 2011
Lynch, Lorenzo, July 27, 2009
McElveen, David, June 22, 2009
McNeely, Ken, March 28, 2011
Martin, Harry, August 21, 2009
Martin, James G., July 13, 2010
Melvin, Jim, October 19, 2010
Michaux, H. M., Jr., September 14, 2009
Mitchell, Burley, September 1, 2009
Morrison, Fred, May 27, 2010
Nieman, Lisa Marie, April 13, 2011
Orr, Robert, September 8, 2009
Piggott, Lucille, August 13, 2009
Patterson, Jane, November 9, 2009
Pollitt, Daniel, August 5, 2009
Rascoe, Donna, March 29, 2011
Ross, Thomas, July 28, 2009
Sellers, Cleveland, February 24, 2010
Shuford, Reggie, March 22, 2011
Smoot, Beth, March 18, 2011
Speight-Buford, Velma, June 20, 2009
Stagner, Deborah, March 18, 2011
Steward, Carl, Jr., August 4, 2009
Storrs, Thomas I., November 2, 2010
Stringer, Ola, June 24, 2009
Swann, Mel, February 17, 2010
Terry, Frederick, August 5, 2009
Watt, Mel, November 2, 2009
Whichard, Willis, August 26, 2009
Woodlief, Alan, March 14, 2011
Wynn, James, February 23, 2011

Interviews by Others

Duke University Perkins Library, Special Collections:
Bluethenthal, Joanne, July 13, 1977 (interview by William Chafe)
Elam, Jack, undated (interview by William Chafe)
Morehead, David, December 19, 1974 (interview by William Chafe)
Walker, James R., October 7, 1976 (interview by Marcellus Barksdale)

Southern Oral History Program, UNC–Chapel Hill Library:
Beech, Harvey, September 25, 1996 (interview by Anita Foye)
Chambers, Julius L., June 5, 2000 (interview by Hugh B. Campbell, Jr.); June 18, 1990 (interview by William A. Link); March 6, 2007 (interview by Judith Van Wyk)
Frye, Henry E., August 21, 1995 (interview by Joseph Mosnier); February 26, 1992 (interview by Amy E. Boening)
Lee, J. Kenneth, September 26 and October 26, 1995 (interviews by Ann S. Estridge)

Periodicals

A&T Register
Aynatee
Crisis
Future Outlook
Greensboro Daily News
Greensboro Record
News and Observer
Rockingham Post

Published Sources

Atwood, J. Howell, Donald W. Wyatt, Vincent J. Davis and Ira D. Walker. *Thus Be Their Destiny: The Personality Development of Negro Youth in Three Communities.* Washington, DC: American Youth Commission/American Council on Education, 1941.
Branch, Taylor. *Parting the Waters: America in the King Years, 1954–63.* New York: Simon & Schuster, 1988.
Brown, Leslie. *Upbuilding Black Durham: Gender, Class, and Black Community Development in the Jim Crow South.* Chapel Hill: University of North Carolina Press, 2008.
Chafe, William H. *Civilities and Civil Rights: Greensboro, North Carolina, and the Black Struggle for Freedom.* New York: Oxford University Press, 1980.
Du Bois, W.E.B. *The Souls of Black Folk.* New York: Dover Publications, 1994.
Escott, Paul, and Flora J. Hatley. *A History of African Americans in North Carolina.*

Raleigh: N.C. Division of Archives and History, 1992.

Fletcher, Winona Lee. *No Way! Memoirs of J. Kenneth Lee, Esq.* Denver: Outskirts Press, 2008.

Frazier, E. Franklin. *The Negro in the United States.* New York: Macmillan, 1957.

Gavins, Raymond. "Behind the Veil," in *W. J. Cash and the Minds of the South,* edited by Paul Escott. Baton Rouge: Louisiana State University Press, 1992.

_____. "The NAACP in NC During the Age of Segregation," in *The Civil Rights Movement,* edited by Jack E. Davis. Malden, MA: Blackwell Publishers, 2001.

Gibbs, Warmoth T. *History of the North Carolina Agricultural and Technical College.* Dubuque, IA: William C. Brown Co., 1966.

Graham, Lawrence Otis. *Our Kind of People.* New York: HarperCollins Publishers, 2000.

Hairston, Otis, Jr. *Greensboro, North Carolina.* Charleston, SC: Arcadia Publishing Co., 2003.

Hanchett, Tom. "Rosenwald Schools and Black Education in North Carolina." *North Carolina Historical Review,* Vol. 65, No. 4, October 1988.

Hayes, Anna R. *Without Precedent: The Life of Susie Marshall Sharp.* Chapel Hill: University of North Carolina Press, 2008.

Huneycutt, James E., and Ida C. Huneycutt. *History of Richmond County.* Raleigh, NC: Edwards and Broughton, 1976.

Kelley, Carrye Hill. "Profiles of Five Administrators." *The Agricultural and Technical College History–Digest.* Greensboro: The Agricultural and Technical College, August 1964.

Link, William A. *William Friday: Power, Purpose, and American Higher Education.* Chapel Hill: University of North Carolina Press, 1995.

Newbold, N.C. *Five North Carolina Negro Educators.* Chapel Hill: University of North Carolina Press, 1939.

Reynolds, Elva S. *Ellerbe Springs Remembers.* Utica, KY: McDowell Publications, 1991.

Spruill, Albert. *Great Recollections from Aggieland: A Human Interest Account of the Development of the Agricultural and Technical College of North Carolina from 1893 to 1960.* Wilmington, NC: Whitehead Printing Company, 1964.

_____. *Historical Tour of North Carolina Agricultural and Technical College.* Greensboro: North Carolina A&T University Archives, 1982.

Taylor, Pat. *Fourth Down and Goal to Go.* Raleigh, NC: Ivy House Publishing Group, 2005.

Warren, Robert Penn. *Who Speaks for the Negro.* New York: Random House, 1966.

Washington, Booker T. *Tuskegee and Its People.* New York: D. Appleton and Co., 1905.

Dissertations and Theses

Braswell, Deborah J. "A History of North Carolina Central University Law School, 1939–1968." Master's thesis, North Carolina Central University, 1977.

McLeod, Frank Daniel, "A Survey of the Public School Facilities for Negroes in Richmond County." Master's thesis, University of North Carolina, 1948.

Mosnier, Joseph L. "Crafting Law in the Second Reconstruction: Julius Chambers, the NAACP Legal Defense Fund and Title VII." Honors thesis, University of North Carolina at Chapel Hill, 2005.

Womack, Olivia Peace. "Study of Windsor Community Center." Honors thesis, N.C. Agricultural and Technical College, 1952.

Index

Numbers in **bold italics** indicate pages with photographs.

Webb, John 210, *216*, *217*, 231; retirement 240
Webb, Kathy 156
Webster, David "Boss" 24
Webster, Nathaniel C. 20
Wells, Wyoming 147, *152*, 154, 175
Wesley Long Community Hospital 78–79
WFMY-TV 255–56
Wheeler, John Hervey 81, 84, 95, 143–44, 147, 154, 191
Whichard, Willis 209, 210, 214, 215, *216*, *217*, 221–22, 231, 240; retirement 240
White, George H. 111
White, Walter 18
white supremacy 10, 11, 12
Whitted, Earl 161
Wilder, L. Douglas 155
Wilkes County 91

Winslow, Ed 252
Winston-Salem State University 161
Winters, John W. 181
Witherspoon, James H. 151
Womble, William F. 99–100
Wooden, Ralph, 113, 114, 118
Woodlief, Alan 224–25
Woolworth store sit-in 69–70
workers safety case 240
Wynn, James A., Jr. 219, 232, 240, *244*

Yadkin River 90–91
Young Men's Christian Association 93
Young Women's Christian Association 93, 104, 169–72 *passim*

Zane, Ed 110